*Entrepreneurship in
Imperial Russia
and the
Soviet Union*

Entrepreneurship in Imperial Russia and the Soviet Union

EDITED BY
GREGORY GUROFF AND
FRED V. CARSTENSEN

Princeton University Press
Princeton, New Jersey

Copyright © 1983 by Princeton University Press
Published by Princeton University Press, 41 William Street,
Princeton, New Jersey 08540
In the United Kingdom: Princeton University Press,
Guildford, Surrey

All Rights Reserved
Library of Congress Cataloging in Publication Data will
be found on the last printed page of this book

This book has been composed in Linotron Sabon
Clothbound editions of Princeton University Press books
are printed on acid-free paper, and binding materials are
chosen for strength and durability

Printed in the United States of America by Princeton
University Press, Princeton, New Jersey

*To Arcadius Kahan,
our colleague and
friend*

Contents

Preface

We would like to thank the R & D Committee of the American Association for the Advancement of Slavic Studies, which provided funding for the symposium where drafts of the chapters that constitute this book were first presented, and the Kennan Institute for Advanced Russian Studies of the Wilson Center, which hosted the conference.

We would also like to express our appreciation to the Academy of Sciences of the USSR, which made possible the participation of Professor Boris Anan'ich, Institute of History (Leningrad).

Harnessing the talents of fifteen scholars to a single task is always difficult, but we have been particularly fortunate in having a distinguished and patient group of contributors who have supported us through this long venture. One of the volume's distinctions is that the individual authors have attempted, successfully, to link their chapters to a common theme and a common set of concerns. Nonetheless, we should make it clear that each author is responsible only for his or her own chapter and specifically not for views expressed in the concluding chapter, for which we assume complete responsibility.

GREGORY GUROFF
FRED V. CARSTENSEN

*Entrepreneurship in
Imperial Russia
and the
Soviet Union*

I

CYRIL E. BLACK

Russian and Soviet Entrepreneurship in a Comparative Context

The purpose of this book, which brings together chapters based on papers discussed originally at a conference held on November 16-18, 1978, at the Kennan Institute for Advanced Russian Studies in Washington, D.C., is to advance our understanding of entrepreneurship in the Russian Empire and the Soviet Union.

The various interrelated functions of entrepreneurship, management, and innovation, which are among the most characteristic features of national development in the modern era, have received relatively little attention in the Russian and Soviet contexts. Conventional wisdom has taught us that Russia was a backward society until the Five-Year Plans were inaugurated in 1928, that a weak middle class accounted for the failure of the Provisional Government in 1917 and the establishment of a socialist administration, and that educated Russians in the nineteenth century were primarily concerned with abstract ideas rather than with questions of management. Entrepreneurship is a skill associated with commerce and manufacturing in relatively free-enterprise economies, and neither Russia nor the Soviet Union was perceived as an environment where this skill was likely to flourish. Research on Russia and the Soviet Union in recent decades has dispelled many of these preconceptions, but the results of this research have remained scattered and unfocused. This symposium seeks not only to bring together what we know about this subject, but also to bring to bear the judgments of scholars currently working on this theme on issues still under debate and calling for further research.

An underlying task of the comparative study of modernizing societies is to distinguish between those aspects of the advancement of knowledge, political development, economic growth, and social integration that are

(3)

common to all societies, and those that reflect the varied heritages of institutions and values of each society. It has taken a good many years to sort out those characteristics of contemporary Western societies that are universally valid, and those that have roots in a premodern England and France to which modernity was no less alien than it has been to Russia, Japan, or China. Our first task here is to focus on those aspects of entrepreneurship, management, and innovation that are relevant to economic growth regardless of its cultural milieu.

Comparative studies of economic development suggest that an underlying feature common to all societies is that as industrialization advances, the role of entrepreneurship, management, and innovation increases as compared with that of capital and labor. Industrialization is the key factor in the productivity of labor and capital and should be regarded as an economic resource as well as a system of authority.[1]

Early definitions of entrepreneurship stressed the role of the entrepreneur as working in an ambience of uncertainty, that is, contracting for a job without knowing in advance the cost of labor and materials—in contrast to salaried officials working within the constraints of a budget. These days we all seem to be working under conditions of uncertainty, and to this extent we may be entrepreneurs, but this is not a very useful definition for the purposes of this symposium.

There is also the narrow definition of entrepreneurship associated with the work of Schumpeter, which stresses innovation as its principal function—the furthering of economic growth through the improvement of technique. Those who simply administer ongoing concerns, under this definition, may be businessmen, capitalists, bureaucrats, or managers, but they are not entrepreneurs. This is too narrow a definition for our purposes, even though we are concerned with both entrepreneurship and innovation. It is very difficult in the modern era—in which change under the impact of the scientific and technological revolution is of the essence— to isolate "innovation" from the other functions of entrepreneurship except in a very specialized context.

Between a very broad and a very narrow definition there remains a large area that includes functions not only of innovation but also of leadership, management, the mobilization and allocation of resources for particular ends, risk taking, marketing, and certainly cost control, a function no less important in a planned than in a market economy.

Studies of entrepreneurship in a variety of settings lead to the conclusion that as economies develop and as enterprises grow in size, an increasingly higher proportion of managerial resources is required. Not

---

[1] Frederick Harbison, "Entrepreneurial Organization as a Factor in Economic Development," *Quarterly Journal of Economics*, 70 (August 1956), 364-79.

only growth but also innovation call for a large investment in managerial skills. Much is made of the role of individualism in the leadership of market economies, but the fact is that management by teams rather than by individuals increases in proportion to the size and complexity of an organization.

Almost universally, enterprises have evolved from family-dominated "patrimonial" businesses to more impersonal, professionally managed, corporations. Although family names have often been retained long after families have lost exclusive control—as with Ford and Chrysler, Mitsui and Toyota, Peugeot and Krupp—size and complexity require a greater range of skills than any single family is likely to possess. As entrepreneurship evolves from the initiative of a single individual or family, investing savings and loans in new enterprises, to that of managers of large organizations, the role of entrepreneur becomes increasingly one of selecting and directing personnel. Innovation becomes less a matter of individuals having bright ideas for new techniques, than of the administration of research departments with large staffs of specialists engaged in basic and applied research.

In addition to being an economic resource, entrepreneurship and management are also systems of authority. In this respect more than in others, entrepreneurs tend to vary rather widely from one culture to another. This variation depends in part on the types of personality that predominate in a culture, and in part on the social status and educational level of the workers.

As a system of authority, management may range from a highly centralized authoritarian leadership, which is still sometimes evident in advanced industrial societies, through varying degrees of paternalism, to enterprises in which management and labor cooperate on a wide range of policy decisions. Although one might think that enterprises, like polities, would evolve from authoritarian to democratic patterns over the years, the prevailing style of management appears to reflect the mores of a society more than its level of development.

Management has tended to be paternalistic in Japan, and also in some West European countries, owing primarily to the continuing influence of relationships prevalent between landlords and peasants before they became managers and workers. In other Western countries, especially in the United Kingdom and the English-speaking countries of the New World, paternalism has given way to a more pluralistic approach that gives labor an increasing role in management. In the later-developing societies, however, the size and limited education of the available labor force have encouraged entrepreneurs to run their businesses with a heavy hand.

In all societies, the authority structure of enterprises depends greatly on the economic status, political culture, and educational level of the labor force. If, to take an extreme case, managers are employing slave labor—the reference here is to twentieth-century examples, not to ancient times or the United States before 1861—the entrepreneurial role is naturally quite different from the situation in which, at the other extreme, the labor force is adequately trained, well-organized, and protected by law in its right to negotiate. Most cases fall between these two extremes, and the available studies show a wide variation by country, by region, by industry, and by personalities of entrepreneurs. What these studies tell us is that the common functions of entrepreneurial leadership—including not only promoting innovative techniques, but also managing both administrative personnel and labor—can be successfully performed in a wide variety of settings.[2]

Although the study of entrepreneurship in Russia and the Soviet Union is a rather recent phenomenon, there are several aspects of the subject on which scholars of various persuasions are likely to agree.

Of these, the most obvious is that there is a continuity from at least the eighteenth century down to the present in the degree to which Russian and Soviet society have been state-centered. Although this is not to suggest that the monarch and his bureaucracy before 1917 achieved anything like the penetration of society that has characterized the Soviet party-state administration, yet in the nineteenth century the state played a large role in directing the economy and in determining the relations between social strata. Neither the church, nor provincial leaders, nor estate or class organizations could influence the policies of the imperial administration in any decisive way.

The Russian economy and society developed rapidly in the last decades of the monarchy, but the state failed to adapt political institutions to changing economic and social realities and in the end it finally succumbed to revolution. The fact remains, however, that in both Russia and the Soviet Union, in marked contrast to the situation in Western Europe, entrepreneurship evolved in a setting where the interests of the state predominated over those of the entrepreneurs. Between actual government ownership and state contracts, the state in the last decades of the empire played a very large role in industrial development.[3] To this extent, the evolution toward a planned economy in the Soviet Union continued imperial policies, although to be sure in a much more intense form, rather than departing radically from them.

[2] Frederick Harbison and Charles A. Myers, *Management in the Industrial World: An International Analysis* (New York, 1959); Sydney M. Greenfield, Arnold Strickon, and Robert T. Aubey, eds., *Entrepreneurs in Cultural Context* (Albuquerque, 1979); and Paul H. Wilken, *Entrepreneurship: A Comparative and Historical Study* (Norwood, N.J., 1979).
[3] William L. Blackwell, *The Industrialization of Russia: An Historical Perspective* (New York, 1970).

In another dimension, however, Russia and the Soviet Union were very dissimilar settings for entrepreneurship. Before 1917, entrepreneurs had no well-defined status in Russian society, and only in the last decades of the empire did they emerge as a well-organized interest group with direct access to the central government. The merchants, tradespeople, and artisans of Great Russian ethnic origin were slow to develop entrepreneurial skills, and national minorities and foreigners played a larger role than in most comparable countries. At the same time, entrepreneurship did not have a high standing in the values of the empire. Only the upper guild of merchants had a status in some ways comparable to that of the noble landowners, and in the popular culture persons involved in commerce and artisanry were held in low esteem. The fact that in dictionaries today the term for tradesperson (*meshchanin*) is a synonym for narrow-minded, vulgar, uncultured, and Philistine, suggests that this is a continuing attitude.

As early as the 1850s, the enterprises in the Moscow region nevertheless began to organize interest groups to press their case with the central government, and they gradually emerged as an influential force in society.[4] After the revolution of 1905, industrial interests began to play an even more active role as a pressure group through the Association of Industry and Trade and other organizations, and were able to exert a strong influence on several of the political parties that emerged in this period. They never felt that their needs were adequately understood by the central bureaucracy, however, and their representatives were among the leaders who urged Nicholas II to abdicate in 1917 in the hope that a government more in tune with industrial needs would result. From what is known of the thinking of leading Russian entrepreneurs at this stage, they would have liked to see a form of cooperation between government and business somewhat along the lines that has recently been developed in Japan.[5]

The situation has of course been very different in the Soviet Union where, especially since the inauguration of the Five-Year Plans in 1928, entrepreneurship, management, and innovation have been the principal concerns of the government. Joseph Stalin might well have echoed, in the very different Soviet context, Calvin Coolidge's assertion that "The business of America is business," and in due course most leaders of the

[4] Thomas C. Owen, *Capitalism and Politics in Russia: A Social History of the Moscow Merchants, 1855-1905* (New York, 1981); and Alfred J. Rieber, *Merchants and Entrepreneurs in Imperial Russia* (Chapel Hill, 1982).

[5] Ruth AmEnde Roosa, "The Association of Industry and Trade, 1906-1914: An Examination of the Economic Views of Organized Industrialists in Prerevolutionary Russia," Dissertation, Columbia University, 1967; and Johan H. Hartl, *Die Interessenvertretungen der Industriellen in Russland, 1905-1914* (Vienna, 1978).

Soviet hierarchy included as part of their training some experience in agricultural and industrial management.

One could of course write at length about the transformation of Russian and Soviet society in the nineteenth and twentieth centuries, but this brief sketch of the continuities and contrasts will suggest the problems faced by an effort to trace the development of entrepreneurship in a country such as this. A particular challenge is represented by the need to distinguish form from function—to discover the essential roles of entrepreneurship that may be concealed under various institutions and titles that may seem alien or irrelevant when viewed from the vantage point of the West.

In seeking to give unity to our subject, we must look for a reasonably consistent set of entrepreneurial functions in a period stretching from the emergence of Muscovy, after the virtual destruction of manufacturing and trade as a result of the Mongol invasions, to the development of a modern industrial economy in the twentieth century. The cast of characters thus ranges from the *gosti*, the merchants whose origins go back to the Kievan period and who survived into the nineteenth century, to the managers of contemporary industrial and agricultural enterprises.

The identification of the specific roles that we should consider as entrepreneurial is one that deserves particular attention. In a society that more than most others has been inclined to label societal actors and provide them with a legally defined status, we should be able to identify those engaged in entrepreneurial activity. If we are going back to the *gosti*, we should also consider the other *posadskie liudi*, including the *kuptsy* who in their various incarnations played a central role until 1917, as well as the *meshchane*. If chairmen of *kolkhozy* are to be considered in the Soviet period, should we not also pay attention to those *pomeshchiki* who ran substantial estates that produced for the market and for export, and the *prikazchiki* who served as stewards or bailiffs on both government and private estates.

The fact that Witte is referred to as an entrepreneur in both his private and ministerial capacities raises the question of the extent to which the term entrepreneurship includes government as well as private activity. This question is even more relevant in the Soviet period, when both state officials and enterprise managers surely work under conditions of sufficient uncertainty to be considered as entrepreneurs.

Once the entrepreneurs have been identified, it is important to locate their position in the social scene. Did entrepreneurs have a high and respected position in society—as in twentieth-century United States, where at least in terms of personal income they are on the top of the pile—or were they assigned a relatively low position—as in Ch'ing China? In other words, did society encourage or discourage entrepreneurship? This ranking should be determined not only in terms of income, but also of legal status as reflected in privileges and restrictions.

In this context, special attention should be given to non-Russians as entrepreneurs. Not only native non-Russians, such as Armenians, Poles, and Germans, but also foreigners played an important role in Russian, and to a lesser extent, Soviet entrepreneurship. Religious minorities, too, notably the Old Believers and the Jews, deserve special consideration.

No less important than the social status of entrepreneurs is the question of their specialized training. How were they prepared by education for their role as entrepreneurs? When and for which groups was in-service and on-the-job training supplemented by formal education in commerce and business practices? It is significant that in the Soviet Union and also in Eastern Europe most heads of enterprises were until the 1960s trained as engineers, and were, at best, amateurs as managers. Is this lack of specialized training a heritage of the past or an idiosyncrasy of the Soviet scene?

In all societies the state has played a critical role in entrepreneurship in modern times, if only, as in the United States, by establishing and enforcing the rules by which rights and privileges are granted, taxes assessed and collected, and competition maintained—and also more indirectly by supporting the training of entrepreneurs through systems of public education.

Yet if the Russian and Soviet experience has a particularly distinguishing feature, it is certainly the role of the state in entrepreneurial activity. Not many public officials in the United States would be considered entrepreneurs—possible exceptions one thinks of are the managers of TVA, the Manhattan Project, and the Port Authority—but this is certainly not the case with either Russia or the Soviet Union. For well-known reasons, the state there has long had a position of much greater importance relative to other institutions than in any Western country.

A central question here is whether the state supported or hindered entrepreneurship and innovation—and when the state took the initiative, was it more effective than private agencies? For the period before 1917 the relevant issues have been discussed at some length in the literature, and Anan'ich's chapter is particularly valuable for its description of the obstacles placed by the government in Alexander III's reign to legislation that would facilitate entrepreneurial activity. In the Soviet period this subject takes on a more technical aspect in the debate over the incentives provided to managers for innovation, as compared with gross output and other objectives.[6]

---

[6] The problems of entrepreneurship in Russia and the Soviet Union are discussed in some detail in M. C. Kaser, "Russian Entrepreneurship," *Cambridge Economic History of Europe*, ed. Peter Mathias and M. M. Postan (Cambridge, 1978), 7, Pt. 2, 416-93, 535-53.

At a more general level under this heading, we should also ask whether state enterprise in the USSR has demonstrated its capacity to match private enterprise. One thinks particularly of private plots' extraordinary production for the market as compared with collective and state agriculture.

All of the above questions, from the definition of entrepreneurship to the contemporary development of managerial skills in the Soviet Union, raise the issue of treating Russian and Soviet developments from what is essentially a Western point of view. From the invitation of Aristotele Fioravanti of Bologna in 1475 to rebuild a new church in Moscow that had collapsed from faulty construction, to the most recent cases of technical collaboration with the West, Russia and the Soviet Union have relied extensively on the West European reservoir of knowledge and experience. There are many references in this volume to Western influence, and one should consider how Russia and the Soviet Union compare with other later-modernizing societies in this respect. More specifically, how efficiently has foreign expertise been used in the development of native entrepreneurial and innovational skills? All such judgments are by nature comparative, and the comparisons here should be not only with Western Europe but also with countries at other stages of development.

The comparative context also calls for reexamining which aspects of entrepreneurship and innovation are universally valid, like mathematics and the natural sciences, and which are culturally relative, like religion and language. When Witte wrote that a country could industrialize under any form of government, was he also saying that a country can achieve vigorous entrepreneurship and a high level of innovation with a diversity of institutions? To put it more directly, is it possible that the large role of the state in Russian and Soviet entrepreneurship and innovation is a consequence more of an institutional heritage of statism than of the policies of a few perverse leaders in the nineteenth and twentieth centuries, and that there is no reason why current Soviet (and Japanese or Brazilian) practices in their native context cannot perform at the same level that Western practices have achieved in theirs?

The challenge of this collaborative study of entrepreneurship is not simply to compare Russia and the Soviet Union with the West. There is no "West," after all, to the extent that the United Kingdom, France, Germany, and the United States, for example, differ significantly in the way they do things—or at least sufficiently so that one cannot envisage their adopting a common legal code in the foreseeable future. The problem is rather to describe the roles and institutions which in the Russian and Soviet settings have performed the functions of entrepreneurship that take a considerable variety of forms not only in the diverse societies of the West but in many others as well.

*The
Tsarist
Period*

II

WILLIAM BLACKWELL
*The Russian Entrepreneur
in the Tsarist Period:
An Overview*

Like the much more familiar Russian sol-
dier or monk, the man who organized and acted for economic rather
than military or religious objectives was ubiquitous to the long span of
Russian history. Until most recent times, however, he was relegated by
scholars to the shadows of a largely political historical stage, and by his
fellow Russians to an "inferior position . . . in Russian society."[1] At the
very beginning, it would seem that enterprise was an important and highly
esteemed activity of the Russians. In the medieval Russia of Kiev and
Novgorod, however much scholars have debated the primacy of commerce or agriculture in the economy, not only did merchants and artisans
have political power and substantial wealth, but almost everyone above
the lowest level of peasants engaged in economic enterprise of one type
or another. The princes, their governors, the boyars, the abbots and their
monks, a numerous community of Russian and foreign merchants, and,
farther down the social hierarchy, a host of craftsmen, were involved in
the organized pursuit of a wide variety of mercenary activities. Liashchenko asserts that not until the fourteenth century did trade as a
profession become "gradually concentrated in the hands of merchant-
specialists."[2]

In such a society of relatively undifferentiated commercial activity,
where landlords traded and merchants owned land, entrepreneurship
must have been a desirable, privileged, and honorable pursuit. Not so,

[1] See Thomas C. Owen, *Capitalism and Politics in Russia: A Social History of the Moscow
Merchants, 1855-1905* (New York, 1981), p. 1. Owen continues, "Bearded, patriarchal,
semi-Asiatic in dress and manner, and fully versed in the arts of haggling and swindling,
the Russian merchants in the early 19th century not only lacked the distinctive urban ethos
of the West, but also clung to their obscurantist cultural traditions."

[2] Peter I. Liashchenko, *History of the National Economy of Russia to the 1917 Revolution*
(New York, 1949), p. 140.

it would appear, after the passage of two centuries of intermittent war in the despotic successor state of Moscow. Samuel Baron, in his essay on the Russian entrepreneur of the sixteenth and seventeenth centuries, cites the English visitor, Giles Fletcher, who in the late 1500s observed an oppressed, taxed, powerless, lethargic group at the bottom rungs of society, hardly better off, in his view, than the serfs. The status of the Russian entrepreneur little improved during the eighteenth and nineteenth centuries. Peter the Great's program to create a class of Russian industrialists out of merchants and craftsmen, with a few notable exceptions, such as the Demidovs, Gubins, and Yakovlevs, became a pork barrel for influential courtiers, generals, and bureaucrats more than any solid foundation for an entrepreneurial tradition. The liquor stills, canvas and woolen shops of the rural gentry in the same period constitute a much more substantial base of entrepreneurship and raise a real question about the traditionally viewed disinclination and incapacity of the nobility in business matters. But their motivation was clearly one of expedient financial desperation rather than calculated entrepreneurial calling. The serf and Old Believer industrialists of the early nineteenth century were scorned: at best, they were seen as golden geese to be plucked by their owners or police authorities; at worst, they were deemed rascals when not condemned as outright criminals.[3] The passage of a generation of rapid industrialization, capital accumulation, and partial Westernization did little to improve the self-image of families, some of whom would maintain a front parlor lavishly furnished in European style for foreign visitors but rarely used otherwise; they chose to seclude their Russian life style in the back rooms. Only in the last moments of the old regime did a stratum of what may be called technologist-entrepreneurs, many of them non-Russians, appear particularly in the new industrial region in the Southwest. This group prided themselves on their modernity and attempted to assert national leadership, but they were too few to break the shell of conservatism and traditionalism that encased the Great Russian entrepreneurial class.[4]

By the beginning of the twentieth century, Russian historians became interested in the entrepreneur. As in Europe and America, the business firms themselves were the first to show an interest in their past. Histories of firms and industries were published, not only to promote business and extol the economic achievements of private enterprise, but also to display

[3] William L. Blackwell, *The Beginnings of Russian Industrialization 1800-1860* (Princeton, 1968), pp. 22-27, 206, 227.

[4] The anecdote about the front parlor and the information on enterprise in the southwest industrial region are taken from Alfred J. Rieber, *Merchants and Entrepreneurs in Imperial Russia* (Chapel Hill, 1982), the most substantial study we have of the Muscovite and regional entrepreneurs of the nineteenth century.

the social responsibility of the Russian entrepreneur.[5] Such a beginning of modern entrepreneurial history, similar to what was soon to flourish, particularly among German and American historians, was cut short even before the Russian Revolution, by the emergence of a dynamic and aggressive Marxist historiography, whose concern with capitalist enterprise was best exemplified by Tugan-Baranovsky's *Russian Factory in the Past and Present*, but also by Lenin's *Development of Capitalism in Russia*. The latter work, for all its limitations, had the original virtue of turning first to the peasantry for observation of the emergence of private entrepreneurship. Nevertheless, a broader interest in the Russian entrepreneur—his origins, motivations, functions, achievements, society, culture, and politics—was overshadowed by a political and ideological preconcern with the bourgeoisie as it played its appointed role on the Russian road to socialism. This approach was carried over into official Soviet historiography, as well as into most non-Soviet interpretation for much of the twentieth century. Only very recently has this dogma been questioned by American scholarship; and at the same time, entrepreneurial history has arrived belatedly to the field of Russian studies in this country, as seen in the appearance of several dissertations, the publication of articles and at least three full-scale studies at the time of this writing, and the interest of scholarly conferences, most notably the symposium held at the Kennan Institute, Washington, D.C., in November 1978, upon which the chapters and comments here are based.

The purpose of this essay, in light of the ample theoretical and definitional statements that have been provided by Cyril Black, Joseph Berliner, and the editors, will be to provide an essentially historical introduction, which will attempt to set the papers that treat the several centuries of the tsarist period into a broader historical and geographical context.

There is a significant *historical geography* of Russian entrepreneurship. The role of geography in the emergence of entrepreneurial activity, as well as the spatial and locational aspects of enterprise during the several periods of Russian history, form a subject that is not restricted to the earliest and most distant times, but assumes crucial importance later on, even in the very last years of the tsarist empire, when entrepreneurship

---

[5] See, among many other works, P. N. Terentyev, *Kratkii istoricheskii ocherk deiatelnosti Prokhorovskoi Trekhgornoi Manufaktury po tekhnicheskomu i obshchemu obrazovaniu rabochikh 1816-1899 gody* (Moscow, 1899); *V pamiat 75-ti letnego iubileia Pervago Rossiiskago Strakhovago Obshchestva Uchrezhdennago v 1827 godu* (St. Petersburg, 1903); Ch. M. Yusimovich, *Manufakturnaia promyshlennost' v proshlom i nastoiashchem* (Moscow, 1915), vol. 1; Ia. P. Garelin, *Gorod Ivanovo-Voznesensk* (Shuia, 1884); K. Golovshchikov, *Pavel Grigorievich Demidov i istoriia osnovannago im v Yaroslavye uchilishcha 1803-86* (Yaroslav, 1887). For other references, see the bibliography, part 3 of Blackwell, *Beginnings of Russian Industrialization.*

was situated in four major and several lesser industrial regions, each with its own character and dynamics.

The earliest Russian states centered at Kiev and Novgorod, as suggested earlier here, were entrepreneurially oriented to a high degree. Situated on the great Eurasian river-trading routes, their lifeblood was international commerce. Most strata of medieval Russian society had a hand in it. The two hundred to three hundred towns so sustained, particularly the larger cities, in turn stimulated a handicraft industry, so that a wide variety of small-scale artisan-entrepreneurs became even more numerous than their commercial counterparts.[6]

The Moscow or Central Industrial Region fostered the oldest continuous tradition of industrial enterprise in tsarist Russia, extending back to the geographical conditions surrounding the formation of the Muscovite state in the Mongol period. Its forested vastness provided a refuge from Mongol raids. The soil, however, was too poor and the climate too cold and dry to provide agricultural surpluses, or even subsistence for the urban population which had grown as a result of Moscow's strategic commercial position on the Eurasian river and portage system. The village as well as the town populace turned of necessity to handicrafts. This turned into an extensive involvement in industrial enterprise engaged particularly in the manufacture of metallurgical implements, which were exchanged for grain, salt, fish, and other food products. Generations of such activity provided a pool, not only of artisanry, but also of entrepreneurial aptitude and experience.[7] Thus, the basis was established for an entrepreneurial cadre as well as an industrial force, a conversion that first occurred in the premodern metallurgical industrialization of the region in the seventeenth century, and was repeated in the development of the Muscovite textile and other manufacturing industries in the eighteenth and nineteenth centuries, and again in the Soviet period. Dmitry Mendeleev grasped the power of this tradition when he reported on Russian industry for the World International Exposition of 1893 in Chicago: "Moscow . . . now concentrates so many enterprising people and forms such an advanced economic center that it will long remain at the head of the extensive manufacturing development destined for Russia."[8]

The great Muscovite industrial entrepreneurs of early modern times,

[6] M. N. Tikhomirov, *Dreverusskogo goroda*, 2nd ed. (Moscow, 1956).

[7] On the forest refuge and the growth of Muscovite craft enterprise, see William L. Blackwell, "The Historical Geography of Industry in Tzarist Russia" (*Essays on the Historical Geography of Russia*, forthcoming, Academic Press); see also R.E.H. Mellor, *Geography of the USSR* (London, 1965), pp. 65-67, 78.

[8] D. I. Mendeleeff, Introduction, *The Industries of Russia* (St. Petersburg, 1893), vols. 1-2, *Manufactures and Trade*, translated by John M. Crawford for the International Exposition, Chicago, p. xix.

if they were Russians, were of merchant background, like Anika Stroganov, or they were craftsmen, like the Tula armsmith Nikita Demidov. Most of them, however, even in this period of a truly national Russian state, were of foreign origin—Englishmen primarily, and then Dutchmen. This foreign participation in Russian enterprise became even more pronounced in the succeeding period of the formation of the Russian Empire, 1700-1850. The tsarist domain became not only a multinational empire in the political sense, but also an economic world of commercial-industrial enterprise, analagous, as Professor Armstrong has indicated in his essay here, to the Mediterranean Arab empire of the seventh and eighth centuries, and in some respects to medieval Western Europe of the twelfth century. With the absorption of the Baltic states, Poland and the Caucasus, the Russian state came to rule over several national minorities who were to play an important if not predominant role in the development of enterprise during the period of industrialization: Germans, Poles, and Jews, most notably. Another geographical development of crucial importance for the evolution of Russian enterprise in the same period was the return and concentration, beginning in the reign of Catherine the Great, of Old Believers in the city of Moscow.[9] The establishment of a new imperial capital at St. Petersburg on the Gulf of Finland was also a crucial geographical factor in Russian entrepreneurial history. The hub of the tsarist administrative apparatus, the empire's greatest port, and a major industrial center less than a century after its founding, St. Petersburg conditioned the emergence of a particular type of entrepreneurship.

By the last decades of the old regime, St. Petersburg may be considered an early version of what is today termed a "world city." An international depot with a spirit that invited experimentation, it bred a cosmopolitan type of entrepreneur, of Western origin—mainly German, but also French, British, Swedish and American—Western in outlook and citizenship. Although there was a noticeable Russification of the staff of St. Petersburg enterprises at middle and high levels, capital continued to be drawn very largely from Europe. The St. Petersburg entrepreneurs were involved deeply in foreign trade, but also in highly concentrated industries, with large working forces, corporate organization, and sophisticated technology. By the turn of the century, another group of banking entrepreneurs in St. Petersburg had formed into a financial oligarchy that "set its sights on controlling the economy of the entire country." In spite of such ambitions and extensive foreign connections, the St. Petersburg entrepreneurs continued to live under the shadow of the Leviathan, and

[9] At the same time, another modernization of the craft tradition into industrial entrepreneurship was taking place at the eastern tip of the central industrial region among the serf craftsmen-entrepreneurs of the Sheremetiev village of Ivanovo. See Blackwell, *Beginnings of Russian Industrialization*, 205-11.

were more closely "intertwined" with the tsarist bureaucracy than any other entrepreneurial group in the Russian Empire.[10]

Less involved with, or subservient to, the government and yet strongly nationalistic and fervently monarchist were the entrepreneurs of Moscow. The old capital and its regions shaped another distinct variant of entrepreneurship in the tsarist empire, what may be considered the most purely Russian type. This came to maturity in the early nineteenth century. It was a wedding of the centuries of entrepreneurial experience of the Muscovite craft tradition to the practice and organization of religious dissent. The Old Believers, who returned to Moscow in great numbers thanks to the tolerant religious policy of Catherine the Great, and settled in its suburbs, wherein a puritanical communal life facilitated capital accumulation as well as labor mobilization for modern industrial enterprise, were a numerical minority of Moscow's entrepreneurs. But they were powerful and wealthy, particularly in the textile-manufacturing sector, and, partly as a result of their tradition of religious study and disputation, highly articulate. As they secularized, this religious background was transformed into traditionalism in business practice, conservatism in politics, and nationalism in culture. Adhering to the older ways of family-controlled firms, loyalty to the tsar, and preservation of Russian culture, particularly religious painting, the Muscovite entrepreneurs never really modernized, even with the challenge presented by progressive, competitive entrepreneurial groups from other parts of the empire and the political storms of 1905 and 1917. The most dramatic image we have of this conservatism is the scene, in a blizzard-swept railway yard in 1918, of the meeting of two "expropriated" Muscovite entrepreneurs, one clutching a family ikon beneath his overcoat.[11]

Foreshadowing the policies of Witte at the end of the century, the dynamic finances minister of the Kingdom of Poland, Prince F. X. Drucki-Lubecki instituted a comprehensive program of capital accumulation and industrialization in the 1820s and 1830s. This provided the basis and incentive for entrepreneurship of a new group of capitalists who involved themselves deeply in the industrial revolution of the Polish region. Ethnically, a few of the new economic leadership were recruited from the declining Polish gentry; but the majority were either Polish Jews, Germans, Belgians, or French. Entrepreneurial activity focused on heavy industry: railroads, iron and coal mining, and steel manufacture, but there was also significant development of the Polish textile industry and

---

[10] Material on St. Petersburg entrepreneurship, and also the information later that deals with the Polish and southwestern entrepreneurs, was derived from the very original treatment of these regions or peripheries in Professor Rieber's book (supra, n. 4), chapters 6 and 8.

[11] This anecdote is presented in Thomas Owen's book (supra, n. 1).

sugar refining, the latter not on estates, but in factories in Warsaw. Financing was done from the same city, where bankers were in touch with the capital sources and markets of Vienna and Berlin. Industry grew in the new centers of Lodz, Huta Bankova, and Dumbrowa.[12]

Riga had the most venerable tradition of entrepreneurship in the Russian Empire, if we exclude such ramparts of the ancient Mediterranean mercantile world as Armenia. The great Baltic port and industrial center was itself an eastern outpost of German culture—of Protestantism, capitalism, German law, organization, and science. Its Baltic German mercantile cadre, through centuries of commercial activity, accumulated the capital and nurtured the capitalist mentality that provided the social and economic foundations for Riga's industrialization in the nineteenth century. The entrepreneurs that financed and superintended the industrialization of Riga were both Baltic Germans and *Reichdeutsch*, with a sprinkling of Russian Old Believers, Jews, and English. Much of Riga's technology and capital also were derived from Germany. Riga's industrial and commercial entrepreneurs thus became part of both the industrial revolution of the late nineteenth century in Germany and the same process in the Russian Empire, the latter providing the market for Riga's industry as well as some of the raw materials and foods.

The newest and most dynamic industrial region during the last decades of tsarist Russia was the Southwestern, embracing the eastern Ukraine and the north coast of the Black Sea in an industrial triangle extending from Kharkov in the north to Krivoi Rog in the west to Rostov on the Don in the east. Geographically, the Southwestern Industrial Region represented a transfer of Russian heavy industry from the stagnant Urals to the emergent west: railroads united the Donets coal mines with the ore of Krivoi Rog, facilitating a massive and rapid buildup of the iron and steel industry. As in the case of almost all the other industrial regions of the Russian Empire—the old Muscovite, the Urals, St. Petersburg and the Baltic, the Polish, and the Transcaucasian—the Southwestern Region was largely developed by foreign entrepreneurs, mainly Belgians and Frenchmen, who traded their advanced technology for high returns. But a crucial role in the development of the area was played by new types of entrepreneurs who were subjects of the Russian Empire. Ethnically, they were a mixed lot: Poles, Jews, Russianized Germans, Ukrainians, and Russians. Functionally, three types of entrepreneurs can be identified. First, there was what John McKay has termed the promoter, essentially a salesman with contacts among Tsarist officials, Russian investors, and European firms. A second type, with representatives among both the

---

[12] In addition to the short account by Rieber, see also G. Missalowa, "Les crises dans l'industrie au royaume de Pologne a lepoque de la revolution industrielle," *Studici historicae economicae*, no. 8 (Poznan, 1973); and my essay (supra n. 7).

foreign and Russian subject entrepreneurs, was essentially a technologist: he was a manager or an engineer, and many of this group had formal training as engineers. A third type of entrepreneur can be seen in the great railway tycoons of the Western and Southwestern regions, involved in the complex effort of financing, constructing, and coordinating railway networks. Some of these entrepreneurs were German, others Jewish, most notably Samuel Poliakov and Ivan Bloch.[13] The Russian entrepreneur of the Southwestern Region can be characterized as mixing a frontier boom-town speculativeness with corporate managerial sophistication and technological expertise. He represents the most advanced stage of entrepreneurship as it appears in the last years of the old regime.

As crucial as geography is to an understanding of the evolution of enterprise in tsarist Russia, Russian entrepreneurship is equally a matter of economic and social history. Many of the essays on the tsarist period are devoted to the elaboration of not only the many impediments to enterprise in Russia, but also the rich variety of entrepreneurial activity over a period of several centuries, involving most social groups and intruding upon the main branches of the economy.

Thomas Owen's essay, "Entrepreneurship and the Structure of Enterprise in Russia, 1800-1880," describes merchants, peasant traders, dealers, industrialists, concessionaires, importers, promoters, salesmen, investors, managers, technological innovators, financiers, and lobbyists during a period of modernization of entrepreneurship at the beginning of Russia's first industrial revolution. It is clear that a genuine entrepreneurial spirit existed in Russia, despite the facts that entrepreneurship was thwarted by the state and the entrepreneur himself was despised by the gentry and intelligentsia. By fusing the spirit of entrepreneurship with nationalist aims it was possible for the Russian entrepreneur to make his calling an honorable one. Samuel Baron, in his "Entrepreneurs and Entrepreneurship in Sixteenth/Seventeenth-Century Russia," gives us a portrait of the premodern, highly diversified, large-scale Muscovite merchants of early modern times, and observes that entrepreneurship in that period was more substantial than has been perceived previously by scholars, given the formidable impediments to economic growth.

Fred Carstensen, in "Foreign Participation in Russian Economic Life: Notes on British Enterprise, 1865-1914," studies the role of British entrepreneurship in Russia before the Witte period, and questions both the statistics and the thesis that minimize British involvement in the Russian

---

[13] John P. McKay, *Pioneers for Profit* (Chicago, 1970), p. 92. Rieber also discusses types of the new entrepreneur, as does Arcadius Kahan in his chapter on Jewish enterprise here. On Bloch, see Blackwell, *Beginnings of Russian Industrialization*, pp. 260, 321, for brief references. There is no full-scale study of this important entrepreneur.

economy in areas other than the state-induced sector of development. He sees a market pull that attracted a significant transfer of British technology.

Political aspects of Russian enterprise in the tsarist period were also extensively analyzed by the symposium. Almost every chapter touches upon the state: it is the "red thread" of Russian entrepreneurial history, as deeply interwoven with this activity as with other sectors of Russian life through the centuries. Boris Anan'ich's essay, "The Economic Policy of the Tsarist Government and Entrepreneurship in Russia from the End of the Nineteenth through the Beginning of the Twentieth Century," probes this theme most deeply, considering the way by which increasing government control and intrusion impeded private enterprise, but also examining government entrepreneurship, as seen in the activities of Sergei Witte, who may be considered both a political and an economic entrepreneur. Ruth Roosa, in "Russian Industrialists During World War I: The Interaction of Economics and Politics," treats another political theme, the political and administrative activities of big Russian private entrepreneurs involved in the war effort, their failure to unite, and again, the retrograde force of the state.

Perhaps the most challenging achievement of the symposium has been its exploration of psychological history. Entrepreneurship, wherever it appears, is the result of material arrangements, but it is also a state of mind, a view of the world, a type of personality, motivation, and ideology. This theme has been developed in a large theoretical literature, extending from the classic articles on the Protestant ethic and capitalism, written over three-quarters of a century ago by Max Weber, to very recent studies by McClelland, Hagen, Strodtbeck, and others, including the essay by John Armstrong included in this symposium. In the broadest sense, it refers to the aggressive and activist attitude toward nature and society seen by many scholars as a key prerequisite for modernization. In the narrower, economic meaning, it is restricted to the profit-seeking incentives motivating entrepreneurs.

Both definitions are useful for an understanding of entrepreneurship in Russian history. As has been noted here and elsewhere, Peter the Great is the example, par excellence, of the secular modernizing mentality that has played so important a role in both tsarist and Soviet Russian history. Less dramatic cases in point would be the tsarist ministers of finances of the late nineteenth century, most notably Sergei Witte. Peter was the first great Russian "political entrepreneur"—which may be defined as the early modern state builder, mobilizer of the national populace, ingatherer and consolidator of new territories, modernizer and manager of standing armies. The survival and growth of modern European states, it is argued, depended upon a "continuous supply of political entrepreneurs,"[14] among other crucial factors.

More than a political entrepreneur, Peter was also the leading economic entrepreneur of early eighteenth-century Russia. He was the large-scale innovator of new techniques, the manager of a vast economic enterprise, the engineer of roads and canals, the founder of scores of factories, the mobilizer of their management and labor force, the builder of cities, the developer of science and technology, and the accumulator of capital through taxation and war.[15]

There was a third aspect of the Petrine mentality and energy relevant to our discussion beyond political and economic entrepreneurship strictly defined. Peter was possessed seemingly of a daemonic impulse to modernize, what has been termed voluntarism—the highly activist belief in the power of the determined human will to overcome all obstacles, to subdue nature, control society, and, indeed, accelerate history.[16] We could dismiss Peter's voluntarism as an accident of personality had it not reappeared in dramatic fashion in Lenin's dynamic brand of elitist communism, and the leadership of Stalin. In the 1930s, Peter's daemonic modernizing voluntarism was repeated with forcefulness and cruelty, with similarly revolutionary economic results. These were the two great enterprises of Russian history in modern times.

Defining the entrepreneurial mentality more narrowly and economically as a quest for profits, it must first be noted that the urge to acquire profits—even seen as rational calculation—is not necessarily congruent with the modernizing mentality. Thus, the Old Believers of early nineteenth-century Moscow, who were relentless and systematic profit seekers and profit makers, were at the same time profoundly antimodern in their approach to almost all aspects of life. Except for the financing and production of textiles in modern factories, the Old Believers, at least the early entrepreneurial generations of the sect, strove to preserve life as it had been in the premodern Russia of the mid-seventeenth century. Inevitably, however, they began to secularize, Westernize, and modernize outside as well as inside of their factories. But to the very end in 1917, they clung to a cultural traditionalism and political conservatism that

[14] Charles Tilly, ed., *The Formation of the National States in Western Europe* (Princeton, 1975), pp. 40-41.

[15] On Peter's role as an entrepreneur, see the recent discussion by M. C. Kaser, "The Impetus from Peter the Great," *The Cambridge Economic History of Europe*, ed. Peter Mathias and M. M. Postan (Cambridge, 1978), vol. 7, part 2, pp. 432-52.

[16] On Peter's daemonic voluntarism, defined as "the daimonic feeling that development was a function of will power translated into pressure and compulsion," see Alexander Gerschenkron, *Europe in the Russian Mirror* (Cambridge, 1970), pp. 71-73, cited in W. W. Rostow, *How It All Began* (New York, 1975) in the chapter "The Politics of Modernization," pp. 55-60; Rostow also sees a dynamic Petrine state entrepreneurship.

retarded the modernization of their enterprises as well as their society, as contrasted to most other groups of entrepreneurs in the last years of the old regime.

Much of the scholarship on the entrepreneurial attitudes of the Old Believers and other religious minorities during the early stages of the industrial revolution in Russia has focused on the social economic aspect seen in the relationship of religion to capitalism.[17] The finding has been that outcast religious groups developed a spirit of cooperation and frugality; that they pooled their financial resources as well as mobilized a labor force, with a resultant rapid growth of industrial and commercial enterprise. These conclusions have been established and need no further elaboration, at least for the groups that have been studied. However, much more can be said about the entrepreneurial personality in this context. The first model that scholars used was the controversial thesis of Max Weber on the Calvinist ethic and entrepreneurship, for the similarities between particularly the Old Believers and European Protestant dissenters were striking. Indeed, they had been noted a generation before Weber's theorizing by the keen French observer of the Russian Empire in the 1880s, Anatole Leroy Beaulieu. Weber had only passing and fragmentary references in his encyclopedic works to some of the Russian dissenting groups seen as progenitors of an entrepreneurial spirit. In allusions that were not elaborated in his studies of the sociology of religion, he joined the Old Believers and Sectarians, particularly noting the Stundists and Skoptsy, with European Pietists, Methodists, Quakers, Calvinists, Mennonites, Baptists, and others, as religious groups linked with rationalized capitalistic development, although in a qualified way and to a lesser degree than the Western sects. He also remarked on the economic role of subordinate or transplanted and pariah minorities, such as the Poles in Russia on the one hand, and the Jews and Gypsies on the other.[18] Arcadius Kahan, in his "Notes on Jewish Entrepreneurship in Tsarist Russia," has elaborated on part of this mosaic with a description of the Jewish entrepreneur in the nineteenth century, the varied sources of his capital and equally wide range of entrepreneurial activity within and outside the Jewish community, and the emergence of more rationalized and sophisticated entrepreneurship, extending from the period of estate stewardship under serfdom to the complex integration of financing, promotion, and management in railroads and other industries during the last years of the old regime. The dynamism that activated Jewish entrepreneurship was its rationality and determination. "It was a group of

---

[17] See William L. Blackwell, "The Old Believers and the Rise of Private Industrial Enterprise in Early Nineteenth-Century Moscow," *Slavic Review*, 24 (1965): 407-24, and Gerschenkron, *Europe in the Russian Mirror* for the main expositions of this approach.

[18] Max Weber, *Wirtschaft und Gesellschaft*, 4th ed. (Tübingen, 1956), vol. 1, p. 292.

rational men, knowledgeable of the realities of the world, of the marketplace and of their own worth and calling."

Other commentators have attempted to develop models of the entrepreneurial personality, essentially along the theoretical lines put down by Weber, most notably Everett Hagen, David McClelland, Fred L. Strodtbeck, and John A. Armstrong, in his essay in this symposium. Armstrong, in "Socializing for Modernization in a Multiethnic Elite," discusses the role of early life experiences of socialization of ethnic minorities in producing an entrepreneurial personality in such groups as the Old Believers, Jews, and Germans, during the crucial formative period of empire and enterprise during the eighteenth and nineteenth centuries. This occurred particularly in the great imperial "melting pot" cities of late tsarist times, seen as breeding places for the entrepreneurial spirit.

As suggestive as this theorization is, it needs the underpinning of more basic research of a purely empirical and historical nature on the entrepreneurial personality in Russia, where availability of sources permit. This is perhaps the most neglected field of Russian entrepreneurial history, more even than its social and geographical aspects, and I can only outline here what I see as four distinct areas that need substantial future investigation. First, we must have a much clearer picture of the religious and ethnic mix of entrepreneurship in the Russian Empire in the period of capitalism, particularly as this is seen in the major cosmopolitan urban "melting pots"—St. Petersburg, Odessa, Warsaw, Riga, and also Moscow. Who were the entrepreneurs in terms of national and religious origin, numbers, location, type of enterprise, and extent of capital? How do we distinguish between "foreign" and "Russian" entrepreneurs? Many entrepreneurs were not Russian, but were not foreign either. The British were an exception; they remained strictly unassimilated. Russia for them was like a colony: St. Petersburg could have been Hong Kong, or Cairo. But it was different for most of the other entrepreneurs who were not born linguistically or ethnically Great Russians. Whatever their origin, they operated on a Russian geographic stage, were part of a Russian community, spoke Russian, thought and believed like Russians, converted to Russian religion, and were loyal to Imperial Russia. Yet we never use the word *immigrant* in discussing them, as in the case of United States history; but perhaps we should not use the term *melting pot* either. Nevertheless, there would appear to have been a many-faceted socialization going on in the multinational cultural entity of the Russian Empire in its great urban centers during the last century of the old regime. Some of these non-Russians became bureaucrats, some revolutionaries, some the avant garde, and some became entrepreneurs.

Second, much more should be known of the specific ethnic and religious minorities engaged in enterprise, their cultural traditions, social organization, and political tendencies. The Baltic Germans are a case in point, in terms of their Protestant and German heritage, their role as *mamluks* rather than *pariahs*, their position as a privileged military, bureaucratic and commercial elite. What was their role in the development of capitalism in Riga and other modernizing cities of the northwest? Intense and active group solidarity was a long tradition with the Baltic Germans, going back at least to the seventeenth century, when they changed allegiance from Sweden to Russia after many generations of what may be considered suffering as a persecuted ethnic minority under Swedish absolutism.[19] To what extent did this experience forge an entrepreneurial personality?

Third, much has recently been learned, but there are still questions to be answered of the life style and attitudes of the large entrepreneurial cadre drawn from the Orthodox Great Russian majority, particularly the Muscovite core. There are now two recently published studies that deal with this subject in great detail, particularly as regards culture and politics.[20] Finally, there is, on the other hand, practically no biographical study of the individual entrepreneur, Russian and non-Russian, in capitalist Russia. To the extent that sources are available (and Arcadius Kahan has indicated in his essay the paucity of these in such cases as Jewish enterprise, although much more material appears to be available for the study of Great Russian, German, and British entrepreneurs), perhaps the greatest need in the field of Russian entrepreneurial history is to probe inside the mind, family life, and social and cultural experience of the individual entrepreneur.

The study of the Russian entrepreneur in the tsarist period embraces a very substantial subject in time and space, social and ethnic complexity, diversity of economic functions, ubiquity of political forces, and a subtlety and richness of psychological nuance. We are involved with a millennium of the history of a very large empire, the interaction of a multiplicity of social, ethnic, and religious groupings of the most diverse origin and purpose, as wide ranging a variation of economic functions as is to be found in any of the major regions of the world, and a perennial and deep entanglement of entrepreneurship and the autocratic state. The historical study of Russian entrepreneurship has hardly begun and its elaboration will require extensive and variegated monographic research, as well as synthesis of a nature and scope comparable to the now substantial achievements of the longstanding traditions of entrepreneurial history of

[19] Mart S. Kuuskvere, "The Baltic German Nobility of Estonia and Livonia, A Political Study: From Crisis to Stability, 1675-1728," Dissertation, New York University, 1976.
[20] See notes 4, 9, and 11.

the United States and Europe, particularly Germany. The virtue of this collection, particularly the essays on the Tsarist period, is its rich diversity, which at the minimum casts light on many of the major problems and aspects of Russian entrepreneurship, and provides a preliminary map for the research that must come.

III

SAMUEL H. BARON

Entrepreneurs and Entrepreneurship In Sixteenth/Seventeenth-Century Russia

If the title of this chapter raises some eye-brows, that is a tribute to the strength of a historiographical tradition which envisages Muscovite Russia as a commercially and industrially backward country in which, necessarily, businessmen and entrepreneurial activity could play only an insignificant role. The tradition owes much to the mutually reinforcing writings of such foreign observers of Muscovy as Giles Fletcher, Iurii Krizhanich, and Johann Phillip Kilburger. Fletcher (1590) portrayed the Russian merchants as a group with low status and no power ("no better than servants or bond slaves"), whom the tsars regularly fleeced; and, since accumulation under these conditions was but the prelude to spoliation, they showed little interest in enterprise. Krizhanich (1663-65), a Croatian Russophile, was dismayed by the Muscovites' ineptness in economic affairs, and fervently hoped to teach them how to improve their performance. Almost a century after the publication of Fletcher's book, Kilburger (1674) wrote: "the Lord God, for unknown reasons, still conceals from the Russians [that] no country can do without a merchantry [and trade], and . . . that their country more than any other in the universe is endowed with the requirements [*udobstva*] for the organization and flourishing of commerce." Fletcher, Krizhanich, and Kilburger all emphasized that the Russian government was excessively involved in economic enterprise, and that it stifled private business effort with inordinate regulation and unmeasured exactions.[1]

---

[1] Giles Fletcher, *Of the Russe Commonwealth*, ed. Richard Pipes and John V. A. Fine, Jr. (Cambridge, Mass., 1966), pp. 22ᵛ, 41, 45ᵛ-47; B. G. Kurts, ed., *Sochinenie Kil'burgera o russkoi torgovle v tsarstvovanie Alekseia Mikhailovicha* (hereafter, Kilburger), (Kiev, 1915), p. 87; Iu. Krizhanich, *Politika* (Moscow, 1965), pp. 382-420, 482-83. On the prevalence in the seventeenth century of the belief that God had so distributed resources

This point of view deeply influenced prerevolutionary Russian historians and, through them, Western writers both past and present.[2] But another and contrary tradition has taken shape in the present century. It had its beginnings with M. N. Pokrovskii, who envisaged the rise of commercial capitalism to predominance—and a concomitant rise in the power of the merchant class—in the sixteenth and seventeenth centuries.[3] After the repudiation of Pokrovskii in the thirties, Soviet historians assumed a less extreme stance, finding in Lenin's well-known remark concerning the role of "merchant capitalists" in the development of an "all-Russian market" the basis for locating the *beginning* of the "transition from feudalism to capitalism" in the seventeenth—or, occasionally, the sixteenth—century. Soviet researches both in Pokrovskii's time and since have produced a considerable amount of material that highlights commercial and industrial development through entrepreneurial activity in the Muscovite era.

In the last two decades, new developments have complicated the historiographical situation. The post-Pokrovskii position failed to convince all members of the Soviet guild, and in the sixties the skeptics directed a well-orchestrated attack against it. Arguing that the dominant conception was unacceptably one-sided, they denied the claims made for the sixteenth and seventeenth centuries, and placed the beginning of the transition to capitalism no earlier than the last third of the eighteenth.[4] Although the critical group clung to various concepts that Western scholars generally are unlikely to accept, its efforts significantly narrowed the distance between the two. In roughly the same years, interestingly enough, a few Western writers who may have been influenced in one way or another by the dominant current of Soviet historiography have challenged the virtual consensus in the West. In reaction to what they perceived as a one-sidedness of *their* colleagues, they contended that commerce, industrial development, and a bourgeoisie were of greater moment in the Muscovite era than Western scholarship has been willing to concede.[5]

---

over the earth as to promote trade, see Jacob Viner, *The Role of Providence in the Social Order* (Princeton, 1972), chap. 2.

[2] Illustrative is the recent work of Richard Pipes, *Russia under the Old Regime* (New York, 1976), chap. 8.

[3] M. N. Pokrovskii, *Russia in World History*, trans. Roman and Mary Ann Szporluk (Ann Arbor, 1970), pp. 70-72. Pokrovskii's views are elaborated more fully in the closing chapters of his *Russkaia istoriia s drevneishikh vremen*, 3rd ed., 4 vols. (Moscow, 1920), vol. 1.

[4] *Perekhod ot feodalizma k kapitalizmu v Rossii* (Moscow, 1969). For a discussion of this "new current," see Samuel H. Baron, "The Transition from Feudalism to Capitalism in Russia: A Major Soviet Historical Controversy," *American Historical Review*, 77, no. 3 (1972).

[5] Jacqueline Kaufmann-Rochard, *Origines d'une Bourgeoisie Russe* (Paris, 1969); Joseph T. Fuhrmann, *The Origins of Capitalism in Russia* (Chicago, 1972); Paul Bushkovitch,

Diversity of views is of course not a bad thing, but it is a source of some puzzlement when those holding differing views have available much the same materials. Differing presuppositions and approaches may not be so important as we are apt to assume, moreover, when rifts are apparent not only between, but also within, the Soviet and Western historical communities. Is it possible, we are impelled to ask, that the well-worn tale of the blind men and the elephant is germane; that neither of the primary contending parties has grasped the whole truth, each having seized a part which it mistakes for the whole? In particular, is it possible that those who have trumpeted the achievements of entrepreneurial activity in our period have tended to ignore the impediments to capitalistic development, while those who have concentrated on the latter have tended to underestimate the former? May not the dissenters on both sides have been groping toward a synthesis that would do justice to both aspects of the story? If their varied efforts have been less than compelling, rather than dismiss them, might it not be preferable to strive for a more accurate and balanced representation? Such unsettling thoughts and questions have occurred to me with increasing frequency since I, an upholder and sometimes contributor to the dominant Western view,[6] lightheartedly undertook to write a paper on the emergence of the entrepreneur in sixteenth- and seventeenth-century Russia.

The discussion that follows may seem at times to be only obliquely concerned with entrepreneurship, but there are good reasons for this. For one, information on many aspects of entrepreneurship in Muscovite Russia is anything but abundant. Moreover, as Barry Supple has so effectively demonstrated for Western Europe in this era, enterprise cannot be divorced from the environment in which it occurs.[7] As the range of factors that make up the environment establishes the framework and limits, and shapes the character, of entrepreneurial activity, these factors must figure prominently in our discussion.

A Great Potential, Minimally Exploited?

Let us begin with Kilburger, who evidently was the first person to pose the problem trenchantly. As he saw it, Russia was blessed with a whole

"The Merchant Class of Moscow, 1580-1650," Dissertation, Columbia University, 1975. These several works are quite different in focus and approach.

[6] Samuel H. Baron, "The Weber Thesis and the Failure of Capitalist Development in 'Early Modern' Russia," *Jahrbücher für Geschichte Osteuropas*, 18, no. 3 (1970); "Vasilii Shorin: Seventeenth Century Merchant Extraordinary," *Canadian-American Slavic Studies*, 6, no. 4 (1972); "Who Were the *Gosti*?" *California Slavic Studies*, 7 (1973); "The Fate of the *Gosti* in the Reign of Peter the Great," *Cahiers du Monde Russe et Soviétique*, 14, no. 4 (1973).

[7] Barry Supple, "The Nature of Enterprise," in *Cambridge Economic History*, 5 vols. (Cambridge, 1941-77), vol. 5.

series of advantages "for the organization and prospering of commerce," and yet it failed to secure a tenth of the gain that it might have were its resources more effectively exploited: (1) It was well furnished with valuable resources, among them furs, leather, and hides, hemp and flax, fish and caviar, train oil, potash, tallow, masts, and grain. On the other hand, it required many things that it did not produce, and thus the essential conditions for a lively and profitable foreign trade existed. (2) Its frontiers were close to four of the world's great seas—the Baltic, White, Black, and Caspian—and, therefore, it was admirably situated to engage in trade with both West and East. (3) Besides, he implied, Russia's geographical situation offered its merchants the opportunity to profit further by acting as middlemen between East and West. (4) Because Russia boasted many navigable rivers, foreign goods could readily be transported into the interior, and native products to seaports, whence they might be shipped abroad. (5) Finally, Russia's people, whether of high estate or low, showed a decided propensity for trade. The merchants were shrewd and able, and their requirements were modest. Therefore, they ought to prosper, to accumulate, and to expand their business operations.

Paradoxically, this apparently auspicious set of circumstances had thus far produced meager fruit because, as Kilburger put it, the Russian authorities "oppress and hinder trade in many ways." He alluded to the tsar's monopolies in the trade of a number of commodities; the failure to support financially those who knew how to develop manufactures; the oppressive activities of the *gosti* (the merchant elite), whom he envisaged as the tsar's factors; and the heavy duties and other hindrances inflicted on foreign merchants. The economy languished for other reasons too: The government deprived itself of the helpful services of foreign specialists because it reputedly dealt arbitrarily with them; and, to compound the difficulty, it would not allow its own subjects to go abroad to study with others. Besides, the Russians failed to give due attention to communications and transportation. They did not keep the roads in proper condition, and they did not build ships, even though they possessed in abundance all the essential materials.[8]

The last point was also stressed by other foreign observers, most notably the Frenchman Jean de Gron, who in 1651 submitted to Tsar Aleksei Mikhailovich a plan for the economic development of Russia.[9] The key

[8] Kilburger, pp. 87-90, 148-50, 152-53. As the next pages of this paper constitute a critique of Kilburger, attention may also be called to my critique of Fletcher's representation of the merchantry in "Ivan the Terrible, Giles Fletcher, and the Muscovite Merchantry: A Reconsideration," *Slavonic and East European Review*, 56, no. 4 (1978).

[9] De Gron's project is printed, though wrongly identified, in A. Viskovatov, *Kratkii istoricheskii obzor morskikh pokhodov russkikh i morekhodstva ikh voobshche do iskhoda XVII stoletiia* (St. Petersburg, 1864), pp. 165-70. It is discussed in N. Baklanova, "Ian de

point in his scheme was the establishment of a shipbuilding industry. This undertaking would stimulate the exploitation of the forests for timber and the growing of hemp and flax for rope and sails. The new industry would soon create a Russian merchant fleet, the means to expand Russian commerce manifold, and this shipping capability would stimulate native export industries. De Gron projected a bustling trade not just with Europe but with such far-flung places as Brazil, India, and China. The fleet could be gainfully employed in carrying the cargoes of other countries as well, and Russia might even sell ships to Portugal, Venice, and France at a handsome profit.

There is obviously more than a grain of the fanciful in De Gron's plan—could anyone seriously expect Russia to be transmuted forthwith into a maritime power capable of carrying on an active trade with Europe, Brazil, India, and China? Elements of Kilburger's analysis call forth objections too. Russia's southern frontier actually lay a considerable distance from the Black Sea and, although part of its northeastern border was close to the Baltic, it had free access to neither, since both were controlled by foreign powers. The White Sea port of Archangel was frozen shut half of the year, and Russia's rivers too were closed for many months. Russia's failure to maintain a good road system is understandable, indeed inevitable, given its well-integrated river system and the prohibitive costs of building a satisfactory road network in such an enormous territory. Foreigners were in fact recruited into Russia's service in some numbers, and only few, usually high-ranking military men, were detained.[10] However, despite such objections, it would seem that Kilburger's analysis and his and De Gron's prescriptions still have considerable merit. In particular, Russia seemed to enjoy real opportunities to expand its commerce if its merchants more vigorously assumed the role of intermediaries between East and West, and if it were to create a merchant fleet of its own. It was not unreasonable to suppose that the growth of foreign trade and shipping would stimulate the exploitation of native resources; and that increased use of foreign experts and the sending of Russians abroad to study would result in the introduction of new, or the improvement of old, industrial methods. Last, but not least, if the tsar gave up his trade monopolies; and, in general, if the government loosened control of economic affairs, would not private initiative be stimulated, and commerce and industry flourish?

If, initially, assent to all this is apt to be readily forthcoming, the more

Gron, prozhektor v moskovskom gosudarstve XVII veka," *Uchenye zapiski Instituta istorii RANION*, 4 (1929): 109-22. Krizhanich (p. 540) also called attention to Russia's shipbuilding capability and the benefits its development would confer.

[10] Samuel H. Baron, trans. and ed., *The Travels of Olearius in Seventeenth Century Russia* (hereafter, Olearius), (Stanford, 1967), p. 200n.

one reflects on these propositions the more do doubts arise. People like Kilburger and De Gron were rather insensitive to what we may broadly call cultural differences and the limits these set on possibilities for change. For that reason, they greatly overestimated Russia's then potential for economic development. Still, they should not be judged too harshly. After all, able Western economists who participated in the emerging field of development economics after World War II were obliged to discover the hard way the truth that, as it was often expressed, "you go into one of these Asian or African countries as an economist, and come out an anthropologist." In other words, to gauge the prospects and find suitable avenues for economic development requires a good understanding of the particularities of the society and culture concerned. Kilburger and other foreign observers of Muscovy were intelligent men, but they were not anthropologists or even economists; and, in the bargain, they apparently knew little about Russian history and the deeply ingrained features of the society it had shaped.

Consider, for example, the expectation of Kilburger (and Krizhanich) that the Russian government might be persuaded to withdraw from, or relax its control of, different areas of economic activity, thus providing a stimulus for private initiative. To both components of this proposition, contrary arguments may readily be adduced. Apropos the first, inasmuch as pretensions to unlimited power (autocracy) and to control of the country's resources (patrimonialism) were fundamental features of the Muscovite political system,[11] the likelihood that a tsar might respond positively to such pleas seems slim indeed. It may be retorted that neither Kilburger nor anyone else advocated a government policy of laissez faire; it was a case rather of favoring intelligent and stimulative over wrong-headed and stifling state action. And if, as such different writers as V. O. Kliuchevskii and the Soviet author A. I. Pashkov have agreed, the Muscovite government "looked upon the economy first of all as a source for replenishing the state treasury, and [accordingly] subordinated its economic policy to fiscal interests," then a tsar's own self-interest should lead him to welcome proposals that promised economic growth and a consequent increase in revenues.[12]

Though this line of reasoning may seem persuasive to us, it would not necessarily have convinced a Russian ruler. What we have designated intelligent and stimulative action implies selective rather than comprehensive state involvement. But a powerful inclination toward total control was a most prominent feature of Muscovite autocracy. Arguments for

[11] Richard Pipes (supra, n. 2) is the most recent of a long line of historians of Russia who have emphasized the patrimonial character of the Russian regime.
[12] V. O. Kliuchevskii, *Sochineniia*, 8 vols. (Moscow, 1956-59), 3:267; A. I. Pashkov, *Istoriia russkoi ekonomicheskoi mysli* (Moscow, 1955), vol. 1, part 1, p. 230.

self-limitation, therefore, were tantamount to arguments for a change in its essential nature. Except for the remarkable A. L. Ordyn-Nashchokin, a voice crying in the wilderness, Russia's governing elements apparently took for granted a direct relationship between the extent and effectiveness of controls and the volume of revenue generated for the treasury.[13] Such an attitude might have seemed to be supported in fact, for revenues had grown as state authority expanded in the course of the sixteenth and seventeenth centuries, notwithstanding the setbacks inflicted upon the economy by the Livonian War, the *oprichnina*, and the Time of Troubles.[14]

Because Russia long stood outside the main currents of European commercial development, its merchants had not experienced the transforming effects of what Robert Lopez has called "the commercial revolution of the middle ages."[15] In the sixteenth and seventeenth centuries, they were in more or less continuous contact with the dynamic merchant capitalism of Western Europe, with its great store of accumulated knowledge, skills, experience, and supportive institutions, but were incapable of competing with it. They evidently recognized their inferiority and saw no hope of overcoming it, especially since West European merchants actively discouraged them. Consequently, they tacitly surrendered a large measure of control over their foreign trade.[16] They did not go abroad to traffic; instead, foreign merchants came to Muscovy to sell European goods and to procure Russian wares for European markets. The Russians did not construct seagoing vessels; instead, their water-borne trade with Western Europe was carried exclusively in foreign bottoms. They eschewed shipbuilding partly out of inertia—Russia had no significant maritime tradition—partly, perhaps, out of the despair they felt about the prospects of participating effectively in West European markets. Kilburger and De Gron emphasized foreign trade when they prescribed programs for Russia, yet this was precisely the area in which the Russians contented themselves with a passive role. It is difficult to see how the relaxation of

[13] Ordyn-Nashchokin argued against sacrificing the welfare of the people to the interests of the fisc. He believed that the state should assist and cooperate with entrepreneurs, while allowing them great freedom of initiative. See the article on Nashchokin in *Russkii biografisheskii slovar'*, vol. 12, esp. pp. 289-94; E. V. Chistiakova, *Sotsial'no-ekonomicheskie vzgliady A. L. Ordyn-Nashchokina* (Voronezh, 1950), pp. 15-40; Pashkov, pp. 214-17, 226.

[14] Thus in the 1660s, when the government was in dire financial straits, it deliberately set out to increase state revenues by establishing a massive economic empire directly under its own control. A. I. Zaozerskii, *Tsarskaia votchina XVII v.*, 2nd ed. (Moscow, 1937).

[15] Robert S. Lopez, *The Commercial Revolution of the Middle Ages, 950-1350* (Englewood Cliffs, N.J., 1971).

[16] I have dealt with this question in "The Muscovy Company, the Muscovite Merchants, and the Problem of Reciprocity in Russian Foreign Trade," *Forschungen zur osteuropäischen Geschichte*, 27 (1980).

government control alone could have galvanized them into action, and enabled them to overcome their backwardness. Perhaps Kilburger was aware of this problem when he pointed to Muscovy's need of foreign specialists and the desirability of sending Russians abroad to study. The reverse side of this attitude, it should be pointed out, is a lack of faith in the value of private initiative left to itself. Finally, the power of conservatism, the attractiveness of tested and more or less efficacious methods as opposed to new ones whose results were bound to be uncertain, should not be underestimated.

On the other hand, let us suppose that the regime accepted counsel of the sort Kilburger proffered. Would private initiative inevitably have been unleashed, with marked and persistent economic growth following? On the basis of the widespread "love of trade" he had observed, Kilburger assumed that this would occur if the government pulled back from commercial operations and gave up all sorts of burdensome regulation of the operations of others. Without a doubt, private merchants could be expected to exploit commercial opportunities made available were the tsar to surrender his trade monopolies in a variety of products. Other than that, however, there are ample grounds for doubting the expectations of Kilburger and his like. He was unaware of the history of the Russian merchantry, of the near disappearance of towns and trade during the long period of the Mongol yoke, and of their subsequent, slow revival within the framework of a Muscovite state well along in the process of unification and centralization. This powerful state easily subordinated the young, small, and comparatively weak merchant element to its own interests and needs. The merchants generally accepted their subservient status rather than struggle for greater independence and self-determination, and their capacity for initiative was accordingly stunted. Yet important though these circumstances were, the posture of the merchants cannot be understood solely in terms of their relation to the government.

The problem of Russia's foreign trade relations involved not Europe alone; an analogous situation existed in its relations with the Orient. Russian merchants traveled to Persia infrequently, and to India or other Eastern lands practically never, choosing instead to trade with Indian and Armenian merchants at Astrakhan. These merchants performed the role of middlemen between Russia and the Orient much as the Dutch, English, and German merchants did between Russia and the West. The matter of oceangoing craft was not an issue here, although Russia evidently lacked vessels capable of negotiating the Caspian Sea easily and safely. While the Eastern countries experienced the commercial revolution of the middle ages no more than did Russia, their merchants may still have enjoyed certain advantages as a result of a long, uninterrupted history of commercial activity. At any rate, as a recent Soviet work has put it, "the Moscow merchants . . . proved less enterprising, and also less prepared for large foreign trade operations, than their experienced Indian competitors, with their wide connections throughout the Near East."[17] The parallelism between Russia's relations with the West and the East causes us to wonder whether, in addition to other considerations, most Russian traders may have shunned foreign travel for religious or cultural reasons.[18]

The belief that Russia possessed a great untapped potential for profitable trade in the role it might play as intermediary between East and West must be examined too. In the first place, some Russian merchants recognized an opportunity here, and sought to cash in on it by trading Oriental wares at Archangel and Western products at Astrakhan or in Persia. The scale of this trade does not seem to have been very great, it is true, and there were those who thought it could be much increased. However, it is well to recall that the tsars from time to time monopolized the trade in such Oriental products as raw silk and rhubarb, but when they allowed others free access to the silk trade, this hardly produced a revolution in the pattern or volume of Russia's foreign trade.[19]

Indeed, it is probable that Kilburger and others greatly overrated the potential for Russia of the intermediary role in trade between East and West. This may be inferred from information at our disposal concerning the efforts of a number of foreign trading companies to capitalize on Russia's geographical position to secure control of part of the East-West trade. The English Muscovy Company (1558-84), a Holstein company (1634-39), and an Armenian one based in Persia (1667-73) all secured from the tsars the right to travel from Archangel across Russia to Persia and back (the reverse for the Armenians). The great expectations of each proved illusory, however. Unforeseen difficulties—whether climatic and navigational, the depredations of marauders, or the rapaciousness of government officials—conspired to produce losses rather than the gains anticipated, or profits insufficient to warrant continuation of the trade.[20] Nor were such disappointments restricted to foreign merchants alone. Russians who sent caravans to trade in Persia in the mid-seventeenth century suffered tremendous losses.[21] Not to speak of other problems,

---

[17] *Russko-Indiiskie otnosheniia v XVII v. Sbornik dokumentov* (Moscow, 1958), p. 13. The entire introduction to this collection of documents is germane to our discussion. Considerations of space prompt us to leave out of our account Russia's trade relations with China, which had their beginning in the mid-seventeenth century.

[18] On prohibitions against and inhibitions of contact between Russians and West Europeans, see Samuel H. Baron, "The Origins of Seventeenth Century Moscow's Nemečkaja Sloboda," *California Slavic Studies*, 5 (1970).

[19] Kilburger, pp. 150-51.

[20] T. S. Willan, *The Early History of the Russia Company, 1553-1603* (Manchester, 1956), pp. 149-55; Olearius, pp. 5-11; Baron, "Vasilii Shorin" (supra, n. 6), pp. 530-31.

[21] *Russko-Indiiskie otnosheniia v XVII v.*, no. 55; S. M. Solov'ev, *Istoriia Rossii s drevneishikh vremen*, 30 vols. in 15 (Moscow, 1959-66), 6:572.

so long as the tsars could not guarantee security on the middle and lower Volga, and the shahs in their domains, the prospects for development of this particular axis of East-West trade were far from auspicious.

The recommendations of Kilburger and De Gron left out of consideration some as yet unmentioned aspects of Russian society that militated against greatly expanded and accelerated economic development. These authors somehow managed not to notice—or at least not to consider worthy of comment—that the mass of the population were serfs, living in an overwhelmingly natural rather than a commercialized economy. As serfs, the bulk of the population had little disposable income and, therefore, minimal purchasing power. As they also produced most of their subsistence requirements, demand for goods was bound to be weak, the market narrow, and the possibility of expanding it decidedly limited. These circumstances compounded the difficulties for the development of an easy, low-cost traffic already inherent in the dispersion of a relatively small population in Muscovy's immense territory.

Kilburger and De Gron, each in his way, anticipated the stimulation of native resource exploitation as one consequence of a more active foreign trade. In fact, Russian production of furs, potash, timber, pitch, and other commodities had grown in response to foreign demand. Some further growth in the production of such goods, and a corresponding increase in commercial opportunities for Russian merchants, may have been within the realm of the possible. But, given the institution of serfdom and the political predominance of the landed-servitor class, the principal results were apt to be intensified exploitation of resources and the peasant labor force under the aegis of the landed class, continuing emphasis on the production of raw materials and foodstuffs, and a further degree of economic dependence upon the mercantile powers of Western Europe. In short, one could foresee the sort of economic development peculiar to Poland in the sixteenth century[22]—and, with some significant variations, of Russia in the eighteenth—but not the emergence of a socioeconomic order featuring the commercialization of the economy and the erosion of local self-sufficiency, the decline of serfdom, and the rise in importance and power of a bourgeoisie.

It may be objected that the line of argument advanced here is excessively bleak; that we have in effect foreclosed the possibility of significant Russian economic development in the era under consideration; that, in any case, our brief is contradicted by the impressive growth registered during

[22] Jerome Blum, "The Rise of Serfdom in Eastern Europe," *American Historical Review*, 62, no. 4 (1957); Marian Malowist, "Poland, Russia, and Western Trade in the 15th and 16th Centuries," *Past and Present*, 13 (1958); Immanuel Wallerstein, *The Modern World System* (New York, 1974), chap. 6.

the reign of Peter the Great. To these objections we reply: First, of course, we believe that our seventeenth-century observers did exaggerate Russia's potential for economic growth but, contrariwise, we will presently argue that they underestimated Russia's *actual* economic achievements. Secondly, as regards the foreclosure of possibilities, we have taken a skeptical view of the kind of economic development that Kilburger and his like seem to have projected for Russia, but not every kind. Thirdly, significant economic advances certainly were made in Peter's reign, but along quite different lines than the seventeenth-century observers envisaged. Most importantly, the spurt of economic growth that occurred was stimulated not by government withdrawal from economic life but, on the contrary, by its more active involvement than ever.[23] In Peter's time, an incipient tendency to substitute the state for what was perceived as an insufficiently energetic commercial-industrial class became much more pronounced and conspicuous. The results are illuminating. Peter built Russia's first navy, and he helped to promote the construction under state or private auspices of the first elements of a merchant fleet. Oddly enough, however, while Russia sold some of the vessels it produced to West European entrepreneurs, Russian merchants still ventured abroad to trade infrequently.[24] Furthermore, so far as we know, in Peter's reign Russia did not succeed in aggrandizing its role as intermediary in the East-West trade to any great extent. The state itself was the most important industrial entrepreneur, and in large part to fill its own needs for iron, weapons, ships, cloth for uniforms, and sails. Moreover, the new industrial sector was grafted onto a society still featuring autocracy, the predominance of the landed-servitor class, serfdom (the new industrial enterprises were manned by serfs!), an overwhelmingly natural as opposed to a commercialized economy, and a small class of commercial-industrial people who were of little sociopolitical significance.

A Limited Potential, Fairly Effectively Exploited

If we set aside as unfounded the view that Russia's potential for economic development in the Muscovite era was enormous, we ought to make some estimate of its actual opportunities and the degree of success with

[23] Peter's encouragement to the merchants to form trading companies (1699) and establish industrial enterprises (1702) met with little or no response. See Baron, "The Fate of the *Gosti*" (supra, n. 6), pp. 502-3; Alexander Gerschenkron, *Europe in the Russian Mirror* (Cambridge, 1970), pp. 69-81; N. I. Pavlenko, "Torgovo-promyshlennaia politika pravitel'stva Rossii v pervoi chetverti XVIII veka," *Istoriia SSSR*, no. 3 (1978). For a somewhat different view, see Arcadius Kahan, "Entrepreneurship in the Early Development of Iron Manufacturing in Russia," *Economic Development and Cultural Change*, 10, no. 4 (1962).

[24] N. N. Repin, "Kommercheskoe sudostroenie v Rossii v kontse XVII-pervoi polovine XVIII veka," *Voprosy istorii*, no. 1 (1978).

which they were exploited. These are difficult tasks hardly susceptible to precise solutions, partly because the sources are extremely limited and fragmentary, partly because of the large number of variables involved, partly because of subjective factors. Be that as it may, I would hypothesize that the Russians did not do badly, that is to say, they made a fairly successful adaptation, given the severe constraints within which they functioned. If their performance was less impressive than some Soviet writers would have us believe, it was a good deal more impressive than people like Kilburger implied. In making the case for a fairly successful exploitation by the Russians of a limited potential, we are obliged to rely upon the handful of Soviet studies of individual entrepreneurs and entrepreneurial families.[25] This presents no great problem, I believe, for on the whole these researches were carried out conscientiously; and, besides, the message they convey largely corresponds with my own findings in a study of the *gost'* Vasilii Shorin. The Shorin case may be used both to illustrate Muscovite entrepreneurial activity, and as a point of departure for its further discussion. It may be of particular interest in that Shorin's business activity attained full flower at about the same time that De Gron, Krizhanich, and Kilburger articulated their ideas.

In the mid-seventeenth century, Shorin (birthdate unknown, died 1678 or 1679) developed a business empire of imposing proportions.[26] He was first and foremost a merchant, although his business activity was not confined to commerce. A major participant in Muscovy's foreign trade, he or his agents dealt with Dutch and English merchants at Archangel,

[25] S. V. Bakhrushin, "Torgi gostia Nikitina v Sibiri i Kitae," *Nauchnye trudy*, 4 vols. in 5 (Moscow, 1952-59), 3:pt. 1; the same author's treatment of Sveteshnikov and the Gur'evs in "Promyshlennye predpriatiia russkikh torgovykh liudei v XVII v.," ibid., vol. 2; and of a Novgorod entrepreneur family, "Torgi novgorodtsev Koshkinykh," ibid.; E. Zaozerskaia, "Vologodskii gost'" G. M. Fetiev (Iz byta torgovykh liudei XVII v.)," *Zapiski istoriko-bytovogo otdela Gosudarstvennogo Russkogo Muzeia*, no. 1 (1929); V. Geiman, "Solianoi promysel gostia I. D. Pankrat'eva v Iarenskom uezde v XVII veke," *Letopis' zaniatii Arkheograficheskoi Kommissii za 1927-1928 gg.*, Vyp. 35 (Leningrad, 1929); K. V. Bazilevich, "Krupnoe torgovoe predpriatie (Bosovykh) v Moskovskom gosudarstve v pervoi polovine XVII veka," *Izvestiia Akademii Nauk SSSR. Otdelenie obshchestvennykh nauk*, Seriia 7, no. 4 (1932); N. A. Baklanova, "O datirovke 'Povesti o Savve Grudtsyne,' " *Trudy Otdela drevne-Russkoi literatury. Institut Russkoi Literatury*, 9 (1953); idem, *Torgovo-promyshlennaia deiatel'nost' Kalmykovykh vo vtoroi polovine XVII v.* (Moscow, 1959); V. A. Aleksandrov, "Sibirskie torgovye liudi Ushakovy v XVII v." in N. V. Ustiugov et al., eds., *Russkoe gosudarstvo v XVII veke* (Moscow, 1961); A. A. Vvedenskii, *Dom Stroganovykh v XVI-XVII vekakh* (Moscow, 1962); E. S. Ovchinnikova, *Tserkov' Troitsy v Nikitnikakh* (Moscow, 1970), chap. 1; M. Ia. Volkov, "Khoziastvo kapitalista-kuptsa Srednogo Povolzh'ia I. A. Mikliaeva v kontse XVII—pervoi chetverti XVIII v.," in S. D. Skazkin et al., eds., *Problemy genezisa kapitalizma* (Moscow, 1970). See also the data on entrepreneurs in northern Russia in the last half of the sixteenth century in N. E. Nosov, *Stanovlenie soslovno-predstavitel'nykh uchrezhdenii v Rossii* (Leningrad, 1969), pp. 240-84.

[26] All the data in this sketch are drawn from Baron, "Vasilii Shorin," supra, n. 6.

with Oriental merchants at Astrakhan, and with representatives of both West and East at Moscow. To some extent he acted as a middleman for the exchange of goods between East and West, but certainly more significant was his role as a purveyor of native products to the foreigners. Furs appear to have been the single most important item he sold to both Western and Oriental merchants, but he also delivered such commodities as hemp, hides, and tallow to the Westerners. On several occasions he sent caravans with thousands of rubles worth of goods to be traded in Persia, and he had plans for the development of trade relations with India. He was at least marginally involved as well in trade with Sweden by way of the Baltic.

Shorin's foreign trade surely constituted a principal element of his business activity, though it is impossible to say whether it predominated. In any case, his external trade required him to procure goods for sale to foreigners and to distribute the wares bought from them. Thus, he repeatedly purchased large numbers of fine furs from the "sable treasury" of the government's Siberian Chancellery (*Sibirskii Prikaz*), and in the major market at Velikii Ustiug. His agents also traveled to Siberia to obtain furs directly from trappers or local jobbers. For these Siberian ventures, Shorin outfitted his agents with so-called Russian goods, a wide variety of foodstuffs, clothing and fabrics, and hardware (axes, weapons, and the like), which were not produced in Siberia and consequently had to be "imported." The procurement of these Russian goods added another element of complexity to Shorin's operations. So did the disposal of such Western luxuries as velvets, satins, damasks, vessels made of precious metals, and writing paper; items of wider use such as needles and inexpensive baubles; and raw silk (and perhaps spices and dyes) from the East. While Shorin sold some of these items wholesale to other merchants, he surely procured various luxury products for individual members of the court and Moscow's upper social strata. Moreover, he had a good many retail shops in Moscow's Kitaigorod section, and he may have had others in different parts of the capital or in other towns.

It should not be supposed that Shorin's domestic trade was merely an appendage to his foreign trade. In fact, he dealt wholesale and retail in a variety of commodities, notably salt, fish, leather and hides, and grain, whose procurement and distribution had either no relation at all, or at most an indirect one, to his foreign business. The lion's share of his internal trade appears to have been connected rather to productive enterprises that he developed or acquired. Shorin was a salt merchant as early as the 1630s, but in the course of his career he became the owner and operator of a number of salt-producing works. One was located at Kostroma, another at Sol' Velikaia, and the four salt-boiling units he ran at Sol' Kamskaia made him one of the more important producers in the country's leading salt-extraction center.[27] For several decades, he controlled the three best weirs in the rich fishery on the Volga north of Astrakhan. Shorin sent quantities of fish up the Volga, and salt from his Sol' Kamskaia works by way of the Kama and Volga to the market at Nizhnii Novgorod, where he possessed a compound and storage facilities overseen by one of his agents. Portions of these products may have been sold at Nizhnii, while others were dispatched to other places. There are records of the sale of Shorin's salt at Moscow and Orel, of his fish in the capital and as far afield as Novgorod.

At Nizhnii, Shorin owned together with another merchant two works that processed hides into leather. The one about which we have some information was fairly impressive in size, boasting seven or eight buildings, employing perhaps twelve persons, and producing thousands of rubles worth of leather each year.[28] Shorin was also a landowner. He possessed two villages near Ustiug, which produced hay and grain crops, at least part of which were sold. He may have had other lands too, but in any case he was involved in the grain trade. He apparently owned a fleet of rivergoing vessels as well to carry his cargoes hither and yon. His carrying capacity must have exceeded his needs, for on occasion he contracted to ship boatloads of state grain down the Volga, probably for the provisioning of troops garrisoned in towns along the river. Parenthetically, it required a small army of people—peasant cultivators, fishermen, salt- and leather-workers, boatmen, warehousemen, salespeople, clerks, and the agents (*prikazchiki*) who oversaw different subdivisions of the whole—to sustain Shorin's business empire.

Finally, we know that Shorin was active as a moneylender, thanks to information available about a few loans which became the subject of litigation. He advanced sums to foreign merchants and native Russians alike, no doubt at the going rate of 20 percent interest per year. Shorin may also have extended small amounts, but the size of those we have run across is arresting. Around 1650, he loaned 2,000 rubles to an English merchant named Osborne. Earlier he had loaned 480 rubles to a court peasant, Artamon Sergeev, and later 2,555 rubles to a townsman-trader, Matvei Pershin.

These sums indicate that Shorin possessed a good deal of capital, and a few other figures may help to drive the point home. Shorin repeatedly purchased furs from the state or at Velikii Ustiug to the value of 4,000-5,000 rubles; he initiated trade ventures to Siberia worth thousands of rubles; and a caravan he sent to Persia reportedly suffered losses of over

[27] On this, see N. V. Ustiugov, *Solevarennaia promyshlennost' Soli Kamskoi v XVII v.* (Moscow, 1957).

[28] With respect to the last point, the evidence is not entirely clear. See Baron, "Vasilii Shorin," pp. 513, 516, and note 40.

17,000 rubles.[29] It is astonishing to learn that the large fur purchases, the loan to Osborne, a trade venture (with a partner) to Siberia with over 6,000 rubles worth of goods, the caravan to Persia, and the acquisition of the Sol' Kamskaia and the Kostroma saltworks all occurred between 1647 and 1654. The tens of thousands of rubles of which Shorin disposed constituted a very considerable sum at a time when the entire state revenue came to no more than 1.3 to 1.5 million rubles per year.[30]

What we have described, it must immediately be added, is based upon a record consisting exclusively of those surviving state papers that reflect the intersection of Shorin's activities with governmental authority. His business records, like those of just about every Russian entrepreneur of the sixteenth and seventeenth centuries, have not been preserved. Accordingly, the image we obtain of the number and scale of his business operations may be a good deal less than complete.[31] More importantly, the surviving documents provide only glimpses of the internal aspects of his operations. As is the case with other entrepreneurs of the period, therefore, we are unable to specify with any certainty or precision such vital matters as the dimensions of Shorin's capital at different points in time, the rates of profit he achieved—and his losses, the relative importance of different sectors of his business activity, the stages in the development of his interests and organization, and the manner in which the several components were coordinated and managed.

Nevertheless, Shorin's case surely demonstrates—contrary to Kilburger and others—that an entrepreneur could flourish in Muscovite Russia. But it also raises many questions, above all, how typical was Shorin, what does his activity tell us about the incidence and character of entrepreneurship in sixteenth/seventeenth-century Russia? Inasmuch as he was a great entrepreneur, by definition there were not many like him, but there was a larger number of substantial businessmen than may be supposed. The *gosti*, the top-level privileged merchant corporation to which Shorin belonged, averaged only thirty members throughout the seventeenth century. The second- and third-level privileged corporations, the *gostinaia sotnia* and the *sukonnaia sotnia*, totaled from three hundred to six hundred at different times (incidentally, most of those elected to

---

[29] At one point, he owed the state treasury over 28,000 rubles. Ibid., p. 533.

[30] For figures on the state revenue, see Kliuchevskii, *Sochineniia*, 3:235-36; Raymond Fisher, *The Russian Fur Trade, 1500-1700* (Berkeley and Los Angeles, 1943), pp. 118-19. Kliuchevskii estimated that the seventeenth-century ruble was worth seventeen times that of the late nineteenth century. Others have criticized his method, but we seem to have no better estimate.

[31] Parenthetically, the state of the sources explains our frequent resort to conjectural language in the foregoing account.

all three groups were obliged to reside in Moscow).[32] Appointment to these corporations went only to conspicuously active and successful men, although there were of course significant differences in wealth both among and within the three groups. In the provincial towns, the townsmen (*posadskie liudi*) were ranked according to affluence and the dimensions of their trade into *luchshie, srednie,* and *molodshie.* The first-named group, from whose number members of the privileged corporations were often recruited, included hundreds of well-to-do persons; and even some of the *srednie* engaged in salt production, the grain trade, or other operations on a scale sufficient to warrant their inclusion in the ranks of the entrepreneurs. Finally, a considerable number of court, patriarchal, and monastery peasants who engaged in production and/or trade were also named to the *gostinaia sotnia* or the *sukonnaia sotnia*—a sure sign that these groups included numbers of substantial operators.[33] Although the data is far from complete, and though the numbers no doubt fluctuated through time, there are apt to have been as many as three thousand entrepreneurs active throughout much of the seventeenth century, probably fewer in the sixteenth.

There appears to have been no lack of rank-and-file townsmen—and peasants—who were alert to opportunities and tried to make the most of them. In salt-rich regions such as Sol' Kamskaia, local residents set up tens of extraction works on lands they occupied. In the seventeenth century, as many as 500 to 1,000 *promyshlenniki* came annually to the Enisei region of Siberia to make their fortune in fur trapping. In the Nizhnii Novgorod region, where grain was abundant, among those who produced liquor were everything from members of the *gostinaia sotnia* through *posadskie liudi* to landless peasants (*bobyli*). At Novgorod in the last half of the sixteenth century there were around 4,400 craftsmen and 645 merchants, large and small; at Pskov, almost 1,500 trade es-

---

[32] According to a document of 1649, there were 600 during the reign of Fedor Ivanovich (1584-98) and 274 in 1649. The reason for the decline in numbers is not at all clear, but it continued. By 1710-13, the *gostinaia sotnia* numbered around 100, and the *sukonnaia sotnia* no longer existed. See *Dopolnenie k aktam istoricheskim*, 12 vols. (St. Petersburg, 1846-75), 3:no. 47, p. 59; M. Ia. Volkov, "Formirovanie gorodskoi burzhuazii v Rossii XVII-XVIII vv.," in *Goroda feodal'noi Rossii* (Moscow, 1966), p. 185; Tsentral'nyi Gosudarstvennyi Arkhiv Drevnikh Aktov (hereafter TsGADA), Knigi Denezhnogo Stola, 1710, nos. 153, 154.

[33] Scattered data show sixteen *luchshie liudi* at Iaroslavl' in 1614, seventeen at Ustiug in 1623-26, and eighteen at Pskov in 1655. See O. P. D'iakonov, "Posadskaia obshchina g. Iaroslavlia v pervoi polovine XVII veke," *Uchenye zapiski Iaroslavskogo Gosudarstvennogo Pedagogicheskogo Instituta*, Vyp. 60 (19), 1947; Ustiugov (supra, n. 27), pp. 56-57; V. A. Bogusevich, "Pskovskie kuptsy XVII v. Rusinovy," *Novgorodskii istoricheskii sbornik*, Vyp. 8 (1940):40. Examples of non-*luchshie liudi* who evidently ran substantial enterprises are found in Ustiugov, pp. 56-57; *Goroda feodal'noi Rossii*, p. 379. On substantial traders who were dependents of ecclesiastical or secular magnates, see *Istoriia Moskvy*, 6 vols. (Moscow, 1952-59), 1:459-60; 2:72-73.

tablishments (shops, warehouses, etc.). And, as Kilburger observed, the Russians' love of trade was manifest in the presence in Moscow of "more shops . . . than in Amsterdam or entire principalities."[34] Needless to say, though many were called few were chosen. But from among the large number of townsmen who engaged in small-scale trade or craft production, some of the more shrewd, energetic, able, or lucky might expand and diversify their operations and move upward in the merchant social order. Numbers of peasants (especially in the north, where serfdom penetrated slowly or not at all, and some who were dependents of monasteries) also ventured into trade, did well, and were advanced into the upper levels of the merchant class.[35] Despite the fact that movement from one social group to another was in principle prohibited in Muscovite society by the mid-seventeenth century, both before and after that time social mobility within the commercial-industrial community was conspicuous.

The history of the Shorin family is instructive in this regard. Vasilii's father was a *gost'*, and of course this conferred definite advantages on him. But the privileged merchant corporations were not closed, hereditary groups. Vasilii was fortunate to inherit a considerable capital, but he was designated a member of the *gostinaia sotnia* rather than a *gost'*. He might have remained that for the rest of his life or he might have squandered his substance and lost his status. He did neither, instead demonstrating the qualities that soon resulted in his promotion to the topmost rank. As a *gost'*, Vasilii far surpassed his father in the range and dimensions of his entrepreneurial activity. On the other hand, one of his sons was utterly incompetent; and the other, who was also named a *gost'*, had an indifferent career, which ended in insolvency. Such cases of downward mobility were by no means exceptional. Shorin's business activity had much in common with that of other major Muscovite entrepreneurs; whether the Stroganovs, the greatest entrepreneurial family of the period, whom alone the tsars dignified with the status of *imenitye liudi* ([merchant] titled persons); other *gosti* such as Grigorii Nikitnikov, Nadeia Sveteshnikov, the Gur'evs, Filat'evs and Pankrat'evs; or members of the *gostinaia sotnia* like the Kalmykovs of Nizhnii Novgorod, the Reviakins of Ustiug, and Sergei Pogankin of Pskov.[36] All of these, and many another,

---

[34] Ustiugov (supra, n. 26), pp. 41-62; V. A. Aleksandrov, "Rol' krupnogo kupechestva v organizatsii pushnykh promyslov i pushnoi torgovli na Enisee v XVII v.," *Istoricheskie zapiski*, 71 (1962); Baklanova, *Torgovo-promyshlennaia deiatel'nost' Kalmykovykh*, p. 106; Bakhrushin *Nauchnye trudy*, 1:142, 144-45; Kilburger, p. 88.

[35] Nosov (supra, n. 25), pp. 240-84; Bakhrushin, "Torgovye krest'iane v XVII v.," *Nauchnye trudy*, vol. 2. The Kalmykovs were monastery peasants.

[36] A good deal of information on the Reviakins occurs in A. Ts. Merzon and Iu. A. Tikhonov, *Rynok Ustiuga Velikogo v period skladyvaniia vserossiiskogo rynka (XVII vek)* (Moscow, 1960). On Pogankin, see E. V. Chistiakova, "Pskovskii torg v seredine XVII v.," *Istoricheskie zapiski*, 34 (1950):226-30.

engaged in both commercial and industrial activity, in foreign and domestic, and wholesale and retail trade. They had far-flung business interests and large staffs to perform the many essential tasks. Most loaned money at interest and also possessed riverboats to transport their goods. Although the similarities are more important, there were differences too. The Stroganovs had very large landholdings, while others had much less or none at all. If the operations of the Stroganovs, Shorin and others reached into almost every corner of the country, and involved almost every type of activity, those of others were more restricted. For example, *gost'* Gavrilo Nikitin was mainly involved first in the Siberian and then the China trade; the Ushakovs' activity was confined chiefly to Siberia, and that of the Kalmykovs to the Volga region and Astrakhan. The mix of enterprises differed from person to person too. Though they had varied interests, the Kalmykovs and the Ushakovs made their fortune principally by way of contracts to supply the government with fish, grain, liquor, and beer. The Koshkins of Novgorod specialized in the importation of metals from Sweden. It is safe to say that the business of nonprivileged entrepreneurs was similar in kind to, if smaller in volume than, that of their privileged confreres.

There is more testimony to entrepreneurial vigor in the period in the recognition and exploitation of economic opportunities which arose thanks to such major contemporary developments as the spectacular territorial expansion of Muscovy and the concomitant growth of the state apparatus. The annexation by Moscow of Novgorod, Tver, Pskov, Smolensk, and Riazan between 1478 and 1517 vastly increased the area wherein productive activity and commerce could be carried on. Perhaps most significantly, the cession of the Republic of Novgorod gave Moscow control of the Pomor'e, an immense territory extending northeastward from Novgorod, which boasted rich fur, fish, and salt resources, navigable rivers, and access to the northern seas. The exploitation of these resources more intensively than ever before made the Pomor'e one of Muscovy's major economic hearths. The development of this region, and particularly the northern Dvina country, gained fresh impetus in 1553, with the opening by the English of a new sea route between Western Europe and Russia, and with Archangel (built 1584) becoming the most important center of an expanding trade with Western Europe.[37]

[37] See Nosov, (supra, n. 25), pp. 240-84 on the development of the Pomor'e; on the development of the Archangel trade, S. Ogorodnikov, *Ocherk istorii goroda Arkhangel'ska v torgovo-promyshlennom otnoshenii* (St. Petersburg, 1890); N. Baklanova, "Privoznye tovary v Moskovsom gosudarstve vo vtoroi polovine XVII veka," in *Ocherki po istorii torgovli i promyshlennosti v rossii v 17 i v nachale 18 stoletiia* (Moscow, 1928); B. N. Floria, "Torgovlia Rossii so stranami zapadnoi Evropy v Arkhangel'ske (konets XVI-nachalo XVII v.)," *Srednie veka*, Vyp. 36 (1973); Bushkovitch (supra, n. 5).

With the conquest of Kazan and Astrakhan in the 1550s, Muscovy gained control of the entire course of the Volga, direct access to trade with Oriental merchants at Astrakhan and in Persia, and the potential to become intermediaries in the exchange of goods between East and West. They also capitalized upon the resources of the lower Volga, among them fish, caviar, and salt.[38] Too, these conquests laid Siberia open to penetration, and it was subjugated by the mid-seventeenth century. Fur trapping grew by leaps and bounds in the sixteenth and seventeenth centuries, and furs became a more important item of trade than ever before.[39] The expansion of Muscovy brought under its sway lands with varied climates and resources, whose exploitation and exchange (e.g., the grain and crafted articles of the central regions for the fish, salt, and furs of the north and Siberia) offered attractive prospects for gain. To a remarkable extent, the activity of Shorin and other Muscovite entrepreneurs was connected with the Pomor'e, the middle and lower Volga, and Siberia.

Finally, the satisfaction of the state's varied and growing needs offered further opportunities for enterprise. As Muscovy expanded, new military-administrative centers were established to govern conquered territories such as the middle and lower Volga and Siberia, and their populations had to be provisioned. Moreover, the government contracted with private persons to furnish it with such other requirements as grain, vodka for the state liquor monopoly, provisions for the army, and transportation services. Then too, and perhaps this was the most important of all, lucrative opportunities existed in serving the needs of the capital. Moscow was not only the political but also the economic center of Muscovite Russia. It was at once the seat of the court, the location of the central government's offices and numerous personnel, the ecclesiastical headquarters, and far and away the most densely peopled place in the country. Though it was not larger than London, as is often asserted, with its population of 100,000 in the sixteenth century and 200,000 in the seventeenth, Moscow was one of the largest cities in Europe, and many times larger than such second-rank Russian towns as Iaroslavl' and Novgorod. Necessarily, great quantities of goods of all kinds flowed from

[38] A good deal of interesting material on the salt and fish industries is given in two articles by I. V. Stepanov: "Khoziaistvennaia deiatel'nost' Moskovskogo pravitel'stva v nizhnem Povolzh'e v XVII veke," *Uchenye zapiski Leningradskogo Gosudarstvennogo Universiteta*, Seriia istoricheskikh nauk, Vyp. 5 (1939); "Organizatsiia solianykh promyslov v nizov'iakh reki Volgi v XVII veke," ibid., Vyp. 8 (1941).

[39] Fisher, *The Russian Fur Trade*. Apropos Siberia, K. V. Bazilevich has written, no doubt with some exaggeration, that Siberia "played in the seventeenth century the same role in relation to the Muscovite state that the American and East Indian colonies did somewhat earlier vis-à-vis France, Holland, and England." See his "Krupnoe torgovoe predpriatie" (supra, n. 25), p. 2.

every part of the country and from foreign parts, both Western and Eastern, to provision the capital. Moscow was also the most important center of exchange of goods coming from all parts of the country. The greatest merchants resided there and, to a large extent, they directed the flow and profited from it.[40]

There has been a great deal of rubbish written apropos Lenin's pronouncement on the formation of the all-Russian market as a result of the activity of the "capitalist-merchants." If this proposition is understood in a properly qualified way, however, it is difficult to see how it can be contested. As we have noted, in exploiting their respective natural resources, people in different parts of the country produced particular kinds of goods while they lacked others. Merchants took advantage of the situation to transfer goods from where they were produced to where they were needed, thus performing a service to producers and consumers alike, and netting gains in the process. In linking different parts of the country into a network of interdependent parts, they created markets where none had existed before, and they undoubtedly helped to stimulate the production of certain goods. This is not to say, of course, that the Russian economy became capitalistic in the seventeenth century. As we know, and as many Soviet scholars readily acknowledge, the economy remained overwhelmingly natural and self-sufficient, the dimensions of the market very narrow and impossible to expand beyond certain limits, and the great majority of the population had little or no connection with the market, either as sellers or buyers.[41]

A few other aspects or achievements of Muscovite entrepreneurship may be briefly noted. The decision of entrepreneurs to invest in many different kinds of activity in widely separate parts of the country speaks for their flexibility and a willingness to take risks when profit lay in prospect. Along this line, it is noteworthy that as the fur yield from Siberia declined in the later seventeenth century, leading merchants shifted away from the fur trade to trade with China, a new field for enterprise as Russia inaugurated relations with the Middle Kingdom.[42]

Relative to business organization, a number of interesting cases of economic integration in Muscovite enterprise may be cited—and there surely were others. The Stroganovs, who began as salt producers, required

[40] An important prerevolutionary historian and Soviet writers agree on much of the substance of this paragraph. See M. V. Dovnar-Zapol'skii, "Torgovlia i promyshlennost' Moskvy v XVI-XVII vv.," in *Moskva v ee proshlom i nastoiashchem*, vol. 6; Bakhrushin, "Moskvia kak remeslennyi i torgovyi tsentr XVI v.," *Nauchnye trudy*, vol. 1; D. Tverskaia, *Moskva vtoroi poloviny XVII veka—tsentr skladyvaiushchegosia vserossiiskogo rynka* (Moscow, 1959).

[41] *Perekhod ot feodalizma k kapitalizmu v Rossii*; A. M. Sakharov, *Obrazovanie i razvitie rossiiskogo gosudarstva v XVI-XVII vv.* (Moscow, 1969), pp. 147-48.

[42] Aleksandrov, "Rol' " (supra, n. 34), p. 158.

all sorts of iron equipment for their works. As the equipment was expensive, they took to mining and smelting iron ore themselves, and soon met not only their own needs but produced a surplus of the metal, which they sold. Shorin acquired the fish weirs on the Volga north of Astrakhan in 1646, and several years later the saltworks at Sol' Kamskaia and Kostroma. Fish was a major item of the Russian diet, and a considerable share of it was fish preserved by salting. It is likely that Shorin secured the saltworks as a means to save on salt used in preserving his fish. The Kalmykovs' main effort went into contracts with the government to provide fish and grain. As the shipment of these commodities was of the first importance, they presently established boatbuilding wharves in a number of towns to provide the necessary conveyances. Just before he died, Klim Kalmykov, who "feared to let slip any opportunity to secure advantage," was looking into the use of mash, a by-product of liquor production (in which he had major interests), as cattle feed. All those mentioned, and many another, engaged in moneylending as an adjunct to their other activities. In particular, they advanced mortgage loans or assumed sureties on loans that others contracted, with an eye to prospective advantage; then, if the loans were not paid off, the creditors obtained properties they envisaged as complementary to their business interests.[43]

Even the briefest account of Muscovite entrepreneurial activity would be misleading if it did not give due attention to the relation between the entrepreneurs and the government, and more particularly the role of government favor. Given the pretensions of the tsars to unlimited power and to proprietorship of the country and its resources, an entrepreneur or a would-be entrepreneur, whatever his abilities, could not go far unless he enjoyed the government's approbation. Government favor was bestowed upon those who had rendered appreciable services or to men on the way up who were likely to do so. In extraordinary cases—the Stroganovs and the Gur'evs come to mind—a family (or an individual) at its own expense had equipped and made available military contingents, taken part in the conquest of a territory, or built a frontier fort. They, as well as others, might have made large monetary contributions or loans to the treasury, or consistently paid very high taxes.[44] More commonly, they served the tsars as factors, tax assessors and collectors, and officials in branches of the administration concerned with finance and commercial-industrial affairs.

[43] Vvedenskii (supra, n. 25), pp. 24-27, 36, 142-43, 298; Baklanova, *Torgovo-pro-myshlennaia deiatel'nost' Kalmykyovykh* (supra, n. 25), pp. 27, 104, 107, 108-23, 200-201; Baron, "Vasilii Shorin" (supra, n. 6), pp. 517-19.

[44] Vvedenskii (supra, n. 25), pp. 34, 52-56, 82, 95, 109-10, 126, 129, 130-31; Bakhrushin, *Nauchnye trudy*, 2:251-53.

For its part, the government had a wide range of benefits to distribute, whether formally (i.e., to members of the privileged corporations) or informally. Those designated *gosti* had the right to travel abroad (although almost none did). They and the members of the *gostinaia sotnia*, alone among the merchants, could own land. These groups were freed from certain tax levies and other responsibilities incumbent on the townsmen generally, they were not to be molested by local officials, and if they became involved in litigation they were to receive special judicial treatment.[45] Of course some of these privileges might be economically advantageous, but other, informal, benefits to which they and other substantial merchants had access may have counted more heavily. The tsars made extensive land grants to some merchant families, with the Stroganovs far and away the most handsomely endowed.[46] The government granted rights to exploit such resources as salt deposits, fisheries, and forests, sometimes as a boon but more usually in return for an annual payment to the treasury. The government let contracts to merchants to provide it with large quantities of vodka and beer, grain and fish for the capital, various military-administrative outposts, and the army. How lucrative such engagements might be is evident from this: the Kalmykovs paid subcontractors eight *altyns*, two *den'gi* for a small bucket (*vedro*) of liquor, which they then sold to the government for 15 *altyns* the bucket.[47] The government occasionally paid subsidies for the searching out of natural resources—metals and salt—for exploitation; and it also made available a kind of commercial credit, of which more later.

Entrepreneurs zealously competed in currying favor, and winning it definitely was an ingredient of entrepreneurial success. In Shorin's case, we either know or strongly suspect that the large fur purchases he made from the treasury, the lease he secured on the Volga fish weirs, his acquisition of some of the Sol' Kamskaia saltworks, and the trade caravan he sent to Persia in 1651 all were done with the government's blessing and/or aid. Moreover, there is reason to believe that because he was well-connected with high-ranking officials he was shown forbearance when he became involved in financial difficulties. The role of government favor is apparent in every case study of a successful Muscovite entrepreneur that we possess.

In addition to land grants, exploiting rights, contracts, and loans, there

[45] For a fuller discussion of the privileges and obligations of the *gosti*, see my article, "Who Were the *Gosti*?" (supra n. 6), pp. 12-19. For a patent that sets forth the privileges of a member of the *gostinaia sotnia*, see Baklanova, *Torgovo-promyshlennaia deiatel'nost' Kalmykovykh*, pp. 205-6.

[46] Vvedenskii (supra, n. 25), pp. 32, 82, 293, 298.

[47] Baklanova, *Torgovo-promyshlennaia deiatel'nost' Kalmykovykh*, p. 107. Of course, the difference was not clear profit, for expenses had to be defrayed.

was another kind of government aid which the merchants sought. They rightly viewed foreign merchants as a threat to themselves, particularly because the tsars had bestowed special privileges on some of them. It was not that the Russians wanted reciprocal rights abroad, for they felt incapable of making such rights effective. Rather, they strove to exclude foreign merchants from Russia's domestic market for their own benefit. They began as early as the 1560s with informal requests, which were satisfied, to bar the English merchants of the Muscovy Company from retail trade within the country, from the resale in Russia (and probably in Persia) of goods they bought there, and from the employment of Russians to buy, sell, and exchange goods for them. By the mid-1580s, Russian merchants secured the cancellation of much of what remained of the extraordinary privileges earlier granted the English Muscovy Company—its monopoly of trade with Russia at the White Sea, and the right to send agents across Russia to trade with Persia. And their influence surely worked to block the grant of such rights to the Dutch, who then began to replace the English as Russia's most important West European trade partner. Then they escalated their demands, and began to call for the restriction of all foreigners to trade at the country's frontiers.[48] In the seventeenth century, the merchants carried on a protracted petition campaign that won them a measure of tariff protection and, in the New Trade Charter of 1667, the apparent fulfillment of their primary objective vis-à-vis the foreign merchants.[49]

The Policy of Accommodation and Its Consequences

We have argued that conditions in Muscovite Russia did not afford so great a potential for mercantile activity, and for privately initiated economic growth generally, as many have supposed; that opportunities were in fact severely limited by a whole series of circumstances; and that, all things considered, Russian entrepreneurs made a respectable showing. Operating in a country whose government asserted a proprietary right to all natural resources and itself engaged in a good deal of commercial-industrial activity, they managed to initiate, promote, or support private exploitation of most of the then accessible resources, and to secure control

[48] See my article "The Muscovy Company" (supra, n. 16).

[49] See P. P. Smirnov, *Novoe chelobit'e moskovskikh torgovykh liudei o vysylke inozemtsev, 1627 goda* (Kiev, 1912); K. V. Bazilevich, "Kollektivnye chelobit'ia kupechestva i bor'ba za russkii rynok v pervoi polovine XVII veka," *Izvestiia Akademii Nauk SSSR. Otdelenie obshchestvennykh nauk*, no. 2 (1932); "Novotorgovyi ustav 1667 g.," ibid., no. 7; "Elementy merkantilizma v ekonomicheskoi politike pravitel'stva Alekseia Mikhailovicha," *Uchenye zapiski Moskovskogo Gosudarstvennogo Universiteta*, Vyp. 41, *Istoriia*, 1 (Moscow, 1940).

of the greatest part of the trade. Functioning under a government embarked upon an extraordinary territorial expansion, they proved adept at developing or capitalizing upon industrial and commercial opportunities in newly conquered regions. Living in an immense country with a very low population density, a country, moreover, whose economy was overwhelmingly natural and self-sufficient, they not only found and exploited opportunities for trade but even linked the widely separated regions of the country into an all-Russian market of sorts. The organization, financing, and transportation of this countrywide trade was no mean achievement.

The small dimensions of the market were offset in some degree by foreign trade and the growth in the needs of the state, whose aspirations and apparatus expanded greatly in the period. Muscovite merchants undertook with alacrity the filling of these varied needs, and reaped the gains this activity made possible. Some of them also took advantage of their close association with the government to increase their capital by diverting state funds to their own pockets.[50] In carrying out these diverse activities, they made effective use of the river network, built vessels appropriate to their requirements, and business organizations which, whatever their shortcomings, made possible the running of much-ramified enterprises.[51] Finally, though evidently incapable of competing in foreign markets, they did not suffer so badly on that account. The government was sufficiently responsive to their needs, and of course powerful enough, to prevent any one country from monopolizing Russia's foreign commerce and setting grossly unjust terms of trade. Besides, what Russia's merchants may have lost because of their nonparticipation in foreign markets was at least partly made up by their rather successful struggle to exclude foreigners from participation in Russia's domestic market. In the age of mercantilism, we should note, Muscovy consistently enjoyed a favorable balance of trade and an inflow of silver.[52]

Despite their economic achievements, which of course required energy, boldness, and skill, the Muscovite merchants were basically wedded to a policy of accommodation. To be sure, they took risks in the pursuit of profit, but always within well-defined limits, which they generally neither challenged nor tried to transcend. They never disputed the proprietary

---

[50] Kilburger, p. 449; Dovnar-Zapol'skii, "Torgovlia i promyshlennost' Moskvy" (supra, n. 40), pp. 32-35.

[51] On business organization and methods, see Bakhrushin, "Remeslennye ucheniki v XVII v.," and "Agenty russkikh torgovykh liudei XVII v.," *Nauchnye trudy*, vol. 2; Baklanova, *Torgovo-promyshlennaia deiatel'nost' Kalmykovykh*, pp. 49-57 and passim; Geiman, "Solianoi promysel," supra, n. 25.

[52] This is the central theme of Artur Attman's *The Russian and Polish Markets in International Trade, 1500-1650* (Gothenburg, 1973).

claims of the state to the country's resources, nor pressed for group autonomy, local self-government, or a voice in the affairs of state. They never campaigned for recognition of that most fundamental requirement of orderly and sustained business activity—security of property. Nor did they challenge the servitor-landowner class,[53] whose predominance ensured the prevalence of policies—for example, the binding of the peasants—which were inimical to their own interests. They did not see fit to challenge the foreign merchants' considerable control of Russia's external commerce and attempt to shift from a passive to an active trade. Rather than confront established institutions, traditions, and forces, the Russian merchants maneuvered around, over, and between these obstacles, to maximize their opportunities, status, and security.

Why they so behaved is not difficult to surmise. How could a smallish group, and an unorganized one at that, oppose itself to the powerful state, to the servitor class, or to a combination of the two, for they were apt to join forces in the face of a threat from a third party. The very idea of principled opposition may have scarcely occurred to the upper-level merchants. Unlike some merchant groups in the West, they had no tradition of political involvement or struggle and, anyhow, they had some reason to think of themselves as beneficiaries of the established order. On one occasion (1584-86), a number of them plunged into a political conflict and paid for their audacity with their lives,[54] an experience that must have powerfully reinforced the merchants' already strong inclination to political passivity. As regards competition in foreign markets, the Russians apparently envisaged the disparity between themselves and foreign merchants as so awesome that they despaired of overcoming it through an offensive strategy, and fell back instead on a policy of seeking exclusive control of the home market. In general, then, the Muscovite merchants took the path of accommodation because their traditions, outlook, numbers, and social position virtually precluded an alternative course. Besides, the risks involved in contrary policies were incomparably greater than the prospects of success.

To appreciate the latter point, one must be aware of the considerable hazards incurred by anyone who did business *within* the limits set by Muscovite conditions. Most of those who cast their bread upon the water failed to make good, while a much smaller number built more or less impressive enterprises and fortunes. Even for this last group, however,

---

[53] For some thoughtful comments apropos the relationship of the upper merchant strata to the ruling servitor class, see E. I. Zaozerskaia, *U istoki krupnogo proizvodstva v russkoi promyshlennosti XVI-XVII vekov* (Moscow, 1970), pp. 179-80. Kaufmann-Rochard (supra, n. 5), pp. 258-59, takes a somewhat similar view.

[54] P. P. Smirnov, *Posadskie liudi i ikh klassovaia bor'ba do serediny XVII veka*, 2 vols. (Moscow, 1948), 1:331-35.

success was often but the prelude to a dramatic collapse. This fate befell the Kalmykovs three to four decades after the beginning of their ascent to prominence. Despite Vasilii Shorin's accomplishments and stature, his business empire declined in his later years. As for his son Mikhail, he presently became insolvent, and the government forthwith confiscated his property.[55] Apropos the *gosti* generally, as I have elsewhere demonstrated, the chances that a member-family would maintain its standing for more than a single generation was only one in four, for more than two generations no better than one in fifteen.[56] Almost none of the great seventeenth-century merchant families survived as such beyond the reign of Peter the Great. Even if lesser entrepreneurs incurred lesser risks and consequently had better survival chances—a plausible if unproven proposition—their risks were still considerable.

Big merchants were often ruined by such accidents as fire or shipwreck, for no such thing as insurance existed. Or their trade caravans fell prey to marauders in such areas as the middle or lower Volga or Siberia, which the state was incapable of policing effectively.[57] Occasionally, urban disturbances in more established parts of the country led to the victimization of more affluent merchants by resentful rank-and-file townsmen. Judging by Shorin's experience, the incidence of nonfulfillment of obligations in the business community—both repayment of loans and delivery of goods according to contract—was distressingly high, and the tissue of commercial relations accordingly fragile and unstable. Similarly, if, as Supple has emphasized, uncertainty and insecurity stemming from inadequate information, discontinuity of markets, and the like, were hallmarks of commercial life in the far more developed West in this era, one can imagine how significantly such disabilities figured in Muscovy.[58] It should be added, perhaps, that spying, informing, vindictive frame-ups, and unscrupulous business practices, partly encouraged by the government-instituted surety system, added further hazards to the conduct of business.[59] The fact that the usual rate of interest was 20 percent per year at a time when it stood at 4 percent in Holland and 8 percent in England testifies eloquently to the high risks and insecurity involved in doing business in Muscovy.[60]

[55] TsGADA, Kontora Kantselariii Konfiskatsii, F340, no. 143.

[56] "Who Were the *Gosti?*" (supra, n. 6).

[57] E. I. Zaozerskaia, "Torgi i promysly gostinoi sotni srednego Povolsh'ia na rubezhe XVII-XVIII vv," in *Petr Velikii* (Moscow-Leningrad, 1947), pp. 232-33; Baron, "Vasilii Shorin" (supra, n. 6), pp. 546-47.

[58] See supra, n. 7.

[59] Horace W. Dewey and Ann M. Kleimola, "Suretyship and Collective Responsibility in pre-Petrine Russia," *Jahrbücher für Geschichte Osteuropas*, 18, no. 3 (1970).

[60] Violet Barbour, *Capitalism in Amsterdam in the Seventeenth Century* (Baltimore, 1950), pp. 80, 81, 85.

The government was of course an important part of the problem. It saddled the more successful entrepreneurs with burdensome service obligations, which were bound to affect their private affairs adversely. It exacted special contributions (tenth- and fifth-pennies) or services in time of war or other emergencies—and they were all too frequent—which cut significantly into the merchants' substance.[61] From year to year it increased the charges for the right to exploit different resources, thus reducing profits and sometimes driving private entrepreneurs out of the field altogether. It not only competed with private businessmen in certain industrial and commercial activities, but it had no compunction about expanding its operations at their expense when it was hard pressed financially, as during the thirteen-year war with Poland (1654-67) and the Great Northern War.[62] It was prone to insist inflexibly on punctual and exact fulfillment of obligations merchants contracted vis-à-vis the state, and to confiscate their property if they failed. It was apt to do so regardless of extenuating circumstances such as harvest failures or its own sometime practice of paying for goods or services with other commodities, which a contractor might not be able to dispose of at a profit. In general, though the government extended privileges to the upper merchant strata, their value was much diminished by the burdens the government imposed and by other practices it engaged in that contributed to the instability of merchant fortunes. Given the numerous hazards inherent in business activity in Muscovy, it is no wonder that entrepreneurs were conservative, cautious, wary of undertakings that would make them yet more insecure; in short, no wonder they embraced a policy of accommodation.

But did a policy of accommodation have to be a policy of complete immobilism? There was a striking contrast between the wide geographical range and the dimensions of Russia's trade and the relative primitiveness of its business methods. Russian merchants were bound to recognize the advantages that foreign merchants enjoyed because—not to mention other things—they possessed seagoing ships, they organized themselves into companies, and (whether they recognized this is more problematical) they had banking and credit facilities. Granted that it was impossible for

[61] For example, between 1654 and 1680, the merchants were obliged on nine different occasions to pay extraordinary levies ranging from 5 to 20 percent of their annual incomes. When in the 1690s Peter I set out to build a fleet, he ordered the *gosti* to organize and oversee the construction of fourteen of the fifty-two ships he demanded. Kliuchevskii (supra, n. 12), 3:235; M. M. Bogoslovskii, *Petr I. Materialy dlia biografii*, 5 vols. (Moscow, 1940-48), 1:356-63, 3:150-53.

[62] K. V. Bazilevich, *Denezhnaia reforma Alekseia Mikhailovicha i vosstanie v Moskve v 1662 g.* (Moscow, 1936), pp. 52-53, chap. 5; P. Miliukov, *Gosudarstvennoe khoziaistvo Rossii v pervoi chetverti XVIII stoletiia*, 2nd ed. (St. Petersburg, 1905), pp. 161-65; *Ocherki istorii SSSR. Period Feodalizma. Rossiia v pervoi chetverti XVIII v.* (Moscow, 1954), p. 133.

Russian merchants to plunge immediately and massively into trade abroad, especially with Western Europe, might they not, without great risk, have taken steps gradually to overcome their backwardness, and to prepare for a later successful challenge? One would think so, but they did nothing of the kind: the Muscovite merchants apparently had little desire to learn from their competitors. Some discussion of this perplexing problem is clearly in order, although we are unlikely to come out with an entirely satisfying explanation.

The taking of steps gradually to overcome their backwardness would have required time, planning, and cooperative action. However, conditions in Muscovite Russia militated against long-term strategies and cooperative endeavors. A long-term strategy is thinkable only in an environment that affords security of property, reasonable assurance of fulfillment of expectations, and, conversely, little likelihood of arbitrary interference in private economic affairs. None of these conditions obtained, and, accordingly, Muscovite entrepreneurs were inclined to eschew long-term planning and to favor the pursuit of short-term advantage. In this, they were at one with their government, which paid little attention to economic development while striving everywhere and always to increase the immediate flow of revenue to the treasury.

As regards cooperative endeavor, which obviously would have been necessary for the formation of companies, the establishment of banking, and the building of a merchant fleet, in the main the Muscovite merchants were alien to it. Their behavior on this score is explicable partly on historical grounds, partly in terms of contemporary circumstances. Except in Novgorod in earlier centuries, Russian merchants simply had no experience of group organization and collective action. They had not formed guilds, which had played so large a part in the socioeconomic evolution of the West and served as forerunners to the trading companies.[63] This is not to say that Muscovite merchants were totally opposed to any kind of cooperation. In fact, there is evidence that two or more of them sometimes pooled their resources in order to launch some venture, and they also loaned money to one another, or signed as guarantors of loans contracted by other parties. As we know, they collaborated politically in efforts first to diminish advantages foreigners enjoyed in Russia, and then to exclude them altogether from the Russian domestic market. But they went no farther.

When merchant organizations came into being—the reference is to the *gosti, gostinaia sotnia,* and *sukonnaia sotnia*—it was at the initiative of

---

[63] Gerschenkron (supra, n. 23), pp. 56-60. For another view, see V. V. Stoklitskaia-Tereshkovich, "Problema mnogoobraziia srednevekovogo tsekha na zapade i na Rusi," *Srednye veka*, Vyp. 3 (Moscow, 1951).

the government and for its purposes.[64] Once they were constituted, the privileged merchants did not utilize their organizations as a springboard for joint economic endeavors, nor, except for the campaign against the foreign merchants, did they promote their interests through political channels. In 1620, when the government solicited their views on an English proposal to help develop Russian resources and to enter into joint commercial operations, they reacted negatively, asserting, among other things, "they act in concert, and we cannot do so." When, in 1699, Peter I published a decree urging the merchants to join together in companies, the better to exploit commercial opportunities at Archangel, Astrakhan, and Novgorod, his plea was unheeded.[65] Perhaps other reasons also figured, but the merchants' disinclination to form companies stemmed principally in the first case from their sense of inferiority to West European merchants, and a consequent fear of being bested in any joint endeavor; and in both cases, from their perception of the government and its relation to them. As a number of foreign observers suggested, the merchants sought to conceal their wealth from a government that unceremoniously laid hands on the substance of others in time of need. They refrained from organizing trading companies because to do otherwise would attract attention and invite trouble.[66]

In the area of banking and credit, where there is general agreement that Russia was sadly deficient, the situation exhibits some other interesting features. Banks did not exist and credit may have been in short supply, but it was available to some extent. Monasteries, landed magnates, merchants both native and foreign, and the government all made loans or extended credit to Muscovite merchants. The fact that many merchants loaned money to others may even raise doubts about the allegedly desperate shortage of capital and credit; or may the explanation be that moneylending was one of the safest investments?[67] In the abstract, an established system of banking would no doubt have been more advantageous in many ways, but even if they had had the resources, the merchants might have been no more enthusiastic about creating banks than creating trade companies, and for the same reason.

In the absence of private initiative in this sphere, the government sub-

[64] Kliuchevskii (supra, n. 12), 8:45-48.

[65] S. M. Solov'ev, "Moskovskie kuptsy v XVII veke," *Sovremennik*, 71, no. 10 (1858): 440. *Polnoe sobranie zakonov Rossiiskoi Imperii (PSZRI)*, 3, no. 1,706; N. N. Firsov, *Russkie torgovo-promyshlennye kompanii v pervoi polovine XVIII stoletiia*, 2nd ed. (Kazan, 1922), chap. 2.

[66] Kilburger, p. 449. Similarly, Krizhanich (supra, n. 1), p. 417, asserted that Russians did not trouble to search for ores for fear that the all-powerful government might deprive them of the fruits of their labor and expense.

[67] S. Ia. Borovoi, *Kredit i banki v Rossii* (Moscow, 1958), chap. 1; Kaufmann-Rochard (supra, n. 5), p. 65.

stituted itself and rendered positive services. It allowed upper-level merchants to take fine furs from the treasury and pay for them later with
interest. When it let a contract to a merchant to provide one good or
another, he was given an advance on future delivery. Now and then, it
granted or loaned a sum to a person to enable him to search for metal
ores, salt deposits, or other resources for exploitation. In all this the
government acted as a kind of commercial and industrial investment
bank:[68] the tsar was not only the country's "first merchant," as foreign
observers repeatedly remarked, but also its chief banker. The merchants
undoubtedly prompted the government to give these kinds of assistance.
They took the state's enormous power as a given and, within narrow
limits, sought to have it serve their needs. For its part, the government
could be forthcoming when there was a probability of gain and almost
no prospect of loss. In the process, however, the merchants made themselves hostages to fortune; once institutionalized, these arrangements
reinforced the power of the state and the merchants' dependence.

Because of the peculiar history of commerce, towns, and traders in
Russia, the merchants entered the Muscovite era as a small, powerless,
and markedly backward group relative to their opposite numbers in
Western Europe. Within the scope that unfavorable demographic, economic, social-structural, and political circumstances allowed, successive
generations of Muscovite entrepreneurs demonstrated considerable re-
sourcefulness and succeeded in advancing the country's commercial development to a respectable extent.

They achieved a good deal less in industry, a realm of undoubted
importance, which considerations of space have obliged us to slight. The
number of salt- and ironworks increased, the amalgamation of smaller
enterprises into larger proceeded apace, and production increased. (Textile production remained primitive.) But little technological advance was
registered, except for what was introduced by foreign entrepreneurs. The
English established rope factories in the sixteenth century, and nationals
of other North European countries set up a number of ironworks in the
seventeenth. Although they pressed insistently against foreign commercial
enterprise, Russian businessmen waged no campaign against foreign industrial activity in Muscovy.[69] They did not probably because they were

---

[68] Another such service was performed by the government too. What with the insecurity
that travelers faced in Muscovy, it was hazardous for merchants to carry large sums of
money, even though they might need cash to carry out their transactions. The government
made it possible for a merchant to deposit a sum with one of its agencies in Moscow (or
elsewhere), and receive in return a document ordering an official in another town to pay
him the same amount upon demand. A document requesting such a transfer is printed in
Nizhnii Novgorod v XVII v. Sbornik dokumentov (Gor'kii, 1961), pp. 77-78.

[69] On foreign industrial enterprise, Erik Amburger, *Die Familie Marselis* (Giessen, 1957);
Fuhrmann, *The Origins of Capitalism in Russia*. Supple (supra, n. 7), pp. 424-25, notes

disinclined to follow the lead of the foreigners and either established no competing native enterprises or those that they established were too small to meet demand. Therefore, they had no reason to call for the exclusion of foreign industrialists, yet Russia also came nowhere near to closing the technological gap between itself and the West.

If Russian entrepreneurs managed to promote commerce, they made no significant moves to transform the environment into one with diminished constraints and risks, one more supportive of commercial-industrial activity. They took the path of caution and conservatism even with respect to business methods, showing little interest in learning from their more advanced competitors. But they should not be blamed overmuch. To transcend their backwardness would have required a bold, determined, energetic, and protracted effort, supported and nurtured in every way possible by the state. The state was not everywhere and always unhelpful, as we have seen, but on balance it figured more as a menace to merchant interests, and therefore it tended to inhibit any aspirations to progressive change that might have appeared. Of course, the state did not deliberately contrive this end, it simply did what came naturally. However, the lamentable results—the obliteration of the upper strata of the Muscovite merchantry and the perpetuation of a narrowly circumscribed scope for commercial-industrial activity under private auspices—were not the fault of the state alone.

Just as the conduct of the merchants was conditioned by the character of the state, so to no small extent the behavior of the state was conditioned by the backwardness of Russian socioeconomic development in general, and of commerce and the merchantry in particular. If Russia's development had not lagged so far behind, its government would no doubt have been correspondingly less autocratic and patrimonial in character. Failing that, those features became increasingly pronounced. The Muscovite state was incapable of effective and sustained support to private initiative; it therefore could not avoid perpetuating and even deepening relatively the backwardness of the private sector, and, by way of compensation, further enhancing its own role in the country's economic life. Even the great Peter could find no way out.

The problems with which we have been concerned persisted well into the eighteenth century, and some Russians at the highest level had by then come to apprehend them. In 1762, Peter III published a remarkable

---

that technology in Western Europe remained simple in large part, with the putting-out system the predominant mode of industrial organization. Zaozerskaia (*U istoki*, pp. 446-50) summarizes Muscovy's quantitative industrial growth and its failure to achieve significant technological progress. For the Russian merchants' disinclination in 1620 to block foreign industrial enterprise in Russia, see Solov'ev (supra, n. 65), p. 440. I have found no evidence that they subsequently reversed themselves on this.

edict designed to free economic activity and promote development. A few months later Catherine II, who succeeded him, confirmed the essentials of the edict. Reading this document, one cannot escape the impression that its author (Dmitri Volkov, the emperor's privy secretary) had been reading Kilburger (or some other source with very similar ideas), was deeply convinced by his observations, and had persuaded his master to take corrective action. Kilburger had written his treatise in 1674. Almost a century later many of the conditions he described remained unchanged, but now a serious attempt to address them was launched.[70]

[70] I am grateful to Victor Kamendrowsky, a graduate student at the University of North Carolina who is working on Catherine II's economic policies, for calling this document to my attention. It is printed in *PSZRI*, 16, no. 11, 489.

IV

THOMAS C. OWEN

Entrepreneurship and the Structure of Enterprise in Russia, 1800-1880

This survey of Russian entrepreneurship has three specific goals: to offer a terminological dichotomy between "traditional" and "modern" forms of business activity; to examine the cultural and economic determinants, in the Russian setting, of what David Landes once called "the structure of enterprise";[1] and to discuss whether and to what extent the Russian merchants qualified as Schumpeterian entrepreneurs in the 1800-1880 period.

One is tempted, in view of Professor Baron's vivid description and analysis of the merchants of old Muscovy, to imagine Shorin or one of his fellows resurrected in the mid-nineteenth century in Kitaigorod (the commercial district near Red Square) or Zamoskvorech'e (the merchant quarter south of the river, opposite the Kremlin), in the role of a *samodur* (merchant patriarch) in a comedy by Aleksandr N. Ostrovskii. The Russian merchants' mode of commerce in this period may be termed "traditional" not only because it had persisted with only slight modifications over several centuries, but also because, in the Weberian sense, the label identifies the past as the source of legitimacy for behavior. Here, "hierarchy is the fundamental ordering principle; patriarchy, personal loyalty, patronage and corporatism are the key forms of human relations; and passivity is the normal political posture of common men."[2] The crucial distinction between tradition and modernity in the economic realm was

* Financial support of much of the research for this article was generously provided by the International Research and Exchanges Board, New York, and by the Louisiana State University Council on Research.

[1] "The Structure of Enterprise in the Nineteenth Century: The Cases of Britain and Germany," Comité international des Sciences Historiques, XIᵉ Congrès international des Sciences Historiques, Stockholm, *Rapports*, vol. 5: Histoire contemporaine (Uppsala, 1960), pp. 107-28.

[2] Michael Walzer, *The Revolution of the Saints* (New York, 1968), p. 311.

not so much between crooked and honest behavior toward customers
and suppliers as between a short-term and a long-term economic outlook.
The same traditional merchant who employed "fraud, forgery, false measures, and false weights" (*obman, podlog, obmer i obves*)[3] as a matter of
principle to fleece gullible passers-by could be scrupulously honest when
dealing with the wholesale suppliers or creditors on whose good graces
his entire operation might depend.[4] In particular, Old Believers (schis-
matics of the Orthodox Church) trusted each other, not because they
held with special piety to the ethical absolute of the Eighth Command-
ment, but because a network of personal relationships, strengthened by
periodic religious persecution, provided crucial financial and commercial
support, including interest-free loans, so that ostracism on account of
dishonesty toward a coreligionist meant economic ruin in the short run.
(The same held true within groups of Jews, Greeks, *skoptsy*, and other
religious and cultural minorities in Russia, regardless of the differences
among their dogmas.)[5] It was, of course, the treatment of outsiders that
molded the public's opinion of Russian merchants, and the historical
record is filled with eloquent testimony that these merchants practiced
the art of cheating with as much virtuosity as their forbears. More unflattering than even the Russian folk-saying, "Shake hands with a Greek
and count your fingers," was the jingle attributed by the former merchant
Buryshkin to the gypsies:

> *Moskovskoe kupechestvo,*
> *Izlomannyi arshin,*
> *Kakoi ty syn otechestva,*
> *Ty prosto s . . . n syn.*[6]

Characteristic of this shortsighted outlook was a strong aversion to
innovation, typical of the peasant milieu from which the leading merchant
dynasties had emerged. Victor Hehn, a Baltic German, noted contemp-

[3] Fundamental'naia biblioteka obshchestvennykh nauk (FBON), Moscow, "Zhurnal
Moskovskogo otdeleniia Manufakturnogo soveta," 1846, p. 148ᵣ.

[4] Two English accounts, one on dishonesty in retail trade in 1805-7 and another on
honesty in wholesale commerce, are given in Peter Putnam, ed., *Seven Britons in Imperial
Russia, 1698-1812* (Princeton, 1952), pp. 275 and 313. A hilarious description of the
"refinement of deception and roguery" achieved by retailers in Moscow is in Robert Lyall,
The Character of the Russians (London, 1823), reprinted in Anthony Cross, ed., *Russia
Under Western Eyes, 1517-1825* (London, 1971), pp. 353-62.

[5] On the importance of religious "solidarity" among Dissenters in English business circles,
see Charles Wilson, "The Entrepreneur in the Industrial Revolution in Britain," in Barry
E. Supple, ed., *The Experience of Economic Growth* (New York, 1963), p. 174.

[6] Pavel A. Buryshkin, *Moskva kupecheskaia* (New York, 1954), p. 27. A rough translation: "Greedy merchant of Moscow, / Dishonest and rich, / You're no true Russian son, / Just
a son of a bitch."

tuously that at the great fair at Nizhnii Novgorod in the reign of Alexander II very few Russians used the bill of exchange to pay for goods;
"this is something that *nemtsy vydumali*, that is, Germans invented."
While Hehn may have been unfair in claiming that the ancient Phoeni-
cians had employed more advanced business practices than did the Russians,[7] the latter certainly lagged far behind earlier European merchants,
who used bills of exchange on a large scale, both at the great medieval
fairs and in Italian cities of the Renaissance.[8] The account books of several
leading merchants of the Moscow region recorded a growing tendency
to accept and draw bills of exchange in the 1840s,[9] but the traditional
merchant routinely offered nothing more than his word to repay his debt
a year later as he departed Nizhnii Novgorod with a load of goods. As
Hehn remarked, "In general, Russian commerce is [simply] petty retailing
on a large scale."[10]

Of course, in the absence of rational bookkeeping, the sudden illness
or death of a merchant plunged his entire family business into chaos.[11]
The need to develop close personal ties with other merchants might be
considered another liability of traditionalism, since long hours of con-
versation in the tavern or on a muddy street corner seemed essential to
the conclusion of a successful deal. Tsarist bureaucrats viewed as irra-
tional the merchants' persistent refusal to desert the tavern and the street,
even in the dead of winter, for various new exchange buildings erected
at government expense, as in Rybinsk (1823) and Moscow (1839).[12] The
merchants' inability to understand or appreciate innovation was best
typified by the experience of a wealthy Moscow industrialist whose first

[7] Victor Hehn, *De Moribus Ruthenorum. Zur Charakteristik der russischen Volksseele:
Tagebuchblätter aus den Jahren 1857-1873*, ed. Theodor Schiemann (Stuttgart, 1892), p.
95.

[8] Max Weber, *General Economic History*, trans. Frank H. Knight (New York, 1927),
pp. 221, 258-63.

[9] Out of 3.7 million rubles in gross income between Easter 1849 and Easter 1850, the
Guchkov textile firm received 1.2 million rubles in cash and 1.7 million in "documents,"
presumably bills of exchange, while 0.6 million was left "pending" (*neokoncheno*), probably
on verbal promises to pay. Gosudarstvennyi istoricheskii muzei (GIM), Moscow, F 122,
file 497, fols. 58ʳ-59ʳ.

[10] Hehn, *De Moribus*, p. 94. Weber's description of the traditional business mentality
(pp. 354-56) applies perfectly here. Note, for example, the case of Gordei I. Chernov, a
wealthy Volga shipowner in the 1880s, who kept bank statements in one pocket and debt
records in the other so that he always knew his net worth without having to hire a
bookkeeper. Karl W. Hagelin, *Moi trudovoi put'* (New York, 1945), p. 173.

[11] Hehn, *De Moribus*, p. 204.

[12] On Rybinsk, Georgii Polilov-Severtsov, *Nashi dedy-kuptsy: Bytovye kartiny nachala
XIX stoletiia* (St. Petersburg, 1906), p. 204; and Prince Vladimir P. Meshcherskii, *Ocherki
nyneshnei obshchestvennoi zhizni v Rossii*, 2 vols. (St. Petersburg, 1868-70), 1:211-18. On
Moscow, see *Moskovskaia birzha 1839-1889* (Moscow, 1889; reprinted Ann Arbor, 1975),
pp. 12-13.

trip on the new railroad ended in humiliation. On his way to Moscow from the capital, he mistakenly changed trains at the rest stop midway, and then, while chatting with his fellow passengers, declared with wonderment: "The same train that is taking you to Petersburg is taking me to Moscow. Devilishly clever, these Germans!"[13] Well into the 1850s, Russians controlled no more than 3 percent of the country's foreign trade; they left this risky business to foreigners: Germans and Englishmen in the north and Greeks, Italians, Armenians, and Jews in the south.[14] In defense of the merchants, one should note that even the Russian gentry landlords who undertook manufacturing on their estates generally preferred the safest course: to produce wool cloth and other crude products for the most stable of markets, the army.[15]

The reasons for the persistence of this traditional behavior may be found in both the political and cultural institutions of the eighteenth century. Catherine II, like Elizabeth before her, strove to dismantle Peter the Great's system of the merchants' monopoly on trade and industry, preferring instead to open the economic field to the gentry and the peasantry.[16] While in principle this policy may have represented a step toward a freer and more vigorous market economy, Catherine's maintenance of the gentry's economic privileges (including serf labor and freedom from guild payments) vitiated her professed desire to encourage the development of a "middle group" in Russian society. Enterprising serfs, called "trading peasants," were ordered by their masters to engage in commerce and industry, for such activity generated increased cash dues (*obrok*) for the landlords. In the case of state peasants, the tsarist bureaucracy likewise benefited. The merchants' bitter complaints of unfair competition[17] failed to reverse Catherine's policy.

In 1824, Finance Minister Kankrin enacted a "guild reform," which required trading peasants to buy an annual certificate entitling them to trade, much as the merchants had long done. However, constant evasions of these payments and various other restrictions prompted cries of outrage

[13] Sergei I. Chetverikov, *Bezvozvratno ushedshaia Rossiia: neskol'ko stranits iz knigi moei zhizni* (Berlin, n.d.), pp. 108-9; and Hehn, *De Moribus*, 95 (quoted).

[14] Michael T. Florinsky, *Russia: A History and an Interpretation*, 2 vols. (New York, 1960), 2:790, citing a report by the Finance Ministry bureaucrat Nebolsin; and William L. Blackwell, *The Beginnings of Russian Industrialization, 1800-1860* (Princeton, 1968), p. 82.

[15] Nina S. Kiniapina, *Politika russkogo samoderzhaviia v oblasti promyshlennosti (20-50-e gody XIX v.)* (Moscow, 1968), pp. 62-64.

[16] Russia, *Polnoe sobranie zakonov Rossiiskoi imperii* (hereafter, *PSZ*), sobranie 1, 46 vols. (St. Petersburg, 1830-39), no. 10,486 of December 1, 1755, and no. 14,275 of March 17, 1775.

[17] "Rukavkin, Danila," *Russkii biograficheskii slovar'*, 25 vols. (incomplete) (St. Petersburg, 1896-1918), 17:435 on complaints in the 1760s.

from merchant leaders, who sought their old monopoly on commerce and industry, rather than a laissez faire policy.[18] Small wonder, then, that the movement of families in and out of the merchant guilds continued at a high rate throughout the eighteenth and early nineteenth centuries, as enterprising peasants and *meshchane* (petty townsmen) entered the guilds, while ruined merchants who were unable to meet the guild payment in a given year fell back into the *meshchanstvo* or the peasantry. In 1873, only 108 of 623 first-guild merchants in Moscow could trace their ancestry back to eighteenth-century merchant families. Between 1800 and 1861, the ancestors of 185 had entered from other social estates, and in twelve years alone (1861-73) 330—more than half—had joined the guild for the first time.[19]

Despite some half-hearted bureaucratic efforts to make the merchants' social position less precarious than in Catherine's time, as in the creation of Honorary Citizen status in 1832,[20] it was impossible for merchants to feel secure. The ownership of real wealth, in the form of populated land (i.e., serfs), remained the exclusive privilege of the gentry, and unpredictable disasters in the form of sudden price fluctuations or malevolent persecution by an insufficiently bribed *chinovnik* could wipe out the fruits of years of shrewd dealing. Thus, the risk of ruin in the generally hostile climate (economic and political as well as atmospheric) impelled the clever merchant to withdraw from his precarious occupation after having amassed a fortune large enough to support his family for the next few decades.[21] The most enterprising merchant best protected his wealth, in other words, by ceasing to be an entrepreneur. Under such conditions,

---

[18] Vasilii N. Iakovtsevskii, *Kupecheskii kapital v feodal'no-krepostnicheskoi Rossii* (Moscow, 1953), pp. 178-79, on a complaint of 1846. On the guild reform, see Pavel G. Ryndziunskii, *Gorodskoe grazhdanstvo doreformennoi Rossii* (Moscow, 1958), pp. 107-28.

[19] Akademiia nauk SSSR, Institut istorii, *Istoriia Moskvy*, 7 vols. (Moscow, 1952-67), 4:145-46. There are no definitive statistical studies of this question, but a high rate of turnover is alleged by two experts, a Soviet historian and a former merchant, for the 1800-1825 period and the entire modern era, respectively. See Ksana S. Kuibysheva, "Krupnaia moskovskaia burzhuaziia v period revoliutsionnoi situatsii v 1859-1861 gg.," in M. V. Nechkina, ed., *Revolutsionnaia situatsiia v Rossii v 1859-1861 gg.* (Moscow, 1965), p. 318; and Vladimir P. Riabushinskii, "Kupechestvo moskovskoe," *Den' russkogo rebenka* (San Francisco), 18 (April 1951):188.

[20] *Entsiklopedicheskii slovar' Brokgauza-Efrona*, 43 vols. (Leipzig and St. Petersburg, 1890-1907), 9:523-24. The law, *PSZ-2*, no. 5,284, was dated April 10, 1832. Merchants with uninterrupted membership in the first guild for ten years or in the second guild for twenty, as well as bearers of various medals and titles for exemplary commercial and industrial activity (e.g., commercial councilors and manufacturing councilors), were eligible to receive Hereditary Honorary Citizen status, which passed to their legitimate offspring in the absence of a conviction for a crime or fraudulent bankruptcy.

[21] FBON, "Zhurnal," 1846, fol. 162ᵛ.

the size of the merchant estate could not grow. In 1811 the merchants of the empire numbered 201,200, scarcely 7.4 percent of the *urban* population, and the membership of the Moscow guilds (the largest in Russia) declined steadily, from 13,442 in 1747 to 1,695 in 1822.[22]

Cultural traditions prevalent in serf and merchant families reinforced the tendency toward short-run maximization of profits. Rare indeed was the serf or merchant who could read or write. Moreover, the proclivity of even the most literate merchants to stud their prose with Biblical homilies attested to the fact that their education had ended with a mastery of the Book of Psalms and the abacus.[23]

The development of modern capitalist institutions in Russia in the mid-nineteenth century represented a major shift away from these patterns. Following Weber, we may briefly note the essential components of "modern capitalism": rational accounting for business, separately from the family's finances; a free market, without formal restrictions on business activities according to an individual's social status; the application of new technology, specifically mechanization, to industry and trade; a legal and administrative system operating without arbitrariness; a free labor force; and the public sale of shares in economic enterprises and property.[24] Russia in 1800 lacked all six of these criteria, due to the traditional nature of agriculture and commerce; the multifarious legal restrictions on serfs, *meshchane*, and merchants; the stagnant industrial and commercial technology; the system of capricious bureaucratic rule; the shortage of industrial labor under serfdom; and the lack of corporate forms of enterprise. By 1850 the first, third, and sixth obstacles had begun to crumble, and by 1880 only two showed no sign of yielding: the arbitrary bureaucratic system and the Emancipation laws, which imposed on most of the industrial workers heavy financial obligations to their native communes in the countryside.

Because the most important changes occurred first in the cotton-textile

[22] Ryndziunskii, *Gorodskoe grazhdanstvo*, p. 283; Iakovtsevskii, *Kupecheskii kapital*, p. 133. To a certain extent, this decline is attributable to the consolidation of up to twenty relatives into a single "household," so that each could legally trade under the one certificate that was purchased by the head of the household.

[23] E. F. Korsh, "Byt kupechestva i meshchanstva," in Moscow, Gosudarstvennyi istoricheskii muzei, *Iz epokhi krepostnogo khoziaistva XVIII i XIX vv: stat'i i putevoditel' po vystavke*, ed. Iu. V. Got'e and N. B. Baklanov (Moscow, 1926), p. 28; and August von Haxthausen, *Studien über die innern Zustände, das Volksleben und insbesondere die ländlichen Einrichtungen Russlands*, 3 vols. (Hannover, 1847-52), 2:517. For examples of such merchant prose, see the memoirs of an eighteenth-century St. Petersburg mayor, Aleksandr P. Berezin, "Sokrashchennaia zhizn' . . . Berezina . . . ," *Russkii arkhiv*, 1879, vol. 1, no. 2, 226-35; the autobiography of a Siberian, and later Moscow, Old-Believer merchant of the late nineteenth century, Nikolai M. Chukmaldin, *Zapiski o moei zhizni*, ed. Sergei P. Sharapov (Moscow, 1902), esp. p. vii; and Riabushinskii, "Kupechestvo," esp. p. 173.

[24] Weber, *Economic History*, pp. 276-78.

industry of the Central Industrial and St. Petersburg regions in the 1840s, it is convenient to date the growth of modern capitalism in Russia from that time. Steam-powered printing, weaving, and spinning factories (*fabriki*) gradually replaced the putting-out system and the nonmechanized workshops (*manufaktury*).[25] Even before Emancipation, the hiring of so-called free workers (i.e. serfs on *obrok*) steadily outstripped the use of less efficient *barshchina* (forced-labor dues), characteristic of the old possessional and gentry-owned enterprises. Also, the search for foreign markets to supplement the weak mass market within the empire led to the establishment of new companies selling Russian textiles in the Caucasus, Asia Minor, Persia, and Central Asia.[26] In the absence of a modern banking system before the 1860s, the problem of financing was met by several expedients. A few liquor-tax concessionaires (*otkupshchiki*), including Vasilii A. Kokorev, Ivan and Nikolai F. Mamontov, and Dmitrii E. Benardaki, amassed millions of rubles, which they poured into new companies; William Blackwell has elsewhere described the various private credit networks among Old Believers, Jews, *skoptsy*, and foreigners.[27] Direct government subsidies also went to new plants and factories, especially in the St. Petersburg area. Most innovative of all, however, was the special line of credit that Ludwig Knoop, the German-born importer of English textile machinery, provided to Russians through his ties with the de Jersey company of Manchester (where his brother worked), and later with Platt Brothers of Oldham (for spinning machines) and Hick Hargreaves and John Musgrave (for steam engines).[28] In the first boom of capitalist enterprise, following the Crimean War, new companies in shipping, railroads, chemicals, and metallurgy attracted not only merchants of various cultural backgrounds but also gentry entrepreneurs and bureaucrats like Pavel P. Mel'nikov and Evgenii I. Lamanskii.

Modern forms of entrepreneurship could not have flourished in Russia without the emergence of a number of educated merchants who were trained in the rudiments of the newly available capitalist techniques. Sons of prominent merchant families like the Botkins (in tea), the Guchkovs (in woolens), the Tret'iakovs (in linens), and the Krestovnikovs, Naiden-

---

[25] Gerhart von Schulze-Gävernitz, *Volkswirtschaftliche Studien aus Russland* (Leipzig, 1899), p. 70n. An excellent account in English is Blackwell, *Beginnings*, esp. pp. 39-53.

[26] The literature on these subjects is immense. See, for example, Petr. I. Lyashchenko, *History of the National Economy of Russia to the 1917 Revolution*, trans. L. M. Herman (New York, 1949), esp. chap. 19; Roger Portal, "Aux origines d'une bourgeoisie industrielle en Russie," *Revue d'histoire moderne et contemporaine*, 8 (1961):35-60; and Viktor K. Iatsunskii, "Krupnaia promyshlennost' Rossii v 1790-1860 gg.," in M. K. Rozhkova, ed., *Ocherki ekonomicheskoi istorii Rossii pervoi poloviny XIX veka* (Moscow, 1959), esp. pp. 177-82.

[27] See Blackwell, *Beginnings*, chaps. 9-10.

[28] Schulze-Gävernitz, *Volkswirtschaftliche*, pp. 91-93.

ovs, and Shchukins (in cotton textiles) obtained a solid preparation in reading, writing, mathematics, English, and German from private tutors or from strict German teachers at the Lutheran Boys' School in Moscow and various boarding schools in St. Petersburg.[29] Trips to Manchester or Alsace to learn the latest textile production techniques invariably bred a taste for European clothes, food, and pretensions to culture; the fabled art collections of the Tret'iakovs, Botkins, and Kokorev began in the 1840s and 1850s. By the early twentieth century, this trend had developed so far that the Moscow merchant leader Grigorii A. Krestovnikov and others of his generation held university degrees. Some wealthy merchants, of course, clung to their traditional way of life; the Old Believer Elisei S. Morozov, winner of medals for excellence in cotton-textile production, withdrew from manufacturing to write a huge study, apparently since lost, on the Antichrist. In many families, however, the rapidity of the cultural change from one generation to the next impressed contemporary observers. In 1853, Fedor A. Guchkov's sons Efim (mayor of Moscow, 1858-59) and Ivan abandoned the Old Belief for the unpersecuted half-way house to Orthodoxy, *Edinoverie*, after returning home from England with strong tastes for expensive London suits and for less fundamentalist religious doctrines.[30]

The decade before the Crimean War thus witnessed fundamental economic and cultural changes. While the "traditional" mores continued to exist among the petty merchants, *meshchane*, and peasants for generations, apparently even into the 1920s, the merchant leaders of the primary economic centers—Moscow, St. Petersburg, the Baltic cities, Poland, and

[29] On the Botkins, Kuibysheva, "Krupnaia moskovskaia," p. 327; and Afanasii A. Fet, *Moi vospominaniia*, 2 parts in 1 vol. (Moscow, 1890), 1:218-19, 408; on the Guchkovs, Blackwell, *Beginnings*, pp. 49, 111, 225-26; on the Tret'iakovs, Aleksandra P. Botkina (née Tret'iakova), *Pavel Mikhailovich Tret'iakov v zhizni i iskusstve*, 2nd ed. (Moscow, 1960); on the Krestovnikovs, Nikolai K. Krestovnikov, *Semeinaia khronika . . .* , 3 vols. (Moscow, 1903-4), 2:12-21; on the Naidenovs, Nikolai A. Naidenov, *Vospominaniia o vidennom, slyshannom i ispytannom*, 2 vols. (Moscow, 1903-5; reprinted in 1 vol., Newtonville, Mass., 1976), 1:15, 83; on the Shchukins, Petr. I. Shchukin, "Vospominaniia," *Shchukinskii sbornik*, 10 vols. (Moscow, 1902-12), 10:272, 370. Buryshkin, *Moskva*, chap. 2, contains a wealth of information on various merchant families and the education of individuals.

[30] Krestovnikov, a graduate of the physical science and mathematics faculty of Moscow University (Buryshkin, *Moskva*, p. 181), was well versed in the chemical processes of textile production. On Morozov, see "E. S. Morozov" (obituary), *Sovremennye izvestiia*, no. 71 (March 13, 1868), front page (no pagination). On the Guchkovs, Pavel G. Ryndziunskii, "Staroobriadcheskaia organizatsiia v usloviiakh razvitiia promyshlennogo kapitalizma," *Voprosy istorii religii i ateizma*, vol. 1 (1950), 246. The contrast between traditional, or "Russian-style," and modern, or "German-style," manners and dress at mid-century is vividly described in Naidenov, *Vospominaniia*, 2:11-12.

Odessa—had made the irreversible transition to "modern" methods of enterprise. An essential part of this transition lay in the adoption of new forms of economic activity, specifically the modern corporation. Because the development of Russian businesses has received scant attention from Soviet historians, on whom we must depend for the painstaking analysis of voluminous corporate archives, the overview offered below must be considered tentative at best. Fortunately, the imperial government's Complete Collection of Laws (*Polnoe sobranie zakonov*) included the officially approved charter (*ustav*) of each major corporation founded through February 1881. This compendium, the next best source to the files of the Ministry of Finance itself, provides concrete evidence on the nature and direction of Russian corporate enterprise in its formative period (see Table 1).

The simplest Russian businesses came under the provisions of an imperial manifesto dated January 1, 1807 (*PSZ*-1, no. 22,418). Registered with the local authorities, these enterprises did not require imperial confirmation (art. 5). Any member of a merchant guild could operate a small business in his own name, with or without the help of his sons, younger brothers, or other relatives. He could also establish, with other merchants of his guild, one of two types of "trading firm" (*torgovyi dom*): a "full partnership" (*polnoe tovarishchestvo*) or a "trust partnership" (*tovarishchestvo na vere*). In both cases, each partner remained "liable for the debts of one firm to the full extent of his property"; the partner of one trading firm could not, therefore, become a partner in another (art. 4). However, membership in a "trust partnership" could be acquired by any firm or citizen, even those not personally enrolled in a guild, through the investment of capital. As long as these outside investors did not become full partners, their financial liability was limited to the size of their investment (art. 3). Any member of the gentry not in active military or civil service could enter the first or second merchant guild in order, without losing his gentry privileges, to become a full partner in a trading firm engaged in wholesale commerce (arts. 6-7).

The primary effect of unlimited liability was to constrict the size of trading firms. Only a few merchants would dare to risk their entire livelihood for the sake of pooling financial resources and business acumen. The typical Russian business remained a purely individual or family affair or a full partnership, unless it developed gradually to include eminent cousins or in-laws, or an outsider well versed in specialized production techniques.

Somewhat puzzling at first glance is the use of two different Russian names for essentially one economic entity: the large corporation. Both the "joint-stock company" (*aktsionernoe obshchestvo* or *aktsionernaia kompaniia*) and the "share partnership" (*tovarishchestvo na paiakh* or

TABLE 1

Forms of Economic Enterprise under Imperial Russian Law

Name	Law	Founder(s), Investors	Method of Founding	Type of Liability	Structure
Individual business (delo)	PSZ-1, 22,418 Jan. 1, 1807	Individual or family in a merchant guild; also Honorary Citizens	Local registration	Unlimited	Individual or family firm
Trading firm* (torgovyi dom)					
a. full partnership (polnoe tovarishchestvo)	PSZ-1, 22,418 Jan. 1, 1807	Guild merchants; Honorary Citizens	Local registration	Unlimited	Partnership
b. limited or trust partnership (tovarishchestvo na vere)	same as a.	Guild merchants, HC (full partners); members of any free estate (investors)	Local registration	Unlimited (full partners); limited (investors)	Partnership with outside investors (like French société en commandite simple)
Share partnership (tovarishchestvo na paiakh or tovarishchestvo po uchastkam)	PSZ-2, 9,736 Dec. 6, 1836	Members of any free estate (after 1884, no holder of one of top three ranks could act as a founder or officer)	Imperial confirmation	Limited	General Assembly, Board; tendency toward expensive shares called pai
Joint-stock company (aktsionernoe obshchestvo or aktsionernaia kompaniia)	PSZ-2, 9,736 Dec. 6, 1836	Members of any free estate (after 1884, same as above)	Imperial confirmation	Limited	General Assembly, Board; tendency toward inexpensive shares called aktsii

* Industry as well as commerce.

tovarishchestvo po uchastkam) guaranteed to managers and investors alike a limited liability on their investments; both sold shares publicly for the purpose of amassing large amounts of capital for significant new undertakings in transportation, commerce, manufacturing, or finance; and both operated under the terms of the restrictive law of December 6, 1836 (*PSZ-2*, no. 9,763), which gave the tsarist bureaucracy immense authority over the establishment and management of Russian corporations down to 1917. The standard Smirnitskii dictionary translated both as "joint-stock company," and leading scholars of Russian capitalism have either ignored the differences between the two forms (Kiniapina, Blackwell) or mentioned them only in passing (Shepelev, Nifontov, Gindin).[31] One legal expert noted that both names meant "one and the same thing" following a Senate ruling of 1898; the only difference was that in Russia "it is customary to call larger units not *aktsii* but *pai*."[32]

A recent study of the corporate charters granted by the tsarist government in the reign of Alexander II showed that the distinctions between these two forms of incorporation reflected crucial cultural, as well as economic, differences in entrepreneurial behavior.[33] The first clue lay in the terminology itself. The foreign origin of the joint-stock company showed plainly in the fact that the French word for share (*action*) became *aktsiia* in Russian, just as *obshchestvo* and *kompaniia* were direct translations of *société* and *compagnie*. In contrast, *tovarishchestvo* derived from the old Russian word for partner or comrade, and connoted therefore a smaller and more intimate institution than the impersonal company; and the word *pai* had been borrowed from the Tatars centuries before. In keeping with the deep-seated cultural differences between the two major centers of economic activity in the empire, *obshchestva* predominated in the more cosmopolitan city of St. Petersburg (where German remained the favored language of the Exchange "during most of the nineteenth century"),[34] while *tovarishchestva* were preferred in the more traditional Moscow.

Real structural differences existed as well. Despite some overlapping

---

[31] Leonid E. Shepelev, *Aktsionernye kompanii v Rossii* (Leningrad, 1973), pp. 22, 53; *Istoriia Moskvy*, 4:134-35 and 213-14. It must be noted that Shepelev, working almost single-handedly, has opened up new lines of research, as in his refreshing article, "Chastnokapitalisticheskie torgovo-promyshlennye predpriiatiia Rossii v kontse XIX-nachala XX vv. i ikh arkhivnye fondy," in Glavnoe arkivnoe upravlenie, *Informatsionnyi biuleten'*, 10 (1958):76-107.

[32] S. I. Gal'perin, *Uchebnik russkogo torgovogo i veksel'nogo prava* (Ekaterinoslav, 1907), pp. 110, 108.

[33] Whitney A. Coulon, "The Structure of Enterprise in the Russian Empire, 1855-1880," M.A. thesis, Louisiana State University, 1979. He counted 678 such corporate charters in the *PSZ* for these years.

[34] Blackwell, *Beginnings*, p. 79.

in the intermediate range, the largest enterprises were called joint-stock companies, and the smallest bore the name of partnerships. The former generally offered to the public a large number of relatively low-priced shares. For instance, the Odessa-Kiev Railroad Company's basic capital of 30 million rubles was divided into 300,000 shares priced at 100 rubles each. (See its charter in *PSZ*, March 21, 1863.) The individual investor, even if he attended the meetings of the stockholders' General Assembly (*Obshchee sobranie*), therefore exercised little influence over the managers, although these were formally elected by the Assembly: the Council (*sovet*), a supervisory body that existed in only the largest companies; and the Board (*pravlenie*), which consisted of three or more directors, often including a president (*predsedatel'*) and executive director (*direktor-rasporiaditel'*). In the typical share partnership, on the other hand, shares were both few and expensive, so that the main founders, by buying large blocks of the firm's capital, often acted as both investors and directors. Moreover, the founders' friends and relatives usually bought shares; and a clause requiring that shares for sale be offered first to other shareholders for a period of from one to six months appeared more often in the charters of share partnerships than in those of joint-stock companies. As long as they had sufficient wealth to exercise their "right of preferential purchase" (*pravo preimushchestvennoi pokupki*), the original shareholders and their heirs could maintain full control of the enterprise. Finally, unlike the many joint-stock companies that were formed to launch a new venture, the great majority of share partnerships grew organically and relatively slowly out of preexisting family firms.[35]

Purely economic factors reinforced the cultural contrasts between St. Petersburg and Moscow. The empire lacked a national securities market that could erase existing regional differences. There was every reason for corporations in the St. Petersburg area to issue low-priced shares, for these would attract capital investments from wealthy landlords and bureaucrats there, who generally had no desire to play a large role in a company. In contrast, the relative shortage of liquid capital in Moscow, together with the old networks of trust among merchant dynasties and the smaller size of textile and other light manufacturing and commercial enterprises of the Central Region, made the share partnership a more attractive choice in most cases.

Important exceptions existed to this general pattern of the Petersburg joint-stock company and the Moscow share partnership. The less Europeanized merchants in the northern capital tended to form share part-

---

[35] Buryshkin, *Moskva*, pp. 58-59. On the various share partnerships established by the four branches of the famous Morozov family, see Chedomir M. Ioksimovich, *Manufakturnaia promyshlennost' v proshlom i nastoiashchem*, vol. 1 (no more published) (Moscow, 1915), 5-36.

nerships, especially for smaller undertakings, and in Moscow by the 1860s traditionalism was fading among the most ambitious and capable merchants. For example, bonds of mutual trust could override ethnic and religious differences, as in two new share partnerships: the technologically advanced Emile Zindel Chintz-Printing Company (*PSZ*, July 19, 1874) and the first private banking company in Moscow (July 1, 1866). Moreover, when a new undertaking required huge amounts of capital, a joint-stock company would be formed even in Moscow, as in the case of the Trinity Railroad (May 29, 1859) and the Moscow Trading Bank (June 12, 1871).

By and large, however, the Muscovites avoided the joint-stock principle, while in St. Petersburg, the other major center of corporate enterprise, founders preferred it. Table 2 displays data on the size and type of the 451 corporations that had their headquarters in these two areas and accounted for almost two-thirds of the companies founded in the

TABLE 2

Joint-Stock Companies and Share Partnerships Founded
in the St. Petersburg and Moscow Regions, 1855-1880
(size of basic capital in thousands of rubles and type of corporation)

	0-500		501-5,000		5,001 and above		Totals	
	JSC	SP	JSC	SP	JSC	SP	JSC	SP
Area								
St. Petersburg[1]	60	50	74	27	34	1	168	78
Baltic Region[2]	13	8	9	6	2	0	24	14
Moscow[3]	12	43	29	52	16	1	57	96
Central Industrial Region[4]	1	6	1	6	0	0	2	12
St. Petersburg area total	73	58	83	33	36	1	192	92
Moscow area total	13	49	30	58	16	1	59	108
Totals of both areas	86	107	113	91	52	2	251	200

SOURCE: Compiled by Whitney A. Coulon.
[1] Province of St. Petersburg
[2] Provinces of Estonia, Livonia, and Courland
[3] Province of Moscow
[4] Provinces of Vladimir, Iaroslavl, Kostroma, and Nizhnii Novgorod

empire between 1855 and 1880. While in the Central Region share partnerships outnumbered joint-stock companies by a margin of 108 to 59,
an opposite pattern—92 to 192—prevailed in and around the northern
capital.[36] The founders of relatively small businesses in the Moscow
region preferred the partnership form, but larger corporations in both
areas tended to be joint-stock companies.

It must be stressed that these data from *PSZ* on the formation of share
partnerships and joint-stock companies do not provide an accurate measurement of real economic development. Some corporations approved by
the imperial government never went into operation. In the case of share
partnerships, moreover, incorporation typically entailed a limited increase in the size of an already existing family firm; legal advantages,
especially regarding taxes, sometimes played as much a role as did economic expansion. Skepticism is also warranted with regard to joint-stock
companies, for incorporation often represented an attempt to grab speculative profits from unwary investors.[37] (Alexander Gerschenkron once
quipped that two or three bankruptcies sufficed to make a man rich in
Russia.)

As for the attitudes that underlay these patterns of entrepreneurial
behavior, no better statement of the Moscow merchants' opinions on
corporate forms of enterprise can be cited than the vivid memoirs of
Vladimir P. Riabushinskii. Although a thoroughly modern businessman
of the eminent textile, banking, lumber, and automobile clan, he idealized
the old trading firm. There, he wrote long after 1917, the boss (*khoziain*)
took full advantage of his total power; "bold, enterprising, and flexible,
[he] did not have to look back." Next best was the family firm like his
own: "brothers polished one another, conflicts were absent, and there
was support and replacement for rest." The European-style joint-stock
company could not function properly in Russia, he asserted, because
managers "*wasted time on explanations, self-justifications, apologies, and
self-glorification.*" An Old Believer proud of his ties with the common
people, he boasted, "We, the Moscow merchants, were essentially nothing but *trading muzhiks, the highest stratum of the thrifty Russian muzhiks.*"[38] As late as 1890, out of 667 factories and plants in the city of
Moscow, 534 were individually owned and 75 belonged to trading firms,

[36] Figures from Coulon's data bank. The geographical terms are based on the official
designations of 1910. For comprehensive maps and geographic categories, see the excellent
study by Thomas S. Fedor, *Patterns of Urban Growth in the Russian Empire during the
Nineteenth Century* (Chicago, 1975), esp. pp. xviii-xix. (Kaluga and Tver provinces are
considered part of the Central Industrial Region in some sources, e.g., the Brokgauz-Efron
encyclopedia.)

[37] I am indebted to Fred Carstensen and Paul Paskoff for clarification of certain economic
factors mentioned in the above four paragraphs.

[38] Riabushinskii, "Kupechestvo," pp. 177, 189; emphasis in original.

while 46 were controlled by share partnerships and only 12 by joint-stock companies.[39] Nor was the Central Region unique in this regard. Of the 53 beet-sugar companies formed between 1855 and 1880 in the right-bank Ukraine, all but one took the form of share partnerships; of another 9 sugar refineries located there but with headquarters elsewhere, 8 were owned by share partnerships and only 1 by a joint-stock company.

The attitudes of the St. Petersburg corporate leaders toward larger issues of business ethics and the ultimate purpose of their activity (beyond simple self-enrichment) remain unclear owing to the lack of diligent research on the entrepreneurial history of that city,[40] but if one may judge by the highly realistic novels of Pavel D. Boborykin—*Del'tsy* (The Wheeler-Dealers, 1872) and *Kitai-gorod* (The Moscow Commercial Quarter, 1882)[41]—a definite contrast existed between the bold and sometimes unscrupulous corporate wizards of the capital city and the more cautious men of Moscow. This hypothesis finds support in the fact that many large companies whose activities took place far from St. Petersburg maintained their headquarters there, for example, the Odessa-Kiev Railroad and the Volga-Don Railroad and Steamship Company (January 12, 1865).

This represented more than a reflection, in the economic realm, of the old bureaucratic habit of directing change throughout the empire from offices in the capital. Corporate leaders saw the wisdom of maintaining cordial personal relations with the bureaucrats who provided essential subsidies, treasury orders, purchases of stock, and even "irregular loans" (*neustavnye ssudy*, granted by the State Bank in violation of its own charter).[42] Many companies owed their very existence to slight changes in governmental economic policy. In 1857, for example, the lowering to 3 percent of the interest rate on deposits in the government's Commercial Bank induced savers to withdraw their funds and to invest them in joint-stock companies instead. The result was the first episode of "stock-exchange fever" (*birzhevaia goriachka*) in Russia, which lasted from 1857 to 1860.[43] It was also at this time that highly placed tsarist bureaucrats began to serve simultaneously as officers of many a new corporation, to

[39] *Istoriia Moskvy*, 4:134.

[40] A graduate student at the University of California at Berkeley, Victoria King, is studying the Petersburg industrialists. The best treatment of the Petersburg merchants before 1905 is still A. G. Timofeev, *Istoriia S.-Peterburgskoi birzhi* (St. Petersburg, 1903). A good example of the avoidance of crucial issues by Soviet scholarship is Pavel G. Ryndziunskii, *Utverzhdenie kapitalizma v Rossii, 1850-1880 gg.* (Moscow, 1978), esp. the chapter on "the bourgeoisie," pp. 229-61.

[41] Buryshkin, *Moskva*, p. 33, called the description of the merchant way of life in *Kitai-gorod* "photographically precise."

[42] Iosif F. Gindin, *Gosudarstvennyi bank i ekonomicheskaia politika tsarskogo pravitel'stva (1861-1892 gody)* (Moscow, 1960), esp. chap. 6.

[43] Shepelev, *Kompanii*, pp. 66-78.

the benefit of their own pocketbooks as well as those of the companies' stockholders. One of the foremost practitioners of this "dual officeholding" (sovmestitel'stvo), Evgenii I. Lamanskii, occupied crucial posts at the State Bank: vice-president, 1860-66, and president, 1866-81.[44] By the 1880s, 370 of 1,006 Transportation Ministry engineers held positions in railroad companies, while 225 officials of the Finance Ministry served as corporate managers. Only in 1884 did the government act to curtail the practice of sovmestitel'stvo.[45]

In a perceptive commentary on the contrasts between the seekers after substantial state help (more often than not the large joint-stock companies of St. Petersburg) and the corporations that were oriented instead toward the mass market (primarily the textile share partnerships in Moscow), Fred Carstensen offered a neat analysis in the form of a paradox. The joint-stock companies, despite their modern form, actually perpetuated the old patrimonial pattern of state domination, while the smaller, less technologically advanced, and apparently less modern share partnerships in fact struggled for an economic livelihood outside the state's control, in keeping with the essence of modern capitalism. This insight correctly emphasizes the persistence of the state's power in spurring the application of advanced technology through large firms, with only minimal concern for the strengthening of the purely capitalist market; however, it minimizes the degree to which the Moscow textile men, even as they produced for the market and not the state, demanded high tariffs, government sponsorship of their banks, and the other forms of aid mentioned above. Perhaps this paradox can best be resolved by recognizing that both the joint-stock company and the share partnership objectified different aspects of modern capitalism—the former, advanced technology; the latter, the free market—and that by 1880 neither had been able to break free of the state's awesome power.

To bring these differences between the traditional and capitalist, and Moscow and St. Petersburg, entrepreneurs into sharper focus, it is useful to ask, finally, to what extent each type corresponded to the Schumpeterian definition of an entrepreneur. Schumpeter recognized the possibility of entrepreneurship in any historical situation where "a sufficient density of population, security, division of labor, adequate wealth," and

---

[44] Gindin, Gosudarstvennyi bank, p. 120n.

[45] Shepelev, Kompanii, pp. 129-33. This situation opened up many possibilities of securing economic advantages through the bribing of officials. While precise data is of course lacking, one scholar alleged in 1879 that "the commerce in favors . . . is, to our great misfortune, practiced in most industrial enterprises." Aleksei Antipov, Obzor pravitel'-stvennykh meropriiatii po razvitiiu v Rossii metallicheskoi promyshlennosti (St. Petersburg, 1879), p. 19.

other prerequisites existed. In fact, he wrote, "the [German] merchant of the eleventh century . . . is therefore different from the merchant of today or of Tacitus' time not because he had a different kind of acquisitiveness, or thought differently about economics, or behaved according to different principles, but because he operated under different relationships and thus faced different problems."[46] What he called "the entrepreneurial function," which differed from pure greed by its "much higher degree of rationalism, cleverness, and energy," consisted of at least one of five specific qualities: "1. the creation and implementation of new products or new kinds of production, 2. the introduction of new methods of production, 3. the establishment of new industrial organizations (for example, trusts), 4. the opening up of new markets, [and] 5. the opening up of new sources of supply."[47] The emphasis here was on innovation, rather than simply the competent management of an existing operation.

Against this strict measurement, the Russian merchants before the Crimean War scarcely qualified as true entrepreneurs. Owing to the technological backwardness of Russian industry relative to that of Western Europe, no Russian deserved credit for a genuine invention or innovation in production, notwithstanding the Stalinist claim that Ivan Polzunov, in an iron plant in the Urals, invented the steam engine in 1763, thirteen years before James Watt's feat.[48] Technological progress occurred in Russia through the importation of French, Belgian, and (after the British government lifted restrictions on exports in 1842) English equipment, notably steam-powered textile machinery. Savva V. Morozov, who outfitted the first Russian cotton-spinning mill to use Knoop's equipment,[49] certainly deserved credit for taking this unprecedented step toward modern capitalist production. However, the crucial financial innovation that made this importation possible was the work of Knoop himself. His opening of the line of credit with de Jersey and other English firms meant that he, not the Russians who bought his machines, best deserved the title of "entrepreneur." One must also credit Knoop with extraordinary tenacity in dealing with the Moscow merchants, who were just then beginning to shed their traditional ways of doing business. Schulze-Gävernitz wrote in 1899: "People who knew Moscow around mid-century have assured me that Knoop owed his success to his strong stomach. He

---

[46] Joseph A. Schumpeter, "Unternehmer," *Handwörterbuch der Staatswissenschaft*, 4th ed., ed. Ludwig Elster, Adolf Weber, and Friedrich Wieser, 8 vols. (Jena, 1923-28), 8:477-88.

[47] Ibid., pp. 482, 483.

[48] Lyashchenko, *History*, pp. 425-26, also credited Russians with inventing the electric light arc, the telegraph, aniline dye, galvanoplasty, etc.

[49] Schulze-Gävernitz, *Volkswirtschaftliche*, p. 92; Ioksimovich, *Monufakturnaia*, pp. 3-4; Buryshkin, *Moskva*, p. 62.

had the ability to be on close terms with the Russian merchants, to drink vodka with them, and to drink many bottles of champagne in taverns and with the gypsy girls—by no means a safe thing to do, since the customs of that time were downright Asiatic, and glasses, bottles, and mirrors flew through the air fairly often."[50]

Well-educated Russians from the gentry also provided crucial entrepreneurial talent that the semiliterate merchants lacked. Because only the most privileged social estate had, since the time of Peter the Great, received instruction in European arts and sciences, it is not surprising that Russians from gentry families took a disproportionately large role in the creation of new capitalist enterprises. In St. Petersburg, for example, Sergei A. Sobolevskii and the Mal'tsov brothers acquired the huge Samson cotton-spinning mill as early as the mid-1830s,[51] while two Slavophile intellectuals in Moscow—Aleksandr P. Shipov, a former guards officer and provincial official in the Ministry of State Domains, and Fedor V. Chizhov, a former mathematics professor and silkworm cultivator—plunged into a myriad of economic-development projects after the Crimean War: railroad construction, banking, and industrial journalism.[52]

In his analysis of the "Moscow entrepreneurial group," Alfred J. Rieber noted the nationalist impulse that lay behind the unusual partnership between merchants and gentry intellectuals.[53] It must also be stressed that because of their vastly different educational backgrounds, the leading role in this merchant-Slavophile alliance belonged to the latter, not the former. Efim F. Guchkov, the famous woolens magnate, bluntly wrote to Chizhov: "I do not wish to meddle in the administration of a railroad," and the exchange president from 1859 to 1865, Aleksei I. Khludov, poured far more money into his huge collection of pre-Petrine religious books and manuscripts than into Chizhov's overly ambitious journal, *Vestnik promyshlennosti* (The Herald of Industry), which closed for lack of funds in 1861.[54] A disappointed nobleman bemoaned the refusal of

[50] Schulze-Gävernitz, loc. cit.

[51] Kiniapina, *Politika*, p. 45.

[52] Thomas C. Owen, "The Moscow Merchants and the Public Press, 1858-1868," *Jahrbücher für Geschichte Osteuropas*, n.s., 23, no. 1 (March 1975):26-38.

[53] Alfred Rieber, "The Moscow Entrepreneurial Group: The Emergence of a New Form in Autocratic Politics," *Jahrbücher für Geschichte Osteuropas*, n.s., 25, no. 1 (March 1977):1-20, and no. 2 (June 1977):174-99. Likewise, in the 1820s and 1830s Count Aleksei A. Bobrinskoi (or Bobrinskii), 1800-1868, a wealthy landowner, single-handedly created the Ukrainian beet-sugar industry by means of his model farms and machine shops, in the face of governmental indifference and hostility. See the informative family history in "Graf Lev Alekseevich Bobrinskoi" (obituary), *Vestnik sakharnoi promyshlennosti*, year 16, no. 13 (March 20/April 11, 1915), pp. 281-83.

[54] Guchkov's letter of November 10, 1862, Gosudarstvennaia biblioteka SSSR im. Lenina, Otdel rukopisei (GBL-OR), Moscow, F332, carton 22, file 33, 1ʳ. On Khludov's collection, see *Russkii biograficheskii slovar'*, 20:341.

the Rybinsk grain traders and Ivanovo textile manufacturers to organize the extension of railroads to their towns in the late 1860s.[55] Even the modern capitalist merchants of the Central Region, therefore, were more distrustful of innovation, as a rule, than were the relatively better educated businessmen in the northern capital.

Only in one perverse sense can the Russian corporate leaders of the 1855-80 period be considered true Schumpeterian innovators. The millionaires Vasilii A. Kokorev, Nikolai A. Novosel'skii, and Petr I. Gubonin[56] were only three of the many Russians who discovered ingenious ways to mine the mother lode: the coffers of the Ministry of Finance. State aid represented the crucial factor in the success of every kind of large commercial, industrial, and financial venture in the reign of Alexander II. Not only was the tsar's signature required on the charter of every joint-stock company and share partnership founded in Russia,[57] but the personal participation of the State Bank vice-president, Evgenii I. Lamanskii, was necessary to launch the first private banks in St. Petersburg and Moscow.[58] Likewise, state orders and subsidies breathed life into the new iron, steel, and railroad companies, so that fair competition was impossible as long as a selected few received such favors.[59] Without the conquest of Transcaucasia and Central Asia by the imperial army, the textile magnates of the Central Region would have lacked an opportunity to demonstrate their talents for opening up new markets and transforming the Ferghana region into a "domestic" source of raw cotton.[60]

[55] Meshcherskii, *Ocherki*, 1:206-7, 169.

[56] Valuable but fragmentary information is in Konstantin A. Skal'kovskii, *Nashi gosudarstvennye i obshchestvennye deiateli*, 2 vols. (St. Petersburg, 1890), 1:154-78 on Kokorev; Skal'kovskii, *Satiristicheskie ocherki i vospominaniia* (St. Petersburg, 1902), pp. 293-302 on Gubonin, and 303-15 on Novosel'skii; and Gindin, *Gosudarstvennyi bank, passim*. The first detailed account of Kokorev's remarkable career is Paula Lieberman's doctoral dissertation, "V. A. Kokorev: An Industrial Entrepreneur in Nineteenth Century Russia" (Yale, 1982).

[57] Shepelev, *Kompanii*, pp. 55-58. On complaints against this bureaucratic tutelage by commercial-industrial leaders from 1860 onward, see Vladimir Ia. Laverychev, *Krupnaia burzhuaziia v poreformennoi Rossii (1861-1900 gg.)* (Moscow, 1974), pp. 42-43. On the government's refusal in the 1870s and 1880s to implement a system of simple registration of newly formed companies, Shepelev, *Kompanii*, pp. 111-21.

[58] Shepelev, *Kompanii*, 130; Naidenov, *Vospominaniia*, 2:108, 116. The first commercial bank in St. Petersburg would have failed at the outset had the State Bank not purchased one million rubles' worth of its stock: Laverychev, *Krupnaia*, p. 22.

[59] On the largest recipient of state favors, the Russian Railroad Company, see Rieber's informative article, "The Formation of La Grande Société des Chemins de Fer Russes," *Jahrbücher für Geschichte Osteuropas*, n.s., 21, no. 3 (September 1973):375-91. A good argument against selective favors, based on the case of the Hughes rail plant in the Donets basin, is in Antipov, *Obzor*, pp. 16-19.

[60] Lyashchenko, *History*, pp. 619, 605-11. For a detailed account, see Mariia K. Rozhkova, "Iz istorii torgovli Rossii s Srednei Aziei vo 60-kh godakh XIX v.," *Istoricheskie*

Even when Russian industrialists displayed certain hallmarks of the modern entrepreneur, such as the careful study of market conditions and the modification of product designs to satisfy consumer preferences,[61] they did so, typically, *through* their patron, the tsarist state. The cotton-textile producers of the Central Region, for example, paid close attention to the preferences of the inhabitants of Central Asia, and won a large share of that Eastern market from the English, whose designs were not so appealing to native tastes. Yet instead of establishing their own sources of market information, they turned to the state with pleas for help from the diplomatic service, especially consuls in foreign capitals.[62]

Indirect government aid had an equally stimulating effect, in the sense that high tariffs represented the single most important measure promoting the prosperity of Russian manufacturing companies. Cries for a prohibitive tariff to stem the flood of European manufactured goods issued with monotonous regularity from various merchant forums, and by 1868 the Finance Ministry had abandoned its experiment with sharply lower import duties (in 1850 and 1857) in favor of gradually stronger protection for the entire range of Russian products.[63]

A vigorous public debate raged in the early years of Alexander II's reign over the precise means of borrowing European expertise and capital to the best advantage. Was it wisdom or folly to allow foreign bankers and managers to reap huge profits from the new corporate enterprises, especially the railroad lines built by the largely foreign-financed Russian Railroad Company? Chizhov, Kokorev, and others in the Moscow group insisted on domestic financing of railroads as a principle of economic nationalism, arguing that no other policy could stem the outflow of

---

zapiski, 67 (1960):187-212. The Swede Ludwig Nobel encountered only apathy among Russian oilmen and shippers when, in 1877-78, he began to transform the Baku petroleum industry by building pipelines connecting the oil field with the refineries and by inventing the oil tanker. Robert Tolf, *The Russian Rockefellers* (Stanford, 1976), pp. 50-55. However, the Russian Spakovskii apparently did invent independently of the English scientist Aydon, in the 1870s, the process of using an oil fuel to power steamships: ibid., p. 70.

[61] Wilson, "Entrepreneur," p. 176, stressed "*a sense of market opportunity*" (his emphasis) as the crucial element of entrepreneurship.

[62] See Timofei S. Morozov's speech on this point in *Trudy vysochaishe razreshennogo torgovo-promyshlennogo s"ezda, sozvannogo Obshchestvom dlia sodeistviia russkoi promyshlennosti i torgovle . . . 1882 g.,* 2 vols. (St. Petersburg, 1883), 1:347-48.

[63] The polemical and scholarly literature on this crucial question is vast. Some excellent accounts are: Iatsunskii, "Krupnaia promyshlennost'," esp. p. 181 on the importance of tariffs to industrial growth before 1861; Naidenov, *Vospominaniia,* 2:66-68, 81-90 for the Moscow merchants' version; and K. Lodyzhenskii, *Istoriia russkogo tamozhennogo tarifa* (St. Petersburg, 1886; reprinted Cambridge, England, 1973); and M. N. Sobolev, *Tamozhennaia politika Rossii vo vtoroi polovine XIX veka* (Tomsk, 1911) for both statistics and policy debates.

Russian specie to Western Europe.[64] On the other hand, the St. Petersburg banker Baron Aleksandr L. Stieglitz, who headed the State Bank until 1866, eagerly cooperated with Pereire, Baring Brothers, and Mendelssohn, despite Chizhov's accusation of economic treason,[65] in hopes of reaping the rewards: technical competence, lower costs, and prompt financing of construction projects of unprecedented magnitude. Of course, when their own financial resources proved inadequate to extend their private railroad from the Trinity Monastery to Iaroslavl', Chizhov and his merchant supporters in Moscow showed no compunction about turning to Finance Minister Reutern for a guarantee of a 5 percent profit, such as the Russian Railroad Company enjoyed. Furthermore, to finance the Moscow-Kursk railroad in 1871, they sold bonds on the European exchanges.[66] The heated rhetoric of these debates over tariff protection and foreign financing of economic development obscured one essential point: the importers, manufacturers, and bureaucrats of St. Petersburg, no less than the Moscow textile and railroad men, hoped to strengthen the Russian economy by drawing on whatever Western skills, techniques, and capital were available to substitute for the relatively scarce entrepreneurial talents and financial resources of the Russian Empire.

One must not, however, underestimate the political importance of these debates. The xenophobia of the Moscow industrialists continued unabated well into the 1880s. Sergei F. Sharapov, the secretary of the Moscow Section of the Russian Industrial Society and editor of the economic column of Ivan S. Aksakov's virulently nationalist periodical *Rus'* (Ancient Russia, 1880-86), hammered out article after article demanding bureaucratic restraints on Polish industry, especially those companies under Jewish or German control. "Moscow's struggle with Łódź" (the title of one of his pamphlets, dated 1889) could be won only by political measures. Notwithstanding his dubious economic arguments, Sharapov's press campaign netted impressive favors from the state, including the closing of Transcaucasia to the foreign transit trade in 1884.[67] There is nothing surprising in this fact, for as Schumpeter noted, the influence of purely political, "non-capitalist elements of society" often has out-

[64] Rieber, "Formation," pp. 384-89; Laverychev, *History*, pp. 38-39; Owen, "Moscow Merchants," p. 33.

[65] "Stieglitz is one of those who is actively promoting our ruin." Paraphrase by Aleksandr V. Nikitenko in his diary, May 14, 1866, *Dnevnik*, 3 vols. (Moscow, 1955-56), 3:34. On the Baron's career, see Blackwell, *Beginnings*, pp. 258-60.

[66] Nikitenko, *Dnevnik*, diary entry of May 8, 1866, 3:32; Naidenov, *Vospominaniia*, 2:99; Arkadii Cherokov, *Fedor Vasil'evich Chizhov* (Moscow, 1902), pp. 41-42.

[67] Laverychev, *Krupnaia*, pp. 204-5; U. A. Shuster, "Ekonomicheskaia bor'ba Moskvy s Lodziu," *Istoricheskie zapiski*, 5 (1939):188-234 on both the Polish and Transcaucasian issues.

weighed "the inner logic of entrepreneurial production."[68] In many other countries as well, state aid proved crucial to the success of large economic projects, such as railroads and canals. In Russia, however, where over the centuries the policies of the autocratic government had determined the structure and activity of social and economic institutions, the political factor remained paramount. (It also assumed special importance because the alliance between capitalists and the autocratic state hindered the development of liberal and radical political movements before 1905.)

One is led to conclude that Russians, especially the Muscovites, used nationalist fervor to make up for their deficiencies as modern capitalists. Lack of expertise in the intricacies of corporate management can be seen as just one aspect of the merchants' cultural inferiority relative to the gentry. Although their economic nationalism kept merchants and Slavophile intellectuals together in corporate undertakings until the death of the major figures (of Chizhov in 1877 and of Aksakov in 1886), several embarrassing episodes marred the collaboration. An especially serious misunderstanding occurred in 1868, when Chizhov grew exasperated with Kokorev's debonair approach to the unsuccessful campaign to purchase the Moscow-St. Petersburg railroad. Although a firm patriot who loudly criticized certain bureaucrats in the Finance Ministry for an alleged lack of economic nationalism, the bearded millionaire had mastered too well for Chizhov's taste "all the ins and outs in Petersburg."[69] Because of his simple Old Believer education, Kokorev did little more than trust his cunning and luck in risky joint-stock companies, and only a sequence of huge "irregular loans" and other favors from the State Bank between 1860 and 1867 saved him from bankruptcy.[70] The meticulous Chizhov, although a Slavophile intellectual who longed to return to his first love, art history, proved to be, in Weberian terms, a more rational entrepreneur than the unpredictable Kokorev. Toward the end of their collaboration, Chizhov "feared him for his endlessly grandiose fantasies and his purely American schemes, and feared being involuntarily drawn in and burned, without serious and fundamental consideration, as he had taught himself [to do] in his own affairs."[71] Kokorev's own feelings about the great cultural gap remain unknown, as he passed over that subject in silence in his wordy memoirs.[72] For his part, the highly influential president of

[68] Schumpeter, "Unternehmer," p. 477.

[69] Naidenov's phrase, *Vospominaniia,* 2:54. Chizhov once wrote disparagingly of both Kokorev and N. I. Putilov: "bribery is their main tool, then lies." Quoted by Laverychev, *Krupnaia,* p. 74.

[70] Gindin, *Gosudarstvennyi bank,* pp. 270-79.

[71] Cherokov, *Chizhov,* p. 39.

[72] Ekonomicheskie provaly po vospominaniiam s 1837 goda," *Russkii arkhiv,* 1887, vol.

the Moscow Exchange Committee, Nikolai A. Naidenov, complained that Chizhov's tendency to staff the Merchant Bank with "persons from the bureaucratic and scholarly world" implied "a lack of confidence in the competence of the mercantile men themselves."[73]

It was not until the early 1880s that two well-educated young merchants turned the tables decisively, when, as new board members of the Moscow district Zemstvo, they introduced the complicated system of Italian bookkeeping, to the utter bewilderment of the older gentry members of the board.[74] It was also at this time that younger and better educated Moscow industrialists first began boasting publicly of the economic ability of native Russians. At the Commercial-Industrial Congress of 1882, Grigorii A. Krestovnikov, then aged twenty-seven, declared that if tariffs were maintained at adequate levels the manufacturers would prove equal to the task. "Capital," he asserted, "needs profit. Show it the ways of profit, blaze the trail to it, and capital will gallantly [*bogatyrski*] rip out from the bowels of the earth all of Russia's incalculable riches."[75]

The attitudes expressed by Chizhov, Kokorev, Krestovnikov, and the other Moscow business leaders constitute what Alexander Gerschenkron termed an "ideology of delayed industrialization," that is, a set of ideas capable of removing "the mountains of routine and prejudice" that had previously impeded rapid economic development. Gerschenkron asserted that in the 1890s Marxism began to fulfill this function in Russia,[76] but the Moscow intellectuals Chizhov, Shipov, and Babst had long before grafted a fervent Slavophile nationalism onto Friedrich List's and Wilhelm Roscher's theories of balanced economic growth, thus creating a powerful ideology of Russian industrialization.[77] Recognition of this fact helps to clear up the apparent contradiction that Gerschenkron perceived between the negative "social attitudes toward entrepreneurs" on the part of the

---

1, no. 2, 245-79; no. 3, 369-82; no. 4, 503-14; vol. 2, no. 5, 130-44; no. 6, 263-72; no. 7, 394-416. His papers, in *TsGIA* F 1639 and *TsGIAM* F 959, have never been systematically studied by either Soviet or Western historians.

[73] Naidenov, *Vospominaniia*, 2:10.

[74] Chetverikov, *Bezvozratno*, pp. 88-90. The two merchants were Chetverikov and his brother-in-law, Nikolai A. Alekseev, the future mayor of Moscow (1885-93).

[75] *Trudy*, 1:265.

[76] "Economic Backwardness in Historical Perspective," in Gerschenkron, *Economic Backwardness in Historical Perspective: A Book of Essays* (Cambridge, Mass., 1966), pp. 22, 24, 25.

[77] Schulze-Gävernitz perceived this several decades after the process had begun (in 1855-60); see his "Der Nationalismus in Russland und seine wirtschaftliche Träger," *Preussische Jahrbücher*, 75 (1894): no. 1, 1-31; no. 2, 337-64; no. 3, 496-528, reprinted with modifications in *Studien (Ocherki)*, chap. 4.

anticapitalist gentry, intelligentsia, and peasantry, on the one hand, and the successful business careers of Russian traders and manufacturers on the other. What Gerschenkron called "the profound malaise . . . of the 'repentant merchant' "[78] was, in fact, far less common than he intimated, even in the 1860s, due largely to the legitimizing function of the merchant-Slavophile ideology of economic nationalism. Entrepreneurship for the sake of Russian power had become an honorable calling, at least among capitalists of the Central Industrial Region.[79]

Several tentative conclusions may be drawn from the brief definitions and descriptions presented above. First, one is struck by the interesting ways in which European capitalist institutions that were introduced in the 1830-70 period underwent important modifications in order to operate successfully in the Russian environment. Immediately evident were the lack of adequate private capital resources for the new companies of the post-Crimean War period; the grave shortage of qualified and honest business managers; and the reluctance of the tsarist bureaucracy to relinquish the firm control over corporate development that the law of 1836 provided. Even when Russian merchants embraced modern forms of enterprise, they continued to look to the state for crucial support in the form of credit, tariffs, subsidies for exports, and other favors.

The second conclusion is that a cruel dilemma therefore faced the Russian government toward the end of the nineteenth century: on the one hand, a laissez faire policy would risk the spread of mismanagement, swindling, stock-exchange speculation, and business failures—the unfortunate side effects of capitalism seen most of all in St. Petersburg; but, on the other hand, the continuation of tight controls would stifle the growth of entrepreneurship or at least pervert the acquisitive talent into an unseemly scramble for special favors from the imperial treasury. Protectionist tariffs and infusions of foreign capital represented no easy solution to the overwhelming problem of creating a dynamic market, which for centuries had been absent in relatively backward Russia.

This observation leads to a final point. One must avoid judging too harshly the foibles of native Russian merchants, particularly their slowness in casting off their traditional ways. Comical and corrupt they cer-

[78] Alexander Gerschenkron, "Social Attitudes, Entrepreneurship, and Economic Development," in *Backwardness*, pp. 59-62; quotations from p. 61.

[79] By 1900, the economic dynamism of America, made famous in Russia by visitors to the great industrial exhibits in Philadelphia (1876) and Chicago (1896), had also become an attractive model. Hans Rogger, "America in the Russian Mind—or Russian Discoveries of America," *Pacific Historical Review*, 47, no. 1 (February 1978):42-45. I am indebted to Samuel Baron for calling Rogger's article to my attention and for making other valuable suggestions on this paper.

tainly seemed to outsiders, as in the unflattering stereotypes of Ostrov-skii's immortal *samodur* and the "arch-swindler" and "crook" (*arkhiplut* and *naduvala*) of Gogol's *Inspector General.* Yet the traditional Russian merchant had simply learned too well for the general good how to survive in a society dominated by an oppressive and arbitrary bureaucracy.[80] Weber noted long ago that modern capitalism was unthinkable without "the rational state" and its "expert officialdom and rational law,"[81] most closely approximated in Britain, postrevolutionary France, and the United States. In view of the fact that, at least in their formative periods, laissez faire capitalism and liberal democracy flourished together in those coun-tries, it was hardly surprising that in Russia the world's most powerful autocratic government coexisted with an economy in which the market forces remained relatively weak. As Witte's policies showed, entrepre-neurial initiative could not be directly stimulated by political and bu-reaucratic substitutions for the market mechanism.

Kokorev's shortcomings as a modern capitalist may therefore be traced directly, if not exclusively, to the pro-gentry policies of the well-educated Catherine II and her privileged courtiers. In search of profits, individual Russian merchants, traditional no less than capitalist, bravely faced nu-merous dangers: overland travel in bitter winters, unpredictable market fluctuations, and attacks from brigands on Central Asian caravan routes, to name a few. The entrepreneurial impulse existed in Russia, but despite the reforms of Alexander II (and, one might also add, of the Soviet government during NEP) it was never freed sufficiently from the heavy burden of bureaucratic controls.

---

[80] Even the corruption of government officials could not be blamed entirely on the merchants. As Kokorev explained to the fastidious Chizhov, it had taken two years for the charter of the Moscow Merchant Bank to receive the government's approval; "In Petersburg it is hard to make your case without incurring expenses." Disgusted with wholesale grafting in railroads in 1868, Aleksandr I. Koshelev wrote that "the immorality, unscrupulousness, and absurdity of the higher administration has surpassed all the swindling and nonsense of the provincial and district bureaucrats." In 1876 the Third Section found one Finance Ministry official who demanded and received from corporate directors payments of up to 100,000 rubles. Laverychev, *Krupnaia*, pp. 41 (quoted), 53 (quoted), and 48-49.

[81] Weber, *Economic History*, p. 339.

V

JOHN A. ARMSTRONG   *Socializing for Modernization in a Multiethnic Elite*

The Russian experience in economic development, like that of other societies, has been highly complex. Certainly one component has been the role of the entrepreneur. Yet, this role itself is a very complex one; failure to separate the many components of the role and to define them analytically has probably caused even more mischief in Russian studies than in examinations of other polities. This chapter rests on considerable thought and a limited amount of research on topics close to the theme of entrepreneurial response. There is no intention, however, of presenting a research report on entrepreneurs in the Russian polity, or even laying an adequate groundwork for such research. Several promising directions that need to be pursued are followed in other chapters of this book. My purpose is to clarify the problem, insofar as that preliminary step can be taken by reflection and discussion. At certain points in the analysis comparisons are introduced. These comparisons are not fully elaborated, but, given the relative isolation in which so much of Russian area studies has proceeded, even preliminary suggestions of novel analogies to developments elsewhere appear to be appropriate. While the focus on the multiethnic character of the polity leads to specific emphases, alternative theoretical viewpoints are suggested where they appear especially relevant.

The special aspect of the entrepreneurial response examined here is its ethnic complexity. In the preceding paragraph the terms *Russian polity* and *Russian* were used repeatedly. These terms are appropriate, both formally and substantially, for consideration of the nineteenth century (the period treated in this chapter), for the Soviet period, and for long periods prior to 1800. Since the end of the sixteenth century the empire's legitimizing symbols, and usually its formal title, have been Russian. A very large majority of members of the ruling elites have accepted this symbolic identification with Russia as a polity even when they were not themselves ethnic Russians, and may not have had a very high regard for Russian culture. Given this identification, it was natural and easy for writers who did consider themselves to belong to the ethnic Russian culture (i.e., who identified with the Russian language and culture in addition to the polity symbols) to imply that the empire consisted of an ethnically homogeneous society comparable, say, to France's. This trend, as Jaroslaw Pelenski has pointed out, became noticeable as early as the sixteenth century, but it seems to have been particularly influential among nineteenth-century economic historians, whether they were dealing with their own or the preceding century.[1] Thus the entrepreneurial biographies based on Ministry of Justice archives and the *Kupechaskaia Uprava* presented by N. Chulkov[2] suggest virtually exclusively Russian ethnic origin. Without questioning the validity of the author's observations, one might expect him to have shown some awareness of the atypical nature of his Moscow sample. More influential writers like Tugan-Baranovskii convey a similar misleading impression through their choice of background materials.[3] For the last forty years at least, most Soviet discussions of eighteenth- and nineteenth-century entrepreneurs have also stressed the Russian component—as have many émigré historians so influential in the direction scholarship has taken in the West.

Up to a point this stress is reasonable. As Joseph Schumpeter once suggested, study of social phenomena in an ethnically homogeneous environment is the logical first step.[4] Ethnic Russian entrepreneurial elements such as the Old Believers and others of peasant origin, as will appear below, are both interesting and important objects of study. Yet a balanced appraisal of the overall course of Russian economic development might do better to take into account Erik Amburger's conclusion that even in the centuries before the empire's greatest expansion native Russian foreign trade was important only in commerce with the underdeveloped lands to the south and west.[5] If this generalization can be extended to the nineteenth century entrepreneurial response, we must scrutinize other ethnic elements. For some purposes—as will appear shortly—ethnic background is not a crucial consideration. To the extent,

[1] Jaroslaw Pelenski, *Russia and Kazan: Conquest and Imperial Ideology (1438-1560s)* (The Hague, 1974), pp. 8-10.

[2] N. C[hulkov], "Moskovskoe Kupechestvo, XVIII i XIX Vekov (Genealogischeskie Zametki)," *Russkii Arkhiv*, 45 (1907), esp. p. 500.

[3] Mikhail Tugan-Baranovskii, *Geschichte der russischen Fabrik*, trans. B. Minzes (Berlin, 1900), esp. pp. 15, 355.

[4] Joseph Schumpeter, "Die sozialen Klassen im ethnisch homogenen Milieu," *Archiv für Sozialwissenschaft und Sozialpolitik*, 67 (1927):1-67.

[5] Erik Amburger, "Der fremde Unternehmer in Russland bis zur Oktoberrevolution," *Tradition*, 2 (1957):337; cf. p. 343.

however, to which entrepreneurial propensity derives from socialization in a specific cultural milieu, the assumption of Russian ethnic homogeneity is highly counterproductive. Nor (despite the essential contribution which Fred Carstensen's presentation makes to this symposium) is the matter entirely one of foreign contributions to Russian-polity entrepreneurial development. It will not do to consider entrepreneurs born abroad to be foreigners, as most Russian historians do, if their early socialization occurred within the empire.[6] The critical problem, which is the main one posed in this chapter, is the way in which distinctive subcultures (or, it may be argued, the cultures of separate societies coexisting on the territory of the Russian Empire) socialized some of their members to become entrepreneurs differing significantly from other entrepreneurs in the developing economy.

Before approaching this problem directly, it is useful to address, briefly, some preliminary questions. What is an entrepreneur? Is early socialization really a critical differentiating factor in producing an "entrepreneurial personality"? Is this personality crucial, as compared to structural characteristics, in a developing economy? What was it about the Russian imperial polity that provided opportunities for culturally diverse entrepreneurs? How did the presence of these heterogeneous elements affect the interaction of economic, social, and political development? These are very large questions; other symposium contributors undoubtedly provide more significant answers to several than I can hope to suggest. Still, clarity concerning my assumptions requires some attempt to answer the questions; it seems preferable to begin with the last ones, which most directly bear upon the whole system.

Certainly a major characteristic of the Russian polity was its slow, uneven development. As I have treated elsewhere the relation of economic development to the extremely uneven Russian social development, I shall not pursue the theme at this point.[7] It will become clearer later in the chapter, however, that uneven social modernization strongly affected the significance of differing entrepreneurial roles. From a somewhat different point of view, though, it was the uneven, "leaplike" nature of Russian development that led to incorporation of different ethnic milieus favor-

[6] See, for example, William L. Blackwell's comment on Russian historians' view of Ludwig Knoop in *The Beginnings of Russian Industrialization, 1800-1860* (Princeton, 1968), p. 242.

[7] "Communist Political Systems as Vehicles for Modernization," in Monte Palmer and Larry Stern, eds., *Political Development in Changing Societies* (Lexington, Mass., 1971), pp. 127-58. For more specific economic and technological unevenness, see Roger Portal, "Das Problem einer industriellen Revolution in Russland," *Forschungen zur Osteuropäischen Geschichte*, 1 (1954):208. For comparative development rates, see Angus Maddison, *Economic Growth in Japan and the USSR* (London, 1969), pp. xvi, 31.

able to entrepreneurial personalities in the Russian polity and provided the field for their fructifying exercise. The inflated romance of the conquest of Siberia, plus the more significant history of the foundations for expansion laid by tsars from Ivan III to Peter I, often obscure the fact that most economically valuable territory was acquired between 1772 and 1815, that is, in a single generation just preceding the beginnings of entrepreneurial expansion. To be sure, Old Believer entrepreneur families had long been subjects of the empire, as had been the Volga Tatars and most of the Baltic Germans. Many more Germans were added during the partition of Poland, as was a notable Polish contingent, and above all the large reservoir of potential Jewish talent, virtually absent from the Russian Empire before the First Partition of Poland.[8] Russian protection for the "Armenian commercial people" in the Transcaucasus was widely recognized to be an innovation with important international economic implications.[9] More important than the incorporation of these new elements, perhaps, was the vast extension of fields for entrepreneurial talent of all backgrounds. The large area of Polish economic activity was within the Russian Empire by 1815, and the old but still valuable Oriental trade routes to the Caucasus were under firm Russian political domination. In addition, a vast region of economic exploitation, never before significantly tapped, lay available in the steppes north of the Black Sea.[10]

The establishment of the Pax Russica alone, making possible rationally calculable commerce in what had been (apart from the early Mongol period) a region of desperate commercial gambles, tended to release pent-up economic energies. The situation resembled the Moslem-Arab conquest of the southern and eastern Mediterranean lands after centuries of barbarian incursions. As the outstanding French economic historian of this period has pointed out, the commercial expansion of the Arab Empires regrouped and utilized the "old peoples of the classic Orient and the Mediterranean. . . . The world of ports, caravans, shops, commercial firms."[11] The process, as an American historian argues, may have been facilitated by the sober, bourgeois commercial qualities inculcated by Islam.[12] The first centuries of Arab expansion, however, were characterized by predominance of minority cultures in commercial expansion. Few—even among the Russian historians mentioned above—would con-

----

[8] S. B. Weinryb, *Neusste Wirtschaftsgeschichte der Juden in Russland und Polen: 1, Das Wirtschaftsleben der Juden in Russland und Polen von der 1. polnischen Teilung bis zum Tode Alexander II (1772-1881)* (Breslau, 1934), p. v.

[9] Hermann von Petersdorff, *Friedrich von Motz*, 2 vols. (Berlin, 1913), 2:323.

[10] See esp. William H. McNeill, *Europe's Steppe Frontier, 1500-1800* (Chicago, 1964), p. 186.

[11] Maurice Lombard, *Espaces et réseaux du haut moyen age* (Paris, 1972), 11th p. of first essay.

[12] Marshall G. S. Hodgson, *The Venture of Islam*, 3 vols. (Chicago, 1974), 1:37, 43.

tend that Orthodox Russians *in the dominant political elite* of the Russian Empire were as fitted by cultural attitudes for commercial and industrial expansion as were the Arab rulers of the seventh century. If anything, the early stages of the Industrial Revolution required more specialized entrepreneurial qualities than did medieval commercial expansion. Nowhere in Western Europe did an elite of bureaucrats, military officers, and landowners, as contrasted to the large native bourgeoisies inherited from the early modern era, play the predominant part in industrial development. It is a trite understatement to remark that the Russian ethnic bourgeoisie was much too small to take adequate advantage of the great opportunities afforded by the coincidence of Industrial Revolution abroad and the huge new areas available within the Russian Empire.

Some of the specific reasons that socialization by Russian merchant families did not produce entrepreneurial personalities fully suited to these opportunities will appear below. Here one need only point out that a major barrier, affecting all European bourgeoisies *in inverse proportion to their weight in the social order*, was lingering feudal denigration of economic activity. Consequently, the bourgeois was constantly tempted, having achieved a modicum of material success, to abandon his entrepreneurial activity (and withdraw his capital) in order to adopt a noble way of life. Because of their small numbers the Russian bourgeois would have been particularly exposed to this temptation to "class suicide" even if all other things had been equal. In fact, things were not equal. Middle-class consciousness was proverbially weak. The Russian imperial system placed a particularly strong emphasis on officially recognized rank, while the *chin* system made access to this rank—over two or three generations—exceptionally easy for financially successful Russian Orthodox families. Almost as significant, toward the end of the nineteenth century, was the disdain for economic activities among the Russian intelligentsia, the counter-"Establishment" that might otherwise have served to promote entrepreneurial capacities.

The master theorist of our subject, Alexander Gerschenkron, has advanced the concept of an inspiring doctrine as a substitute for entrepreneurial socialization in countries like Russia: "To break through the barriers of stagnation in a backward country, to ignite the imagination of men, and to place their energies in the service of economic development, a stronger medicine is needed. . . . Even the business man, even the classical daring and innovating entrepreneur, needs a more powerful stimulus than the prospect of high profits. What is needed to remove the mountains of routine and prejudice is faith."[13] David McClelland makes

[13] Alexander Gerschenkron, *Economic Backwardness in Historical Perspective* (Cambridge, Mass., 1962), p. 24.

very much the same point: "There is no real substitute for ideological fervor. A country or at least a significant portion of its elite has got to want economic achievement badly enough to give it priority over other desires."[14] While writers like these are ready to specify the development ideology (Legal Marxism for Gerschenkron, List's doctrines for Theodore Von Laue),[15] their propositions are more useful for explaining how a favorable climate for entrepreneurs can arise than in locating the origins of entrepreneurial talent. In effect, what Gerschenkron and Von Laue argue is that the *structural* requisites for industrial take-off were developed in late nineteenth-century Russia because the regime was affected by favorable ideologies, although (as will appear shortly) Von Laue also allows for the intervention of personality attributes.

More generally, resort to structural explanations of Russian economic development is the dominant mode in the historiography of the subject. This is one reason that information on entrepreneurs' personalities is a relatively neglected topic, which requires considerable digging and interpolation even in a preliminary sketch. Gerschenkron's and Von Laue's ideological explanations would probably be labeled "idealist" by most Marxists, but official Soviet Marxism is also essentially a structuralist explanation. Social forces (the well-known relationships of production) resulted in circumstances conducive to economic enterprise; at that point in history the requisite personalities appeared. It is possible to translate this type of analysis—prescinding from the specific "forces" posited by Marxism-Leninism—into the language of role theory. One might hypothesize that the societal structure produced certain types of entrepreneurial roles, which in turn molded the appropriate behavior of those recruited (or self-selected) for the roles.[16] Indeed, it would appear that the most recent trend in role analysis has been to emphasize the dominant effect of role definition upon any holder (within an indeterminately broad range of acceptable personalities) as contrasted to the formative effect of early socialization. For example, it is argued that a body like the U.S. Senate structures its roles in such a way that an astounding variety of personalities among those elected senators (a few obvious deviants come to mind) accommodate. The process of accommodation is a learning process, but in contrast to theories of the dominance of early socializing experiences, the role-dominance hypothesis assumes a large measure of conscious choice in individual accommodation to the role definitions. In

[14] David C. McClelland, *The Achieving Society* (Princeton, 1961), p. 430.

[15] Theodore H. Von Laue, *Sergei Witte and the Industrialization of Russia* (New York, 1963).

[16] I discuss this complex sociological problem at some length in *The European Administrative Elite* (Princeton, 1973).

his chapter in this symposium, David Granick presents the role-dominant assumption very forcefully.

The student of entrepreneurial behavior should be aware of the alternative theoretical ways of approaching role and personality, but the subject is obviously too vast—and too much in flux—for treatment here. Instead, I shall concentrate on the earlier theoretical position, which posited the dominance of early socialization. Although, as elaborated at the end of this essay, there was considerable scope for ethnic cultural differentials in adult role accommodation in the actual circumstances of the Russian polity, early socialization affords the strongest and most obvious opportunity for developing peculiar ethnic personalities. In his famous exposition of the cultural basis for the entrepreneurial personality, Max Weber discusses at length the influence of Calvinist and similar religious milieus, but he always assumes the dominance of early socialization: "the chances of overcoming traditionalism are greatest on account of the religious upbringing."[17] More recent exponents of the basic Weberian model such as David McClelland, Everett Hagen, and Fred L. Strodtbeck are nearly all adherents of schools of social psychology that posit the dominance of socialization in childhood and adolescence, if not infancy.[18] Even restricting these assumptions to a minimum (by assuming that adolescence may be the most critical period), one is left with a powerful school of interpretation that necessarily accords priority to differential ethnic influences where strong ethnic subcultures exist. Strodtbeck's interpretation, essentially faithful to the Weberian model, ascribes the following attributes to the entrepreneur:

1. Rejection of a mystical, personal relationship with God which might lead to efforts at advancement by "magical" manipulation.
2. Belief, on the contrary, that God's decisions are eternal and orderly, hence a stable basis for rational calculation by anyone who understands the revealed order of the universe.
3. Belief that the individual's transcendental fate is predestined and that the nature of this predestination is ascertainable by the extent to which strict performance of duty is crowned by worldly success.
4. High achievement motivation arising from dissatisfaction with accomplishments ("no defined stopping place"), hence concentration on the secular role performance in areas where material results are readily apparent.

[17] Max Weber, *The Protestant Ethic and the Spirit of Capitalism*, trans. Talcott Parsons (New York, 1957), p. 63.

[18] David C. McClelland, et al., *Talent and Society* (Princeton, 1959), pp. 135-94. For an especially cogent critique of Weber's neglect of political, social, and material factors in favor of "internal history" see Fernand Braudel, *Ecrits sur l'Histoire* (Paris, 1969), p. 269.

While Weber appeared to assume lifelong attachment to a peculiar religious milieu, it is clear that he believed the individual would persist in anxious performance even after long separation from the religious milieu (particularly the family) in which he had received his socialization. The classic example is Benjamin Franklin. In David Riesman's expressive phrase, the Calvinist type of personality was extremely "inner-directed."

Strodtbeck and his colleagues question whether the Calvinist model is fully appropriate for the structural conditions of highly developed economies—for even the most extreme model based on cultural influences cannot ignore structural change. In the English-speaking countries and Northwest Europe, where Weber derived his models, economic development eventually entailed a drastic shift from the small-scale, independent entrepreneur to large organizations. For the later stages of development the revised Weberian model may include the following attributes (I follow Strodtbeck less closely here than in his interpretation of the original model):

1. Rational calculability, as in 1 and 2 of the original model, though perhaps with less conscious religious underpinning.
2. Dissatisfaction with any given level of accomplishment, leading to a constant "future orientation." As in the Weberian model this dissatisfaction derives indirectly from early socialization; but the concern is commonly attributed to the immediate reference group, i.e., one's peers' evaluation of one's role performance; thus the trait corresponds to Riesman's "other-directedness."
3. A correspondingly high degree of concern for interpersonal relations of an instrumental nature at the organizational level, with cultivation of the communication skills (verbal and nonverbal) requisite for effective relations.[19]
4. Continued concern outside the organizational context for a specific reference group established as dominant early in one's socialization. Because this concern is not (at least consciously) instrumental but affective, the personality retains a strong "inner-directed" component. In the multi-ethnic polity one can expect most of this affect to be directed toward ethnic cultures, but the trait is not essentially different from the persistent adherence of an Englishman to the norms inculcated by his adolescent public-school peer group.
5. High geographic mobility, involving (despite the persistence of inner-directedness based on initial socialization by the family) rejection of familist values like unwillingness to face physical separation

---

[19] I discuss the communication advantage of "mobilized diasporas," which is probably more salient in commercial and administrative activities than in strictly entrepreneurial work, in "Mobilized and Proletarian Diasporas," *American Political Science Review*, 70 (1976):393-408.

or emphasis upon extended family well-being at the expense of personal advancement. Obviously the mobility factor is especially important in a very large polity.

I shall examine the application of these models in more concrete terms shortly; it has been necessary to present them at some length here because their features are crucially related to peculiar structural aspects of the Russian polity. Largely because of the authoritarian political intervention, economic organizations were exceptionally large in early stages of Russian industrialization. It may well be, as Bert Hoselitz and others have argued, that such contrived structures are "functionally" important for conserving scarce entrepreneurial talent in Roman Catholic and Orthodox polities where the dominant religious culture is not conducive to entrepreneurial qualities.[20] Whatever the functional significance (if any) of Russian resort to organizational "gigantism," it anticipated in important respects a much later stage of bureaucratic economic organization in the West. This structural anticipation required, therefore, much of the role emphasis on interpersonal relationships at a rather superficial level, as posited in the revised Weberian model. The requirement for communication skills was obviously enhanced by the polyglot nature of imperial society, and in a rather more subtle way by the necessity for temporary, instrumental bridging of cultural chasms.

The special organizational mode of development in the Russian polity suggests that the entrepreneurial role there may have been complicated in other ways as well. It has always been hard to define a complicated role like the entrepreneur's. While the classic entrepreneur was concerned with founding, owning, and directing an enterprise that constituted a small portion of a given area of production, the typical Russian businessman operated in an oligopolistic organization like those in modern capitalist economies. He was often a manager rather than an owner, and (as Schumpeter pointed out a half century ago) the managerial role tends to become subdivided among roles with professional attributes.[21] This professionalization of the entrepreneurial role poses numerous problems. One is the extent to which the manager in a large organization differs from the bureaucratic administrator. The difficulty is especially severe in examining the Russian Empire, where much enterprise was carried on by large organizations that were either government bureaus or under close governmental supervision. A second problem concerns the degree to which one must consider, as components of the managerial role, specialized professions like engineering and the type of socialization these

---

[20] *Capital Formation and Economic Growth: A Conference of the Universities-National Bureau Committee for Economic Research* (Princeton, 1955), p. 390.
[21] Schumpeter (supra, n. 4), p. 22.

professions entailed. Elsewhere I have discussed these problems from the point of view of public administration; here I shall endeavor to keep the focus as sharply as possible on entrepreneurial role as set forth in the models outlined above. But one should never lose sight of the fact that in the revised Weberian model, particularly as applied to the Russian polity, the entrepreneur is essentially an analytic category.

Another line of interpretation suggests that persons who are marginal in status are attracted to roles (such as entrepreneur in the Russian imperial polity) that the dominant group neglects, but that are otherwise rewarding. A classic variant of this interpretation has entire subcultures turning to such roles when excluded from dominant status. Everett Hagen identifies various types of "withdrawal of status respect," which lead to marginality; one type is "denigration of valued symbols," which he applies specifically to Russian Old Believers. Hagen also argues that the deviant (marginal) group fosters innovative individuals by protecting them from censure by the larger society.[22] Probably in the present context the marginality interpretation and social-psychological interpretations embodied in the revised Weberian model cannot be distinguished in operational terms. Indeed, some such mechanisms as those posited in Weber's model are essential as intervening variables if the marginality hypothesis is to be developed into a fully explanatory theory. The most important consideration here is that the values held by the dominant Russian ethnic elite relegated *some* other ethnic groups to marginal positions throughout the nineteenth century, and *all* other ethnic groups to marginality during parts of that century. One should never forget, therefore, that the values and perceptions of the dominant Russian ethnic elite constitute a major factor in the dynamics of entrepreneurial response even among non-Russians. In the following outline application of the revised Weberian model to specific ethnic groups, the dynamic element (i.e., change over time) cannot be elucidated fully, but it is crucial to note that the model is adaptable to a dynamic context.

Lack of space precludes even sketchy attention to three of the groups mentioned earlier as potential suppliers of entrepreneurial talent—Poles, Armenians, and Volga Tatars. Alexandre Bennigsen is preparing a major analysis of the last group, and considerable research on the roles held by Poles in the broader empire is under way.

Analysis of Armenian entrepreneurial activity would be especially useful because that experience might be compared directly to numerous other adaptations of Armenian culture to foreign polities. I must confine myself

[22] Everett E. Hagen, *On the Theory of Economic Change: How Economic Growth Begins* (Homewood, 1962), p. 249.

to the three cases where materials are readily available; fortunately, these were the most important sources of nineteenth-century entrepreneurial talent.

Since our symposium member William Blackwell is the outstanding American authority on the Russian sectarian component of nineteenth-century entrepreneurial talent, I would be presumptuous to discuss this topic at length. In particular, I shall prescind from discussing the extent to which various sectarian doctrines coincided with the Calvinists'. Omission of credal analysis appears to be legitimate also because, as noted earlier, the alternative marginality interpretation explicitly identifies Old Believers (the most significant sectarian group) as a subculture that tended to produce innovators like entrepreneurs. What is more important, therefore, is to summarize the ways in which the actual entrepreneurial performance of sectarians accords with the two entrepreneurial models.

There seems little doubt that community and familial milieu of the Moscow Old Believers inculcated traits of frugality, orderly calculation, and curiosity, which were conducive to capitalist enterprises. Ethnic Russians played the major part in the development of the textile industry, a classic instance of small-scale, independent initiative, in which the entrepreneurial role was dominant and well defined. Only a small proportion of the Moscow region textile manufacturers were Old Believers; before 1850, however, most textile manufacturers in the Moscow region who were not Old Believers themselves came from similar artisan or peasant backgrounds and from families which appear to have followed similar life styles.[23] Independent generation of capital resources (often on a communal basis) later enabled these families to establish banks and to embark upon somewhat larger entrepreneurial ventures.[24] Continuing strong adherence to the religious peculiarities that had constituted the basis for their socialization in entrepreneurial qualities is indicated by the fact that many successful Old Believer industrialists provided religious training for their employees.[25]

On the other hand, sectarian entrepreneurs exhibited several characteristics that were ill-adapted to the organizational type of enterprise associated with major early Russian development as well as the revised entrepreneurial model. The high degree of familism apparently militated against strong individual initiative. Familism also probably contributed to relatively low geographical mobility, though the Old Believers also

---

[23] Blackwell (supra, n. 6), pp. 189ff.; Pierre Kovalevsky, "Le 'Rascol' et Sa Rôle dans le Développement Industriel de la Russie," *Archives de Sociologie des Réligions*, 2, no. 3 (1957):37-56; Roger Portal, "Industriels Moscovites: Le Section Cotonnier (1861-1914)," *Cahiers du Monde Russe et Soviétique*, 4 (1963):28.

[24] Portal (supra, n. 23); Blackwell (supra, n. 6), p. 212.

[25] Ibid.

encountered difficulties getting official travel and residence permits.[26] But the intense pride in their Moscow traditions appears to have limited the activities of this entrepreneurial component, especially in the crucial St. Petersburg and Odessa "melting pots" discussed below. Ethnic Russian entrepreneurial families also tended to reject professionalism. Few considered it necessary for their sons to obtain higher engineering education.[27] In this respect the Russian textile industrialists closely resembled contemporary native French textile-manufacturing families, which also found formal higher education superfluous.[28] In both cases, however, this insistence on the undifferentiated entrepreneurial role limited the extent to which early entrepreneurial families could play a major role in large, impersonal economic organizations. Hence one can at least hypothesize that major ethnic Russian elements were unsuited for transition from small-scale, individualized local enterprise to the expanding economy. Moreover, apart from their sectarian affiliation, by the late nineteenth-century these native Russians who faced no ethnic disabilities were also particularly susceptible to the attraction of official careers in the *chin* system. Some established Old Believer families did convert to official Orthodoxy to attain these privileges for their children. Several Russian authors do, indeed, consider the draining off of talent to bureaucratic and aristocratic activities to have been the prime limitation upon cumulative development of an ethnic Russian bourgeoisie.[29]

The significance of these observations concerning the ethnic Russian entrepreneurs or at least their sectarian members becomes evident as one examines contrasting Jewish patterns. An immense amount of work should be done on the sociological history of East European Jews. Arcadius Kahan's chapter in this volume, modest though his claims are, is truly pioneering in its scrutiny of the place of Jews in the final century of imperial Russian economic development. Much of the earlier historiography on the subject is diffuse and anecdotal, partly because (as a recent historian of East European Jews in Germany remarks) members of the community with more analytic interests have preferred to examine anything but their own group.[30] Several of the most penetrating analyses

[26] Portal, "Industriels" (supra, n. 23), p. 28.

[27] Ibid., p. 37.

[28] Jean Lambert-Dansette, *Quelques familles du patronat textile de Lille-Armentières (1789-1914): Essai sur les origines et l'evolution d'une bourgeoisie* (Thesis, University of Paris, Faculté de Droit) (Lille, 1954), pp. 522ff.

[29] Josef Kulisher, "La Grande industrie aux XVIIᵉ et XVIIIᵉ siècles: France, Allemagne, Russie," *Annales d'Histoire Economique et Sociale*, 3 (1931):17; P. A. Berlin, *Russkaia burzhuaziia v staroe i novoe vremia* (Moscow, 1922), p. 30; cf. the biographies in Chulkov (supra, n. 2).

[30] S. Adler-Rudel, *Ostjuden in Deutschland, 1880-1940* (Tübingen, 1959), p. 103: "those whose calling so frequently consisted of observing and describing human, political, and

have been conducted as explorations of the backgrounds of American Jews, with correspondingly little concern for temporal and geographic variations among Jews in the nineteenth-century Russian polity.[31] Nevertheless, enough material is readily available to permit tentative generalizations about the relation of distinctively Jewish socialization to the entrepreneurial models.

Until 1772 Jews were few and severely discriminated against in the Russian polity; but the million Jews incorporated during the Polish Partitions had two centuries of experience in commercial and artisan occupations in Poland, which prepared them for broader roles—despite continuing severe restrictions—in the Russian Empire. From the standpoint of the marginality interpretation, of course, the very severity of occupational restrictions tended to push Jews into roles that more-favored ethnic groups neglected. Geographic restrictions on travel and residence were less ambiguous in their effect, but the most enterprising element among the Jews succeeded in overcoming them. The characteristics of sober frugality, rational calculation, and desire for material progress salient in the original Weberian model were certainly well established. So was the strong achievement motivation arising from constant dissatisfaction with one's accomplishments. Most Jews remained poor laborers; but (as a recent student of economic relations in the Jewish Pale points out): "the Jewish journeyman by no means considered himself permanently a wage earner. As he saw it, were he compelled to suffer the insults of his master one day, the next he might himself become an employer, the master of his own shop. For such changes in status were fairly common practice."[32] To put the matter another way, the Jew was socialized to the entrepreneurial role because its holders constituted his salient reference group. His chances of joining the group might be low; they were not negligible. In this respect the Jew differed drastically (as will appear) from most of the comparably numerous Germans of the Russian Empire, and probably from the great majority of Russian sectarians who remained peasants, little acquainted with the entrepreneurial accomplishments of a small minority of their co-religionists in Moscow.

---

social occurrences nearly incidentally referred to the fate of their own group." Jakob Lestschinsky, editor of *Schriften für Wirtschaft und Statistik* (Berlin, 1928), remarked (p. 11) that all previous Jewish historiography had been descriptive with little concern for economic factors in the Jewish communities themselves; Salo Baron's recent lengthy treatments continue to rely for economic and social data primarily on Lestschinsky's work and the forty-year-old work by Weinryb (supra, n. 8).

[31] For example, some of the material in the chapter by Strodtbeck in McClelland et al. (supra, n. 18); Mark Zborowski, "The Children of the Covenant," in David C. McClelland, ed., *Studies in Motivation* (New York, 1955); and Natalie F. Joffe, "The Dynamics of Benefice among East European Jews," *Social Forces*, 28 (March 1949):239-47.

[32] Ezra Mendelsohn, *Class Struggle in the Pale* (Cambridge, 1970), p. 9.

In other respects, the modal Jewish personality resembled the revised rather than the original Weberian model. Relations with non-Jews necessarily remained superficial in most cases, but within that limitation the Jewish entrepreneur was obliged to be intensely concerned with interpersonal relations. The negotiating and selling skills that he (or his reference group) had acquired as agents for Polish landlords, as merchants, as tavern keepers, or as wagoners, could be applied to large-scale organizational activity such as railroad companies. There is some evidence that East European Jews lacked, at the start of the nineteenth century, the extraordinary oral linguistic facility that had characterized other Jewish communities such as the Sephardic.[33] On the other hand, near-universal male literacy (in Hebrew or Yiddish) was readily converted into general literate accomplishments; there is no doubt that the Jews became proficient in the languages of the Russian Empire as they moved into a broader range of activities. The high respect for "book learning" was also eventually converted into the professional expertise associated with effective direction of large economic organizations. It is true that Jewish communities at first strongly resisted secular educational opportunities, even when these were available, for fear of loss of Jewish ethno-religious character.[34] One reason Jews preferred German higher educational institutions to Russian was that the former did not require a secondary educational certificate instead of the traditional Jewish preparation in the yeshiva.[35] As the century drew to an end, however, Jewish enrollment in imperial secondary and higher educational institutions, particularly law and engineering, increased rapidly. This trend was particularly noticeable in areas of intense economic activity peripheral to the Pale, such as the great port cities of Riga and Odessa, to which Jews were eventually admitted with only minor restrictions. A trickle of Jews has always converted to Christianity in order to take advantage of opportunities in the major Russian imperial centers. Some outstanding entrepreneurs like Jan Bloch, developer of the Southwestern Railway, still found conversion to be acceptable (it did not keep Tsar Alexander III from referring to his railway as the "Jew road").[36] Certainly entry of Jews into the economic life of the Russian polity was far from complete by the end of the nineteenth century. It would be very hard to draw up a balance sheet of their importance, particularly since the role of converted Jews would have to

---

[33] Salo W. Baron, *A Social and Religious History of the Jews*, vol. 16 (New York, 1976), p. 439, note 53.

[34] Abraham J. Brawer, *Galizien wie es an Österreich kam: Eine historisch-statistische Studie über die inneren Verhältnisse des Landes im Jahre 1772.* (Leipzig, 1910), p. 104; Jewish attitudes in Courland and Livonia in the early nineteenth century were similar.

[35] Adler-Rudel (supra, n. 30), p. 12.

[36] Von Laue (supra, n. 15), p. 50.

be identified; but the results would probably be highly revealing. In a tentative way one can suggest that Jews had a dominant part in crucial export commodities like grain and timber; a strong but regionally restricted position in textiles and banking; and a modest but significant part in transportation and heavy industry.[37] It is even riskier to speculate about the position of Jews in professional roles peripheral to the entrepreneurial role, in organizations that were not founded or dominated by Jews. Certainly this position was still very weak in 1900; but Jews in the professions appear to have been increasing at least in the Pale and adjoining western and southwestern regions. In other words, the Jewish position, overall, was one of preparation for major participation in entrepreneurial direction, or in a broader context of activities, for what I have termed elsewhere "a succession of mobilized diasporas."

The third ethnic group to be considered, the Germans, was in a very different situation. On the one hand, Germans saw their privileges eroding rapidly toward the end of the nineteenth century. Superficially, this erosion was due to the pressure of ethnic Russian xenophobia; but many Germans perceived their loss as partly due to replacement by Jews and other minority groups. This perception—which I intend to treat at greater length elsewhere—gave rise to mixed feelings, by no means unequivocally anti-Semitic. Many German writers recognized that the extent of their privileges up to mid-nineteenth century had militated against that condition of marginality which pushed other ethnic groups (and foreigners) into entrepreneurial activity. Indeed, a Slavophile writer in 1862 termed the Baltic Germans "the Mamelukes of the Empire." Probably the writer was aware that the Turkic-Circassian Mamelukes had monopolized military, political, and top administrative posts in Egypt for three centuries, but he may not have been aware that during much of that time they ruled in symbiotic relation with a native stratum of merchants and tax farmers.[38] The peculiarity of the German position was that while they (primarily the Baltic and St. Petersburg minorities among them) did indeed occupy a very large proportion of imperial posts usually associated with ruling status, Germans also provided a very substantial share of the technical and lower administrative skills required to keep the Russian polity going. In terms of economic development, the nature of their contribution was complicated by the social stratification within the German ethnic group.

[37] For very incomplete statistics, see Lestschinsky (supra, n. 30); Weinryb (supra, n. 8); and A. I. Iuditskii, "Evreiskaia burzhauziia i evreiskie rabochie v tekstil'noi promyshlennosti pervoi polovine XIX v.," *Istoricheskii sbornik*, no. 4 (1935):107-33.

[38] Quoted in "Wir und die Anderen," *Baltische Monatsschrift*, 7 (1863):457; cf. Walter J. Fischel, "Über die Gruppe der Karimi-Kaufleute: Ein Beitrag zur Geschichte des Orienthandels Ägyptens unter den Mameluken," *Studia Arabica*, 1 (1937):78.

The great majority of Germans were peasants in the southern parts of the empire. Although they were exemplary farmers and highly important in small-scale local activities like milling, the peasants had little impact on larger areas of economic development. Low geographical mobility and caution if not suspicion concerning higher education appear (studies now being pursued under the direction of Sidney Heitman may throw more light on this subject) to have kept the peasant Germans from providing a significant flow of recruits even for German ethnic institutions in the empire. The considerable stratum of noble landowning families centered on the Baltic provinces but scattered to some extent in adjoining *gubernii*, occasionally exhibited a pragmatic willingness to initiate industrial enterprise. For example, a member of the distinguished Ungern-Sternberg house in Estonia started a textile factory in 1831 to supply cloth to the military.[39] While attracted by aristocratic professions like the military and diplomacy, few Baltic nobles even trained for careers peripheral to economic development in science, medicine, or pharmacy. Instead, these fields, where Germans provided a very significant fraction of the empire's professional manpower, were the special preserve of the peculiar Baltic German stratum known as the *Literati*. Very different from the Russian *intelligent* in political ideology, the conservative *Literati* families shared his antipathy to commercial dealings: "These good people smell frightfully of copper coins" a *Literati* woman scornfully wrote.[40]

Since Baltic shopkeepers frequently took the *Literati* as a reference group in higher education and upward status mobility, the effect of their depreciation of business was considerable. On the other hand, all the Baltic groups had a keen sense of the unusual career opportunities afforded by the vast Russian Empire. As one wrote in 1870, "we saw a broad field in which our sons and younger brothers had always been able to make a way and a career for themselves with slight effort." A recent Balt historian also stresses the "risk-taking propensity" required for setting out on careers in distant, alien environments.[41] Certainly, geographic mobility was nearly optimal, and (judging from intermarriage and conversion to Orthodoxy at all levels of Germans living among Russian ethnic populations) intergenerational family ties were not so strong as to constitute restricting factors. Despite superficial accommo-

[39] L. A. Loone, "Iz istorii promyshlennogo perevorota v Estonii," *Voprosy Istoriia*, no. 5 (1952):87.

[40] Reinhard Wittram, *Drei Generationen: Deutschland-Livland-Russland, 1830-1914* (Göttingen, 1949), p. 243. For a more extended analysis, see my chapter on "Mobilized Diaspora in Tsarist Russia: The Case of the Baltic Germans," in Jeremy Azrael, ed., *Soviet Nationality Policies and Practices* (New York, 1978), pp. 63-104.

[41] E. B., "Zur Lage," *Baltische Monatsschrift*, 19 (1870):8; Wittram (supra, n. 40), p. 254.

dation (especially while they were university students) to noble life styles, most professionals continued to stress the traditional German burger's virtues of orderliness, discipline, frugality, calculation, and orientation to the future—all components of the Weberian entrepreneurial model. Medicine, science (especially chemistry), and pharmacy often led to minor entrepreneurial ventures in related fields, but infrequently (apparently) to major undertakings. Excessive caution and the strong feeling that a man should stick to his *Fach* appear to have been inhibitors. In fact—as far as evidence thus far available goes—Germans in both strictly entrepreneurial roles and top managerial roles in economic organizations (other than certain government hierarchies such as the Ministry of Finance) appear to have been either of foreign origin or men who were unusually detached from their ethnic origins. I shall not attempt to analyze the role of Reich Germans, especially in St. Petersburg; although the Baltic Germans constituted a significant reference group for these foreigners, social relationships in the first generation were cool.[42] Those German immigrants who eventually did assimilate to the German ethnic group (most apparently returned to Central Europe; many assimilated as ethnic Russians) commonly sent their sons to the Baltic German Dorpat University or to similar institutions, where they adopted the professional but nonentrepreneurial values of the Baltic reference group.

As hinted in the preceding paragraph, among Germans born in the Russian Empire it was precisely those who were most detached from the German ethnic milieu who appear to have developed the strongest entrepreneurial spirit. On the surface this suggestion implies that German cultural background had a negative relation to entrepreneurial response. In fact, the situation seems to have been much more complex. As just noted, numerous features in that background were fully consonant with both the original Weberian model and its revised version; other elements of the dominant German socialization pattern, especially in the Baltic, negated their effect. Often this negative pattern persisted throughout the lifetime of an individual even though his career was spent at a great distance from the original Baltic reference group. It would be very difficult to demonstrate this proposition by anything resembling a representative sample, since in the nature of the case ethnic Germans detached from their group are hard to identify. Hence one is compelled to resort to anecdote.

The career of Sergei Witte appears to exemplify both entrepreneurial spirit and detachment from the group to extraordinary degrees.[43] Cul-

---

[42] Julius W. A. von Eckardt, *Aus der petersburger Gesellschaft*, 3rd ed. (Leipzig, 1881), p. 11.

[43] Von Laue (supra, n. 15), esp. pp. 35-49; *The Memoirs of Count Witte*, trans. Abraham Yarmolinsky (New York, 1921), pp. 75ff.

turally Witte's paternal ancestors were typical Baltic Germans; his father had attended German educational institutions, including (according to Witte's own assertion) the core Baltic institution, Dorpat University. In the face of this heritage, Witte's claim that the family was originally Dutch is hardly relevant, since many thoroughly acculturated Baltic German families had originated in non-German areas of Northwest Europe. Vastly more significant was the influence of his mother's noble Russian family; but the failures of both his maternal grandfather and his father in a mining enterprise related to their official duties in the Caucasus suggests that neither ancestral line was deeply imbued with entrepreneurial values. Witte was in fact a self-made man, supplementing his strong future orientation and intense devotion to work with scorn for polite society and "culture" and a preference for material and financial manipulation. It appears significant that he developed, or at least brought to fruition, these personality traits in the Odessa melting-pot milieu, where he was not only catholic in his ethnic associations but positively cultivated persons like Jewish businessmen.

It is equally suggestive to note how the Odessa environment (taken as the paradigm of urban melting pots in the Russian polity) served to accentuate Jewish personality traits conductive to large-scale entrepreneurial activity while suppressing traits negative from this standpoint. In this case, too, one is obliged to resort to anecdote at this stage of our knowledge. Fortunately, the recent biography of Alexander Helphand (Parvus) is rich in suggestive incident.[44] His family's move to Odessa from a rigidly segregated Jewish community in Belorussia brought the youthful Helphand into contact with Ukrainians and Russians as well as Jews of a more cosmopolitan culture. Historiography has understandably focused on the multiethnic revolutionary ferment of Odessa in the 1880s as preparation for Parvus's curious relation to the Bolsheviks. But Helphand's strikingly successful career in international commerce preceded his revolutionary exploits: "And when he set out on the road to becoming a rich man, he did so in the manner of the Odessa merchants: grain trade along the shores of the Black Sea was the foundation of his financial success."[45] It is also highly significant that Helphand's intense attachment to German culture (which in 1916 led him to acquire Second Reich citizenship) began in Odessa, whence he proceeded (in 1887) directly to Basel University. The "Odessa connection" appears to have exercised a peculiarly inverse effect on Witte, for whom German culture was a neglected heritage, and on Helphand, for whom it was "the gateway out of the east European spiritual ghetto." One may speculate that Witte, who

[44] Z.A.B. Zeman and W. B. Scharlau, *The Merchant of Revolution: The Life of Alexander Israel Helphand (Parvus), 1867-1924* (London, 1965).

[45] Ibid., p. 192.

did not speak German well,[46] instinctively rejected immersion in cosmopolitan elite high culture because it might have accentuated the personality traits that would have limited him to a mediocre career.

The real linguistic accomplishments of Baltic and St. Petersburg Germans made them valuable to the empire, not only in foreign diplomacy but in Asian proconsular activity. Witte's youth had been spent in the latter environment; ultimately he saw it reduce both sides of his family to genteel poverty, though their accomplishments in the Caucasus had been real. Just as often, however, complacency in cultural attainments, pride in a cosmopolitan linguistic veneer, were surrogates for achievement motivation in both Russian and German upper-class families. Such cultural emphasis was not even unambiguously valuable in interpersonal relations, for it tended to isolate the upper classes from middle-class foreign businessmen and technicians, energetic men rising from the lower classes, and despised but capable minorities like the Jews. Given his inherited status, Witte could afford to cultivate all of these elements in his shrewd, blunt manner, though he made numerous enemies among the old elites.

For mobile Jews, precisely the opposite tactic was (perhaps instinctively) most productive: cosmopolitan culture complemented their irrepressible achievement drive with credentials as intermediaries between the Russian polity and foreigners and between the old elites and the rising minorities. Decades before Helphand arrived in Odessa, Jewish communities in the region had seriously considered "standardizing" Yiddish as New High German in order to bring East European Jews into what they understandably regarded as the vanguard European culture.[47] It challenges the historical imagination merely to suggest the outburst of achievement in economic, cultural, and political spheres that a coalescence of Germandom and East European Jewry might have produced.

More prosaically, one should note that the actual contexts in which this coalescence, tragically abortive though it proved to be, appeared possible were provided by the *structures* of the Russian polity. In the nineteenth century Old World no other polity provided the dynamically cosmopolitan melting pots that Odessa, St. Petersburg, Riga, and even Warsaw constituted. More consciously structured educational institutions also fostered coalescence of achievement-motivated elements. Though the St. Petersburg Technological Institute, Odessa University, and the Richelieu Lycée in the latter city made a larger contribution to technology

---

[46] Von Laue (supra, n. 15), p. 38. Boris Ananich has pointed out to me that Witte did speak French, but it lacked, as did his Russian, St. Petersburg polish.

[47] Alexander Orbach, "The Russian Jewish Press of Odessa, 1860-71: Towards a Secularization of Jewish Culture in Tsarist Russia," Ph.D. dissertation, University of Wisconsin, 1975, pp. 8, 131.

than directly to entrepreneurial achievement, their activity supported economic development. Although the entrepreneurial response in the nineteenth-century Russian Empire largely depended on non-Russians, it can be argued that the Russian creation of a great polity was an indispensable precondition.

Much remains to be learned from the nineteenth-century Russian *imperial* experience, which until recently has been viewed predominantly as a facet of the evolution of the Russian *nation*. Yet that experience constitutes an integral part of the backgrounds of the Jewish, the Armenian, and to a lesser extent the German nations. As diasporas within the Russian Empire, members of all three ethnic groups occupied key roles, which influenced and continue to influence their national identities. Even more important, the experience of the Russian Empire, at a time when it was still supranational, and not merely multinational, provides critical perspectives on the potential for ethnic interaction within contemporary emerging polities. Not the least important of these perspectives is the way in which entrepreneurial talent, as limited in the Third World as it was in nineteenth-century Russia, can be maximized or dissipated by varying kinds of ethnic interaction.

VI

ARCADIUS KAHAN *Notes on Jewish Entrepreneurship in Tsarist Russia*

It is incumbent upon an economic historian dealing with a particular area of economic activity to put the activity and the participants of the economic process not only in a historical context but also within categories of a body of economic theory. Thus, by focusing upon the phenomenon of entrepreneurship of individuals who shared a common religious, cultural, or national heritage, in this case the Jewish one, it is still necessary to explain, or argue in which sense their activities can be considered entrepreneurial.

Economists and economic historians have variously described the entrepreneurial function emphasizing different aspects of those functions as risk taking, innovation, and so on. Entrepreneurial activity was described as one that grows out of the ability of certain individuals to deal with disequilibria in the market.[1] Such disequilibria are not necessarily limited to short-term discrepancies between two sets of prices, nor do they necessarily consist of unanticipated profit opportunities arising out of the difficulties in discounting the effects of market situations. Entrepreneurial activity arises often as a byproduct of technological change, out of changes in factor prices, and so forth, and concerns the reallocation of resources, the reorganization of production or distribution, based upon the entrepreneur's perception of change and foresight about its direction. It is therefore convenient to focus upon the element of economic change as both the cause and the effect of entrepreneurial activity. Economic change can often be quantified, and the effects attributed to changes of particular factors. Therefore, it is possible to study entrepreneurship within the context of economic change using some of the tools provided by economic growth theory. The Jews constituted within each of the political

[1] See Theodore W. Schultz, "The Value of the Ability to Deal with Disequilibria," *Journal of Economic Literature*, 13, no. 3 (1975).

(104)

units a minority of the population and were, therefore, acting according to behavioral norms or patterns characteristic of a minority. Jewish entrepreneurship might have had different effects upon the Jewish community—the "economy of the Jews"—than upon the community at large.[2] The difference owes to the minority position of the Jews and to their discriminations. The vast majority of the Jewish population and also the chief areas of their entrepreneurial activities were located in the so-called Pale of Settlement, a territory outside of which Jews could not settle in Russia. Thus, only a detailed knowledge of the economy of this region provides the background for an evaluation of the Jewish entrepreneurial activities, and for the economic structure of the Jewish community. But while largely confined to the Pale of Settlement, Jewish entrepreneurs attempted to break out of the existing discriminatory position of their settlement with increasing strength. Thus, during the latter part of the period entrepreneurial activities undertaken by individual Jews outside the Jewish Pale of Settlement become more frequent and their effect upon the Jewish community weaker.

A special problem for the study of entrepreneurial activity by Jewish businessmen is the paucity of data that could throw sufficient light on the family and social backgrounds, education, source of capital, and scope of activities of a large number of the entrepreneurs to permit the construction of representative samples for the different categories of Jewish entrepreneurs.[3] Without such data a student of Jewish entrepreneurship runs into the danger of generalizing from a very small and often unrepresentative sample and using anecdotes as a substitute for evidence. The availability of biographical material would certainly enhance our ability to categorize Jewish entrepreneurs in terms of observed patterns of entrepreneurial activity whose origins may be either in commerce or banking, in technical expertise pertaining to industry, or in the accumulation of experience and capital leading from craft to larger-scale industrial enterprise. Such data could presumably explain the entrepreneurs' ability to adapt foreign models for their activity and help us to understand their complex motives as well as their attitudes to the different economic and cultural environments within which they operated. Certainly, the absence of detailed data on most of the entrepreneurs severely limits the analysis of their role and activity.

[2] On the conceptual and analytical problems of such treatment see Arcadius Kahan, "A Note on Methods of Research on the Economic History of the Jews," in *For Max Weinreich on his Seventieth Birthday: Studies in Jewish Language, Literature and Society* (The Hague, 1964); and Salo Baron, Arcadius Kahan, et al., *Economic History of the Jews* (New York, 1976).

[3] Published sources and bio-bibliographical dictionaries were biased in their emphasis on data for Jewish scholars rather than businessmen.

Since a discussion of the historical background for Jewish entrepreneurship in Russia is outside the scope of this essay, it is perhaps necessary to point out a few of the changes in the legal and social status of the Jews that had a direct bearing upon the activities of actual or potential entrepreneurs. While the Pale of Settlement for Jews in Russia was to a large extent a de jure recognition of the de facto settlement that the Russian Empire inherited as a result of the partitions of Poland, the only exception for Jewish settlement on the "Russian" territories was made with respect to the provinces adjacent to the Black Sea. Those provinces, an object of Russian colonization policies of the eighteenth and nineteenth centuries, were opened for Jewish agricultural and urban settlement, while the rest of the empire remained closed for the resettlement of Jews.[4] However, until 1850 not all provinces within the Pale of Settlement were treated alike, since until that year the territory of Congress Poland had its own tariff and until about 1860 the legal status of the Jews in the Polish provinces was based upon the legislation of Congress Poland, while in the Lithuanian, Belorussian and Ukrainian provinces the imperial legislation prevailed. Given the limited autonomy of the Polish provinces and their attempts to industrialize during the early decades of the nineteenth century, Jewish businessmen were treated perhaps more favorably than in the rest of the Pale, although this treatment was not expressing a recognition of their rights but a more lenient extension of individual privileges granted by the authorities. Within the other provinces of the Pale, the Jewish entrepreneurs suffered the most from disabilities imposed upon the whole Jewish population until about the beginning of the reign of Alexander II (1855). The general liberalization of government policies during the late 1850s and the 1860s had also affected the Jewish entrepreneurial group, providing the merchants of the first guild with permission to conduct their business outside the Pale, at least for part of the year, or for Jews with higher secular education, or especially "useful" skills to practice within or outside the Pale. While there existed a certain dichotomy between the rights granted and the enforcement of such rights, which was left to the local administration, the general liberalization trend made possible an increase in the participation of Jews in industrial entrepreneurship and in the acquisition of higher-quality skills. However, given the enthusiastic response to the opening up of new economic and educational opportunities, during the 1880s the trend of governmental policies toward the Jews was reversed and caused a number of economic dislocations in the employment structure of the Jewish community.

The story is well known and should not be repeated here. It is enough

---

[4] At one point the Russian government considered opening up Siberia for Jewish colonization, but quickly changed its mind.

to say that while during the previous period new economic opportunities had a favorable economic effect and even contributed to an impressive rate of increase among the Jewish population, the growth of the market in the Pale of Settlement was insufficient to provide employment and incomes for the growing Jewish population. The restrictions on rural settlement and rural trade imposed by the government legislation of the 1880s further aggravated the high intensity of competition in the trade sector and hastened the shift from trade into crafts and industrial employment for the Jewish population within the Pale of Settlement. It also intensified the process of spatial migration within the Pale and the urbanization process. Last but not least, it provided additional momentum to the migration abroad, the latter presumably depriving Russian Jewry of a mobile, enterprising element within the population. Thus, both the changes in governmental policies toward the Jews during its more "liberal" and more restrictive periods contributed to processes of employment shifts, changes in regional and demographic distribution of the population, income differentiation, and the formation of a Jewish bourgeoisie and a Jewish industrial proletariat. It is important to keep this background in mind while discussing the problems of Jewish entrepreneurship.

Given the space limitations of this chapter, only the following aspects of the problem and experience of Jewish entrepreneurship in Russia will be considered:

1. The personal and social background of the entrepreneurs and their attitudes toward the different milieu.
2. The origin of capital of the Jewish entrepreneurs.
3. The role of Jewish entrepreneurs in the transition from nobility to capitalist enterprises.
4. The entrepreneurs in service of governmental policies.
5. The entrepreneur's role in fostering vertical integration:
   a. within the economy at large;
   b. within the "Jewish economy."
6. The entrepreneurs in the corporate sector and the fostering of competition.

The first two topics will address the problems of recruitment into entrepreneurial activity and the means to carry on such activities, while the other topics will serve to categorize the functions performed by the Jewish entrepreneurs.

The Origin of Capital of the Jewish Entrepreneurs

One of the "classical" theses about the origin of capital that was at the disposal of Jewish entrepreneurs follows closely the analogy with non-

Jewish entrepreneurs in economically backward countries, or at the early stages of industrial entrepreneurship, preceding the development of a banking system. Government contracts and tax farming played an important role in this process of capital accumulation. Government or army supply contractors as well as alcohol tax farmers invested in textile-mills, tanneries, or distilleries to assure themselves a portion of their supplies or to derive an additional profit. Beginning with the end of the eighteenth century, Jewish army contractors in Poland and, during the first half of the nineteenth century, Jewish alcohol tax farmers in Russia followed this practice.[5] However, it would be mistaken to generalize from a very small population. A much more plausible case for the origins of capital is presented, at best, for the first half of the nineteenth century, by the profits derived from foreign trade. The participation of Jewish merchants in the foreign trade, especially along the western borders, was significant and exhibited a tendency to grow. However, there were limitations to this growth imposed by the slowly growing demand of Russia's western neighbors. Therefore, reinvestment in foreign trade had its constraints. At the same time it could be observed that a number of merchants engaged in foreign trade were investing in textile factories and tanneries, and included some of their output in the commodities subsequently exported.[6] If we should assume that only a half of the profits in foreign trade (assumed as 10 percent of the trade turnover) was invested in industry, this would clearly exceed any estimate of growth of capital in Jewish industrial enterprises.[7] Thus, both the direct evidence of capital transfers from foreign trade to industrial entrepreneurship as well as the volume of profits in foreign trade, in addition to the locational proximity of capital accumulation in foreign trade and establishment of industrial enterprises during the first half of the nineteenth century make foreign trade activity a plausible source for capital used by Jewish entrepreneurs.

[5] Starting with the famous Shmul Zbytkover in Poland, the forefather of the Bergson family and the famous Ginzburg in Russia, the evidence for the type of origin of capital for industrial entrepreneurship was at hand.

[6] The evidence is available from a comparison of the lists of merchants whose foreign trade turnover exceeded 50,000 rubles. Such lists were published yearly by the Ministry of Finance under the title *Vid na vneshneiu torgovliu za . . . god.* The coincidence of names of Jewish merchants, their location with lists of Jewish industrialists in Volynia and Grodno gubernias suggest the plausibility of the above contention.

[7] The estimated 5 percent of the turnover in foreign trade by Jewish merchants gives us the yearly average over five-year periods in silver rubles: 1830-34, 430,000 rubles; 1835-39, 400,000 rubles; 1840-44, 430,000 rubles; 1845-49, 502,000 rubles; 1850-54, 650,000 rubles; and 1855-59, 1,150,000 rubles. These estimates were derived from the yearly reports on foreign trade by separating the names of Jewish merchants. Although the data were not deflated by the price index, and the growth during the last five-year period might be less in terms of the purchasing power of money, there is no doubt that these sums exceed the volume of possible investments in industry.

Given the socioeconomic structure of the Jewish population, internal trade appears to be the most widespread, if perhaps not the most abundant, source of capital for entrepreneurial activities. If one would take into account the fact that entrepreneurial activity was spread out over a large territory, originally perhaps with a low density and often outside of existing nuclei of a future capital market, the thesis of internal trade as the major source is appealing. Perhaps also the pattern of entrance into industrial entrepreneurship from the commercial or financial side of industrial activity points to the importance of domestic trade as a source of capital. The only major problem is that such reasoning has to be based upon an assumption or upon a testable hypothesis that the rate of return to the capital in industry was higher than in trade. The data on about 350 industrial establishments owned by Jews in the textile centers of Bialystok and Łódź for the period of 1861-1900 seem to lend support to this hypothesis, at least as far as the textile industry in those locations was concerned. The data on the growth of output and of capital in a large portion of those textile enterprises over time imply a rate of return that exceeded the profit rate in trade achieved by Jewish merchants in a number of gubernias as reported in the works by Jan Bloch and Subbotin for the 1880s. If we should also assume that intense competition in trade tended subsequently to lower the profit margins, it would follow that during the later period the rate of return to capital in industry exceeded the one in trade and made a transfer of capital not only plausible but also economically advantageous where such opportunities existed.

Large-scale industrial entrepreneurship, however, required credits of substantial size, not only for the initial capital outlays, but also for the purchase of raw material, for wages, storage, transportation, and credit to customers, outlays that are classified as operating capital. Such credits, both long and short term, could be provided only by banking institutions. During the first half of the nineteenth century industrial entrepreneurs would typically obtain bank financing by taking in the private bankers as partners in their enterprises. Since most of the private banks owned by Jews were located originally in trade centers rather than in industrial areas, and the banks were apparently engaged in lending to landowners and to the government, and so on, that is, extending loans to low risk customers, the instances of financing of industrial entrepreneurs were not numerous. By mid-century the situation began to change in two directions. On the one hand, Jewish bankers in some financial centers became more amenable to the idea of extending at least short-term credit to industrial entrepreneurs, and on the other hand, industrialists began to support the idea of establishment of commercial banks in the industrial centers to serve the growing industries. The new banks, established in the 1870s with active participation of Jewish businessmen, found their task facilitated by the growing vertical integration of Jewish enterprises, and thus served both the producers and distributors of the manufactured goods. In turn, the balances of the merchants and industrialists enabled the new banks to increase greatly the scope of their lending operations without having to expand their capital accordingly.

To the extent that there was a scarcity of capital in the "Jewish economy," the Jewish banks made a special effort to attract savings from non-Jews and to borrow from Jewish banks abroad. In both endeavors, they appeared to be quite successful. As the record of the Jewish participation in private banking in Russia, to be discussed later, indicates, the banks were capable of paying high interest and dividends and their connections with the Jewish banks in Germany and later in France, resulted in capital imports and transfers to Russia.[8]

Our discussion on the origin of capital of the Jewish industrial entrepreneurs would be incomplete without mentioning the gradual, incremental self-financing by industrialists themselves. The plowing back of profits, typical of small-scale enterprises in general, took place on a massive scale among Jewish entrepreneurs. In a large number of cases, especially among the small-scale industrialists, the available data permit us to follow this process. Given the relative scarcity of capital and the limitations upon investment opportunities, a high savings ratio in the form of plowing back profits appeared to have been a rational economic decision followed by many entrepreneurs.

Recruitment into Entrepreneurial Activity

In the absence of biographical data for a representative sample of Jewish entrepreneurs, it is more prudent to discuss certain traits and characteristics of the entrepreneurs for which data are available than to pretend that a collective portrait of entrepreneurs can be presented.

If we would agree with the prevailing view of entrepreneurship as an innovative activity, then perhaps we would also have to assume that the self-recruitment into this group was heavily biased toward individuals who possessed character traits or behavior patterns harmonious with the "innovative personality." This is not to say that such individuals had a lower than average risk aversion, but perhaps more accurately that they perceived regularity in phenomena which appeared to the majority as

---

[8] The participation of Jewish private banks in Prussia in lending operations on the territory of the Polish provinces annexed by Russia goes back to the 1790s. The establishment of Jewish banks in the Polish provinces was also greatly influenced by the immigration of Jewish bankers or their agents from Prussia. Needless to say, kinship relations between Jewish bankers in Warsaw and those in Berlin and Frankfurt, which were mentioned before, facilitated transfers of loans across national boundaries.

predominantly random. They perceived real opportunities where others could see primarily uncertainty. However, it would be exaggerated to consider entrepreneurs as deviants from prevailing social norms or as conscious rebels against the social order. While emerging at times and places of disequilibria, acting as agents of change, the entrepreneurs' historical role was of restoration of equilibrium, often related to a considerable advancement of their own economic and social status. Within the Jewish milieu, entrepreneurs and entrepreneurship were regarded not as undermining the established order but as forerunners of adjustment processes which, based upon the historical experience, were considered inevitable and processes which had to be internalized, as had so often happened in the past. Entrepreneurs were not judged within the Jewish community on the basis of their economic activity but as individuals in relation to the net benefits that their activities provided for the Jewish community at large. Thus, there was no reason to assume a prima facie conflict between the Jewish community and the Jewish entrepreneurs.

There was hardly an area of entrepreneurial activity from which Jewish entrepreneurs were successfully excluded. Apart from the manufacturing industries in the Pale of Settlement, one could have encountered them at the oil wells of Baku, in the gold mines of Siberia, on the fisheries of the Volga or Amur, in the shipping lines on the Dnepr, in the forests of Briansk, on railroad construction sites anywhere in European or Asiatic Russia, on cotton plantations in Central Asia, and so forth. Their mass was concentrated in the Pale, with a much lower density outside. Thus, the ones in the Pale were the most typical, and they differed from the ones operating outside of the Pale by degree only, not in kind. They came mostly from the so-called middle strata, from a merchant rather than craftsman background, and possessed above average education. The ones who came from a poorer background must have possessed even more talent, discipline, drive, and perseverance to overcome some initial disabilities. The acquisitive instincts of some made them proverbial. Some would seek publicity, some anonymity. Only a minority, ones who rose from the ranks of craftsmen mostly, gained a reputation within the Jewish milieu as ruthless exploiters. The acquisition of status within the Jewish community followed with a substantial time lag the rise in wealth. The traditional leadership within the community was not eager to share power and influence with the newcomers, the plebeian masses had a traditional distrust of the rich.

Some historians have assumed that eighteenth- and nineteenth-century Jews involved in entrepreneurial activity or intensive business contacts with Gentiles created a dilemma for themselves involving a choice between assimilation and traditional Jewish culture. The relatively high percentage of religious conversions and strong assimilationist tendencies among German Jews or Warsaw Jews who were involved in high finance colored the views of such historians. Broadening of the informational base about Jewish entrepreneurs sheds considerable doubt upon this traditional view. For the majority of first-generation Jewish entrepreneurs such a dilemma did not seem to exist. It is true that some of them operated in two distinct worlds, one of intensive business contact with the outside and the other of the organized Jewish communities. But very few of them considered those two worlds mutually exclusive, for the following reasons. First, the typical large urban Jewish community with its concerns for education, training, welfare, and religious needs was a modern and not medieval institution. Second, the religious and cultural values of their heritage were not considered trifles to be exchanged for an approving nod of the Gentile world, but a rich spiritual heritage. Third, the experience of the 1880s taught Jewish entrepreneurs that the acquisition of a Russian cultural veneer would be insufficient to protect them against persecutions and discrimination and that language assimilation alone would not earn them the status in Russian society to which they felt entitled by the criteria of wealth and cultural sophistication. Thus, they opted for a combination of the indigenous culture with their adaptation of elements of European culture. The disapproval of the larger environment was discounted by the satisfaction derived from philanthropic or cultural activity within the Jewish milieu, and the disapproval of the ultraconservative elements within the Jewish community was countered by their activity in modernizing certain features of Jewish life. Therefore, Jewish entrepreneurs appeared occasionally impervious to slurs and slights suffered from Russian bureaucrats, accepted as inevitable some insults from their competitors, but cherished an inner pride in their own accomplishments. Above all, it was a group of rational men, knowledgeable of the realities of the world, of the marketplace, and of their own worth and calling.

Certain behavioral traits that also prevailed in the traditional society from which these men hailed were discernible in their business and personal relations. The reliance upon kinship ties also in their business, the arrangement of the proper homages that would maximize their business opportunities, were a part of the behavior of business-oriented groups in many cultures, and we find it also among the Jewish entrepreneurs.[9] The sense of noblesse oblige among owners of inherited wealth toward the Jewish community did not weaken with social advancement.[10] How-

[9] The family and kinship ties within the Warsaw Jewish business elite in the nineteenth century are documented and would make a fascinating study. The same is true of their connection with German-Jewish banking families.

[10] Examples of subscriptions by second-generation christianized grandchildren to Jewish philanthropies started by their grandparents were not unusual.

ever, the generational change produced some dichotomies between the first generation of Jewish entrepreneurs and their children. Some of their children remained in the businesses and followed successful business careers, some opted for the professions, some the arts, and some became leading personalities in the revolutionary movements,[11] but most of them moved away from the Jewish milieu.

The Role of Jewish Entrepreneurs in the Transition from Serf to Free Labor in Industry

That Russian industrial production was based largely on serf labor in the eighteenth and first half of the nineteenth century is well-known to students of economic history. Not only in metallurgy but also in textiles and food-processing industries a large proportion of the employed labor force consisted of serfs. Most of the industrial enterprises used the raw materials produced on the estates and the available labor, with a minimum of capital expenditures. Even enterprises established by nonnoblemen tried to receive from the state an allotment of serf-labor resources at a relatively low price.

It is therefore of considerable interest to find already during the first decades of the nineteenth century in a number of regions Jewish entrepreneurs who acted originally as administrators of industrial establishments of the gentry or leased such establishments for various periods of time. It may not be an exaggeration to state that among the first schools of industrial management for Jewish entrepreneurs were the gentry-owned industrial establishments. It is in such regions as Volyn, Grodno, and Podol'e that we find a heavy concentration of Jewish entrepreneurs engaged in industrial activities in the woolen industry. The data for 1828-32 show that among nonnobility industrial enterprises in Volyn 93.3 percent belonged to Jewish entrepreneurs and in Podol'e 32 percent. Most of the enterprises belonged to Jewish merchants of the first guild, while, among the burgher-entrepreneurs the participation was relatively smaller, 75 percent for Volyn and 43.8 percent for Podol'e.[12]

As lessees of the landlords' establishments, the Jewish entrepreneurs excelled the often absentee owners by heavier concentration on the financial aspects of the enterprises, by their ability not to rely exclusively upon the demand of the state for military wool cloth, and by seeking new markets either in the Ukraine or abroad (even in the Chinese trade). Jewish entrepreneurs could also utilize some of the skills already acquired

[11] The Wissotsky family of tea merchants and entrepreneurs provided the brothers Gots; other families supplied their share of revolutionaries.

[12] See Alexander P. Ogloblin, *Ocherki istorii ukrainskoi fabriki, predkapitaisticheskaia fabrika* (Kiev, 1925), pp. 47-49.

by Jewish weavers in the Grodno region by the end of the eighteenth century and through the training factory established in Kremenchug in 1809. Thus, we find definite migration patterns for Jewish skilled workers from Grodno and Kremenchug to the Jewish-leased or Jewish-owned woolen enterprises beginning in the first decades of the nineteenth century. However, the main differences between the landlord-owned and the Jewish-owned, or for that matter also Ukrainian-owned, enterprises was the greater flexibility of locations of such enterprises,[13] the reliance on a free labor force, and use of technological improvements which, while using more capital, economized on the costs of labor and decreased the costs of production of woolen cloth, thus making it more competitive in the market, capable of competing with the cloth from serf-based landlord factories.[14]

The competition between the two types of woolen industry, the serf-based enterprises and the one based upon free labor, took place at two levels: on the one hand, by competition within the same region; on the other hand, in the form of interregional competition. In both types of competition Jewish entrepreneurs were pitted against the serf-based enterprises. Not only were the Jewish woolen mills of Volyn and Podol'e capable of underselling the serf-based enterprises within the regional or even local markets, but the Jewish merchants and textile industrialists of the Bialystok region (of Grodno *gubernia*) were successfully competing in the Ukrainian market with the serf-based enterprises located in close proximity to those markets. As a result of this competition, in the late 1850s even before the emancipation of the serfs, there were no serf-based woolen establishments left in operation.

A similar pattern of Jewish entrepreneurship, begun in the first half of the nineteenth century, became discernible in the sugar industry. The Russian sugar industry, based upon the domestic production of sugar beets, started in the early years of the nineteenth century and centered in the estates of the large landowners. The provinces of Poland and of the Ukraine witnessed the early expansion of this industry, with the share of the Ukraine rising secularly. As in the case of woolen cloth, the initial entrance of Jewish entrepreneurs in the sugar industry took place in the form of extending loans to nobility owners of sugar mills, or by leases and partnerships with nobility owners. This was the "apprenticeship" period for Jewish entrepreneurs to learn the intricacies of the particular

[13] They could be established not necessarily in the rural areas on estates, but near commercial centers.

[14] As an example of competitiveness in Jewish-produced woolen cloth, already in 1817 three partnerships of Jewish suppliers received government contracts for the output of their enterprises for the sum of 1,280,750 rubles. See A. Yuditski, *Yiddishe burzhuazi un yiddisher proletariat*, in Ershter Helft 19 Jh. (Kiev, 1930), p. 23.

industry. The establishment of their own sugar mills followed and succeeded by their paying particular attention to the technical side of the enterprises, to the use of most modern equipment and technology as well as to the expanded supply of the raw material base, and by forward contracts with both estates and peasants. The system of forward contracts permitted both the improvement of the quality of the raw materials as well as the quality of the differentiated products.

While some of the Jewish entrepreneurs possessed usable experience in alcohol-distilleries, many entered the field from trade or finance and therefore turned to innovations in the area of distribution rather than production. This type of activity coincided with the expansion phase of the sugar industry and the search for markets and marketing techniques was timely. The Jewish sugar entrepreneurs, contrary to the customs prevailing among the nobility producers, who would sell the output either at the mills, or at the nearby railroad stations, introduced on a large scale a system of forward sugar contracts, negotiated at the exchange in Kiev, and the larger producers began to develop separate sales networks, based upon established warehouses located in the major urban and mercantile centers of Russia, and employing itinerant salesmen working on a commission basis for the particular major sugar companies.[15]

Not only did free labor replace serf labor in the sugar industry of the Ukraine, but the various forms of corvée-type labor that existed during the first decades after the serf emancipation quickly disappeared following the example of the Jewish entrepreneurs in sugar production. Both technological improvements and higher skill requirements necessitated a free, mobile labor force that could adapt itself to the demands of the industry.

The relative success of Jewish entrepreneurship in the sugar industry could be illustrated by the data which are available for the Ukraine on the eve of World War I. About one third of the sugar mills belonged to Jewish owners and produced about 52 percent of the refined sugar. In the corporate sector of the industry, Jews constituted 42.7 percent of the board members and 36.5 percent of the board chairmen.[16]

The employment opportunities for Jews created by Jewish entrepreneurs in the sugar industry were substantial, although exact figures are not available. Given the existing severe limitations upon Jewish settlements in the rural areas, especially after the legislation of 1882, and the availability of cheap rural labor for most of the menial occupations in sugar production, one would not expect a high participation rate of

---

[15] This system was later copied by a number of other industry branches, such as the oil industry, the agricultural-implement and the sewing-machine industries. It was first developed for the sugar industry by the firm of I. Brodskii and Sons.

[16] H. Landau, "Der Onteil fun Yidn in der Russisch-Ukrainisher Tsuker-Industrie" in *Shriftn for Economik un Statistik* (Berlin, 1929), vol. 1, pp. 103-4.

Jewish workers in sugar mills. The only exceptions were a few cases in which Jewish entrepreneurs acquired land earlier in the century and then settled Jewish families on it to provide workers for the sugar mill.[17] Jews were more likely to be employed in jobs requiring higher technical skills and in the offices of the mill administration.[18]

There were a number of industries in which the distinction between serf and free labor was less significant than the existence of a dual economy. Alongside many small craftlike enterprises, operating with primitive techniques, there existed highly specialized large-scale enterprises. This type of situation existed in such areas as flour milling, leather tanning, tobacco, and in fisheries and wood-processing.

The industries relied upon the raw-material supply of the primary sector, a supply poorly organized and dependent upon a fluctuating demand in markets about which the majority of producers had a very poor notion. The intermediaries in the trade did not expand their networks, and their role remained quite passive, especially in the cases in which they established local monopolies. The supply of capital, even when available to the few large enterprises, did not trickle down to the smaller producers. Needless to say, the Jews as a mercantile element serving as intermediaries between the villages and the cities had first-hand knowledge of the intricacies of those processing industries, starting with the supply of raw materials and ending with the marketing of those goods. It was, however, the change in economic conditions, the new technological possibilities, the growth of a transportation network, and increased availability of capital that made it possible for them to utilize the new opportunities to embark upon entrepreneurial activity.

In order to achieve success, the entrepreneurs had to overcome a number of obstacles. The first was in the area of raw-material supply. For goods that were produced in small quantities and had to be collected over an extensive territory, it was not easy to rely upon the existing network of trading peasants, often labeled as kulaks, who possessed a monopoly in the different localities and paid prices to the producers that did not always reflect the market conditions or serve as sufficient incentives to increase production.

The Jewish entrepreneurs, operating with a longer time horizon, had to break the local monopolies and through their agents entered into

---

[17] The reference is to the settlement of Morgunovka, a sugar-mill village acquired in 1848 by the Jewish owner of the sugar mill and used for the settlement of Jewish families who were employed by and for the sugar mill.

[18] Shortly before World War I, in the sugar mills of the Ukraine 79 out of 283 chemists were Jewish, 62 out of 240 overseers of beet plantations, 71 out of 302 bookkeepers, 68 out of 423 deputy directors, and 53 out of 341 mill directors; Landau, ibid.

competition with the local kulaks. As a rule the primary producers benefited from this new competition between the old and new intermediaries and often responded with an increase of their marketed output. Alongside of the organization of raw-materials supply, the use of the byproducts in the processing of the raw materials often became an important concern of the entrepreneurs. The case of the Azov Sea and Volga fisheries provides a good example of this type of activity of the Jewish entrepreneurs.[19] Until Jewish entrepreneurs entered the fisheries industry, only the high-priced fish varieties were processed, while a large part of the fish catch would simply be thrown out or used for fish oil. It was their use of the less expensive varieties of fish that increased the value of the catch very substantially. The use of the raw materials for the production of new goods, such as modern ties for the railroads, broadening of the assortment of uses made of raw materials, finding alternative uses, and the decrease of the waste of raw materials created new sources of incomes and profits. The standardization of the product and its preparation to suit the taste of the clients was another area of entrepreneurship: the instances of hundreds of skilled Jewish fish processors and packers (*uborschiki*) employed in Astrakham to suit the tastes of the western Russian and foreign consumers, the employment of thousands of Jewish overseers (brackers) skilled in the production of ties for the railroads and construction materials for the taste of German and British importers, were examples of the significance attributed to product improvements. Last, but not least, the opening up of West European markets for frozen fish from the Amur River in the Far East of Siberia illustrates the ability of entrepreneurs to utilize the latest developments in refrigeration technology, to increase production, and to broaden the market for their products.

The Entrepreneur in Service of Governmental Policies

The subordination of economic interests to the interests of the state was a tradition of old standing in Russia, and the use of various social groups for the achievement of government objectives continues there to this day. Whether the state tried various combinations of incentives, persuasion, and force depended to a large extent upon the degree to which the interests of the state were congruent with the interest of a particular group and upon the urgency behind particular policies or services demanded by the state.

The important role of the contractor serving the military or the central or local government is well known in the historical literature and does

[19] For the achievements of Jewish entrepreneurs in the Russian fisheries see, I.M. Bikerman, "Rol' evreev v rybnom dele," in *Ocherki po voprosam ekonomicheskoi deiatelnosti evreev v Rossii* (St. Petersburg, 1913). vyp. 1, pp. 127-230.

not require special elaboration. The Jewish contractors were not given priority in any kinds of contracts, but had to compete in terms of either price or quality. If the various government institutions would have followed the practice of the marketplace, their decisions, even including a taste for discrimination, would have followed a middle course in awarding the contracts; but as quasi-monopolists, in fact, institutional decision-makers most probably engaged in discrimination of a broad spectrum. This forced the entrepreneurs among the Jewish contractors to devise means to reduce their costs by comparison with non-Jewish competitors. One way was to organize a network of subcontractors, and another was to speed up their operations, which tended to diminish the cost of capital.

The real test of contracting ability was not at the level of commodity-supply contracts to the military, even though contractors were sometimes forced to organize their own manufacturing facilities of goods for which no reliable supply could be obtained, but at the level of large construction projects involving railroad and port facilities. Such projects involved not only hiring vast labor forces and procuring new types of producer goods, but also very substantial capital outlays and organization of credit flows.

The first experience for Jewish entrepreneurs in this new kind of contracting was the construction of the Warsaw-Vienna railroad[20] and involved a consortium of Jewish contractors and financiers of Warsaw. Jewish contractors gained additional experience in the construction of the Moscow-Smolensk and Moscow-Brest Litovsk railroads. This accumulated experience was utilized and epitomized in the entrepreneurial activity of Samuel Poliakov, who built the Kozlov-Voronezh-Rostov line, the Kursk-Kharkov-Azov line, the Oriol-Griazi, the Bender-Galatz lines, and participated in the construction of others. The "secret" of Poliakov's success was his ability to obtain credits from Russian and foreign banks, to organize the system of subcontracting and the speed, if not necessarily the quality, of construction and exploitation.[21] In a situation of scarce capital and relatively low wages, this was probably an optimal strategy for an entrepreneur.

The participation of Jewish entrepreneurs in large-scale construction projects had a number of effects both upon the employment of Jews in the Pale, from among whom the subcontractors were drawn, creating a

[20] The first two railroads in Russia, the St. Petersburg-Tsarshoselsk Railroad and the Nikolaev Railroad connecting Moscow with St. Petersburg, were built directly by the government, supported by ad hoc and chaotic arrangements with contractors. The construction of the 609 verst of the Nikolaev Railroad lasted for almost nine years (1842-51).

[21] Poliakovs Kursk-Kharkov-Azov line of 763 verst was built within twenty-two months, which enabled him to receive the government subsidy paid at the completion of the construction period, to begin exploitation which provided revenues, and to make all necessary adjustments and repairs out of a revenue-paying enterprise.

kind of backward linkage, and for the Russian economy, for which the participation of foreign capital, not only in the sale of railroad bonds but also in lending operations for construction, was important.

The Entrepreneurs as Promoters of Integration and Efficiency

During the early stages of industrial development, the chief function of the industrial entrepreneur, in the Schumpeterian sense, was the creation of new productive capacity by bringing about a combination of production factors in order to increase output of old and new industrial goods. Simultaneously, the entrepreneurs operating in the commodity and financial markets facilitated the growth of the market for goods and factors of production.

At a more advanced stage of industrial development, a new field of entrepreneurial activity opened up, namely, the integration of existing industrial and productive capacities with the existing social overhead and system of distribution, and to achieve out of these combinations higher levels of efficiency. To use the analogy with a railroad system would be to create out of various existing unplanned railroad lines an efficient, unified network.

This field of entrepreneurial activity opened up in Russia between 1908 and 1917.[22] As in other countries of Europe, this process of integration of industrial firms, elements of overhead capital, and business services in Russia was taking place with the assistance of the financial institutions, the banks. The case of Jewish entrepreneurship in the area of water transportation provides an interesting example of this new field of entrepreneurial activity.

The mass participation of Jewish entrepreneurs and Jewish employees in the fields of overland and water transportation on the territory of the Pale of Settlement was of long standing and could be explained by their participation in the commodity trade. Thus, already by the middle of the nineteenth century one could find well-organized enterprises in river transportation on the Vistula, Neman, and Dnepr, the most important waterways on the territory of the Pale.[23] The interests of the Jewish entrepreneurs were not limited to the area of the Pale with its meagre resources and expansion possibilities. By 1876, the banking firm of E. Ginzburg founded the Shipping Company for the Skeksna River, which

[22] In a certain sense, this process was revived during the period of the NEP and provided some of the efficiency increases which marked the NEP period by comparison with the prerevolutionary period.

[23] By the middle of the nineteenth century, E. Fagans established his transportation firm on the Vistula, followed by the firms of Rogozik and Friedman. Margolin reorganized the water transportation of the Dnepr during the 1880s and 1890s.

provided an opening to the Volga River waterway. By the end of the 1870s the entrepreneur Grigorii A. Poliak established his transportation firm in Nizhnii Novgorod for Volga shipping and entered in the 1880s the field of water transportation of oil and oil products on the Volga and the Caspian Sea. The field of oil tankers and the transfer of oil from the tankers to the railroads attracted the activities of the successful entrepreneurs Dembot and Kagan, who expanded further Jewish participation in the production, transportation, and trade in oil.[24]

The entrepreneurial activity of interest to us, however, was not the one of founding of shipping companies, construction of docks and warehouses, or even shipbuilding in which Jewish firms were engaged, but the attempts to bring order into the poorly coordinated area of water transportation. This later activity coincided with the government's vision of increasing the Russian share in goods transportation at the expense of foreign shipping companies in both internal and foreign trade. However, for the entrepreneurs there were two areas of immediate concern. The first was to gain control over a sufficiently large number of ships in order to modernize the carrying capacity and to redistribute them over the waterways to conform to the demand of the commodity flow. The second task was to improve the structure of insurance rates for the goods in transit. The expectations of the entrepreneurs were that because of the economies achieved in both areas which would, at least in part, be passed on to the users of the services, the total volume of shipments would increase and thus justify the investments in the improvement of the services. Two Jewish entrepreneurs, the brothers Hessen, succeeded with the help of the banks to gain additional control over the shipping on the waterways that connected the Caspian and Baltic seas as well as to control some major insurance companies.[25] The practical operation of the Hessens' scheme, begun in the war period, was interrupted by the Revolution and ultimately carried out according to the original blueprint during the NEP, no longer as a voluntary, but as a government-sponsored, scheme.

Another attempt, albeit unsuccessful, to create an integrated structure of industrial companies, railroad construction, insurance, and foreign trade enterprises, using federated banks and interlocking directorates, was one by the Poliakovs. The Poliakovs, heirs of the railroad builder and banking entrepreneur S. Poliakov, were probably the first in Russia

[24] Such activities resulted in the expansion of Jewish employment in the trade and production of oil at various levels of their mercantile and technical skills.

[25] Their scheme was supported by the Russian-French Bank of Commerce, the Odessa Merchant Bank, and the Union Bank. They gained control over the "Eastern Company," "Caucasus & Mercury" shipping companies, and over the insurance firm "Volga," having earlier secured the cooperation of the First and Second Insurance Companies.

to attempt the creation of a conglomerate out of their diverse investments and operating firms, to be controlled by their banks. Their scheme, undertaken at the downswing of the business cycle, failed. Although the State Bank helped to prevent the ruin of the Poliakovs' business empire, the Poliakovs were forced to divest themselves of some of their enterprises.[26] A more modest but successful attempt at integration of diverse companies was carried out later by the Russian entrepreneur Vtorov.

Still another attempt to improve efficiency within an entrepreneurial context was provided by a "Jewish" bank, Azov-Don Bank. Already in the early 1890s this bank began to petition the Ministry of Finance for permission to move its headquarters from Taganrog to St. Petersburg. The chief argument in favor of the move was the correct observation that as a bank heavily involved in grain export financing its business suffered from violent fluctuations. The sharply fluctuating demand and supply of money in the region of its operation, and the inefficiencies involved in its correspondent relation with the St. Petersburg banks in its foreign exchange dealings, made its position suboptimal. The Azov-Don Bank argued that its banking efficiency would be improved by the proximity to the St. Petersburg exchange, where there was an outlet for its idle funds and closer connections with foreign bank representatives, who could provide the short-term credits that were needed for its seasonally marked loan operations. The petitions of the Azov-Don Bank made it clear that the transaction costs of the provincial banks were apparently higher than for the St. Petersburg banks, and subsequent discussions related to liquid assets, discounts of commercial paper, and transfer of funds by the provincial banks point to shortcomings in the operation of the banking system. The Azov-Don Bank was able to preserve its degree of specialization and also move its headquarters to St. Petersburg. As far as other provincial banks were concerned, a number of them could not survive the competition of the branches of the St. Petersburg and Moscow banks as banking became increasingly concentrated in the capitals. The lack of data prevents one from judging the extent to which the subsequent improved access to the St. Petersburg money market alleviated the fluctuations in the volume of credits extended by the Azov-Don Bank to the grain producers in the area of its operation. For the country as a whole, the seasonal fluctuations in the size of the money supply, provided by the State Bank in response to the grain harvest, persisted until at least the late 1920s.

[26] It is interesting to note that the majority of the banking community in Russia viewed the Poliakovs' attempt as a case in which "the selfish interests of a business dynasty came into conflict with the proper criteria for banking operations and was, therefore, an abject lesson how not to abandon traditional criteria of sound banking." See I. Levin, *Aktsionernye banki* (Petrograd, 1917), p. 281.

Some Responses of Jewish Entrepreneurship to Policies of Discrimination

Given the existence of discriminatory legislation against Jewish business, as a component of general anti-Jewish legislation, Jewish entrepreneurs had to behave in a manner that would provide them with alliances that could counteract the strict enforcement of the legislation. Toward the end of the nineteenth century, the only group that could enter into an alliance with the Jewish entrepreneurs was the Russian business community. Beginning in the 1880s the incidents of defense by organized Russian business interests of Jewish entrepreneurs were rising. Somehow the Jewish entrepreneurs had to act so that Russian businessmen would overcome their taste for discrimination against the Jews and take the Jews' side when the tsarist bureaucracy strengthened its taste for discrimination.

A number of cases can be cited for the territory outside the Pale, perhaps the most interesting being the case of Siberia. Of all places, it was in Siberia that Jewish entrepreneurs as individuals and a "Jewish" bank, the Siberian Commercial Bank, gained a great deal of support from the local Russian business community. The Siberian Commercial Bank gained its notoriety by being different from the Russian banks operating in Siberia.[27] While most of the banks operating in Siberia were concentrating on financing mining industry, the Siberian Commercial Bank branched out into the areas of commodity trade, and in turn, served also the interests of Siberian agriculture. Given the large distances in Siberia and the low population density, the Siberian Bank nevertheless expanded greatly its branch network serving communities of different sizes and thereby contributed to a more even growth of the Siberian economy. Instead of specializing in a few areas of the economy, the Siberian Bank was acting as a development bank, responding to the needs of various sectors, on a broad front. And, although adversaries have accused the Siberian Bank of attempts to achieve monopoly in various regions and branches of the Siberian economy, some evidence points to the abandonment of specialization and diversification of its operation to foster the growth of the Siberian economy and to purchase good will from a broad spectrum of the business community. Jewish entrepreneurs also benefited from the bank's policies and during the early twentieth century developed a vigorous activity in different branches, starting with the primary industries and finishing with housing construction.

A somewhat different response to discrimination was the ready ac-

---

[27] The Siberian Bank was the brainchild of A. Soloveichik, who founded it in 1872 and who was succeeded in the directorship by his son, M. A. Soloveichik, who died in 1916. The bank had its headquarters in Ekaterinburg and later in St. Petersburg.

ceptance of the corporate status and structures by the Jewish entrepreneurs. There were three basic reasons for the acceptance of the corporate form by Jewish entrepreneurs. The first was capital scarcity and the hope to attract capital for their ventures. The second was to avoid some of the more blatant forms of discrimination that operated against individual or family firms, but not against corporations. The third was the opportunity to cooperate within corporate firms with non-Jewish associates. While corporations were permitted to discriminate against any "undesirable" group, by specifying the exclusion of such a group, whether in share ownership or in the administrative bodies of the corporations, one could discern a trend among non-Jewish corporations to lower the discriminatory barriers. Before World War I, very few corporations indeed prohibited Jews from owning shares. Most of the corporations trading their shares on the stock exchange eliminated this provision. The general prohibition of Jews from participating in the elected bodies (boards of directors) of the corporations was often mitigated by stressing the recruitment of Jewish business leaders living in the capitals. Thus the rules barring the Jews from the Pale admitted Jewish financiers from the capitals. The developing interlocking directorates between the banks and the industrial enterprises, along the lines of the German model, increased the incidence of participation of Jewish experts in the management of non-Jewish corporations and of representatives of firms and institutions in the previously predominant Jewish-owned corporations. Thus, the corporate form of business organization was less suitable for the exercise of discrimination than the family-owned firm, an additional reason for the Jewish entrepreneurs to prefer to deal with, and within, the corporate sector of the Russian economy.

Conclusions

Jewish industrial entrepreneurs made a significant contribution to the industrial development of Russia, primarily in the early stages of industrialization in the area of the Jewish Pale of Settlement. They contributed to the transition of industry from the stage of reliance upon serf labor to the stage of freely hired labor. By concentrating in processing of agricultural raw materials they contributed to the growth not only of commercial agriculture but also of the consumer-goods industries. It was the growth of the consumer-goods industries which created a demand for capital goods (machinery and equipment) and for the subsequent rapid growth of certain branches of machine building. It was to some extent due to the efforts of Jewish entrepreneurs that the provinces of the Pale became industrialized ahead of other provinces of the Russian empire. It was also due to some extent to the activities of the Jewish entrepreneurs that the industry branches (particularly textiles) developed in the Pale could withstand the competition with other economic regions of the empire. Inside and outside the Pale Jewish entrepreneurs engaged not only in the development of primary production but participated actively in the construction of the substantial overhead capital in Russia. Through their links with the trading and banking sectors, the Jewish entrepreneurs were able to introduce a higher degree of efficiency in their operations and to build an effective network of business relations that economized on scarce resources. Like other industrial entrepreneurs, they provided employment and helped raise the skill levels of the labor force, while at the same time creating a demand for capital and providing high returns on capital.

Within the Jewish milieu the role of the Jewish industrial entrepreneurs was even more significant than for the economy at large. On the one hand, they were instrumental in mobilizing the savings of the community and providing a high rate of return, but the capital resources of the community became insufficient when entrepreneurship developed on a large scale. Borrowing from the outside became necessary, and this "import" of capital helped to raise the production output of the community. On the other hand, and most importantly, the Jewish entrepreneurs provided the bulk of employment opportunities for Jewish workers. The spread of industrial employment within the Jewish community took place under conditions of a decline of wages or incomes of skilled labor in the "Jewish economy." It was owing to a general decline of income in other branches of employment that Jewish wage earners and the self-employed turned to factory labor. Jewish entrepreneurs were also unenthusiastic about employing Jewish factory labor. However, the net result was the growing Jewish factory employment in the Pale of Settlement, an opportunity provided primarily by the Jewish entrepreneurs at a time when employment shifts and discrimination threatened large segments of the Jewish population with outright poverty, an opportunity that affected the social structure and the degree of mobility of the Jewish population. Finally, the activities of Jewish entrepreneurs tended to raise the costs of anti-Jewish economic discrimination and perhaps even, to a limited extent, tended to improve the economic structure of the Jews in the Russian empire prior to World War I.

VII

BORIS V. ANAN'ICH

The Economic Policy of the Tsarist Government and Enterprise in Russia from the End of the Nineteenth through the Beginning of the Twentieth Century

The reforms of the 1860s created conditions necessary for the development of capitalism in Russia. The construction of railroads and the growth of industrial enterprises, banks, and joint-stock companies were conducive to the emergence of a new type of businessman and the rise of entrepreneurial organizations.

Having exerted a tremendous influence on the country's economic structure, the reforms of the 1860s had little effect on the system of state government. Until the first Russian Revolution (1905-07), there was neither a unified government nor a representative institution in Russia. In the 1860s, as in the beginning of the 1900s, the tsar and his associates determined the internal and foreign policies of the state. The contradiction between developing capitalistic attitudes and an absolutist form of state government became increasingly evident. This contradiction was further complicated by the crisis of the Russian autocracy, which had worsened in the second half of the nineteenth century. Once embarked on a course of reforms, the tsarist government found itself incapable of simultaneously managing a restructuring of the government mechanism and the processes of the country's economic development. The reforms of the 1860s were incomplete, a fact that manifested itself in vestiges of feudalism in the economy and unresolved problems of the class system (*vsesoslovnost'*) and the government (*predstavitel'stvo*). The Russian peasantry, which comprised a large part of the Russian population, remained the class with the fewest rights, although it assumed the principal tax burden in the form of redemption dues. Moreover, the existing pass-

(125)

port system restricted the peasantry's freedom of movement, as did the mutual guarantee (a form of collective responsibility) for payment of taxes and various duties. The incompleteness of the reforms was the subject of discussion in official circles during the reign of Alexander II. To an important degree, the result of this discussion was the so-called M. T. Loris-Melikov Constitution. Then, in the 1880s, Alexander III's government began to artificially impede transformations that the reforms of the 1860s had initiated. The period of counterreform ensued. As Lev Tolstoi wrote in March 1901, "Not only did the government decide not to advance (*sootvetstvenno obshchemu razvitiiu zhizni*), neither did it stand still for twenty years, but rather went backward by this overt movement, separating it all the more from the people and their needs."[1]

The nationalistic reactionary course followed by the government of Alexander III, whose ideologists were K. P. Pobedonostsev and M. N. Katkov, only intensified the crisis of the autocracy. In the 1880s and 1890s, the government openly refused to complete the 1860s reforms and initiated a series of measures designed to preserve existing conditions in the countryside. The government, however, lacked the power needed to stop processes flowing from the reforms of the 1860s. From the 1890s until the early 1900s, the peculiarity of government policy was that although the government did not want to implement reforms, it could not abandon its reformist work. Therefore, the very nature of the reforms during the reign of Nicholas II was more limited than in the 1860s, and the development of reforms was delayed for decades.

Contradictions between development of capitalistic relations and the absolutist form of power entered a critical period. To a great extent, this determined the nature of the government's economic policy in the post-reform period and the government's relationship to private enterprise and entrepreneurial organizations. This chapter focuses on that problem: to determine the place of private enterprise in government economic policy from 1880 to the beginning of the twentieth century.

In postreform Russia, the Ministry of Finance's role in the system of state institutions was significantly expanded. In the second half of the nineteenth century, the state machinery of the Russian Empire was imperfect and poorly run.[2] However, from the 1860s through the 1890s, eminent statesmen such as M. Kh. Reutern, N. Kh. Bunge, I. A. Vyshnegradskii, and finally S. Iu. Witte headed the Ministry of Finance. Bunge and Vyshnegradskii were also internationally known scholars. Although the direction of government economic policy was usually guided by a general political course whose direction the Ministry of Finance did not

---

[1] L. N. Tolstoi, *Polnoe sobranie sochinenii*, vol. 34 (Moscow, 1952), p. 240.

[2] See P. A. Zaionchkovskii, *Pravitel'stvennyi apparat samoderzhavnoi Rossii v XIX v.* (Moscow, 1978).

directly influence, there is no doubt that these ministers still greatly influenced that direction. Naturally, this relationship of the government to owners and entrepreneurial organizations was reflected in documents originating from the financial department.

Exactly what role was assigned to private enterprise in the empire's industrial development, and how did the representatives of official circles who were responsible for the direction of political policy evaluate the significance of private initiative?

The state had a rather significant role in the economy of the country during the postreform period. State intervention was especially important in the iron-metallurgy industry and in construction of the railroads.[3] In this area of the country's economic life, the contradictory nature of the government's relation to private enterprise had already become apparent. Railroad construction promoted industrial development and concentration of capital in the hands of major financiers and manufacturers. Speculative railroad enterprise in the 1860s and 1870s created a number of "railroad kings" and bankers who were not of noble extraction, but who had formerly been small-scale contractors or tax farmers. "The main source" of their newly acquired wealth was "state funds."[4] At the same time, the concession system and its attendant corruption became the source of profit for a large number of representatives of the bureaucracy and the nobility. As a result, as V. Ia. Laverychev believes, "with the help of railroad construction, the government transferred enormous funds to the top ranks of the privileged gentry, objectively delayed the accumulation of capital on a purely bourgeoise basis, and limited the freedom of entrepreneurial initiative."[5]

Judging from appearances, the opinions of M. Kh. Reutern (Minister of Finance, 1862-78) on the role of private enterprise are distinguished by their contradictory nature. From 1868 to 1870, Reutern supported development of stock operations and "advocated not only private initiative in banking institutions, but also competition among banks."[6] In the 1860s, the change from a restrictive to a nonrestrictive system of institutionalism in the major European countries stimulated the development of a bill in Russia intended to give private initiative broader scope

---

[3] I. F. Gindin, *Gosudarstvennyi bank i ekonomicheskaia politika tsarskogo pravitel'stva (1861-1892)* (Moscow, 1960), p. 44. On this problem see also Theodore von Laue, *Sergei Witte and the Industrialization of Russia* (New York, 1963), and John P. McKay, *Pioneers for Profit: Foreign Entrepreneurship and Russian Industrialization, 1885-1913* (Chicago, 1970).

[4] Gindin, ibid., p. 43.

[5] V. Ia. Laverychev, *Krupnaia burzhuaziia v poreforemennoi Rossi: 1861-1900* (Moscow, 1974), p. 59.

[6] Gindin (supra, n. 3), p. 45.

in the establishment of joint-stock companies.[7] However, Reutern's concept was not realized. Moreover, in 1874, evidently influenced by the stock market crash in 1873, Reutern ordered that "no further action be taken on the bill"[8] and supported limitation of joint-stock institutionalism. In 1877, Reutern came out generally in support of the utilization of government means for a fight against stock speculation, and regulation of the exchange rate of the ruble, and securities, and thereby, as I. F. Gindin pointed out, proposed a government policy of "artificial control of free competition." On the basis of this, the practice of government support of "solid" businesses and banks came into existence, which included payment of nonregulatory loans out of the State Bank.[9] Thus in the 1870s, a series of measures of State intervention were worked out, and the government's relationship to private enterprise was clarified. Reutern also influenced a change in government policy to strict protectionism and the attraction of foreign capital.[10]

Reutern's views on the state's role in economic policy were for the most part adopted by his successor. This does not mean, however, that economic policy in subsequent years remained totally unchanged. That depended mainly on the general direction of political policy and on the individual minister. In this regard, the views and work of N. Kh. Bunge are highly significant.

As a scholar and an economist, Bunge was quite familiar with contemporary Western economic theories and could indeed evaluate the pattern of economic development in the United States and Europe. In his papers and departmental memoranda, he gave significant place to determining the role of private enterprise and the state in the country's economic development.

In September 1880, not yet having assumed his ministerial post, Bunge sent a memorandum to Alexander II, in which he advocated taking steps of a general nature to raise Russia's national economy. "To assist the manufacturing industry and the factory and trade enterprises," wrote Bunge, "it is not so much material aid that is required from the government as the establishment of a better system by the issuance of laws adapted to the modern development of the economy. Russia has failed to keep pace with all of Western Europe in this respect by almost half a century." The industrial development of Russia "has been held back" by "the absence of modern factory-and-works legislation in this country."

---

[7] L. E. Shepelev, *Aktsionernye kompanii v Rossii* (Leningrad, 1973), p. 112.

[8] Ibid., p. 116.

[9] Gindin (supra, n. 3), pp. 46-47.

[10] Ibid., pp. 48-49.

Bunge initiated the development of this legislation.[11] He considered it necessary to revise the joint-stock legislation and to create conditions for the general establishment of joint-stock commercial banks.[12] Bunge's ideology corresponded to a certain extent with the spirit of the reforms of the 1860s. From 1882 to 1886, Bunge carried out the abolition of the head tax. He was for a class system in taxation policy, abolition of mutual guarantee, revision of passport legislation, introduction of a uniform passport for all classes, stipulation of terms for freedom of movement for the peasants, and a change from communal landownership to farm-steads. In his opinion, this would assure development of productive forces in the countryside. Finally, Bunge linked the country's economic development to the necessity for changes in the system of state government and raised the question of a unified form of government.

From 1888 through 1889, in his lectures to the heir to the throne, the future Emperor Nicholas II, Bunge emphasized the state's right "to participate actively in industrial matters" and "to supervise . . . businesses of a public nature." However, he warned his pupil about extremes in this respect, and, as a negative example, cited economic policy during the reign of Nicholas I. Bunge contended that in assisting private enterprises, the government must proceed on the basis of three principles:

> 1) The state should aid private enterprise only when actual state interests, not the interests of private economy, require it. 2) The state should control consumer-oriented businesses—communications industry, banks, harbor construction, etc., especially if a real reduction in production costs can be achieved by this. 3) It is necessary to grant private individuals a share in public economy when private enterprise runs cheaper and better than the bureaucratic administration.[13]

Bunge noted with a certain uneasiness the expansion of "direct government participation in industrial matters," as well as its controlling activities. As minister of finance, Bunge himself was responsible for the founding of the Peasant Land Bank (1882) and the State Gentry Land Bank (1885), the redemption of seven thousand versts that had belonged to private railroad companies, and for subjecting city and public banks to government supervision (1883). Similarly, he proposed another series

[11] See Laverychev (supra, n. 5), p. 59. Bunge's memorandum to Alexander II in 1880 was published by A. Pogrebinskii in the periodical *Istoricheskii arkhiv*, no. 2 (1960).

[12] Shepelev (supra, n. 7), p. 120. In 1857, in the *Zhurnal dlia aktsionerov*, N. Kh. Bunge wrote: "Of all the types of companies, we give preference to the companies based on shares; of all their services, we consider credit to be the most expansive, the most powerful in influence. Of all the conditions necessary for the successful development of companies, we recognize freedom of industry as being the most important." (nos. 25-26), p. 140.

[13] Otdel rukopisei, Gosudarstvennaia publichnaia biblioteka imeni Saltykova-Shchedrina, f. 550, (OSRDK), (238), ll. 596-98.

of measures of a political nature that were undertaken after his resig-
nation; in particular, state regulation of railroad tariffs; involvement of
railroad companies in grain-trade operations, including the issuance of
grain loans at the expense of the State Bank; and state stimulation of
domestic industry.[14]

However, Bunge failed to carry through many of his ideas in practice.
He was a cautious and indecisive politician. Many of the reforms he
outlined either were not fully realized or were not upheld. Bunge's ministry coincided with a sharp change in general political policy. One of
the ideologists of the new policy, the editor of the *Moskovskie vedomosti*,
M. N. Katkov, began a campaign against Bunge in his newspaper. His
assistant in this campaign was I. A. Vyshnegradskii, a professor of mechanics at the Petersburg Technological Institute, also well known in the
business world as one of the chief figures in the Petersburg Waterworks
and chairman of the board of the South-West Railroad Company.

It is difficult to determine to what extent Vyshnegradskii and Katkov's
collaboration was dictated by career considerations and to what extent
by a concurrence of the political views of a prominent scholar and of an
editor of the most influential conservative newspaper in Russia. However,
it was precisely because of this collaboration that Vyshnegradskii became
the minister of finance after Katkov succeeded in obtaining Bunge's res-
ignation through the newspaper campaign. Vyshnegradskii became the
head of the Ministry of Finance in January 1887. But in July of that year
Katkov died; therefore, it is difficult to determine whether or not Katkov
had a direct influence on Vyshnegradskii's economic program while the
latter was minister of finance.[15]

Vyshnegradskii's assumption of leadership in the Ministry of Finance
cleared the way to government service for the manager of the South-West
Railroad, S. Iu. Witte, who took Vyshnegradskii's side, without question,
in his polemics with N. Kh. Bunge. Witte's bureaucratic career began
with the backing of the *Moskovskie vedomosti*.[16] In 1889, Witte was
named director of the Department of Railroad Affairs of the Ministry of
Finance and in August 1892, because of Vyshnegradskii's illness, became
minister of finance.

At first glance, Vyshnegradskii's economic policy, and subsequently
Witte's seems to represent a direct continuation of Bunge's policy, but
this is not really the case. In the first years of their activities as ministers

[14] Ibid., p. 12.

[15] See Akinori Kanda, "Ekonomicheskaia programma dvorianskoi reaktsii i politika
I. A. Vyshnegradskogo," *The Journal of Asahikawa University*, 5 (March 1977):195-214.

[16] For details, see B. V. Anan'ich and R. Sh. Ganelin, "I. A. Vyshnegradskii i S. Iu.
Witte—korrespondenty *Moskovskikh vedomostei*," *Problemy obshchestvennoi mysli i
ekonomicheskaia politika Rossii XIX-XX vekov* (Leningrad, 1972), pp. 12-34.

of finance, Vyshnegradskii and Witte attempted to adapt economic policy to the general political doctrine during the reign of Alexander III. From the end of the 1880s until the beginning of the 1890s, the government implemented a series of legislative measures directed at strengthening the peasant commune (*obshchina*). In 1889, the institution of land captains (Zemstvo chiefs) was introduced, strengthening the gentry's control over the peasants' agencies of local self-government. In the 1880s, voices resounded in government circles for the abolition of article 165 of the articles of regulation of February 19, 1861, which allowed peasants to leave the peasant commune with the consent of the "village community" (mir) or by paying off the redemption debt ahead of schedule. Debates on this subject lasted for almost ten years. As a result, two laws were passed that strengthened the peasant commune system of land ownership. The first, on July 8, 1893, concerned limitation of the right of land reallotments. It established a twelve-year period for reallotments and gave Zemstvo chiefs permanent control over reallotments. The second, on December 14, 1893, prohibited peasants' leaving the commune without consent of the mir even when redemption debts were paid off ahead of schedule, and also prohibited the sale, transfer as a gift, or mortgaging of land allotments.

With the preparation of these bills, conflicts in official circles over the peasant commune finally came to light. Those who advocated preservation of the peasant commune saw the bills as a means of saving the Russian peasantry from proletarianization and of saving Russia from social revolution. Opponents of the peasant commune considered the process of its dissolution inevitable and saw creation of small, stable, individual farmsteads as the way to salvation from proletarianization. In the beginning of 1893, during the State Council discussion of the bill which limited land allotments to a twelve-year period, the minister of the Imperial Court, I. I. Vorontsov-Dashkov, and Bunge (who, after resigning from the post of minister of finance, was appointed chairman of the Committee of Ministers) spoke out against communal ownership of land. "In examining the facts of the situation such as famine in the past (the effects of which still have not been erased); the necessity of feeding the people yearly in this province or another at the expense of the state; the impoverishment of the masses and their trend toward overpopulation, one is forced to admit," Bunge contended, "that a change from communal land ownership to farmsteads is increasingly urgent."[17]

This time Vorontsov-Dashkov's and Bunge's opinions on the peasant commune met opposition not so much from representatives of the Min-

[17] Tsentral'nyi gosudarstvennyi istoricheskii arkhiv SSSR (hereafter TsGIA), f. 1449, op. XI, 1899, d. 47, l. 68.

istry of Internal Affairs, traditionally advocates of the peasant commune, as from the minister of finance, who presented an extensive report in defense of communal landownership. In this report, S. Iu. Witte, speaking in strict accordance with the official political doctrine, called the peasant commune a "bulwark" against socialism and the Russian peasantry "the conservative strength" and "mainstay of order."[18] From the very beginning of his activities as minister of finance, Witte declared himself an advocate of the abolition of mutual guarantee and the implementation of passport reform (measures that had undermined the system of communal landownership). Until at least 1896, S. Iu. Witte remained the most orthodox defender of the peasant commune and actively participated in carrying out legislative measures that strengthened it. Vyshnegradskii and Witte's agrarian policy until the end of the 1890s represented a step backward from the policy that Bunge proposed, and it undoubtedly was an obstacle in the development of capitalistic relations in the countryside. At the same time, from the end of the 1880s until the beginning of the 1890s, the action on such imminent reforms as the passport reform and the abolition of mutual guarantee was frozen, and in the realm of joint-stock legislation there were essentially no significant changes. The conservatives' stand in agrarian policy began in the 1880s and lasted until the beginning of the 1890s. It combined with increasing government intervention in the country's economic life. This was an integral part of Vyshnegradskii and Witte's tariff policy. Along with strengthening protectionism, a policy that found expression in the customs tariff of 1891, the Ministry of Finance established a system of state regulation of grain tariffs in 1889. To do this, former railroad promoters who had been entrepreneurs and were now ministers, had to overcome the opposition of landowners in the central and western provinces and the owners of the railroad companies and show them in practice that, as Vyshnegradskii reported to Alexander III in July 1890, "it is incumbent only on state power to deal with the economic fortunes of the state."[19] The tariff legislation of 1889, drawn up under Vyshnegradskii, was further developed from 1893 to 1897, when Witte was minister of finance. In these years, the state's role in the regulation of grain trade was greatly strengthened.

It was just this unlimited state intervention in the grain trade that prompted Bunge to speak again with conviction about Vyshnegradskii and Witte's policy. He did so in the second half of the 1890s, in his "Beyond the Grave" notes. Reviewing the problem of state intervention

[18] I. V. Chernyshev, *Agrarno-krestian'skaia politika Rossii za 150 let* (Petrograd, 1918), p. 257.

[19] T. M. Kitanina, *Khlebnaia torgovlia Rossii v 1875-1914 gg.*, (Leningrad, 1978), p. 95.

in retrospect, Bunge wrote that on the eve of the Crimean War the government "excessively limited the private principle" in the area "of spiritual and material life":

> The administration and the government institutions not only had to supply private business, but even had to replace it. . . . The disappointment everyone felt during the Crimean War led to an internal policy . . . which expected everything of private initiative. However, we were insufficiently prepared for this initiative, and it sometimes became apparent in such regrettable ways, that intelligent people again began to demand supervision, state control, and even the replacement of private business by state business. We have continued in this direction, and now, whenever it wants, the state is extensively engaged in grain trade and supplies grain to the millions in the population. It seems impossible to go any further, unless the state is allowed to plough, seed, reap, and then publish all the newspapers and periodicals, write stories and novels, and pursue the arts and sciences, as Bellamy suggests (*Looking Backward*).[20]

In the second half of the 1890s, to a certain extent under the influence of Bunge's criticism, Witte changed his opinions on the peasant commune and became an adversary of communal landownership. In 1898, he raised the question of the necessity of revising the government's agrarian policy in order to expand the internal market. However, V. K. Plehve, with the support of K. P. Pobedonostsev and I. N. Durnovo, defeated Witte's attempt to put this issue before the Committee of Ministers. In 1899, the law that partially abolished mutual guarantee (which Witte termed a "lifeless" institution, hindering the development of "private initiative and enterprise"[21]) was passed, largely due to the initiative of the minister of finance. At the end of 1893, in his speech on the state's commercial and industrial policy, Witte spoke cautiously of foreign capital and also expressed fear that "Russian enterprise sometimes found itself unable to compete with foreign enterprise" despite "a customs barrier."[22] At the end of the 1890s, Witte openly supported unlimited attraction of foreign capital, emphasizing that for Russia, "capital, knowledge, and enterprise" were necessary for industrial development, i.e., he considered foreign capital basic for the development of Russian enterprise.[23]

As minister of finance, Witte first attempted to increase the amount of paper money in circulation by a special issue of "Siberian" rubles for operating expenses connected with the construction of the Trans-Siberian

[20] TsGIA, f. 1622, op. I, d. 721, l. 52.
[21] M. A. Simonova, "Otmena krugovoi poruki," *Istoricheskie zapiski*, 83:182-84.
[22] TsGIA, f. 1152, op. XI, 1893, d. 447, l. 140b.
[23] *Materialy po istorii SSSR*, vol. 6 (Moscow, 1959), pp. 181-82.

Railroad. However, under Bunge's influence, Witte became a staunch supporter of gold-money circulation, and three years later implemented a currency reform formulated by his predecessors over many years. Toward the end of the 1890s, Witte's policy became concrete and purposeful. He sought to catch up with the more industrially developed European countries within about ten years and to secure a stable position in the markets of the Near, Middle, and Far East. Witte planned to ensure acceleration of industrial development in Russia by (1) attracting foreign capital in the form of loans and investments; (2) mobilizing internal resources with the help of the government alcohol monopoly and the strengthening of indirect taxation; (3) safeguarding Russian industry against Western competitors and stimulating Russian export with customs.

Perhaps no minister of finance in the postreform period relied as much on state intervention as Witte. To achieve his goals, he resorted to help from state institutions, especially those such as the State Bank or Credit Office. The basis of Witte's policy was profoundly contradictory, because he used means and conditions born of the existing absolutist system of state government in Russia for the capitalistic development of the country. State intervention in economics was often justified by the necessity of support for private initiative, which was not yet firmly established; however, in reality, it went far beyond these limits and hindered the natural development of capitalistic relations in the country. Relying heavily on state economic activity not only to solve internal economic problems, but also in the fight for foreign markets (where at times the state acted as the owner, competing with private Russian trade firms), Witte simply did not carry out or was unable to carry out general reforms that would have created the conditions necessary for freer development of private initiative. Thus, he did not succeed in changing radically the existing system of joint-stock legislation or in advancing solutions to the peasant problem. In the liberal circles of Russian society, it was not by chance that "Witte's system" was perceived as "a grandiose economic diversion of the autocracy," a diversion that distracted various strata of the population from socioeconomic and cultural-political reforms.[24]

From the end of the 1890s, when Witte became an advocate of review of the peasant question and became convinced of the need for completing the 1860s reforms, his views and policy conflicted with the general direction of internal policy and met opposition from the Ministry of Internal Affairs and, in particular, from V. K. Plehve, who strictly and consistently adhered to official doctrine.[25] Thus, two directions of internal policy

[24] *Osvobozhdenie*, 2, no. 26 (1903):24.

[25] The difference in the understanding of the country's internal position and the task of government policy became distinctly apparent in an argument between the two ministers in an unofficial situation in Yalta 1902. See "Otryvki iz vospominanii D. N. Liubimova (1902-1904)," *Istoricheskii arkhiv*, 6 (1962):81-82.

resulted. The differences between Witte's and Plehve's solutions to the peasant question reflected themselves in the work of the Editorial Commission of the Deputy Minister of Internal Affairs, A. S. Stishinskii, and of the Special Conference on the Affairs of the Agricultural Industry, under the chairmanship of S. Iu. Witte. The ministers' difference of opinion on the solution to the labor problem became apparent in the fight between the Ministry of Finance and the Ministry of Internal Affairs for factory inspection and in different approaches to the policy of trusteeship.[26]

Having been involved in private enterprise, Witte, of course, understood not only the interests of the representatives of the industrial class, but also the importance of private initiative and experience to the empire's industrial development. Therefore, from the very beginning of his ministerial activities, instead of going along with Russia's existing system of promotion by rank, Witte placed people from the private sector of the economy in the Ministry of Finance to promote more effective intervention by state institutions in the country's economic life. In the beginning of 1895, Witte wrote to Nicholas II,

> In Russia, because of the conditions of life in our country, state intervention has been required in the most diverse areas of public life, whereas in England, for example, private initiative and private enterprise are granted everything and the state only regulates private activities. . . . Therefore, the functions of the state in these two countries are completely different, and, as a result, the demands made on the people who make up the government service, i.e., the officials, must also be different. In England, the officials only have to direct private activities, while in Russia, in addition to directing private activities, they must participate indirectly in many areas of socioeconomic activity.[27]

While stimulating private initiative and enterprise, Witte strove at the same time to keep it under strict control; therefore, the representative organizations of the bourgeoisie he wanted to keep, above all, advisory organs. The All-Russian Industrial-Trade Conference in Nizhni Novgorod in 1896 and its preparation were revealing in this respect. The Ministry of Finance decided to hold the conference; the Department of Trade and Manufactories prepared the agenda, working out in advance a list of problems to be discussed. Addressing the participants at the opening of the conference, the chairman, D. F. Kobeko, a member of the Council

[26] V. I. Laverychev, *Tsarizm i rabochii vopros v Rossii (1861-1917)* (Moscow, 1972), pp. 146-151.

[27] B. B. Dubentsov, "Popytki preobrazovaniia organizatsii gosudarstvennoi sluzhby, v kontse XIX v. (Iz praktiki Ministerstva finansov)," *Problemy otechestvennoi istorii*, Part 1 (Moscow-Leningrad, 1976), pp. 216-17.

of the Minister of Finance, declared that "the conference has been convened by the direct order of the government, and not at the discretion
of private companies. . . . In the Ministry of Finance, some proposals
concerning conditions which regulate the industrial-trade life of the country are being developed. However, the Ministry of Finance considered it
necessary to first familiarize itself with the views of representatives of
the industrial-trade class on the problems which interest them most."
The conference was presented as proof of the "active communication"
established between the Ministry of Finance and the trade class.[28] On
the other hand, the Ministry of Finance regarded the emergence of one
of the strongest representative organizations—the Petersburg Company
of Factory-Owners and Manufacturers (whose procedure of official registration was delayed for almost three years)—without any special enthusiasm.

Although the tsar still had the final word on decisions about important
economic problems, it is difficult to determine the roles of both Alexander
III and Nicholas II in the development of the general economic program
of the government, and even more, their relationship to enterprise. It is
also difficult to establish the extent of their knowledge in this area. It is
only known that in the second half of the nineteenth century, the preparation for heirs to the throne stipulated their completing a special course
in the history of economic thought and the history of the national economy. The extent and nature of the studies can be judged by the published
course of lectures which Witte read to Grand Duke Mikhail Alexandrovich when he was an heir;[29] and by Bunge's lectures from 1863 to
1864 presented to the elder son of Alexander II, Crown Prince Nicholas,
as well as Bunge's lectures to the future Emperor Nicholas II from 1888
to 1889 (preserved in the Saltykov-Shchedrin State Public Library). A
sample of a test completed by Nicholas II has also been preserved, indicating that the studies were not passive. Finally, the future heir, Nicholas II, was supposed to develop practical skills in the study of economic
activities by serving in the capacity of chairman of the Committee on the
Affairs of the Siberian Railroad. (Bunge was the vice-chairman and actually directed the work of the Committee.)

However, in his convictions, Nicholas II remained, like other Roma-
novs, above all a substantial landowner. During the census of 1897, it
was not by accident that Nicholas II called himself "a landowner" and
"the landlord of the Russian soil." The tsar was the wealthiest person
in Russia. Management of the emperor's properties and those of the

[28] *Trudy vysochaishe uchrezhdennogo Vserossiiskogo torgovo-promyshlennogo sezda
1896 g. v Nizhnem Novgorode,* vol. 1 (St. Petersburg, 1896), p. 2.

[29] S. Iu. Witte, *Konspekt lektsii o narodnom i gosudarstvennom khoziaistve* (St. Petersburg, 1912).

tsarist family was under the authority of the Ministry of the Court and the Cabinet. Supervision of sizable territories of land and forests in the Altai, Zabaikal, and Poland, as well as mountain enterprises in Siberia belonged to the Cabinet. Feudal rent was collected on the lands that belonged to them. The Cabinet received the duty paid in kind (*iasak*) and collected quitrent from the populations of Siberia and the Arkhangelsk and Perm provinces.[30] Nicholas II managed his personal property like a substantial landowner, maintaining antiquated forms of feudal exploitation. In the very beginning of Nicholas II's reign, the Minister of the Court, I. I. Vorontsov-Dashkov, cautiously brought to the tsar's attention the question of restructuring the Cabinet's economic activities. In his account to the tsar for 1895, Vorontsov-Dashkov wrote, "The capitalistic structure of production on which all industrial-trade accounts are now based, especially in the coal and iron metallurgy industries, makes it necessary for the Cabinet either to act on a new basis as an independent owner, by building large-scale factories, constructing underground tracks, etc., or to attract outside capital to mine the natural resources of the Altai and Nerchinskii regions, offering such capital the exploitation of these resources on the basis of tenant right." However, having proposed such an alternative, Vorontsov-Dashkov hastened to oppose the expansion of the Cabinet's entrepreneurial activities, in view of the necessity "for extremely large initial expenditures and the unavoidable risk in every industrial-trade enterprise."[31] Judging by the minister of the Court's account, at the end of the 1890s, the Cabinet's profits from industrial activities were quite insignificant. Only the gold industry in the Altai and Nerchinskii regions brought in substantial profits. It remained "the most important branch of the Cabinet's mining and metallurgical exploitations." However, in the Altai region, land quitrent exceeded it in profitability.[32] More than 4/5 of the gold in the Altai region, and a significant part of the gold in the Nerchinskii region was mined by industrialists who had paid the Cabinet a fixed tax percentage of the extraction. The Cabinet did not try to concern itself with entrepreneurial activities, and in 1895, Vorontsov-Dashkov spoke out in support of "attracting new enterprise" to mine coal and iron ore in Siberia, facilitating private initiative, as far as possible, in the gold industry, and providing conditions under which that industry could work most advantageously for itself and for the Cabinet.[33]

As a landowner and proprietor, Nicholas II obviously conducted his

[30] G. P. Zhidkov, *Kabinetskoe zemlevladenie (1747-1917)* (Novosibirsk, 1973), pp. 56, 59, 258.

[31] TsGIA, f. 468, op. 43, d. 1378, ll. 47-48.

[32] Ibid.

[33] Ibid.

business in a manner generally characteristic of the Russian gentry. As P. A. Zaionchkovskii justly notes, "The Russian gentry, as a whole, was not capable of engaging in commercial matters, and if they did, it was as patriarchal landowners," because, at that time, "participation in business activities by higher officials" was often linked with corruption.[34] As an entrepreneur and a stockholder, Nicholas II, along with other representatives of the Romanov family, was involved in some Bezobrazov's enterprises. In 1900 and 1902, he was involved with the floating 5 percent Persian loans. In both cases, his actions were in no way a business risk, because the state backed the tsar. Thus, for example, capital belonging to the Cabinet and some of the members of the tsar's family, in the sum of 30 million rubles, was invested in the 5 percent Persian loans of 1900 and 1902. In particular, "by the highest command," the entire sum (1 million rubles) of Princess Elena Vladimirovna's dowry (she was the daughter of Vladimir Alexandrovich and the granddaughter of Alexander II) was invested in the 5 percent loan of 1902.[35]

It is possible that these actions were dictated by state interests, as Nicholas II understood them to be, but at the same time this was a profitable operation, guaranteed by the State Bank, which had assumed responsibility for the floating of the loan.

At the end of the nineteenth century, the purchase of soundly guaranteed securities by members of the tsar's family was a common occurrence. Moreover, this did not prevent Nicholas II from controlling the freedom of the joint-stock institution. The tsar remained deaf to the complaints made in this connection. Thus, during World War I, in September 1914, I. Kh. Ozerov, a political economy professor at Moscow University and a member of the State Council on Elections to the Universities and the Academy of Sciences, delivered a special memorandum to the tsar through the minister of finance, P. L. Bark, in which he simply asked for "the removal of the obstacles to the development of the productive forces of the country," and urged the tsar to follow the example of the United States in creating conditions necessary for industrial activities. Ozerov wrote: "In this country . . . the businessman's word is almost considered an oath. . . . Lately, because of the red tape involved in opening our new joint-stock businesses, the Russian people have begun to set up these businesses in English and French territory, according to the laws of those countries. Why does it take six to nine months or even longer here, when there, the same thing can be accomplished in several days?"[36] However, this warning, like many others similar to it, did not convince

[34] Zaionchkovskii (supra, n. 2), pp. 104-5.

[35] B. V. Anan'ich, *Rossiiskoe samoderzhavie i vyvoz kapitalov* (Leningrad, 1975), pp. 43-45, 200.

[36] TsGIA, f. 560, op. 38, d. 191, ll. 111, 117.

Nicholas II to change his attitude toward the problem of the joint-stock establishment.

In an article he had prepared for the brothers Granat's encyclopedic dictionary, V. I. Lenin wrote: "At the end of the nineteenth century in Russia, the sharpest contradiction between the requirements of complete social development and serfdom was found."[37] This contradiction explains the dual nature of the government's economic policy in the post-reform period. The government's basic goal was the strengthening of autocratic power in Russia. But to achieve this goal, the government was forced to support industrial enterprises, banks, and railroad construction; and in this way, promote the development of capitalistic relations. The government stimulated private enterprise and private initiative, but only to the extent that this did not affect the political interests of the autocracy and on condition that control of industrial development was concentrated in the Ministry of Finance and other state institutions. Also, the support of individual businesses had to compensate for the overall lack of entrepreneurial freedom in Russia.

Translated by CAROLE RYCZEK

[37] V. I. Lenin, "Agrarnyi vopros v Rossii k kontsu XIX veka," *Polnoe sobranie sochinenii,* 17:80.

VIII

FRED V. CARSTENSEN   *Foreign Participation in
Russian Economic Life:
Notes on British Enterprise,
1865-1914*

Russian economic historians have often given special emphasis to the role that the government assumed in the period 1885-1903 in shaping Russian economic development. In the absence of a vigorous, competitive market which would develop the creative, developmental energies of native businessmen, the government itself undertook to provide economic leadership and to draw into Russia the energy of foreign enterprise. Minister of Finance Witte argued that successfully attracting foreign enterprise would force the emergence of a native entrepreneurial spirit, a spirit which would eliminate the need for government initiative and foreign enterprise. Thus foreign enterprise—capital, technique, personnel—was central to government policy and central to the development process within only a relatively brief period of a decade and a half. Though foreign individuals and firms were of obvious significance in Russian economic life in this period, their participation often began before 1895 and remained after 1903; the impetus for their participation was often not the result of government initiative but was more prosaic and understandable: the opportunities intrinsic to a large, increasingly integrated market with steadily rising aggregate demand. This chapter briefly reviews the common Western view of foreign participation, its conceptual and evidentiary shortcomings, and then sets out the histories of nearly a dozen British enterprises in Russia. These histories suggest that, to use Olga Crisp's felicitous terms, the autonomous sphere of the economy was at least as attractive to foreign enterprise as the induced sphere of government initiative, and that the contributions of

* The author acknowledges grants-in-aid from the American Philosophical Society and the Economic History Association.

(140)

foreign enterprise to Russian development often came through this channel.

Interpreting the Role of Foreign Enterprise

In 1899 Minister of Finance Sergei Witte assured Tsar Nicholas in a secret memorandum that "the influx of foreign capital" was the "sole means" by which Russian industry could develop rapidly and provide the country "with abundant and cheap goods." Witte argued that "each new wave of capital, sweeping in from abroad," brought effective competition, knocking down the "immoderately high level of profits" to which Russian businessmen were accustomed, forcing industrialists to invest in new, lower-cost technology. This process would reenforce pressure for lower prices and expansion of the economy. Russia's "natural riches" would thus be "utilized to a considerably greater extent"; the economy would thrive. It would "be difficult then to say whether foreign capital or [Russia's] own productive forces, invigorated and given a chance by foreign capital, [would] have the greater influence over the further growth" of industry.[1]

When Witte wrote the tsar, Russia had in fact just experienced one of the most successful decades of industrial growth ever recorded: industrial output had expanded more than 8 percent every year. (The rate was exceptional before World War II; since then several countries, most notably Japan, have surpassed this rate.) Witte, building on the work of his predecessors, N. C. Bunge and I. A. Vyshnegradskii, had pushed Russian industrialization with particular vigor. Tariffs had been brought to a high protective level in 1891. Then Witte, relying on monetary reforms to get the ruble on the gold standard, special incentives for industrial expansion—subsidies, credits, inflated prices on government orders, direct guarantees of profit—and an extensive public relations campaign, tried to attract foreign capitalists and entrepreneurs who would provide the necessary ingredients for successful and sustained economic growth: "capital, knowledge, and the spirit of enterprise."[2]

The effectiveness of such government policies in promoting this growth is open to question. The need to turn to foreign sources for investable funds and business talents arose in substantial part from stifling indig-

---

[1] T. H. von Laue, "Document: A Secret Memorandum of Sergei Witte on the Industrialization of Imperial Russia," *Journal of Modern History*, 26 (1954):69. Subsequently published in Akademiia Nauk SSSR, Institut istorii, *Materialy po istorii SSSR*, vol. 6 *Dokumenty po istorii monopolisticheskogo kapitalizma v Rossii* (Moscow, 1959), pp. 173-95.

[2] Ibid., p. 68. See also O. Crisp, "The Financial Aspects of the Franco-Russian Alliance, 1904-1914" (Ph.D. dissertation, University of London, 1954), and von Laue, *Sergei Witte and the Industrialization of Russia* (New York, 1963).

enous development. In addition, the protective tariff lacked refinement and discrimination, the result of fiscal needs taking priority over development. It resulted in the paradox that importers of capital goods, the goods central to industrialization, had to pay much higher prices for those goods, negating the value of tariffs on final goods. Government orders for industrial goods, though important for some firms, were comparatively small. Sale of government bonds competed directly with industrial shares and bonds for funds in both domestic and foreign money markets.[3]

Whatever the role of government policy, there is no question that foreign enterprise—capital, technique and personnel—did play a special role during the burst of activity in the 1890s: foreign personnel met much of the new demand for technical, managerial and commercial skills; foreign entrepreneurs and firms accounted for perhaps half of all new industrial investment made in that decade. Witte's projection for the subsequent pattern of Russian development—the emergence, in the face of this competitive pressure from the foreigner, of a native entrepreneurial/capitalist class with the spirit and capacity to undertake new investments—does have substantial validity in the description of Russian economic development during the next decade and a half. Thus, for the years 1885 to 1914, the dynamics of the Russian economy have been seen in terms of a shift in the sources of entrepreneurial energy and ability, a shift from the foreigner, perhaps attracted to Russia by vigorous government actions before 1900, to the Russian, operating, after the hiatus in growth between 1900 and 1906, primarily through the rapidly expanding commercial banks. To some scholars, the foreigner then came to play not simply a relatively smaller role, but a different one, becoming a passive provider of capital needed by Russian entrepreneurs.[4]

A Critique

Despite Witte's understanding that the foreign role involved the importation of a complex of productive factors, verification of that foreign role has relied exclusively on the quantitatively impressive statistics of foreign ownership—typically misrepresented as foreign investment—in Russian corporate shares and bonds. Such information, when accurate, is useful

[3] A. Kahan, "Government Policies and the Industrialization of Russia," *Journal of Economic History*, 17 (1965):460-77.

[4] Alexander Gerschenkron is the most important expositor of this approach, but he gave little attention to the role of foreigners. McKay subsequently argued that government was less influential, and highlighted aspects of the foreign role but followed the same broad chronological pattern and conceptual paradigm of shifting entrepreneurial sources. See A. Gerschenkron, *Economic Backwardness in Historical Perspective* (New York, 1962), and J. P. McKay, *Pioneers for Profit: Foreign Entrepreneurship and Russian Industrialization: 1885-1913* (Chicago, 1970).

in suggesting the regional and sectoral concentrations of foreign ownership and indicating the variation in pattern of ownership among firms and individuals from particular nations. But these statistics reflect only ownership of corporate assets, not commercial or manufacturing assets generally, and thus reveal as much or more about the changing legal and fiscal environment of Russian business as any change in the role or level of foreign participation in such business. In either event, such statistics say nothing of the Russian balance of payments: did Witte's program in fact attract to Russia new assets, or were foreign investments offset by purchases of monetary gold or other equivalent capital exports? Perhaps more important, statistics of foreign ownership of Russian corporate assets reveals nothing of the motivations and perceptions that led foreign investors, entrepreneurs, technicians, managers, and companies to come to Russia, of the problems they faced and the responses they made as they dealt with Russian bureaucracy, Russian laws, Russian labor, and the Russian market. The mere coincidence of a foreign influx with the announced intentions of the government to attract foreigners does not establish a causal link.

P. V. Ol', who compiled the statistics of foreign ownership of Russian corporate assets, was an economic nationalist and thus concerned about the implications for Russia of a foreign influx; he wanted to measure foreign influence in Russian corporations and thereby in the Russian economy. To that end Ol' used the nominal or face value of corporate foundation capital—the shares issued as stipulated by the statutes of incorporation—and of corporate bonds to compile a comprehensive, firm-by-firm list of foreign ownership as of 1916.[5] Then, presumably using the same technique, Ol' developed an annual series for the years 1860 to 1915.[6] Ol' neither attempted nor intended to measure the real flow of foreign funds into these companies or the true value of foreign-owned assets. He specifically noted that he did not reconstruct corporate balance sheets or examine actual stock and bond transactions. He warned his readers against using his compilation as anything other than an index of foreign influence: "In reality the sum of nominal foundation and bond capital does not correspond to the sum of capital actually brought into the majority of companies."[7]

When subsequent scholars, like Diakin, Lebedev, McKay, and Greg-

---

[5] P. V. Ol', *Inostrannye kapitaly v Rossii* (Petrograd, 1922). For a more detailed discussion of the problems with Ol''s estimates, see Fred V. Carstensen, "Numbers and Reality: A Critique of Foreign Investment Estimates in Tsarist Russia," in *La position internationale de la France: Aspects economiques et financiers XIXᵉ-XXᵉ siècles* (Paris, 1978), pp. 275-83.

[6] P. V. Ol', *Inostrannye kapitaly v narodnom khoziaistve dovoennoi Rossii* (Leningrad, 1925).

[7] Ol', *Inostrannye kapitaly v Rossii*, p. 143.

ory,[8] treat Ol''s statistics as if they are measures of real investments, they make each incorporation of an enterprise effectively the actual beginnings of that enterprise, and each new share or bond issue coincident with new, real investments. Yet incorporations often represented only a change in the legal status of existing firms—from 1901 to 1913, nearly two-thirds of all incorporations were of this type[9]—or creation of new companies to acquire assets of established concerns, a practice common among French companies operating in Russia.[10] Expansions of nominal capital were often the result not of new investments but of efforts to reduce the effective rate of taxation on business profits.

The principal reason for both conversions to the corporate form and many of the large expansions in foundation capital was the Russian corporate profits tax. Before 1899, corporations and registered share partnerships that published annual balance sheets were subject to a flat rate of taxation on profits.[11] Other businesses (excluding those subjected to excise taxes) paid an apportioned tax. The government set the total to be collected; that amount was then divided among all companies liable to the tax. Its incidence on individual firms was thus unpredictable; as it grew in size during the 1890s, many businessmen realized that a fixed, flat rate of taxation on corporate profits was preferable to this uncertain but relentlessly growing apportioned tax. In 1893 there were but 432 corporations operating in Russia; by 1900 there were over 1,000.[12] Beginning in 1899, corporations paid a progressive tax levied on profits as a percentage of the nominal value of foundation capital. On profits of less than 3 percent, companies paid no percentage tax (they still paid a small tax on capital); on profits of 10 percent or more, they paid a marginal rate of 11 percent. In 1906 the progressivity of the tax was

[8] V. S. Diakin, *Germanskie kapitaly v Rossii* (Leningrad, 1971); P. R. Gregory, "The Russian Balance of Payments, the Gold Standard, and Monetary Policy: A Historical Example of Foreign Capital Movements," *Journal of Economic History*, 39 (1979):379-400 (Gregory's unpublished technical appendix shows he relied either directly or indirectly on Ol', though he seemed unaware of the common source; McKay, *Pioneers*; V. V. Lebedev, *Russko-amerikanskie ekonomicheskie otnosheniia (1900-1917 gg.)* (Moscow, 1964).

[9] *Promyshlennost' i torgovlia*, December 15, 1912, p. 254; January 1, 1915, p. 20.

[10] Crisp, "Financial Aspects," pp. 213-15; "French Investment in Russian Joint-Stock Companies, 1894-1914," *Business History*, 2 (1960):87; McKay, *Pioneers*, p. 41; W. L. Blackwell, *The Beginnings of Russian Industrialization, 1800-1860* (Princeton, 1968), pp. 251-52; P. A. Orlov, *Ukazatel' fabrik i zavodov evropeiskoi Rossii* (St. Petersburg, 1881), p. 367.

[11] The flat rate was introduced for some corporations in 1885, extended in 1887, and raised from 3 to 5 percent as of 1893. *Svod zakonov rossiiskoi imperii* 5 (1885), no. 2664; 7 (1887), no. 4898; 22 (1892), no. 9181.

[12] L. E. Shepelev, "Aktsionernoe uchreditel'stvo v Rossii," *Iz istorii imperializma v Rossii* (Leningrad, 1959), p. 151. Also Shepelev, *Aktsionernye kompanii v Rossii* (Leningrad, 1973).

increased sharply, the marginal rates reaching 24 percent on profits that exceeded 16 percent of nominal capital.[13] To reduce taxes, a company only needed to increase its capital. Thus in the period 1898-1900, when the number of new corporations being formed was dropping and the number of liquidations rising, there was a greater expansion in nominal capital of existing corporations than in all the years from 1874 to 1898. In 1906, 1907, and 1908, after the tax rates were increased, expansion of nominal capital exceeded the nominal capital of new corporations; in 1912 and 1913, after Russian industrial output—and presumably profits—had begun a period of rapid growth, capital expansions reached the remarkable level of about 350 million rubles in each year.[14] Between 1911 and 1914, the nominal value of all corporate shares increased 55.6 percent.[15] If this value had been translated into real growth in corporate output, which accounted for perhaps half of Russian industrial activity, it would imply that there were no other sources of funds, be they bonds sold by Russian corporations, bank loans, internal financing, or growth among the nearly 40,000 unincorporated industrial enterprises.[16] But few Russian corporations or registered share partnerships in fact sold shares publicly.[17] Shepelev estimates that, at most, 35 percent of the nominal value was real investment.[18] Nominal capital values thus reflect more about the legal and tax environment than about real patterns and rates of investment.

Even if Ol''s procedure recorded accurately the changing pattern of foreign ownership or even investment, confirming a dramatic increase in those characteristics during the 1890s, this would not demonstrate that such activity generated a new flow of capital into Russia. Only an analysis of Russian balance of payments can reveal the net contribution of foreign capital to Russian development. Such an exercise—developed in detail in another essay elsewhere—for the period 1861 to 1914, using 1883 as the base year, suggests that between 1887 and 1897 accumulation of gold reserves effectively offset all foreign investment. If Russia had elected to hold a constant reserve of gold and returns on equity investments were

---

[13] *Svod zakonov*, 18 (1898), no. 15601; 26 (1906), no. 27178; 28 (1908), no. 30056; 29 (1909), no. 32837; 31 (1912), no. 36254; F. fon Tsur-Miulen, *Poloshenie o gosudarstvennom promyshlovom naloge . . . ,* 8th ed. (St. Petersburg, 1913), pp. 778-92, 1018-23, 1027-28.

[14] Shepelev, "Aktsionernoe," pp. 140-43.

[15] *Sbornik svedenii o . . . aktsionernykh obshchestvakh . . .* (St. Petersburg, 1914), p. vii.

[16] Gindin found Ol''s figures inconsistent with the volume of activity of commercial banks and concluded that Ol' substantially overstated the inflow of foreign capital. I. F. Gindin, *Kommercheskie banki* (Moscow, 1948), p. 403.

[17] The tax law created a clear incentive for companies attempting to raise capital through public markets to place shares rather than bonds.

[18] Shepelev, "Aktsionernoe," p. 305.

10 percent, it would have been a net exporter of capital in every one of those years; if Russia had elected to accumulate reserves at only half the pace it actually did accumulate gold, and equity returns were 20 percent, it would also have been a net exporter on balance for that ten-year period. Under varying assumptions of return on equity investments, with or without changing Russia's gold reserves, the dramatic periods of net imports of capital came, if ever, before and after the years of the Witte program.[19]

If the Witte program did not apparently succeed in attracting new capital resources to Russia, it may nevertheless have attracted the other two elements of enterprise—personnel and technique—which Witte sought. (Perhaps Witte understood Hymer's proposition that the three elements of enterpise normally only move together.[20]) Statistics of foreign ownership and investment—even of the balance of payments—can say little about such matters. Though not definitive, consideration of those British firms and individuals active in Russia for which I have uncovered records may throw some light on the general questions of timing, motivation, impact, and duration of foreign participation in Russian economic life.

Notes on British Enterprise in Russia

The traditional picture of the distribution of foreign enterprise in Russia puts it predominantly in the high profile growth sectors, specifically mining and metallurgy, engineering, municipal development (principally various utilities and urban transportation), and credit institutions (banks and insurance companies). The highest ranking traditional sector was textiles, allegedly taking only 8.6% of foreign ownership. Ol' shows the British holding down second place with Rs. 507,479,800 or 22.6% of foreign ownership of corporate assets, compared to Rs. 731,746,600 (32.6%) for the French and Rs. 441,593,200 (19.7%) for the German. Ol' argued 60.6% British capital was devoted to mining. Within that broad category, ownership of oil companies accounted for well over half, with copper, gold, silver, and lead mining taking another third. Textiles ranked a distant second, accounting for only 13.7% of British ownership.[21] The British register of Russian claims shows a rather different picture, both in quantity and in industry distribution. Total British claims registered with the Board of Trade were three times larger than Ol''s

[19] I am working with Randall Olson on this study. The numbers presented are from our initial estimates from a simple model of Russian balance of payments.

[20] S. H. Hymer, *The Multinational Corporation: A Radical Approach* (Cambridge, 1979), p. 139.

[21] Ol', *Inostrannye kapitaly v Rossii*, passim.

estimate, exceeding 1.7 billion rubles.[22] The Board of Trade itself thought that at least half of these claims were legitimate. Among these legitimate claims, textiles ranked first. British individuals and firms had controlled 37 textile firms in Russia, not the 20 that Ol' found. Moreover, the British claims of Rs. 221,364,000 are larger than Ol''s estimate of the total foreign ownership in textile firms. Much of the balance of British claims was distributed among engineering firms, saw- and papermills, soap and oil mills, distributing trade, and other commercial enterprises.[23] The information available for these firms suggests that many were involved in the Russian market before the Witte program was articulated; most came to Russia because of market opportunities that lay principally in the traditional, autonomous sphere of the Russian economy. It would appear the government rarely had much direct influence on the decisions of British entrepreneurs to come to Russia.

DE JERSEY AND THE KNOOPS

The preeminent source of British influence in Russian textile development was Ludwig Knoop, Bremen-born agent of de Jersey, who came to Russia in 1839 at the age of only eighteen. De Jersey was a major exporter of Manchester's yarns and already had a market among Russian weavers. Knoop, a man of unusual personal charm and business acumen, quickly established close contact with Moscow's leading merchants and industrialists. In 1841 he met Savva Morozov, scion of what would be Russia's leading textile family. Knoop ultimately got Morozov both credit and textile machinery from de Jersey. Soon Knoop was the one man with whom anyone wanting to work in cotton textiles needed to deal; he could provide the credit, machinery, plants, and skilled and supervisory workers recruited from England. In 1857 Knoop himself began construction of his own Krenholm mill in Narva. Before his death in 1894, Ludwig Knoop would be credited with establishing almost two-thirds of Russia's textile mills, 120 in all.[24]

It is normally assumed that Knoop operated primarily for himself after the first few years and that his sons did not take an active role in the Moscow textile industry. However, the Knoops always kept their affiliation with de Jersey. In 1917 de Jersey held a £S 6 million interest in twelve Russian textile mills, all Knoop-associated properties. De Jersey itself had sent William Hannay, son-in-law of London merchant banker Robert Fleming, to Memphis in about 1900 to operate a cotton-purchasing syndicate to supply Krenholm and other Knoop mills. Moreover,

[22] Evelyn Hubbard to Department of Overseas Trade, September 23, 1921, Public Record Office, Foreign Offices Series 371, V6928: N1600/9395/38 (hereafter, PRO: FO—:V—).
[23] Ibid.
[24] A. P. Buryshkin, *Moskva kupecheskaia* (Moscow, 1914), pp. 61-64.

de Jersey handled all of the Knoop orders for machinery and recruited all technical and some commercial staff for the Russian mills from English textile centers. Though de Jersey and the Knoops were not, after the turn of the century, involved in development of new mills in Russia, they remained active in the development of their Russian properties.[25] Moreover they apparently continued to recruit English staff for other mills, including the Morozovs'.[26]

J & P COATS

J & P Coats was already a multinational enterprise, with marketing and manufacturing operations on both sides of the Atlantic by 1865, when it first became interested in the Russian thread market. By 1884 the company's representatives had penetrated as far as the Irbit fair and net sales revenue was over Rs. 1.25 million a year. The business was such that the Glasgow management decided to have its own Moscow house to supervise and push the trade. The following year a second agency was added in St. Petersburg. The business was so successful that, with an increasingly threatening tariff environment, Glasgow began considering local manufacture by 1887. The first purchase of land and a small mill were completed in 1889. Coats quickly solidified its position with additional purchases of minority but strong holdings in three competing thread mills. Coats owned none of its Russian mills outright, but it had effective control over operations and handled all sales. By 1907 it had twenty Russian central agencies and perhaps two-thirds of the Russian thread market; its factories were by far the largest thread mills in Russia, employing over 9,000 hands, producing well over Rs. 20 million worth of thread annually, representing an investment of £S 8 million.[27]

Though the record on Coats is, like so many others, thin, it seems clear that movement into manufacturing was the natural strategy to protect an already developed Russian market. The management did clearly see the danger in the unpredictable but increasingly protectionist tariffs; only to that extent did government policy influence its decision. And like other

[25] De Jersey & Co., Ltd. to Comptroller General, Dept. of Overseas Trade, August 15, 1921. PRO: FO 371: V 6874: N9813/62/38. Interview with A. S. Redmen, retired de Jersey employee, London, September 1974.

[26] Interview with Redmen. He claimed that all Knoop mills were staffed by recruits that de Jersey sent from England. Such international reference networks were long common to British textile suppliers. See J. S. Fforde, *An International Trade in Managerial Skills* (Oxford, 1957).

[27] J P Coats, Ltd., to Foreign Office, November 28, 1921; PRO: FO 371: V 6928: N13130/9395/38; *Russian Review*, August 1936, p. 42; V. Ia. Laberychev, *Monopolisticheskii kapital v tekstil'noi promyshlennosti Rossii (1900-1917)* (Moscow, 1963), pp. 145-47.

British textile companies, Coats apparently continued to rely on imported managerial and technical workers for its Russian mills.

VORONIN, LUETSCHG & CHESHIRE

In 1868 a domestic weaver by the name of Cheshire left Manchester to join a Russian cloth merchant, J. A. Voronin. Cheshire undertook to weave imported English yarns; Voronin sold the unfinished gray cloth at fairs and through retail merchants. The firm was increasingly successful through the 1870s, and expanded into spinning on the one hand and finishing on the other. By the end of the nineteenth century Cheshire's grandson, Charles Cheshire, was a leading Russian textile merchant. The Cheshire family owned seven textile mills: the Viborg Side Spinning Mill, Nicholskii Weaving Mill, Vassili-Ostrov Print Works, the Sampson Spinning and Weaving Mills, the Resooi Ostrov and Petrogradskii Weaving Mills, and the Rochehusolmskii Spinning Mill. Because the Cheshire mills were, among other things, major suppliers of heavy cloth for the construction of the ubiquitous Russian rubber galoshes, Cheshire had also come to own a major share of Treygolnik Rubber in 1910 in lieu of accounts due.[28]

From what little is known, the Cheshires appear to follow a pattern typical of British families in Russia. They themselves retained close ties to the traditional family roots in the Manchester area; they relied on an all-English technical staff in their mills right to the Revolution, though they always kept the commercial side in the hands of Russians, as it was with Voronin. Their claim of £S 1.2 million (Rs. 11.4 million) for their factories with 100,000 spindles, 4,000 looms, and 16 printing machines was third largest,[29] behind only J & P Coats and de Jersey.

W. & T. FLETCHER; SIMON MAY & COMPANY

In Hamburg, in 1842, Simon May and Phillip Simon organized a small mercantile house specializing in textiles. It quickly found good markets for lace and concentrated increasingly on that good. Because of the principal source of supply of lace was Nottingham, Jacob Weinberg moved there in 1849 to open a branch. Over the next three decades the firm remained headquartered in Hamburg; in 1886, with the death of the last partner still in Hamburg, the firm shifted headquarters permanently to Nottingham. In the following decades Simon May established itself as the premier lace-trading house in the world. It played a leading role in spreading both the product and its production to France, South America, Canada, the United States, and Russia.

---

[28] Based on interview with William Cheshire, September 1974.
[29] Ibid.

While still a Hamburg firm, in 1876, Simon May began selling lace into Russia. It was so successful that by the mid-1880s Paul Meyer, managing partner in Nottingham, began to look for a manufacturer who would build a Russian factory to supply Simon May's existing sales organization there. William and Thomas Fletcher had separated from their father's lace business in 1871 to establish their own mill. Over the next decade and a half they were increasingly successful, and unquestionably were in regular and close contact with Simon May. In 1887 the brothers, with financial assistance from Simon May, established a lace mill in Moscow. The mill remained a Fletcher operation until the Revolution; its skilled lace designers and lace makers apparently were all English. Throughout, Simon May apparently handled all marketing.[30]

Paul Meyer, besides inducing the Fletchers to undertake the Moscow venture, visited Russia fifty-six times in the 1880s and 1890s to promote the trade. By 1894 Simon May carried accounts with 164 Moscow merchants and with 1,165 merchants in other Russian cities and towns; by 1914 the total number of accounts had grown to 1,443. Simon May had twenty-two travelers in the field to serve these merchants; total sales reached Rs. 4 million. Between 1909 and 1914, the only years for which information is available, profits averaged close to 5 percent on sales.[31]

FRANK REDDAWAY & COMPANY

In 1872, eighteen-year-old Frank Reddaway developed a new procedure for making the "perfect woven hose." Existing machinery could not reproduce his process, so it took Reddaway several years to develop a commercially viable hose. By the late 1870s, he was selling the only fire hose that contemporary pumpers could not burst. In the meantime Reddaway had developed high quality industrial belting made from camel hair. The success of this product was such that Reddaway, even before the successful development of his hose, was looking for foreign markets. In 1876 he already had a primary European branch office in Hamburg and a subordinate branch in Stockholm.

By the early 1880s Reddaway's success in weaving and marketing compound cloths led him to seek new markets. In 1883 he himself visited Russia, "travelling through the country . . . , examining into the capabilities of various towns and centres for consumption of goods" made at Manchester. In 1884 he opened a branch office in Moscow. "By continuous personal attention to Russian requirements," Reddaway developed "a business large enough to induce" him to begin domestic manufacturing. Such a step would both avoid the heavy import duties

[30] Based on private letterpress books and ledgers of Simon, May & Co., Ltd., Nottingham. Inspected by author, September 1974.
[31] Ibid.

on his products and permit a more extensive development of the Russian market. In 1887 Reddaway bought fifteen acres at Spass Setun, near Moscow, for his new Russian works. Originally capitalized at Rs. 600,000, Reddaway, by the early 1890s, had put nearly Rs. 4 million into the development of the works. It made machinery belting, hose piping, table covers and, chiefly, a specially impregnated heavy duck used to cover railway cars, as well as a "very flexible oilcloth table covering" popular with the peasantry. Simultaneously Reddaway built a large marketing organization, employing 250 people with offices and warehouses at Moscow, St. Petersburg, Ekaterinburg, Saratov, Baku, Kiev, Rostov, and the Nizhni Novgorod and Irbit fairs. Reddaway himself visited Russia two or three times a year, spending four to six weeks working at the mill or with the sales force.[32]

In the early years the factory relied on skilled workers brought from Lancaster and Manchester. "The brighter Russians proved very adept pupils and became highly skilled, even in hand block printing" used for special oilcloth products. Thus Russians replaced many of the skilled English workers, but most key workers, foremen, and supervisors were English.[33]

From the mid-1890s to 1914 the Russian operations generated fairly even profits of £S 25,000 to £S 30,000 (Rs. 236,000-284,000), about a 6 percent return.[34]

THOMAS FIRTH & SONS

Firth, a leading Sheffield hardware manufacturer, sent its first foreign representative, James Fretwell, to Russia about the middle of the nineteenth century. Changing his name to Freshville, he established offices in St. Petersburg and began developing the market for Firth's files and tool steel. Firth maintained its market position for the next several decades, ultimately having separate St. Petersburg agents for engineering and manufacturing consumers on the one hand and merchant business on the other; a third agency handled Moscow and environs. By the early 1890s Firth was looking at the potential of the growing south Russian market; a company director persuaded John Crookston, a Briton then resident in Odessa, to take the company's agency.

Development of Russian sales reached the point by the late 1890s that Firth began to examine the feasibility of local manufacture of tool steel for files. The company first purchased a small works in Riga in 1901. The continuing rapid expansion of sales apparently kept the company

[32] Frank Reddaway papers, privately held, Newcastle upon Tyne. Inspected, September 1974.
[33] Ibid.
[34] Ibid.

alive to the potential for future expansion. When, in 1903, the partially completed Salamander Steel Works, just outside Riga and adjacent to a J & P Coats thread mill, went bankrupt and was offered at auction, Firth bought the plant.

With the acquisition of these works, company management gave the Russian market special recognition: Crookston was appointed manager at Riga and made special company director for Russia. When finished in 1907, Salamander's file factory was "undoubtedly the largest and best equipped in Europe." Its products were sold in Russia, Siberia, Persia, and Manchuria. Demand expanded so swiftly, the company's historian claims, that Sheffield had to help meet the flood of orders. After 1908 Firth expanded the works with the addition of two shell shops, which made armor-piercing artillery shells for the Russian government. For both the file plant and the shell shops Firth relied on British engineers and managers, with the exception of one Polish engineer; skilled workers came out to Riga to train local workmen.[35]

RICHARD W. CARR & COMPANY

Carr was a latecomer to Russia. Three colleagues, who had served their apprenticeships together, organized the firm in Sheffield in September 1902. The previous summer they had visited Russia together. Their collective belief in the potential of the Russian market for tool steel provided the motivation for organizing the company. After securing crucible-melting furnaces and a file works in Sheffield, the new firm registered its "Car" trademark—the outline of an automobile—in Russia. To facilitate development of the Russian trade, Carr & Company built a small steelworks outside Moscow in 1904; stocks of tool steels were carried in Moscow, Warsaw, and Lodz.[36]

R. SMITH & COMPANY, MOSCOW.

Richard Smith was born August 11, 1824, in West Arthurlie, Renfrewshire, the eldest of eight children. At sixteen he went to Greenock to serve an apprenticeship in boilermaking and shipbuilding. Joining other Scottish and English craftsmen, he sailed for St. Petersburg in September 1847 to take charge of a small ironworks. In March 1848, he moved to the government's railway works to supervise steam-engine construction for the Nikolaevski Railway. For eight years Smith managed the locomotive works at Kolpino; in 1856 he decided to set up his own business in Moscow. On lands next to the Danilovski Sugar Refinery, close to the Moskva River, Smith built his boiler works. His father and

---

[35] *The History of Firth's* (privately printed, 1924), pp. 84-96.
[36] Pamphlet history of Richard W. Carr & Co., given author by firm, 1974.

younger brother James soon joined him. The Smiths would run this works through three generations.[37]

Little exact information on the firm is available. Until the 1890s it concentrated almost exclusively on production of larger steam boilers and the large, cylindrical, vertical fuel-storage tanks. The steam boilers, Cornish (single-flue) and Lancashire (double-flue) types, were comparatively high pressure boilers used as primary power plants for factory machinery. Beginning in the early 1890s, as demand for these boilers fell off, the construction of multistory apartment buildings in Russia's emergent urban centers created a new market for low-pressure boilers for hot water or steam-heating systems.[38]

At its largest, Smith & Company employed perhaps two hundred men. The welders, the plant's highest skilled workers, were, by the end of the century, all Russian. Richard Smith had brought three experienced welders from Britain soon after he founded the company; they trained Russians for the work. By 1902 the plant embraced five sections: power plant, heavy machine shop, welding and blacksmith shop, boiler shop, and light machine shop. Sometime between 1870 and 1880 Richard Smith apparently won a gold medal at a Moscow exhibition for the quality of his Cornish boilers; he claimed in a letter home to Greenock that his works were better than any in Scotland, as fine as any in England.[39]

Apparently the Smiths, who always remained British citizens, returning regularly to visit relatives, sending sons back for quality English public-school education, developed their Russian enterprise entirely on the basis of the accumulated income first from the work at Kolpino, then from the growing boiler works itself.[40] By maintaining their British ties they kept in touch with the evolving technology in boiler construction; they needed to import neither financial nor human capital to augment their own.

MORGAN CRUCIBLE COMPANY

Morgan Crucible, a manufacturer of graphite crucibles, graphite brushes, and other fireproof industrial wares, had developed enough Russian trade in crucibles by 1909 to have a resident agent, Frank Thompson, in St. Petersburg. On November 23, three directors of the English company and Thompson signed a partnership agreement to establish a firm to manufacture and sell graphite products. In July one of the partners had purchased 1,738 square fathoms of land on the Vyborg Quay facing the Bolshaya Nevka River; on December 15 the partnership took control of

---

[37] Autobiography by Henry Smith, manuscript. Given author, 1975.
[38] Ibid.
[39] Ibid.
[40] Ibid.

this land, immediately beginning construction of a crucibles factory. Once established in the crucible market, Morgan began pushing its graphite brushes as well. By 1912 sales were approaching perhaps Rs. 30,000, enough to justify adding a brush factory to the crucible factory. In 1915, the first year for which complete figures exist, sales of crucibles reached Rs. 2.7 million, sales of brushes over a quarter million, returning a handsome net profit on sales of 28.33 percent.[41]

A. M. LUTHER AND VENESTA LIMITED

In Reval sometime in the 1880s, Christian Luther saw a three-ply American chair seat in a store window. With his brother, Carlos, he soon developed a lathe to cut such veneers and reproduce the plywood. Thus, Venesta later would claim, the plywood industry was born in Europe. But the plywood would fall apart in rain, which made plywood chair seats unusable in open cafes. Carlos Luther determined to develop a casein-based waterproof adhesive. Soon Luther registered a patent for his successful glue in every major European country.

Meantime, in London E. H. Archer was building a specialty trade of tea chests made of thin metal sheets. Though successful by 1895 in providing chests for carrying tea from Ceylon and India to European blenders and grocers, the boxes were of no subsequent value—the blenders and grocers could not even burn them. When Archer came across American plywood, he thought he could use it for his chests, but the samples he got in London were not waterproof, their glues dissolved quickly. A little research brought Archer and Luther together; Archer provided the £S 20,000 to build a tea-chest board factory in Reval for the Luthers to operate. The Venesta tea chest was immediately successful; Venesta Limited came into being January 15, 1898.

Venesta did not confine itself to the tea-chest trade. It sought ways of extending the market for plywood products. To this end Venesta set up a sample shop near their factory in Limehouse, which helped convince first motorcar builders and then railways and shipbuilders of plywood's usefulness. Venesta also helped spread the use of cheaper plywoods into the furniture trade. In 1907 Venesta built its own large English factory for cutting veneers. And in 1909 A. M. Luther added a major factory at Staraya Rossiya in the Novgorod area. By 1912 the business of the two companies reached nearly £S 1 million per year, with Luther doing primarily manufacturing, Venesta handling sales, which were predominantly in Western Europe and South Asia. The two companies then decided on

[41] Morgan Crucible Company papers, Morgan Crucible Co., Ltd., London. Inspected, September 1974.

a formal reorganization: Luther became a wholly owned subsidiary of Venesta.[42]

The relationship here between British enterprise and Russian development is unusual: the Luthers provided the technical and manufacturing skill, Venesta provided the capital and the marketing skills.

R & T ELWORTHY, GEL'FERICK-SADE, AND JOHN GREAVES & COMPANY

British enterprise occupied an unusually strong position in the Russian agricultural-implement industry. Apparently this position grew out of Britain's early dominance in the importation of more sophisticated agricultural machinery between 1855 and 1880. Ransomes, Sims and Jeffries was selling its portable agricultural engines in Russia by 1856. It established its first exclusive agency in Odessa in 1857 and opened its own Moscow office in 1868. Ransomes maintained its commercial presence in Russia until 1914, but apparently it never contemplated moving into domestic manufacture.[43]

Clayton and Shuttleworth had similarly built a trade from at least the 1870s in its engines and threshers. Before undertaking any manufacturing investment in Russia it had already established a branch factory in Vienna. In 1902, in the face of what it saw as an increasingly unstable tariff environment, Claytons purchased a 31 percent interest in the old, established firm of Gel'ferick-Sade.[44] Founded as a merchant house in 1853 by a German-born trader, it had acquired knowledge of the agricultural-implement trade through its agencies for Marshalls and Ransomes as well as Claytons. In 1879 it established its own agricultural-implement factory in Kharkov.[45] It had, however, continued principally as a merchant house selling others' goods, including serving as Claytons' principal Russian agent. Purchase of the substantial minority position gave Claytons an assurance both that unanticipated tariff changes would not block it from the Russian market and that Gel'ferick-Sade would not itself abandon Claytons and commence all its own manufacturing. Claytons soon selected an English manager for the Russian operations.[46] By 1914,

---

[42] Ms. history of Venesta International, Ltd. Literally retrieved from the trash bin of the bankruptcy trustee, August 1978.

[43] Ransomes Company papers, Reading University Archives; R. Munting, "Ransomes in Russia: An English Agricultural Engineering Company's Trade with Russia to 1917," *Economic History Review*, vol. 31 (1978):2, pp. 257-69.

[44] Clayton & Shuttleworth records, with Marshall Sons & Company papers, Lincolnshire Records Office.

[45] *Ukazatel' deisvuiushchikh v imperii aktsionernykh predpriiatii i torgovykh domov* (St. Petersburg, 1905), "opolnitel'nyia svendiia . . . ," pp. 110-11.

[46] Clayton & Shuttleworth records.

Gel'ferick-Sade was the fourth ranking implement manufacturer in Russia.[47]

The second ranking manufacturer was also an English firm, R & T Elworthy & Company. Thomas Elworthy, who presumably came to Russia late in the 1860s or early in the 1870s to work in the implement trade, established his own repair shop in 1874. In 1907 his sons incorporated what had become a substantial factory. By 1913 they employed over two thousand workers, produced more than Rs. 5 million worth of implements, and had a retail organization of twenty-eight stores.[48]

Similarly John Greaves, whose firm ranked fifth in Russia, began in that country with just a trading house. In 1883 he established his own factory in Berdiansk to provide some of his own goods. In 1899 he reorganized his company under Belgian law, in part apparently to avoid some Russian corporate profits tax.[49]

The pattern of British expansion from the implement trade into manufacturing was also the pattern for Russia's largest manufacturer and seller of farm machinery, the International Harvester Company.[50] In each case manufacturing was, first, the natural development from an established trade, and, second, the obvious device to provide some assurance both to foreign manufacturers like Claytons and to domestic traders like Greaves and Elworthy that they would have supplies of implements for their sales organizations.

Observations

Case studies provide a test of the general characterizations of the role of the state in attracting foreign enterprise to Russia. Though the record is far thinner than would be desirable, it seems clear that British participation in textiles, agricultural implements and boiler manufacture both antedates the widely proclaimed programs of the Witte period and was a response primarily to the potential of the Russian mass market, not to government enticements. In textiles, de Jersey and Knoop served as the primary actor, helping presumably to recruit from Lancashire textile experts like J. S. Boon, who would work in Tver until the Revolution,

[47] *Zemledel'cheskaia gazeta*, no. 23 (1914):7.

[48] *Sbornik svedenii*, p. 176; *Adresnaia kniga zavodov, masterskikh i skladov sel'skhoziaistvennykh mashin i orudii* (St. Petersburg, 1912), passim.

[49] R. R. Dennis, *American Agricultural Implements in Foreign Markets* (Washington, D.C., 1913), p. 69; *Fabrichnozavodskiia predpriiatiia rossiiskoi imperii* (St. Petersburg, 1914), no. 896B.

[50] Fred V. Carstensen, "American Multinational Enterprise in Imperial Russia" (Ph.D. dissertation, Yale University, 1976), provides a case study of International Harvester (forthcoming from University of North Carolina Press, *American Enterprise in Foreign Markets: Studies of Singer and International Harvester in Imperial Russia*).

Edwin Lunn at Balashikha, the Charnock brothers at Ivanovo Vosnes-sensk, the Ratcliffes at Bogorodsko Gloukhovo, Charles Hastie and others at Moscow. Later, the J. M. Sumner Company would supplement de Jersey's activities, providing machinery, credit, and English textile work-ers.[51] Clearly, Reddaway and Fletcher began Russian production to pro-tect and develop further established markets. The Hubbard family had been trading in Russia for sixty-seven years before it began developing its spinning, weaving, and prints mills from 1842.[52] In the flax industry, another English firm played the role that de Jersey played in cotton textiles; White, Child and Beney provided, from the late 1870s or early 1880s, the machinery and credit for Russian flax processors to develop their mills. By 1900 it found it needed a small Odessa factory to provide exhaust fans for its client flax mills.[53] A similar pattern of market de-velopment preceding manufacturing investment emerges in the agricul-tural-implement sector and in tool steel. Other British families, like the Millers and Gibsons at Nevski Stearine, the Hartleys in textiles and trading through Oborot, and Muir and Merrilees with their prestigious Moscow department store, came to Russia before 1860; their descendants maintained their enterprises right to the Revolution.[54]

That a substantial share of British participation in Russian economic life should have its roots in the autonomous sphere is hardly surprising. Many of these firms sold goods—textiles, candles, farm implements, boil-ers—for which the government orders did not constitute a substantial market share. Moreover, businessmen normally must acquire commercial knowledge—what and where to sell—in order to be successful. Acqui-sition of commercial knowledge about the development of markets in Russia would lead to manufacturing. The government is not unimportant in this process: its provision of legal services, maintenance of a monetary system, and promotion of internal transportation development help cre-ate a wider effective market area in which business can operate. Its manipulation of tariff schedules also induced firms to protect their po-sition with manufacturing facilities. As the size and attractiveness of the Russian market expanded from the 1840s to the 1900s, it continued to attract additional British enterprises.

In most cases British enterprise appears to have been beneficial for Russian development. It brought new products and the skills necessary to produce them. Though there was a remarkable persistence of English managerial and technical personnel in virtually every industry in which

[51] Henry Smith, ms. autobiography.

[52] *Times Russian Supplement*, no. 1, December 15, 1911, n.p.

[53] Information provided in private correspondence by author with White, Child & Beney, Ltd., Manchester, July 1978.

[54] *Times Russian Supplement*, no. 1, December 15, 1911, n.p.

the British were active, they nevertheless attempted—successfully in most cases—to transfer a substantial share of skill to native workers. Only the highest positions—chief carder and weaver, factory engineer, lace designer—remained predominantly British through 1914.[55]

The case studies presented remind us of the diversity and long presence of foreign enterprise in Russian economic life and development; they remind us how Russia, as with all developing countries, needed to import a wide range of human skills. Indeed, the persistence and continuity of British involvement suggest that neither the Witte program of the 1890s nor the subsequent emergence of aggressive Russian commercial banks played such a prominent role in reshaping or displacing foreign participation. Possibly the relative weight of foreign enterprise declined after 1906, but in an expanding economy, the question would not necessarily be one of replacing foreign with domestic entrepreneurs, nor would it imply an inherent shift of foreigners into a passive investor role. Equally important, that so much of the British activity was in those consumer-goods industries in which Britain was the traditional leader argues for differentiating among foreign actors by both national origin and economic sector. The growing literature on multinational enterprise already recognizes the importance of these distinctions and the clearly differentiated patterns for British, American, German, and French firms. The construction of a full typology of foreign enterprise (indeed, as Thomas Owen's chapter suggests, of domestic enterprise as well) would provide a much clearer picture of such activity and give fuller recognition to its sectoral, spatial, and temporal patterns. Finally, the strong concentration of the firms discussed here in the consumer-goods sector argues for the robustness of the nongovernmental or autonomous sector of the Russian economy. That foreign entrepreneurs should find the Russian market so attractive invites a broad reconsideration of the presumed necessity of massive government intervention. Perhaps Russian economic welfare would have been better served by state policies designed to strengthen and expand this autonomous sphere, particularly by policies intended to enhance the growth of domestic enterprise, than it was by Witte's concentration on selected heavy industries.

[55] Ibid.; R. M. Odell, *Cotton Goods in Russia* (Washington, D.C., 1912), *passim*.

IX

RUTH AMENDE ROOSA   *Russian Industrialists during World War I: The Interaction of Economics and Politics*

The outbreak of World War I came at a critical time for the Russian industrialists. Their relations with a government that appeared to them to be singularly unsympathetic to their problems were strained as they had not been since 1905, while longstanding tensions with the landowning and laboring classes were also rapidly increasing in severity. Underlying these difficulties, but by no means explaining their source, which lay deeply imbedded in the Russian entrepreneurial past, was the new period of industrial expansion that began in 1910—a period marked by shortages in key industrial commodities, spiraling prices, and a growing militancy in the labor force. Nothing could better illustrate the interaction of economics and politics, even in such an autocratic state as was tsarist Russia, than the problems associated with this period of rapid economic growth. Charges, not wholly unjustified, of speculation and monopolistic controls over output led both to an increase in the hostility toward industrial enterprise that was endemic in Russia among all other social elements and to officially enacted measures that constrained private enterprise. The response to these pressures included an increase in antigovernment feeling and a limited upsurge in political activity among the "trading industrialists," who, during the last two years of peace, became increasingly persuaded of the necessity for at least a modicum of political reform.

The outbreak of the war also found the industrialists intensely concerned with the question of Russia's economic future. Keenly aware of the threat to the empire's economic, and even political, independence that was posed by its increasing dependence on an expansionist Germany, the industrialists were convinced that the answer to most of Russia's manifold economic problems lay in the elaboration of a program for the broad development of the national economy. This program was also expected to provide the foundation for the enhancement of the empire's position as a great world power.

The industrialists with whom this chapter is concerned had as their organizational spokesman the empire-wide Association of Industry and Trade (*Sezd' Predstavitelei Promyshlennosti i Torgovli*). Founded in Petersburg in 1906 in the aftermath of the revolution of the preceding year and headed since July 1907 by N. S. Avdakov, the Association was made up of the many organizations based on regional, local, or specialized lines that represented large-scale industrial, and to a lesser extent commercial, enterprise. The most influential of these member organizations were those representing the coal and metallurgical interests of the south, the Baku oil industry, sugar production and, of course, the diverse forms of industrial enterprise in Petrograd and Moscow. Although the industrial interests of Petrograd, organized in their own Society of Mill and Factory Owners, were influential in the affairs of the Association, they were not, as has frequently been suggested, dominant. Moscow, the recognized center of the empire's business class (*kupechestvo*), had as its principal representatives the powerful Exchange Committee and the Society of Mill and Factory Owners of the Moscow Industrial Region.

Although the Association was commonly referred to as the organ of "united industry," there were many divisions within its membership based on conflicting economic, social, and political interests that were to play an important part in the history of Russian entrepreneurship during World War I. The scope of this chapter does not permit a discussion of these interrelationships, but no consideration of its major theme can be complete that does not include some attention to the distinctive part played by the liberal industrialists of Moscow. Under the tensions of wartime and impatient with the Association's conservative leadership, one influential element among the Moscow industrialists that centered on the liberal Progressist party was increasingly roused to assume leadership in the world of industry and trade and, indeed, in the Duma and in the country as a whole.

It has been customary not only for most historians but for much of Russia's prerevolutionary intelligentsia as well, regardless of political hue, to ascribe to the industrial bourgeoisie a fatal political weakness that was largely responsible for the ultimate success of the Bolsheviks. The industrialists, it is suggested, should have provided the nucleus for a strong and liberal middle class that would have been prepared, in the Western tradition, to assume the reins of political power. The industrialists were well aware of this criticism and stressed, in at least partial self-exoneration, their enforced dependence on the state and the difficulties that faced them in attempting to break loose from the many governmentally imposed constraints that limited their freedom of action in both the economic and political spheres. But the impact of the war and its related problems obliged even the Association to take a more positive stand on the political issues that confronted the country.

The outbreak of war was attended by an all-engulfing wave of patriotic sentiment that for the moment united government and people and gave to Russian tsardom its last great opportunity to forestall the approaching revolution. Strikes and labor unrest fell dramatically, and the burgeoning expressions of political discontent among the diverse elements in Russian society that had marked the immediate prewar period were suspended in the interest of a united war effort. The most optimistic among the businessmen also hoped that the war would spur the "authorities" to grant a measure of liberalizing reforms at once, and even the most pessimistic among them believed that a victory would assure the attainment of basic political reform after the peace. But the focus of their attention was upon the economic aspects of the war effort. Only later, when the Russian war economy was visibly foundering, did the industrialists turn in desperation, but still only with much hesitation, to political action.

Contrary to the usual portrayal, the Russian industrialists, with the exception of certain groups in Moscow, did not initially welcome the war with enthusiasm. On the contrary, they viewed the beginning of hostilities with much anxiety, painfully conscious as they were of Russia's unpreparedness and the country's heavy dependence on foreign, and especially German, sources of capital, techniques, and manufactured goods. Yet the prospect of winning a war with Germany was enticing, and after the early military victories a period of enthusiasm did burst into flame and burn brightly, if only briefly. It was during this wave of expansive optimism that the industrialists first declared that total victory over Germany was the only alternative to national ruin. It was, in fact, seen as necessary not only for the establishment of Russia as a truly great power in world affairs but also for the final attainment of the long-suppressed sociopolitical aspirations of the trading-industrial class: "The future is for us; for life moves forward and in place of the old there advances the new."[1] At the same time, fears that the government might be unwilling to carry the war to a successful conclusion were already a source of anxiety and of what was to become a continuing distrust of governmental intentions.

The Association met the practical demands of the war with sober realism. On July 24, 1914, N. S. Avdakov, its chairman, told the executive

---

[1] "Staroe i Novoe," *Promyshlennost' i Torgovlia* (hereafter cited as *PiT*), 24 (168), December 15, 1914, p. 575.

council of the organization that its work on national economic development "must inevitably be put aside and all efforts must be directed toward the tasks of the present day."[2] During the first weeks of war the organization foresaw with extraordinary accuracy what were to become the principal, and ultimately the fatal, problems of Russia's war economy. Indeed, it would seem that organized industry perceived the magnitude and complexity of the economic problems confronting Russia and the importance of the economic rear in modern warfare more clearly and more promptly than did the government itself.

Yet well before the end of 1914 and increasingly throughout the spring of 1915, industry was widely charged in the press and among the articulate public with an essentially unpatriotic, "business-as-usual" approach to the war effort. The explanation for this seeming contradiction is complex. Despite its keen awareness of the country's needs, industry probably did not appreciate the full magnitude of the effort that would be required to meet the demands of what was at first expected to be a brief war. Indeed, it was assumed that the maintenance of normal economic conditions was a part of industry's basic duty. Undoubtedly, the expectation of a short war also led to a reluctance of some industrialists to start expanding production rapidly. While speculation and profiteering certainly played a part, the innate hostility of much of the articulate public toward business enterprise undoubtedly also contributed to the low esteem with which the latter was commonly portrayed in the contemporary press.

But it was basically industry's unsatisfactory relationship with the government that accounted for its apparent lapse into a business-as-usual philosophy. This, too, had numerous facets. First, private industrial enterprise, with the limited exception of a few Petrograd arms manufacturers and some textile producers in the Moscow region, was kept from participating directly in the war economy. Orders for arms and munitions were heavily concentrated in state-owned factories and in relatively few of the largest private enterprises. The impact of this situation was aggravated by the fact that longstanding government policies, inimical to private entrepreneurial interests, continued to be pursued and, indeed, in some cases intensified. One such issue was that of "state socialism" and what the industrialists saw as a new official effort to expand the role of state-owned enterprise at their own expense. As early as September 17, 1914, *Industry and Trade*, the Association's journal, observed bitterly that in government circles "there is recommended a system of state socialism and repression of private enterprise."[3]

---

[2] "Dnevnik Soveta," *PiT*, 15 (159), August 1, 1914, pp. 132-33.

[3] *Tsentral'nyi gosudarstvennyi istoricheskii arkhiv* (hereafter cited as TsGIA), f. 32, op. 1, d. 23, ll., 117-22.

Most significant of all was the early failure of industry's effort to forge a cooperative relationship with the government for the promotion of the war effort. The industrialists, seeing an opportunity to advance their own class interests, broadly understood, acted quickly on the outbreak of the war to proclaim their hope of contributing "organizational and creative" work, in addition to productive activity, in cooperation with the government on behalf of victory. They confidently welcomed the opportunity that the war seemed to offer to win recognition as an "equal" and responsible partner with the government in confronting the national emergency. In this they were soon to be disillusioned. Indeed, these very initiatives, inspired also by genuinely patriotic motives, underlay the government's early distrust of entrepreneurial intentions and its fear of the political motives that might underlie the new assertiveness of the industrialists. Ultimately, this fear was transformed into a mutual distrust, which increasingly hampered the successful prosecution of the war effort.

The first weeks of war, however, were replete with organizational endeavors on the part of industry, which were apparently welcomed by the government in a seemingly remarkable atmosphere of official cooperation and good will. Frequent governmental conferences with industry's representatives were held, and committees, both joint and parallel, for the study and implementation of the economic tasks of wartime multiplied, most often on industry's initiative. These efforts proved, however, to be of brief duration and very limited success. In mid-September the Association, while noting the government's more favorable attitude toward organized industry, stressed the necessity of solidifying the relationship and assuring that industry's voice would indeed be taken into account in the formulation as well as in the implementation of economic policy. Moreover, governmental inefficiency and failure to pursue the task at hand with sufficient vigor were already giving rise to disquiet within industrial circles. Reflecting its uneasiness, the Association on September 12 endorsed a statement issued by the Society of Mill and Factory Owners of the Moscow Industrial Region, which asserted, "In general, in the opinion of trading-industrial Moscow, the government should devote much more attention to questions of industry and trade than it is doing at the present time."[4] Three days later, *Industry and Trade* pointed to "a certain lack of resolution" and the need for a more decisive approach to Russia's many pressing economic problems. While "the government listens very willingly to the statements of the industrialists and learns much about current problems, the tangle of artificially disrupted economic relations becomes more and more confused."[5] Clearly,

[4] Ibid., l. 114.
[5] "Ekonomicheskiia zadachi mirovoi voiny i russkaia promyshlennost'," *PiT*, 18 (162) September 15, 1914, p. 259.

mid-September marked a fatal turning point in industry's relations with the government. It was at once the peak of their short-lived improvement and the beginning of an inexorable downward course, interrupted only by an ultimately unsuccessful attempt at renewed cooperation that followed the establishment of the war-industries committees in May 1915.

Industry's retreat into an apparently business-as-usual philosophy followed the rejection of its hopes for participation in the formulation of wartime economic policies. Yet at the same time, the alarming decline in production in such key industries as coal and metallurgy, sparked in large part by shortages of skilled labor, attributable to overzealous conscription into the armed forces, and by the inadequacy and mismanagement of the empire's railroads, caused organized industry to voice increasing concern. Late in December the Association once more attempted to take a limited initiatve, to step into the void created by governmental inaction. In a memorandum addressed to the chairman of the Council of Ministers, it urged the adoption of emergency measures both to increase the supply of rolling stock and to counter the prevailing disorganization in transport services. It also created its own Special Conference on transport, which recommended the creation of an official Supreme Commission with extraordinary powers to deal with the situation.[6] No results were forthcoming, however, and the Association met the new year with its confidence in Russia's future badly eroded.

The first five months of 1915 were a time of steadily mounting embroilment between industry and the government. The emerging confrontation now began to assume political as well as economic aspects. Added to the many causes of industrial dissatisfaction was the growing, and ultimately critical, crisis in the supply of arms and munitions.

Already of serious concern to the highest military authorities in the fall of 1914, the existence of any shortage in this area was nevertheless persistently denied by government officials. On January 1 the government did establish the Special Regulatory Commission on Artillery, which was designed to coordinate action between the military authorities and the government organs that were responsible for the supply of war materials. Nevertheless, later in the month the war minister, V. A. Sukhomlinov, responding to inquiries by members of the Duma, again denied that any shortage existed. But despite the official posture of optimism, the increasingly critical position in military supplies, long suspected, became common knowledge during the first month of the new year. In part, this was a result of a visit to the front and to the headquarters of the commander in chief that was undertaken in late December by M. V. Rod-

---

[6] "Dnevnik Soveta," *PiT*, 1 (169), January 1, 1915, p. 54.

zianko, president of the Duma, and A. I. Guchkov, leader of the Octo-brists and a member of a prominent Moscow industrial family. While at headquarters, they informed the grand duke of the industrialists' urgent desire to begin the mobilization of industry in order to increase the country's output of arms and munitions. This met with a warm response from the commander, who had himself sent repeated appeals to the government for an increase in military production by private industry.

The beginning of the new year saw a renewed effort by the industrialists to initiate an organized joint effort on the part of private industry and the government on behalf of the war effort. After consultation with the major metalworking and machine-construction enterprises in the Pet-rograd area, the Association on January 12 sent to the Council of Min-isters a memorandum setting forth its suggestions for alleviating the approaching arms crisis. It proposed that orders for military materiel should be sent directly from the High Command to the large producing plants, rather than through the War Ministry as was currently the prac-tice. These plants, the number and location of which should be expanded beyond the narrow circle of Petrograd-based firms, should be empowered to allocate orders to smaller plants, which should be brought into the war-production effort. Skilled workers, technicians, and engineers should be released from military service for work in the plants. And, finally, it was recommended that a Special Council be established with broad su-pervisory powers over the allocation of orders and the organization of the entire production process, including the authority to assure priority in the supply of metals, fuel, and transportation facilities to firms engaged in war production. Soviet historians have rightly credited these proposals with directly inspiring the establishment by the government in May 1915 of the Special Council for the Coordination of Measures to Guarantee the Supply of Munitions and Other Materials to the Army, itself a pre-cursor of the Special Council on Defense that was established in August.[7] However, the Association's proposal was rejected by the Council of Min-isters and no official recognition was ever given to its suggestion.[8] Despite the failure of its effort to confront the developing arms-supply crisis, however, the mobilization of industry became the self-proclaimed slogan of the industrial leadership of the country.

[7] T. D. Krupina, "Politicheskii krizis 1915 g. i sozdanie osobago soveshchaniia po obo-rone," *Istoricheskie zapiski*, 83 (1969):59-62. The Association's initiative is also recognized by Lewis Siegelbaum in his unpublished doctoral dissertation, "The War-Industries Com-mittees and the Politics of Industrial Mobilization in Russia, 1915-1917" (Oxford), p. 32. A more traditional account, attributing the formation of the Special Council entirely to Rodzianko, is presented by Raymond Pearson in his *The Russian Moderates and the Crisis of Tsarism, 1914-1917* (London, 1977; and New York, 1977), p. 40.

[8] TsGIA, f. 1276, op. 11, d. 814, ll. 1-17. This also contains the text of the Association's memorandum.

But, at the same time, the Association's continued interest in Russia's economic future caused it to turn once again to its old project for national economic development, which it had put aside at the outbreak of the war. On January 3 the organization appointed a Special Commission, headed by Vice-Chairman V. V. Zhukovskii, to consider how best to promote Russia's long-term economic growth. The commission met regularly until the convening of the Ninth Congress of the Association in May, and the fruit of its labors was the monumental report *On Measures for the Development of the Productive Forces of Russia*.[9] The overall task was increasingly coupled with the specific problem of how best to cope with all the major economic problems that were now seen as likely to confront Russia in the postwar world. Indeed, as *Industry and Trade* had observed in its new-year issue: "Let us not forget that not only must the war be won . . . but it is necessary to utilize the economic results of the war."[10] In these thoughts the Association was not alone, as the connection between economic growth and national power became increasingly recognized by broad elements in Russian society. Particularly gratifying to the organization were the interest and concern for the nation's problems that were evinced by the legislature during its brief, three-day session at the end of January. *Industry and Trade* noted approvingly the words of the chairman of the Duma's Budget Commission, in which he called for a completely rejuvenated Russia after the war. Nevertheless, one consequence of the Association's concern for economic growth was a still further increase in derisive charges leveled by the general press at industry's allegedly business-as-usual approach to Russia's critical economic problems.

One significant outcome of the generally inconsequential legislative session was the evidence of its concern for the state of the Russian economy, which was manifested in its decision to create an Economic Conference (*Soveshchanie*) composed of one hundred or more members of the State Council for the purpose of conducting an ongoing discussion of economic issues. Among the twelve members of its presidium were N. F. fon Ditmar, head of the powerful Association of Southern Mine Owners, and S. P. Glezmer, chairman of the Petrograd Society of Mill and Factory Owners—both influential members of the All-Russian Association.[11] The former took an especially active part in the meetings of the Conference, as did Avdakov and other representatives from the business world.

[9] Sovet sezdov Predstavitelei Promyshlennosti i Torgovli, *Doklad Soveta o merakh k razvitiiu proizvoditel'nykh sil' Rossii* (Petrograd, 1915).

[10] "Blizhaishiia perspektivy i polozhenie promyshlennosti v 1914 godu," *PiT*, 1 (169) January 1, 1915, p. 5.

[11] *Rech'*, January 31, 1915, p. 5.

The spring of 1915 was a time of mounting trial for the industrialists, and the issues, largely connected with spiraling prices and growing shortages in fuel and transport, began to assume a political aspect. In the sudden dismissal in February of S. I. Timashev, minister of trade and industry since 1909, the dwindling supplies of coal that were reaching factories and urban centers were seen as the precipitating cause. Although his departure had long been anticipated and was not entirely unwelcome, its timing came as a surprise to the industrialists, who waited nervously to see what the new minister, Prince V. S. Shakhovskoi, would do. His background was not such as to instill confidence in the entrepreneurial world. At thirty-nine he was relatively young for the post; he had only a very limited experience in industrial affairs and his appointment was mainly welcomed in agrarian and nationalist circles. The industrialists' fears were soon realized. On February 28 Prince Shakhovskoi made known his intention of visiting the Donets Basin, and out of this investigatory journey came a major confrontation between the government and the entrepreneurial class.

The affair centered in the Economic Conference of the State Council and had its beginning at its meeting on March 26. At the two previous sessions fon Ditmar, with the full support of Avdakov, had presented reports which maintained that stocks of coal in the Basin were adequate for Russia's needs and that difficulties in supply stemmed almost entirely from the inadequacy and disorganization of railroad services. When Shakhovskoi took the floor he rejected the coal men's explanation, which had been received with sympathy by much of the Conference's membership, and attributed the problem instead to low levels of production, which he ascribed to labor shortages caused not by military conscription but by low wages and poor living conditions at the mines. A series of sharply worded debates between Shakhovskoi and members of the Conference ensued, concluding with the passage of a resolution fully supporting the representatives of the coal industry. During the course of these exchanges, the broader issue of the relationship between the government and private enterprise in general had also been raised. On April 1, the government acted; the Conference was abruptly dissolved by Goremykin.[12] The exceptional bitterness of this dispute left a lasting impression in trading-industrial circles, and perhaps it was not a coincidence that on the evening of April 1 Progressist members of the Duma, backed

---

[12] Ibid., March 24-27 and 29-31, and April 3, 1915. Cf. the account in Pearson (supra, n. 7), p. 32. The sources Pearson cites do not support his description of this episode, or the industrialists position in favor of industrial mobilization, as "a public relations exercise." In fact, the Economic Conference (or Commission) is not mentioned in one of the sources he refers to, namely S. O. Zagorsky, *State Control of Industry in Russia during the War* (New Haven, 1928), pp. 76-77, 82, and 87-88.

most notably by the liberal industrialists of Moscow, decided to begin a
campaign for the early recall of the legislature. Indeed, from that time
on, the industrialists were virtually unanimous in demanding the recall
of the Duma.

The nature of the problem was well illustrated by the disorganization
in railroad transport, which during the early months of 1915 was an
increasing cause for concern among the industrialists as well as among
the public at large. A month after the Association's fruitless approach to
the government in December, *Industry and Trade* printed an article
chronicling industry's efforts since 1906 to persuade the government of
the need to improve the supply and capacity of freight cars. Its concluding
words clearly attributed the current situation to political influences: "the
thickening, God forbid, of the political horizon brings in its wake a
complete blow to the economic organism."[13] The article led to an unofficial reply by the Ministry of Transport in a polemical article published
in the conservative *New Times* (*Novoe Vremia*), which flatly denied the
existence of any shortage in freight cars. *Industry and Trade* countered
with its own indignant article, which ended with a plea to the minister
to take action while it was still not too late.[14] There was no reply, and
the urgent petitions that the Association addressed to the government
later in the month and again in mid-March and in mid-April remained
unanswered.

Early in April the journal angrily addressed itself once again to the
question of Russia's economic crisis. While conceding that a measure of
self-criticism was called for on the part of industry, the article lamented
the closing of the Economic Conference and charged the daily press,
inspired by "political and personal motives and by demagoguery of the
most vicious hue," with a major responsibility for industry's unenviable
position in the public eye. But it was the government that was found to
be most responsible for the empire's now critical situation. While maintaining that the economy was fundamentally sound, the article also contended that a state of crisis indeed prevailed, attributable largely to mismanagement at the highest level.

The defeats on the Galician front revealed the full magnitude of the
arms and munitions crisis. Even the emperor himself and his war minister,
Sukhomlinov, were finally driven to conclude that Russia's position called
for drastic measures and that only cooperation between the government
and private industry could offer any hope of easing the critical shortages
in military supplies. The result was the creation early in May of the
Special Council on Supply chaired by the minister of war. Although

[13] R., "Razrukha zheleznodorozhnago khoziaistva," *PiT*, 3 (171) February 1, 1915, p.
130.
[14] "Otvet Ministerstvu Putei Soobshcheniia," *PiT*, 4 (172) February 15, 1915, p. 178.

Rodzianko claimed to have been its originator, its establishment, as has already been noted, has been traced by historians with remarkable unanimity to the Association's initiative in January.[15]

The first meetings of the Special Council were held on May 14 and 18, only shortly before the convening of the Ninth Congress of the Association on May 26. Included in its membership, in addition to representatives of the war and navy ministries, were four members of the Duma and three members of the Petrograd banking and industrial world—A. I. Putilov, A. I. Vyshnegradskii, and V. P. Litvinov-Falinskii (recently dismissed after long years as a high official in the Ministry of Trade and Industry), all of whom had close connections with the Association. At its third meeting on May 28, perhaps in an effort to appease the Congress, membership in the Council was expanded to include representatives from the ministries of finance and trade and industry as well as the State Control. Representation of banking and industrial interests was increased to eleven, all of whom were still drawn from the Petrograd area. The primary interests of the new members were in banking and finance, however, and their connections with the Association were slight.[16]

The establishment of the Special Council has been described by Soviet historians as a great victory for the industrialists. A. L. Sidorov, for example, observed that it gave them "the right to decide on a basis of equal rights all questions of material provision for the army."[17] It is true, of course, that the creation of the Council represented potentially a partial fulfillment of the hopes for an active share in the formulation of economic policies that the Association had nourished since the first days of the war. But it was far from a culmination of industry's highest hopes, and the industrialists' attitude toward the Council was mixed. The Association's more conservative elements, especially Avdakov, clearly hoped that the Council could be utilized as a channel for expanded industrial influence. But the fact that the representation of business interests on the Council was entirely drawn from the financial-industrial world of Pet-

[15] "Krushenie imperii," *Arkhiv Russkoi revoliutsii*, 17:92-95. The events leading up to the creation of the Special Council are extremely complex and the record is obviously incomplete. Cf. n. 7, above.

[16] G. A. Krestovnikov, the conservative chairman of the Moscow Exchange Committee, where he was soon to be replaced by the Progressist leader P. P. Riabushinskii, was apparently appointed as a member from the State Council but was unable to serve because of illness. The Council was no doubt very well aware of the state of his health, which had been highly publicized.

[17] A. L. Sidorov, "Bor'ba s krizisom vooruzheniia russkoi armii v 1915-1916 godakh," *Istoricheskii zhurnal*, nos. 10-11 (1944):42. Sidorov's statement is of questionable validity, not only in view of the subsequent history of the Special Council but also because all powers within the Council were concentrated in the hands of its chairman, the minister of war. Members of the Council were given only consultative votes.

rograd and consisted of men who were already engaged, directly and indirectly, in supplying the army could only have been a major source of irritation not only to Moscow and other industrial centers but to the Association itself, which had long preached the need to draw all of industrial Russia into the war effort. In fact, as Sidorov acknowledged, the industrialists "demanded a radical change in the existing relationship between the War Department and private enterprise," insisting "first of all on the broad participation not only of individual mills but of the whole of industry in work for the army, as well as on the composition of a plan of 'unified work by private mills.' "[18] Of equal concern was the fact that the rights and potential influence of the businessmen who were members of the Special Council were by no means clear, while even the place of the Council itself within the government was still at issue, as the Council of Ministers sought to subordinate it to its own control.

The Association had always been reluctant to engage in political discussion—a product, no doubt, both of governmental restraints imposed at the time of its founding in 1906 and of its own painful awareness that the industrialists were not a politically united class. But in mid-February growing public criticism of industry's apolitical stand combined with the mounting challenge from the government to extract from *Industry and Trade* carefully guarded statements with political implications. Baron G. Kh. Maidel', the director of the Association's secretariat, voiced industry's dissatisfaction with the government and its hopes for a change in political leadership as a product of military victory. Proclaiming the need for confidence in "the great Russian people" and its future destiny, he declared: "Let us have confidence that when the military threat is over, when the tasks of peaceful prosperity have come to the fore, there will be at the helm of the state new and strong men who will be capable of resolving the powerful demands of life."[19] Perhaps this emerging willingness to touch on the political aspects of Russia's problems reflected in some measure the growing influence of the Moscow Progressists and particularly of their leaders, A. I. Konovalov and P. P. Riabushinskii, both of whom were active members of the Association. Konovalov was also a member of the State Duma. Another prominent member of the organization, A. A. Bublikov, was also a Progressist (although not a Muscovite) and a member of the Duma.

Quite obviously, disillusionment with the political leadership of the country was also causing the industrialists to turn in increasing desperation to the commander in chief, Grand Duke Nikolai Nikolaevich, who had long supported their aspirations for an enhanced role in the war

[18] Ibid., pp. 41-42.

[19] Baron G. Kh. Maidel', "Graf S. Iu. Vitte, kak zheleznodorozhnykh [sic] deiatel'," *PiT*, 6 (174), March 15, 1915, p. 302.

effort, as a potential national leader and champion of the cause of national self-fulfillment. Even Avdakov was moved by the appointment of Prince Shakhovskoi as minister of trade and industry to observe that, in contrast with the economic "war" where confidence in victory was low, the military effort was "led by a man of unshakable will, who possesses all the capacities of genius, in whom and in the success of whose work all Russia has faith."[20]

Strong as the political feelings of the industrialists might have been, however, they did not go beyond a desire for a change in the personnel of the government and a number of modest reforms including recognition of the principle of "legality," the implementation of civil liberties, and abolition of restrictions based on religion and nationality—all issues that had long been demands of the Association. Moreover, the Association's attitude toward the State Duma was not without ambivalence. Its firm belief in the need for a strong and authoritative legislature was matched by its continuing discontent with the predominant influence in the Duma of agrarian elements which, it felt, were basically hostile to entrepreneurial interests. Yet, despite these misgivings, the industrialists' growing anxiety during the spring of 1915 caused them to place their hopes on the Duma as the only body that could possibly exercise a beneficent influence on the government.

All these uncertainties notwithstanding, however, the Association clearly believed that the future of Russia lay in the hands of its own entrepreneurial class. But even its dedication to its own future predominance was now subject to qualification. *Industry and Trade* put it succinctly: "There stands before business Russia, when it is able to organize and understand itself, a great future."[21]

The Ninth Congress of the Association of Industry and Trade, held in Petrograd on May 26-28, was a large and influential assembly, including representatives of the business world from all parts of the empire as well as members of the legislature and government officials. It opened against a background of continuing defeats on the Galician front and in an atmosphere tense with potential political conflict. From its proceedings there emerged not only the decision to take the initiative in attempting to alleviate the now critical shortage in arms and munitions by the creation of the War Industries Committee but also the beginnings of an active movement of political protest among the industrialists.[22] In ad-

[20] "Predsedatel' Soveta Sezdov N. S. Avdakov ob ukhode S. I. Timasheva," *PiT*, 5 (173), March 1, 1915, pp. 230-31.

[21] "Graf Sergei Iulevich Vitte," *PiT*, 5 (173), March 1, 1915, p. 233.

[22] According to Pearson (supra, n. 7), p. 34, "The Ninth Congress was planned as a giant publicity-stunt for industry."

dition, it witnessed a rise in the status of Moscow, always acknowledged to be the heartland of mercantile and industrial Russia, to a position of leadership rivaling that of the Association itself. This rise to political prominence was a clear reflection of the increasing activism of the industrially backed Progressist party, and was symbolized by a change in the chairmanship of the Moscow Exchange Committee from the conservative G. A. Krestovnikov to the Progressist leader, P. P. Riabushinskii.

Much has been made by historians of the conflict that allegedly occurred at the Congress between a conservative Association and a liberal and activist Moscow. Yet the limited record that is available suggests that the areas of agreement and cooperation between the two centers far outweighed their differences. Both had long proclaimed the necessity for the mobilization of industry on behalf of the war effort, although the Muscovites had advanced the slogan with particular vigor during the days immediately preceding the Congress. And on the need for a government that would have the confidence of the people virtually all industrial elements in the empire were in agreement. The differences between the Association and the Moscow men would seem, in fact, to have been mainly tactical, centering on the role of the Special Council. Yet Moscow's manifest anger at the creation of an institution whose industrial representation was limited almost exclusively to Petrograd, and with which the Association was eager to work, was countered not only by the fact that the Association itself had urged the need to broaden the representation of industrial interests, but also by Moscow's own recognition that cooperation with the government was essential to the success of industry's effort.

Moscow, indeed, had genuine grievances, if not with the Association then with its Petrograd base, that were inseparable from the traditional antagonisms between the old capital and the new. One primary cause of outrage was the fact that, except for its largest textile firms, Moscow had not shared in the largesse of war orders which the biggest firms in Petrograd had enjoyed. Petrograd had also been favored, as Moscow saw it, in the allocation of fuel and raw materials. Finally, Moscow's undisputed position as the center of national, liberal, and activist sentiment in entrepreneurial Russia contrasted sharply with the apathy and apparent indifference of many of the Petrograd magnates. Yet there were differences, on the political issues at least, among the Muscovites, for not all of them shared the views of the "young men"—the Progressists. Moreover, within the Association's own leadership, the waning influence of the conservative Avdakov and the rising star of the energetic and liberally inclined Polish member of the Second and Third Dumas, V. V. Zhukovskii, were starkly revealed at the Congress.

The first day of the Congress, at which Riabushinskii was not present, having been delayed at the front, was dominated by the Association's leadership. In addition to Avdakov and Zhukovskii, their numbers included M. M. Fedorov, a Progressist who was active in Petrograd financial and industrial circles but who was also close to the Moscow leaders, and Iu. I. Poplavskii, vice-chairman of the Society of Mill and Factory Owners of the Moscow Industrial Region and, in Riabushinskii's absence, the leader of the Moscow delegation. Together they raised the slogan "All for the War."[23] The day closed with the adoption of a resolution that not only called upon industry to devote itself to supplying the army but also proclaimed the need for increased industrial representation on the Special Council. In addition, the session declared the urgent need for the immediate convening of the legislature.

Riabushinskii's moving speech the following morning was the turning point in the proceedings of the Congress. Although he did not outline a specific plan for the creation of the War Industries Committees, as he is often credited with doing, he did declare his confidence that "the need will be proclaimed . . . to create some kind of committee"[24] which would direct industry's war effort. But he did not call for a movement that was totally separate from the government, nor did he seek a political confrontation with the government. Rather, he stressed the need, as the Association had done since the outbreak of the war, for cooperation between government and industry. The prime need, he insisted, was to organize the rear and to draw into the effort "strong, knowledgeable, experienced persons" both from the government and from every stratum of the population without regard for political differences. At the same time, he appealed for greater governmental understanding of the country's needs: "And we would like to say to our government with a pure heart: it is already late, but listen to us at last; try now to learn a little in order to draw closer to the people, in order to give yourself the possibility even at this moment, a dangerous moment, to help us emerge with honor from the immediate situation that has been created."[25] His final words were an emotional and colorful appeal for national unity: "let us hold out firmly in our places, let us forget our personal affairs, let us concentrate on helping the state in this difficult time. And may the many-headed German snake, which is winding around us . . . , feeding on our vitals, be destroyed."[26]

After a lengthy debate, the Congress decided to act upon Riabushin-

---

[23] TsGIA, f. 32, op. 1, d. 61, l. 11. Cf. Rodzianko's account, in which he claims to have initiated the slogan ("Krushenie imperii," [supra, n. 15], p. 95).

[24] TsGIA, f. 32, op. 1, d. 61, l. 9.

[25] Ibid., l. 11.

[26] Ibid. A slightly different version of Riabushinskii's speech is to be found in TsGIA, f. 32, op. 1, d. 34, ll. 116-19.

skii's proposal and, in Fedorov's words, "to put together a suitable committee, chosen from among the best people of the trading-industrial class, which would be in a position to devise an organization necessary for the creation of the means of defense, for their delivery to the front."[27] Zhukovskii was chosen to head the organizing committee, which was made up of some forty persons representing all the major industrial and commercial centers of the empire as well as those members of the legislature who represented or were members of the business class. On the third and final day the Congress accepted, to the cries of "Bravo, Bravo," Zhukovskii's suggestion that the resolution drafted by the committee be adopted unanimously and without debate. It proposed the establishment in Petrograd of a Central War Industries Committee, which should coordinate the work of district committees in adapting enterprises to production for defense, elaborating plans for the delivery of output according to a regular schedule, and determining needs for raw materials, transportation, and labor. The Association was entrusted with the task of organizing this Central Committee, with the proviso that it should include representatives from trading-industrial organizations, the railroads and shipping lines, the learned and technical professions, and the All-Russian Unions of Zemstvos and Towns.[28] The Association for its part agreed to assign 25,000 rubles from its own funds to meet the initial organizing expenses.

Political issues were never far from the surface at the Congress. Riabushinskii touched on them only lightly, but industry's grievances were clearly present in his reference to the limitations that had thus far impinged on society's right to organize and the need to give recognition to the importance and capacities of "the most important sector" (i.e., the trading-industrial class) of Russia's population. The suggestion that a delegation be sent to the Emperor to acquaint him with the full magnitude of Russia's problem was evidently valued not only for its economic content and possible political overtones but also as a reflection of the class pride of the industrialists. As Poplavskii declared, by taking "such an extraordinarily audacious step" the Congress would simultaneously be taking action that would have great and lasting importance for the future of its own class. For "at this moment we shall come forward as a completely independent class in the political life of the country."[29]

Allowing for the inadequacies of the printed record, there would seem to have been no real disagreement on political issues among the great majority of the Congress's membership. Rodzianko's claim to have ad-

[27] TsGIA, f. 32, op. 1, d. 61, l. 30.

[28] "Rezoliutsiia, priniataia IX Ocherednym Sezdom po voprosu ob udovletvorenii nuzhd gosudarstvennoi oborony," *PiT*, 11 (179), June 1, 1915, p. 544.

[29] TsGIA, f. 32, op. 1, d. 61, l. 25.

dressed the gathering on its first day with the specific purpose of deflecting "radical" political demands planned by the Moscow industrialists[30] is highly suspect, if only because he in fact addressed the Congress only on its last day in a speech devoted to an already routine appeal to the industrial class to work with the Special Council and to lend its support to a broad program of governmental reform. Moreover, there is no evidence that even the most liberal of the Moscow industrial leaders harbored "radical" political demands. It remained for Prince S. P. Marsyrev, the left Kadet leader soon to join the Progressists, to introduce the one note of political discord which marred an otherwise largely harmonious consensus. To applause from back-benchers, he bitterly accused the government not only of indifference to Russia's fate but of wholesale corruption as well, and invited the assembled industrialists to take "the path of struggle . . . whatever this may cost us."[31]

The succeeding disarray was finally silenced by Zhukovskii, who as chairman declared that this was a time not for "echoes of internal revolution and all kinds of political movements" but for cooperation with the government in the interest of the war effort. To cries of "Correct, Correct," he told the gathering, "It is impossible to conceive of ourselves here as both a congress and a national assembly which chooses a government"; rather, "we can only talk about a struggle with a common enemy. . . . We must in solidarity with all our strength go to the aid of the government, our native land and the TSAR (*sic*)."[32] Zhukovskii's intervention was perhaps made easier since his own political philosophy with respect to postwar Russia had already been set forth in the Association's report to the Congress on economic development. There, speaking of the need for basic reforms, he continued: "But such a reforming role will be within the strength not of a police state, not of a bureaucratic state, not of a class (*soslovnomu*) state, but of an economic state, a state which not only bases its work upon the public but works through the public, a state that would know how to unite all the vital forces of the people, that would not oppress but would base its work on the free individuality."[33] In the end the only overt political act of the Congress was the reiteration of its earlier resolution declaring its belief in the necessity of "the convening without delay of the Legislative Institutions."[34]

[30] "Krushenie imperii" (supra, n. 15), pp. 95-96.

[31] TsGIA, f. 32, op. 1, d. 61, l. 29.

[32] Ibid., ll. 29 and 32-33.

[33] Sovet Sezdov, *O merakh k razvitiiu*, pp. 7-8. See also: I. Glivits, "Politiko-ekonomicheskie vzgliady V. V. Zhukovskogo," *PiT*, 42 (235), October 22, 1916, p. 308.

[34] "Rezoliutsiia" (supra, n. 28), p. 542.

The events of the Congress produced a brief period of exhilaration, renewed self-confidence, and frenzied activity, both economically and politically oriented, among the industrialists. But *Industry and Trade* solemnly warned that "even mobilized industry cannot work if it is not told precisely and definitely what it must produce. . . . The fulfillment of the task of the War Industries Committee requires not only initiative on the part of industry but also the active cooperation of the organs of government power."[35]

The Association lost no time in proclaiming with unprecedented forthrightness its political ideals. The legislature was now deemed to hold the key to Russia's future, and the industrialists joined their voice to those of liberal political leaders and the Unions of Zemstvos and Towns in an insistent demand that the Duma be reconvened. In mid-June *Industry and Trade* wrote:

> Under the blows of the mailed German fist the new Russia of the future is being forged. We are fighting for a new civil state [*grazhdanstvennost'*], for the broad rights of the people's representatives to participate in state life. The people, bearing on their shoulders the weight of the gigantic struggle, cannot fail to be called to [participate in] the broadest state construction, the reconstruction of the entire obsolete state system. We are awaiting the calling of the Legislative Chambers without delay in order that the entire country in the person of its elected representatives may bear witness to the great words of the Rescript of the Gosudar: "The enemy must be demolished. Until then there can be no peace."[36]

But industry's interest in the convening of the legislature was not entirely selfless. Out of the Congress the industrialists had emerged with a new sense of their own importance to the state, a consciousness of their maturity as a class and a conviction of their mission to serve the state in "a great historical moment." In the surge of public approval that followed the Congress, a meeting of the Duma was seen as a means of finally confirming their new unity with society as a whole: "The imminent calling of the legislative institutions can, no doubt, play a decisive role in the process of the spiritual rapprochement of society with the trading-industrial class. The legislature should fix the shift in the public temper, the psychological upheaval with respect to industry."[37] The campaign,

[35] "Reshenie IX Ocherednogo Sezda Predstavitelei Promyshlennosti i Torgovli," *PiT*, 11 (179), June 1, 1915, p. 546.
[36] "Griadushchaia pobeda," *PiT*, 12 (180), June 15, 1915, p. 604.
[37] "Obshchestvennoe mnenie i promyshlennost'," *PiT*, 13-14 (181), July 1-15, 1915, p. 3.

in which all of liberal Russia shared, finally met with success when the legislature was again convened on July 19.

In the same spirit of enthusiasm the Association energetically began the work of organizing the War Industries Committees. But despite its organizational success, the Association's activities during the interim between the Ninth Congress and the First Congress of War Industries Committees, which met at the end of July, served only to exacerbate the growing tension between certain key elements in its top leadership and Moscow. In part, the trouble was traceable to divisions within the Association itself and specifically between Avdakov and Zhukovskii over the functions of the committees. While the former argued that these should be limited to measures designed to increase productivity, Zhukovskii successfully insisted that their function should also include the allocation and filling of war orders and the adaptation of smaller factories to war production.

An important cause for irritation from Moscow's point of view was the clear intent of the Association to establish a close working relationship between the Central War Industries Committee and the government organ that controlled the issuance of war orders—the Special Council, now reorganized as the Special Council for the Coordination of War Supplies and headed by the newly appointed war minister, the well-liked General A. A. Polivanov. The Council had also been expanded to include additional representatives from the government and the legislature as well as from trading-industrial organizations. Avdakov and V. I. Timiriazev, the first chairman of the Association and the current chairman of its mercantile counterpart, the Association of Exchange Trade and Agriculture, sat as representatives of the State Council, while Guchkov, Zhukovskii, and Maidel' represented the Central War Industries Committee. Konovalov also sat on the Council as a kind of permanent guest, formally representing no constituency but actually serving as spokesman for the Moscow War Industries Committee. After receiving assurances from Goremykin and Prince Shakhovskoi of their intent to cooperate with the Central Committee, the latter invited the membership of the Special Council to participate in its own meetings. In turn, the Central Committee became during its first month the authorized agent of the War Ministry in the allocation of orders among munitions manufacturers. Thus the initial prospects for a cooperative working relationship between the Central Committee and the Special Council appeared to be promising.

When the First Congress of the War Industries Committees met, however, these prospects were already fading rapidly. The Congress, meeting from July 25 to 27, marked a victory for the activist and liberal circles of Moscow, as well as for the principle of the participation of the public in general in the war effort, over the Avdakov group in the Association.

It is noteworthy that Moscow's victory, additionally, over the entrepreneurial interests of Petrograd itself reflected the essential indifference of the latter, who sent a delegation of only minimal size to represent their interests.[38] The majority of the participants at the Congress represented smaller enterprise from the provinces and were basically in alliance with Moscow. Moscow's successful challenge to the Association, which resulted in the replacement of Avdakov and Zhukovskii as chairman and vice-chairman of the Central Committee by Guchkov and Konovalov, denoted success for those who wished to create an organization that would be broadly based in Russian society and would operate in at least semi-independence of the Special Council.

Yet, once again, there were exceptions to this picture. Zhukovskii, in contrast with Avdakov (who welcomed, at least for the public record, the formal separation of the Association from the Central Committee), announced that he personally considered it his duty both as a businessman and as a Polish patriot to continue his work with the Committee. The introduction of a group of labor's representatives to membership in the Central Committee—the single most important step that was taken toward broadening the public base of the War Industries Committees—in fact owed much to his personal efforts in cooperation with Konovalov, who was its principal initiator.[39] Moreover, the Association, with its ten delegates to the Central Committee, still, if one excepts labor's ten delegates, had greater representation than any other single organization or group; and leading managerial posts in the Central Committee continued to be occupied by members of the Association and its staff. Finally, the Moscow leadership at the Congress, despite its insistence on independence from the Special Council, was no less vociferous than its Petrograd-based colleagues in the Association in its insistence on the necessity for government cooperation if the War Industries Committees were to suc-

[38] This fact was reflected in the composition of the Congress. Of the approximately 230 members of district and local committees present, 23 represented Moscow but only 11, apart from representatives of the Association, came from Petrograd. Of the latter, only 3 were delegates of the Petrograd War Industries Committee, and of these only one, E. L. Nobel, was prominent in entrepreneurial circles. There is no evidence that he took part in the general debates at the Congress. (Tsentral'nyi Voenno-Promyshlennyi Komitet, *Trudy Sezda Predstavitelei Voenno-Promyshlennykh Komitetov 25-27-go iiulia 1915 goda* (Petrograd, 1915), pp. 279-88.

[39] There is general agreement among historians that Konovalov was the main force behind the decision to admit the workers to the committees. Yet, at the time of his death Zhukovskii was widely credited for having initiated the movement for workers' representation. At his instigation, reportedly, Guchkov saw to it that an appropriate statement on the subject was issued through the Special Council. "Obzor pechati," *PiT*, 36-37 (231), September 17, 1916, p. 207. See also: Lewis H. Siegelbaum, "Workers' Groups and the War-Industries Committees: Who Used Whom?" *The Russian Review*, 39, no. 2 (1980):155.

ceed in their self-appointed task of supplying the army and organizing the rear.

In fact, it was the relationship with the government that was the principal cause for concern. It was already apparent that industry's initial hopes for cooperation with the Special Council had not been borne out, as Avdakov himself conceded in the first session of the Congress. Requests for information concerning military needs had not been honored. Although the Central Committee's statement on the need for a definite program in the supply of raw materials had been approved in principle by the Council, no additional materials had actually been forthcoming. Similarly, there had been no improvement in supplies of fuel and labor; nor had industry's requests been honored for samples and models on which to base its work on the few contracts that had been received from the Special Council by any enterprise or local or district war industry committee. Indeed, as Baron Maidel', still the secretary general of both the Association and the Central War Industries Committee, reported, the entire project was sunk in a morass of "bureaucratic indecision."[40] In fact, the problem of relations with the government was all the more threatening since the Special Council was once again undergoing reorganization, this time assuming its final form as the Special Council on Defense. In this form it not only was endowed with enhanced powers over industry and the national economy in general but industry's representatives, except for the Central War Industry Committee, were excluded from membership.

Underlying the gloomy prospect for economic cooperation with the government was the political imbroglio that marked the summer of 1915. Two factors undoubtedly contributed to the government's growing unwillingness to have industry help formulate economic policies: one was the industrialists' new political activism that developed rapidly after the Ninth Congress; the other was the suspicion, soon to be confirmed by the emergence of the Progressive Bloc, that the reorganized structure of the War Industries Committees reflected a budding political alliance of the center parties as well as an effort to establish an affinity with organized labor. For industry, the government's position was a cause for near despair. As Riabushinskii affirmed during the course of the debates at the Congress of War Industries Committees, the need was for a strong government; but "Who governs Russia at the present time? . . . We do not know."[41] The desire for a government that would have the confidence of the people ran like "a red thread" through the proceedings of the Congress.

[40] Tsentral'nyi Voenno-Promyshlennyi Komitet, *Trudy*, p. 13.
[41] Ibid., p. 35.

Almost equally troublesome, however, was the attitude of the State
Duma. Its action in approving the exclusion of industrial representatives
from the Special Council was received with understandable bitterness at
the Congress. As A. A. Bublikov, a Progressist member of both the Duma
and the Association, declared, the Duma's stand demonstrated once again
its innate hostility toward industry—an observation that Litvinov-Falinskii expanded to include the fundamental enmity of the press and of
the general public.[42] Yet the Duma remained, perforce, industry's only
hope. After the Ninth Congress the Association's leadership was virtually
unanimous in demanding, as a minimum, a government that would have
the confidence of the country, although the more assertive Progressists
clearly preferred a government that would be responsible to the Duma.
Yet the latter's own continuing dissatisfaction with the Duma was revealed in mid-August at a meeting in Moscow sponsored by Konovalov
and Riabushinskii, where the suggestion was made that representatives
of "public" organizations should avoid channeling their statements and
actions through the Duma but instead should issue them directly.[43]

Despite these misgivings, the creation of the Progressive Bloc in mid-
August had the enthusiastic support of business circles. Resolutions adopted
by the city dumas and exchange committees of both Moscow and Petrograd, as well as by numerous trading-industrial organizations, called
for a change in ministers and the formation of a government that would
have the confidence of the country. The Association itself sponsored an
enlarged meeting of its Council, attended by such prominent liberals as
Riabushinskii, Bublikov, and fon Ditmar, where the need was stressed
for it, "as the organization responsible before the trading-industrial circles
of all of Russia" to "come forward in such a critical moment with its
own authoritative word." The assembly unanimously decided to send a
telegram to the emperor, pointing out "that the war must be waged to
a victorious end, that for this purpose unity is required between the
authorities and the country, that no such unity exists at the present time,
and in order that it should exist it is necessary . . . to change the composition of the government at once and to call to power men who enjoy
the confidence of the public."[44] The telegram elicited no response, however, and the hopes that had been aroused proved to be short-lived.

The year and a half that remained before the collapse of the empire
saw a shift, from what indeed may have been only "bureaucratic indecision" on the part of the government at the time of the War Industries

[42] Ibid., pp. 26 and 29.
[43] V. S. Diakin, *Russkaia burzhuaziia i tsarizm v gody mirovoi voiny* (Leningrad, 1967),
p. 104.
[44] "Dnevnik Soveta," *PiT*, 19 (186), August 29, 1915, pp. 222-23.

Congress, to a policy of open confrontation, not only toward the committees, but toward the business community in general. For industry the results were disastrous. Not only was the work of the war industries committees rendered far from satisfactory; industry's new political orientation was to become progressively weaker in response to official harassment during the remaining months of tsarist rule. A further result of political and other pressures was the steady decline in the class unity that the industrialists had worked so hard to achieve.

September marked a fatal turning point for industry—and, in fact, for the cause of bourgeois liberalism as a whole. On September 3 the Duma was once again adjourned, thus dealing an ultimately fatal blow to the aspirations of the Progressive Bloc. And the election of four new representatives of trade and industry, among whom were Guchkov and Riabushinskii, to replace the current incumbents in the State Council, although vigorously reaffirming the support of business elements throughout the country for the Bloc and the liberal program in general, was also painfully revealing of the continuing discord that rent the trading-industrial class on other grounds. Finally, there was the death of Avdakov, for so long the authoritative leader of the Association of Industry and Trade, which led to a prolonged crisis within the organization over the choice of a successor as well as an intensive debate both within industrial circles and among the public at large regarding the political tasks and responsibilities of "united industry." In this debate the question was not infrequently raised, as it had been before and has been since, as to why the bourgeoisie, and especially the industrial bourgeoisie, had failed to become the bearer of political liberalism in Russia as it had presumably in Western Europe.

Both the crisis over the succession to Avdakov and over the political role of the Association were sparked by Zhukovskii's startling and ill-timed address at the memorial ceremony held in Avdakov's honor on October 1. The address openly revealed the many differences that had plagued the relationship between the two men during the preceding months, centering on the controversial issue of Avdakov's allegedly subservient approach as a "petitioner" to government officials; more important, it proposed that the Association now set off on an entirely new course. In a word, it should become politically activist and should, moreover, join forces with one of the established political parties, presumably the Progressists.[45] The only real alternative, it was later suggested, was to form an independent party of industrialists. Unrealistic though it undoubtedly was, the proposal was soon followed by the unanimous decision to offer the chairmanship of the Association to Konovalov, the Moscow Pro-

---

[45] TsGIA, f. 32, op. 1, d. 143, ll. 12-14.

gressist and vice-chairman of the Central War Industries Committee. But much to the confusion and disappointment of the organization, the offer was refused and Zhukovskii's proposal for an alliance with one political party was rejected most vigorously by the Moscow Progressists themselves.

The weeks dragged on and no one, regardless of his background or political position, proved willing to assume the chairmanship of the Association. For this there was no doubt a broad variety of explanations. Zhukovskii's own candidacy was never seriously considered, influential and highly respected though he was, and, in fact, he early disavowed any ambition to assume the post on grounds of his Polish nationality. Nevertheless, he was recognized as acting chairman of the organization until his own premature death the following August. His political proposals, however, had only the immediate effect of introducing still greater divisions into the business world, where there were wide differences as to their desirability and feasibility. The most telling argument against their adoption was that adherence to any political party would fatally splinter the organization of "united" industry, whose members represented a broad range of political views, while the formation of an independent party of industrialists offered no hope of success. By the beginning of the new year it had clearly been resolved that the Association should continue its former emphasis on the grave economic issues that confronted Russia and, still more, its postwar future.

Yet, despite its abandonment of an openly political role, the Association's position was not one of indifference to political issues. In an editorial comment during the autumn of 1915, *Industry and Trade* bluntly declared that "to create industry in the absence of political influence on the part of the trading-industrial class is impossible," while also acknowledging that "the question of the means by which to attain this influence is an acute problem."[46] Later N. F. fon Ditmar, a prominent member of both the Council of the Association and the State Council, observed that the Association had in the past exerted political pressures and would undoubtedly continue to do so in the future. "Industrial organizations," he declared, "will always be on the side of those parties which stand for progressive measures and reforms for the good of the population and for the prosperity of the native land common to all our nationalities."[47] And the Petrograd *Financial Gazette* observed, for its part, that "it must be clear that the gravitation of the Association . . .

---

[46] Sh., "Politicheskoe ob'edinenie torgovo-promyshlennago klassa," *PiT*, 26 (193), October 17, 1915, pp. 448-50.

[47] "Obzor pechati," *PiT*, 5 (207) January 30, 1916, 131.

toward a certain sector of benches in the Tauride Palace is as natural as it is necessary."[48]

The Association never regained its former stature as the representative of all-Russian "united" industry, for the divisions separating the various entrepreneurial elements had become deeper and more apparent than ever. In Moscow by the end of 1916 Riabushinskii was on the point of relinquishing his chairmanship of the Exchange Committee to a new coalition of more conservative forces headed by its former chairman, G. A. Krestovnikov, while in Petrograd the differences in interest between the Association and entrepreneurial interests indigenous to the area became increasingly evident with the rise of a new organization of the metalworking industry.[49]

Nevertheless, under Zhukovskii's leadership the Association did succeed in reestablishing much of its standing as the principal leader of industry's efforts to represent its interests in government circles and to initiate governmental planning for the day when the war would be over and Russia's problems of financial indebtedness, industrial backwardness, and economic independence in a highly competitive world must be squarely faced. During this period, moreover, the organization exhibited a remarkable and unprecedented objectivity in its assessment both of the role of the government and of private enterprise in the wartime economy. Although, for example, its comments on the Second Congress of the War Industries Committees in February were highly critical of the lack of governmental cooperation that had contributed so much to the poor performance of the committees, it was also critical of the committees' own performance. Although they had indeed failed to obtain the number of orders from official sources that was considered necessary to sustain the war economy, they had also been notably slow in filling those that had been received; and while difficulties in obtaining the necessary raw materials, fuel and transport facilities were largely responsible for these delays, the latter also owed much to the inefficiency of the committees.

The anniversary of the Ninth Congress produced a clear admission that the earlier hopes for a transformation of the war economy had disappeared—an admission couched in an unparalleled acknowledgement of the inadequacy of Russian industry itself: "And it must be recognized that the fault does not lie only with the disorganization of our transport and our general economic disorder. The mobilization of industry could not attain a broad scope among us because the very cadres

---

[48] *Finansovaia gazeta*, December 16 (29), 1915, p. 1. These words were later quoted in *Industry and Trade*: "Obzor pechati," *PiT*, 1 (203), January 2, 1916, p. 14.

[49] The first congress of the Association of the Metalworking Industry was held in Petrograd in the late winter of 1916. Cf. Sezdy predstavitelei metallo-obrabatyvaiushchei promyshlennosti. 1-yi. *Trudy* (Petrograd, 1916).

of industrial enterprise are too few and scattered, because we have no industry in the European sense of the word."[50] Yet when two months later *Industry and Trade* noted with alarm that the economy was showing increasing "elements of decline and of threatening catastrophe," it also declared that "as before, the leaders of our economic policy have neither an awareness of the necessity nor a readiness to embark upon a decisive reform of our obsolete economic way of life."[51]

Meanwhile, the suspicion and hostility endemic in official circles toward private enterprise became more and more evident. The increasing stringency of the censorship of the Association's journal and the arrests of several industrial leaders in the winter of 1915 and again in the autumn of 1916 were assessed by the organization as "a systematicness of action directed with sufficiently clear purpose against the industrialists."[52] Still more serious was the increasing intervention in business affairs of ministries having no direct responsibility for the economy, particularly the Ministry of Internal Affairs. The growing evidence that the government was seriously considering the subjection of private industry to direct state control led one contributor to *Industry and Trade* to the bitter observation that Russia constituted a living refutation of the Marxist thesis that everything springs from economic factors. In an outraged, if confused, melange of tongues, he declared: "U nas la politique c'est tout" ("Among us, politics is everything").[53]

It was clear, however, that the events of the past year had created a new attitude of assertiveness, if not of confidence, toward the government. The Association, for example, demanded that the War Industries Committees be recognized by the government as autonomous organizations endowed with a measure of power commensurate with their responsibilities. Indeed, it went further and insisted that they be recognized as the voice of industry alone. "Responsibility and power are indivisible,"[54] it declared, and both should be vested solely in industry, unconstrained even by the voices of the public elements on the committees. This return to a narrowly industrial outlook was perhaps one of the Association's greatest mistakes. But clearly the days of a "petitioning" industry were gone. As *The Day* (*Den'*), a Petrograd newspaper closely affiliated with the interests of industry and trade, asserted in September 1916: "The time has passed when Russian industry and trade approached the min-

[50] "Nashi budushchiia ekonomicheskiia zadachi," *PiT*, 20 (222), May 21, 1916, p. 563.
[51] "Dva goda voiny," *PiT*, 28-29 (227), July 23, 1916, pp. 45 and 48.
[52] "Deiatel'nost' Soveta Sezdov Predstavitelei Promyshlennosti i Torgovli v 1916 godu," *PiT*, 1 (254), January 7, 1917, p. 57.
[53] Gr. Kvasha, "Ekonomicheskaia politika novago Ministra Vnutrennykh Del'," *PiT*, 26 (193), October 17, 1915, pp. 451-54.
[54] "Itogi Voenno-Promyshlennogo Sezda," *PiT*, 15 (182), August 1, 1915, pp. 63-64.

isterial chancelleries bowing and scraping. Now they have grown up and, rightly, they no longer beg but demand for themselves a real place in the state life of the country and in its administration. And this fact must be stated with authority."[55]

Political pressures and growing differences among the industrialists on how best to cope with the situation undoubtedly contributed to the political diffidence of organized industry that also marked most of the final year before the revolution. No doubt the divergent response to such pressures included the self-interested desire on the part of some to ensure the reception of government contracts and the continued pursuit of entrepreneurial profits through a policy of accommodation. At the same time, the expanding strike movement and the increasing militancy of labor doubtless also played a part in a new mood of quiescence that appeared to characterize some entrepreneurial circles. Although the Central War Industries Committee continued to uphold the cause of its own and other groups of labor's representatives against governmental attempts to restrict their activities, the issue became an increasing cause for division among the industrialists. Nevertheless, the position taken by organized all-Russian industry and trade was clear. In a memorandum addressed to the government and issued jointly by the Association of Industry and Trade and its commercial counterpart, the Association of Exchange Trade and Agriculture, the business leadership of the country warned that the war "has created such a sharp demand for a new order and a new way of life that the most rapid satisfaction of this demand by the state authority is necessary in order to avoid very serious complications."[56] Thus labor's new activism was seen within the entrepreneurial leadership as an added reason for urgency in propounding the need for both political and economic reform.

The last weeks before the Revolution were a time not only of weariness and discouragement for organized industry, as they were for all of Russia, but also a time of renewed activity and belated efforts to create a new class solidarity in opposition to the government and in anticipation of the crisis that all saw approaching. Early in 1917 *Industry and Trade*, declaring that "our native land is in the position of one who is seriously ill," observed that the cause of the affliction was well known: "The public forces that burst forth in time of war are unable to tear away the tight bonds that prevent the Russian people from building its own future in accordance with merit and national resources (*sic*)."[57] Russia's economic problems were still soluble, but "their solution presupposes the presence of conditions which as yet we do not have: an organized governmental

[55] "Obzor pechati," *PiT*, 36-37 (231), September 17, 1916, p. 207.
[56] "Deiatel'nost' Soveta Sezdov . . . v 1916 godu" (supra, n. 52), p. 60.
[57] "1916 god," *PiT*, 1 (245), January 7, 1917, p. 1.

authority which enjoys the confidence of the people."[58] In its absence, the Association turned once again to the State Duma as Russia's last hope.

The turn of the year found the Moscow Progressist leaders, Riabushinskii and Konovalov, attempting to create the framework for an effective entrepreneurial role in the legislature. Their efforts included the establishment of a more comprehensive organization of the business elements in the country. Late in January, however, an attempt to hold a congress in Moscow with the aim of creating a union of all commercial and industrial enterprise, middle-sized and small as well as large-scale, was thwarted by the government, which prohibited not only the convening of the congress but the holding of any private conference in its place. Nevertheless, on the appointed day, January 25, delegates from all over Russia met in private conference at Riabushinskii's home, where they proceeded to elect an organizing commission with Riabushinskii at its head. In view of the ban on the congress, however, the Association decided, in an unprecedented act of open defiance of the government, to call its own executive Council together for the purpose of convening the Tenth Congress of the organization. The agenda, it announced, would be essentially the same as that of the congress that had been forbidden to meet. It was further provided that if the Tenth Congress were also banned, the Council of the Association would meet "with the broadest participation of the representatives of industry and trade."[59] Thus, on the eve of the collapse of the empire, the Association and the industrial leaders of Moscow, whatever their differences may have been in the past, were solidly united in support of what they saw as the salvation of Russia and the advancement of their own entrepreneurial class.

As the revolutionary storm drew nearer, it had at its disposal not only a hungry and rebellious working class and a land-starved peasantry, as well as disaffected landowners and members of the liberal intelligentsia, but also a trading-industrial class that was closer to open rebellion than it had ever been before. The Association was not in the vanguard of these forces but it was fully prepared to move with them. Committed as it was to stability and order, as well as to limited political reform, it had been driven to this position not so much by the state of Russia's wartime economy, or even by the government's lack of cooperation, as by the blind resistance to change of any kind on the part of the entrenched authorities. Above all, the government's refusal to take the industrialists into its confidence and to allow them to participate in the formulation

[58] Ibid., p. 5.

[59] "Dnevnik Soveta," *PiT*, 4 (248), January 28, 1917, pp. 94-96, and 5 (249), February 4, 1917, pp. 118-19. Also: "Iz deiatel'nosti obshchestvennykh uchrezhdenii po promyshlennosti i torgovle," *PiT*, 5 (249), February 4, 1917, p. 121.

of economic policy was for them a cause of great bitterness. As we have seen, the industrialists were dedicated to the elevation of their own class to a position of national preeminence. Yet their reluctance to assume a position of genuine political leadership in a time of national crisis after their brief burst of activity in the late spring and summer of 1915 and their timidity in the face of subsequent governmental harassment must be regarded as a disastrous retreat from their own self-proclaimed objectives.

The collapse of the tsar's government appears to have been welcomed with great joy by most of the industrialists. The old restrictions and constraints were gone and new vistas of opportunity were open to them at last. In alliance with the Zemstvo men and the liberal intelligentsia, the industrialists held positions of influence in the Provisional Government. In its first composition Guchkov served as minister of war and navy, Konovalov as minister of trade and industry, and M. I. Tereshchenko, a young and relatively unknown sugar industrialist from Kiev, as minister of finance. Following the first reorganization of the government in May, Guchkov dropped out while Tereshchenko replaced Miliukov as minister of foreign affairs—a position he continued to occupy until the October Revolution. Konovalov stayed on only briefly, resigning toward the end of the month over differences in economic policy; but later he once again entered the government, serving during its last weeks not only as minister of trade and industry but also as deputy prime minister under Kerensky. Other prominent industrialists also occupied positions of influence either in official posts or as advisers to the government. Yet even during their heyday the industrialists as a class never rose to a position of political leadership, and it was left primarily to the Zemstvo agrarians and the intelligentsia to act out the role of the middle class as the bearer of liberal ideals.

After the Bolsheviks came to power virtually all of the big industrialists found their way to the West. The great majority of them settled in Paris, where they founded an organization known as The Russian Financial, Industrial and Commercial Association (L'Association financière, industrielle et commerciale russe). It remained active until well into the nineteen thirties, battling for the lost cause of Russian private enterprise.

*The
Soviet
Period*

X

JOSEPH S. BERLINER   *Entrepreneurship in the Soviet Period: An Overview*

A decade before the Bolshevik Revolution *Il Giornale degli Economisti* published an article by Enrico Barone entitled "The Ministry of Production in the Collectivist State." In the article, which eventually became a seminal work in the development of the economic theory of socialism, Barone proved that in a collectivist society that wished to maximize the welfare of its people "all the economic categories of the old regime must reappear, though maybe with new names: prices, interest, rent, profit, saving, etc."[1] Barone did not deal with entrepreneurship, but had he done so he would surely have come to the same conclusion. However, while economic theory could provide some counsel on the ways in which prices and interest should be determined in the collectivist state, it had little to offer on the conditions that would be required for the flourishing of entrepreneurship, for that "factor of production" is so intertwined with political and social forces that the abstractions of economic theory do not carry one very far.

At the inception of the Soviet regime, one might have held two views about the prospects for the development of vigorous entrepreneurship in the new socialist society. If one were optimistic about the prospects for socialism, one would have expected a bright future for entrepreneurship. While Marx paid a generous tribute to the achievements of capitalist entrepreneurship in the progressive period of that social system, the thrust of the Marxian view was that in its declining years capitalism becomes a fetter on entrepreneurship. The rate of profit declines, monopolistic restriction on output increases, and technological advance slows down. The abolition of capitalism and the profit motive removes these restrictions on the creative energies of the people, and entrepreneurship should be expected to flourish under socialism at a higher level than had been possible before under the increasingly restrictive regime of capitalism.

[1] E. Barone, "The Ministry of Production in the Collectivist State," in Alec Nove and D. M. Nuti, eds., *Socialist Economics*, London, 1972, p. 73.

If one were pessimistic about socialism, however, one would have been quite gloomy about the capacity of the new society to generate entrepreneurship. The essence of entrepreneurship under capitalism is the autonomy of the businessman, whose command over resources for the purpose of introducing new ideas is limited only by his ability to convince holders of capital that by investing in his venture they can expect a higher return than elsewhere. Central to the entrepreneurial process is the wide dispersion of the ownership of capital by businessmen seeking to put it to the most profitable use. If the ownership of the society's capital is now both socialized and centralized the ensuing bureaucratization would sap entrepreneurship of all of its vitality. Moreover, the socialist society is unlikely to develop an incentive as powerful as capitalist profit has proven to be in generating a high level of entrepreneurial effort. From this perspective the prospects for entrepreneurship under socialism would have been fairly grim.

In the event, history found a path well within these two extremes. The rapid industrialization of the USSR could not have occurred had the pessimistic version proven to be the case. Nor does the economic history of the USSR bear any resemblance to the picture drawn by the optimistic version. It is clear that the Soviet system has found a way of stimulating a significant level of entrepreneurship in its population, but nevertheless those who carry out this function operate under a variety of restrictive conditions. It is the nature of entrepreneurship in the Soviet era of Russian history to which the following essays are directed.

The historical perspective of this volume invites consideration of the historical roots of entrepreneurship in the Soviet period. The preceding essays report a variety of aspects of entrepreneurship in earlier periods that suggest counterparts in the Soviet period as well. In ruminating over the fact that Russian foreign trade had long been conducted by foreign entrepreneurs residing in Russia rather than by Russian traders traveling abroad, one thinks of the insulation of Soviet engineers and executives from the larger world of travel and commerce in products and ideas. The reputation of the Russian merchants for dishonesty is reminiscent of the present-day "second economy," and of the pressures on Soviet executives to engage in illegal acts in order to fulfill plan targets. The dominating thread of historical continuity, however, is the central role of the state in the promotion of economic progress.

The fact of the state's domination of the economy is of major importance in shaping the nature of Soviet entrepreneurship, but more than state domination is involved. As Alexander Gerschenkron has shown, in the process of economic development generally, the greater the backwardness of a country relative to the most advanced, the greater the tendency for the state to take the lead in launching and then guiding the process of catching up. In this sense the domination of the state in Russian economic development is not simply the product of Russian culture but derives from the extreme backwardness of the Russian economy.[2] Similar processes were at work in such un-Russian instances as Hungary (pre-1945) and Japan. Because of the importance of the state in the economy of those nations, the nature of entrepreneurship in their economic history was different from that in England or Germany, in which the state played a lesser role. But the differences among all the aforementioned countries are relatively small compared with the difference between all of them on the one hand and Soviet Russia on the other. For in all those cases the entrepreneurial function was carried out in a private-property market-economy context, while in the Soviet case it has been carried out in the context of a centrally planned socialist economy. It is this that has made the grand difference, not the fact of state domination alone.

Hence, as the reader of this volume moves from the preceding chapters to the ones that follow, while noticing the threads of continuity, he will surely be struck by the sharpness of the discontinuity. The nature of entrepreneurship is vastly different, as are the economic problems associated with it. To put the proposition in the boldest terms, perhaps the best background reading for understanding the nature and problems of entrepreneurship in Soviet Russia is not a book on the economic history of Russia but rather a book on the economy of Communist China.

For this reason one of the major problems with which the authors of the following chapters have to grapple is the basic question of what one ought to understand by the term *entrepreneurship* in the Soviet context and at what points in the system is it to be located. Not that the question is easily answered in the context of a market economy. Several of our authors discuss the difference between the Marshallian view of capitalist entrepreneurship as a response to disequilibria and the Schumpeterian view of capitalist entrepreneurship as the bringing about of "new combinations." Moreover the diffusion of functions in the modern corporation makes it much more difficult to identify the locus or loci of entrepreneurship than in the case of the classical owner-entrepreneur. But in the Soviet case, the categories of economic activity differ so greatly from those of a capitalist economy that the problem is vastly more difficult. The essays reflect the diversity of locations in the system at which the entrepreneurial function may be found. The managers of the production units, both factory and farm, possess certain entrepreneurial functions, which are discussed in the chapter by Roy and Betty Laird, as well as in the other chapters that deal primarily with the nonagricultural

---

[2] Alexander Gerschenkron, *Economic Backwardness in Historical Perspective* (Cambridge, Mass., 1962), pp. 16-21.

sector. This is the locus of entrepreneurship that corresponds most closely to what is regarded as the primary locus of entrepreneurship in capitalist economies. The correspondence is purely formal, however, for the content of entrepreneurship at this level differs greatly in the two systems. Western research has concentrated on this level of management because of the abundance of data, but we have been aware that the entrepreneurial activity of the ministries and the state apparatus, about which little is published, is of vast consequence for the operation of the economy. David Granick studies entrepreneurial behavior at that little-explored level. His chapter is notable also in that the object of investigation is the creation of new organizational structures, rather than the creation of technological combinations which is most often the object of study. The Western literature has devoted considerable attention to organizational innovation, for ability to design and introduce new organizational forms has been found to be an important feature of successful technological innovation. A third locus of entrepreneurship is in the scientific and technical establishments and in the research-and-development (R & D) organizations, which are explored primarily in the chapters by Paul Cocks and Gregory Guroff, as well as in other chapters. That this source should be a special subject of investigation in the case of the USSR springs from the Soviet practice of separating the R & D organizations from the producing units, which gives the former a larger degree of autonomy relative to the producing units than is found in capitalist economies, where "in-house" R & D is standard practice. Gregory Grossman's chapter on the Party as entrepreneur takes us into a fourth locus of entrepreneurship that involves the greatest break with the Russian past. Finally, his and several of the other chapters consider a fifth locus of entrepreneurship that analysts find perhaps the most intriguing—the second economy.

The character of entrepreneurship is influenced by both the socialist basis of the economy and the practice of central planning. The effects of these two features of the economy are somewhat different and they are best treated separately. It is the socialist basis of the economy, for example, that is the source of one of the distinctive problems of entrepreneurship in the Soviet period—the Red-expert problem. As Gregory Guroff observes in his chapter on the subject, the controversy evoked that grand theme of earlier Russian history, that the purpose of economic activity is the furtherance of the state's interests. But we now know from the Chinese and Cuban experience that the Red-expert problem confronts all socialist governments and is not uniquely Russian. It is useful to distinguish what may be called the transition problem from the long-run problem. The source of the transition problem is that the stock of entrepreneurial skills available to a revolutionary government resides in people who are often hostile to the new order. In the course of time the transition problem is solved as the prerevolutionary experts are replaced by young people who grew up under the new order. There remains, however, the long-run problem of the professional; the political leadership is always dependent upon persons with a monopoly of professional expertise (physicians, generals, engineers), which gives the latter a certain form of power. Professionals also tend to have a world view and a set of values and commitments that differ from those of nonprofessionals and which may lead to the vesting of interests in certain institutional arrangements. Some analysts regard this matter as of major political importance, to the point of arguing that the technical-managerial elite, in pursuing its own interests and its own brand of rationality, will eventually dig the grave of communism. One need not subscribe to the grave-digger hypothesis, however, to recognize the existence of a certain permanent tension between the state and the entrepreneurs in a socialist economy.

The socialist character of the economy also affects the nature of the incentives that are provided in order to elicit entrepreneurial effort. The original socialist notion was that moral incentives would eventually replace material incentives and that socialist entrepreneurs seeking to improve the welfare of all the people would greatly outperform capitalist entrepreneurs motivated primarily by personal gain. Had that indeed come about there would have been a large discontinuity indeed between the Soviet period and the Russian past. Unfortunately, the possibility of a true test of the effectiveness of moral incentives vanished with the reinforcement of material incentives in the 1930s following Stalin's attack on "equality-mongers." The incentive system since then has been a mixture of material and moral incentives, with the former evidently playing the more significant role.

The structure of material incentives permits a sufficient degree of inequality to make it possible for wages to reflect roughly the relative productivity of different classes of workers, and perhaps to reflect differences in the performance of managerial officials as well. One may question, however, whether that structure permits sufficient income differentiation to reflect the relative performance of entrepreneurs, or of managerial officials in their capacity as entrepreneurs. Schumpeter regarded the critical feature of entrepreneurial incentives to be the "lottery" nature of the profits of innovation; that is, it is not the average level of profits earned by innovative activity but the large profits earned by the most successful innovations that are the major spur to entrepreneurial effort. The fact that Soviet financial authorities have employed lottery bonds rather than fixed-interest bonds as the instrument for mobilizing savings suggests that the lottery principle applies to economic behavior in the USSR as well. If so, the socialist character of the economy may weaken the ability of the state to elicit a high level of entrepreneurial effort, because it would require an incentive system that would produce such high incomes for successful entrepreneurship as to be unacceptable by the normal socialist standards of distributive equity.

The level of entrepreneurship is affected not only by incentives, however, but also by the level of risk, and in this respect, too, the socialist character of the economy involves a sharp break with the nonsocialist Russian past. The high profits earned by the top winners of the capitalist entrepreneurial lottery reflect not only the return to pure entrepreneurial ability but they are also a return to the high level of risk borne by the financiers of the innovation. In the socialist economy, however, the risk is borne by the state. If a certain innovation proves to be obsolescent by the time production begins, as evidently is sometimes the case, no individual bears the cost of the wasted capital. The hapless entrepreneurs may suffer a diminution of income and perhaps a demotion, but there is no lawful way in the socialist economy to transfer the risk of entrepreneurship from the state to individuals. Since the return to innovation under socialism must reward only ability and not risk, the appropriate level of returns to entrepreneurship need not be as high as in a private-profit economy in order to elicit an equivalent level of entrepreneurial effort.

While there are no lawful ways for individuals to bear the risks of entrepreneurship, there are unlawful ways. Much of the activity of the "second economy" consists of entrepreneurship of the classically Marshallian kind—redirecting resources toward an equilibrium state. Gregory Grossman discusses the entrepreneurial role of the Party in this capacity, but the agents of the second economy also serve this function. The difference between the two is that the Party does it legally while the second economy does it illegally. Because it is illegal, the risks are high, but the returns are evidently correspondingly high, and the combination has succeeded in generating what may be regarded as the most vigorous sphere of entrepreneurship in the Soviet economy. It may be argued, therefore, that the social ownership of productive property diminishes entrepreneurial effort by reducing the risk borne by the entrepreneurs, much as penny-ante poker fails to produce the highest-quality gambling behavior.

Socialism, we now know, does not require central planning. It was also known in 1917, one might say, by socialists of the anarchist and syndicalist persuasion, but they had not made a case for the economic viability of their notions about a society of small communes and cooperatives. The economic theory of a decentralized socialism did not appear until the mid-1930s, almost thirty years after Barone laid the groundwork. It was therefore quite natural for the revolutionary leadership to regard some sort of central planning as the appropriate way of running a socialized economy; and perhaps the Russian historical tradition of centralized government contributed to that decision. The institution of central planning is a major determinant of the nature of Soviet entrepreneurship.

For one thing, central planning as a way of managing a nation's economy calls for qualities that differ from those normally associated with entrepreneurship. Entrepreneurship derives from uncertainty, and indeed increases the level of uncertainty in the system. *Stikhiinost'*, or spontaneity, has long been regarded as a bad thing in Soviet history; it is the opposite of control, and planning requires control. The logic of planning requires that once the plan is made, fulfillment of the plan must be the primary objective of all economic agents. But innovation cannot be reduced to such time schedules. The enterprise manager who has assumed the entrepreneurial role and is engaged in the act of "bringing about new combinations" cannot be sure that the innovation will work the first time around. Innovators tend to underfulfill plans: if their projects are ultimately successful they may yield large benefits but in the interim they disrupt plan schedules.

Innovation also requires the kind of autonomy that is difficult to make available to economic agents in a planned economy. One of the most important kinds of "new combinations" that characterizes Schumpeterian entrepreneurship is the creation of new organizational structures; merging enterprises in a way that increases efficiency, or changing the organizational structure to suit the requirements of a new technological process. Central planning, however, leans toward uniform structures. Once a certain organizational structure is decided upon for a certain type of enterprise, a statute is issued that requires all enterprises of that type to employ that structure. In the early days of the production-association reform this practice appeared to be changing; no statute was issued, and a considerable variety of organizational forms appeared. But as Paul Cocks reports below, that diversity has evidently been unsettling to the central planners and the move is on to force them all into a common mold. To deprive an innovator of the power to adapt organizational structure to new technology is to increase the difficulty of implementing innovation successfully.

Perhaps more important than autonomy over the organizational structure of existing production units is the power to bring entirely new production units into operation. This entrepreneurial function is indeed carried on in the USSR, by officials of the ministry. But only they have that power. In capitalist economies the formation of new companies is one of the most important vehicles of technological advance; in many instances such companies are formed because the conservative manage-

ment of existing companies is unwilling to take the risk of introducing
a new product. Soviet ministries are unlikely to be less conservative in
their technological and economic judgment than capitalist corporations,
and their monopoly over the right to establish new production units
reduces the number of innovations that might otherwise appear.

Socialism and central planning are two features of the domestic Soviet
economy that have influenced the nature of entrepreneurship. In concluding this introduction, we should direct our attention to a feature of
the external environment that has exerted a major influence on entrepreneurship in the USSR: the high rate of technological progress in the
outside world. It has influenced the contribution that entrepreneurship
has made to both the static efficiency of the economy and to its dynamic
growth.

The contribution of entrepreneurship to static efficiency corresponds
roughly to the Marshallian notion discussed by Granick and Grossman.
Even in the absence of technological change an economy may expect to
be in disequilibrium much of the time, a centrally planned economy
perhaps more than a decentralized economy. The entrepreneur is the
agent who discovers that certain products currently sold in market *A*
could command a higher price in market *B*, and he takes the risk of
redirecting the resources in a manner that reduces the extent of disequilibrium. If planning were perfect there would be no need for entrepreneurship of this kind; indeed the early proponents of socialist central
planning held the view that the omnipresent disequilibria in the capitalist
economy reflected the "anarchy of the marketplace," and the advantage
of central planning is precisely that it could more rationally allocate
resources toward the desired ends. The socialist society therefore would
have no need for the kind of entrepreneurship that consists of making
up for the mistakes of the market. As it turned out, however, perfect
planning is not of this world, and the judgment of most analysts is that
the centrally planned economy tends to generate greater disequilibria of
this kind than the market economy. The planning system itself, however,
has not succeeded in generating an effective form of entrepreneurship to
eliminate these "nonmarket failures," in the felicitous phrase of Gregory
Grossman. The society has found a partial substitute in the form of Party
intervention, which is the subject of Grossman's essay. The evidence of
the incompleteness with which the function is carried out is the vitality
of the second economy, which comes as close as one can imagine to pure
Marshallian entrepreneurship, for that activity consists precisely in de-
tecting and correcting the disequilibria generated by the imperfections of
the planning system.

If imperfections in planning were of small proportions, the weakness
of this type of entrepreneurship would be of little importance. Planning

imperfections are, however, of large proportions, and part of the reason is the pace of technological progress. If all technological progress ceased, for example, the central planners would eventually get to know the full detail about the production possibilities of all enterprises and the productivity of all resources in all of their possible uses. Planners would approach, in effect, the ideal state of perfect knowledge of the economy. But technological change causes old knowledge to lose its value, and it takes time for the planners to acquire knowledge of the new production possibilities, new equipment, new materials, and so forth. The more rapid the rate of technological change, the more imperfect the planners' knowledge of the potential demand and supply of all commodities, and the greater the degree of error in economic planning. And the more imperfect the planning system, the greater the need for the kind of Marshallian entrepreneurship to which the system has not been hospitable. It is in this sense that technological progress abroad, by forcing the pace of technological change within the USSR, has contributed to the problem of entrepreneurship within the economy.

The major impact of technological progress abroad, however, has fallen not on Marshallian entrepreneurship but on the Schumpeterian kind—the bringing about of "new combinations," which is the essence of technological progress. It is interesting to wonder what the pace of technological progress would have been in the USSR if, say, all technological progress in the advanced capitalist world had ceased in 1917. One might expect the pace to have been fairly rapid at first, as the developing Soviet economy replaced its old capital stock with new and drew abreast of the now-stationary technological level of the advanced countries. David Granick finds that Soviet technological progress of this kind was in fact fairly rapid in the 1930s. How rapidly, however, would the USSR have pulled ahead of a technologically frozen world? Certainly the R & D institutes would have continued to develop new products and new technology, which ministries and managers would eventually have incorporated into production. But one suspects that the pace is likely to have been relatively slow. In this sense the actual achievements of Soviet entrepreneurs in promoting technological progress are due in large measure to the pressure upon them of the advancing technology of the capitalist world. There are few exceptions to the generalization that Soviet technological progress has been largely derivative of that originated in other countries.

The derivative nature of technological progress in the USSR ought not be regarded necessarily as evidence of the weakness of its entrepreneurial quality. The proper strategy for an underdeveloped country is to borrow heavily from abroad; to reinvent the computer is no less foolish than to reinvent the wheel. It is nevertheless surprising that with all the resources devoted to technological advance, so few genuinely new innovations can be credited to the USSR, particularly in the postwar period when the Soviets began to draw abreast of the world technology in a growing number of fields. That, however, may be too high a standard to apply in evaluating the Soviets' innovative performance. Even the Japanese, who in other respects have demonstrated a remarkable capacity to generate new technology, have not been distinguished in the number of genuinely original innovations. What Japanese entrepreneurship has succeeded in doing, however, is to approach the level of the best world technology in an extremely short period of time and in that way to become a powerful competitor in world markets. That performance is far beyond what the Soviets have managed to attain.

Various of the essays that follow, particularly that of Paul Cocks, discuss the difficulties the Soviets have faced in promoting technological progress. One contributing factor merits notice as a concluding observation because it reflects a feature of historical continuity. The foreign commerce of Muscovy, we have learned, was conducted primarily by foreigners residing in Moscow. The knowledge possessed by Russian merchants about products for trade available abroad was therefore limited to that brought to their attention by foreigners. One must suppose that the gains from trade would have been greater had the Russian merchants been in the custom of scouring foreign cities for objects of commercial trade. At any rate, one is struck by the similarity of the Soviet stance with respect to the acquisition of foreign technology. By and large Soviet managers and engineers have relatively little first-hand knowledge of the advanced technology available in the outside world. Except for the limited foreign travel of trade delegations and more recently from scientific and cultural changes, that knowledge had been acquired primarily from books and periodicals and from the efforts of foreign businessmen coming to Moscow as of old to sell their products and machines and factories. Again the contrast with Japan is striking. A century ago Japan was more insulated from contact with the outside world than was Russia at that time. Once the commitment to modernization was made, however, Japanese students and entrepreneurs began to travel the world in growing numbers, and in the postwar period they have appeared as residents and travelers in other countries with the same frequency as their competitors from the United States, West Germany, Sweden, and elsewhere. When technology is advancing rapidly, a nation whose entrepreneurs are not a full part of the international intercourse in ideas and information cannot expect to keep abreast of that advance. Soviet entrepreneurship has thus inherited some of the legacy of the merchants of Muscovy.

XI

GREGORY GUROFF

The Red-Expert Debate: Continuities in the State-Entrepreneur Tension

In his brilliant though controversial history of Russian culture, James H. Billington describes the period of the 1930s as the "Revenge of Muscovy." This cogent analysis is also in many ways descriptive of the changes that were taking place in the sphere of economic activity at the end of the twenties. The Stalin period has often been described as the second revolution—in Lenin's terms, the political revolution had been secured so attention could now be turned to the economic revolution and the creation of a new society and the new Soviet man. Although it would be fascinating, I will not discuss the specific economic policies adopted to herald this revolution, but rather I intend to focus upon the decisions regarding the nature of economic and political activity embodied in the Red-expert debate. This debate was ostensibly resolved by the expulsion of the old specialists and their replacement by a new cadre of Red-experts.

Rather than affirming a new principle, however, this second revolution first rejected the developments of the late imperial period in which economic activity and decision making had first crept beyond the confines of government circles. Then it reaffirmed the peculiar Russian administrative order which viewed economic and political functions as inextricably intertwined and supported the proposition that economic activity was primarily for the benefit of the state apparatus. But the reaffirmation of this model and its underlying principles did not necessarily imply a return to the particular policies of the tsarist era; rather, it represented a convenient framework for dealing with a number of specific issues that came to the fore in both the political and economic realms at the end of the twenties.

Several aspects of this debate make it critical for understanding the

Soviet experience. In the first instance, the Red-expert dichotomy has become a classic problem associated with socialist transformations, whether in the Soviet Union, China, or Cuba. All societies in which a transfer of power occurs face substantial problems of social reorganization. But is the Red-expert dichotomy a generic socialist problem equally applicable to all socialist transformations? Or is it a peculiar Russian phenomenon which has been projected in that curious amalgam known as Marxism-Leninism onto all others who attempt to follow a socialist path? If the former is the case, then the debate and its resolution have critical importance for other postrevolutionary socialist societies. But, even if we acknowledge that the problem is a generic one for socialist societies, the possibility still exists that its resolution in the Soviet case is idiosyncratic and that rather than being a model for other socialist societies it may well have become a straitjacket to the extent that it is directly imitated.

Second, the specific resolution of the issue paved the way for the creation of a new Soviet elite. As Sheila Fitzpatrick[1] has pointed out, we have devoted enormous energy to studying the victims of the Great Purges but much less time and effort concerning ourselves with the beneficiaries—and beneficiaries there certainly were. In fact, in the crucible of activity flowing from the decisions concerning the Red-expert debate the careers of much of the post-Stalin leadership were to be formed. Many of them were to come from the *vydvizhentsy* (workers promoted within the apparat)—adult workers who were provided the opportunity to return to crash courses to improve their technical training and to increase their chances of rapid upward mobility, or as Stalin promised, they could become "builder[s] of the new life, . . . and a real replacement of the old guard." The decision to train the new political leadership as engineers with technical specialties was unprecedented. Such future luminaries of the Soviet Union as Nikita Sergeevich Khrushchev, General Secretary Brezhnev, Defense Minister Ustinov, former Premier Aleksei Kosygin, and Foreign Trade Minister Patolichev were to join thousands of other young adult workers in returning to school.

During the period roughly from the Shakhty trial of 1928 to the Piatakov trial in 1937 the battle continued, but the Party apparatus, with the General Secretary in the lead, had already decided that Soviet Russia would be liberated from the hands of the non-Party specialists who could hoodwink their technically unskilled Communist bosses by a newly created class of Red-experts, who were presumably more loyal to the Soviet regime and who had adequate technical training to deal with the issues of the economy themselves.

[1] Sheila Fitzpatrick, "Stalin and the Making of a New Elite, 1928-1939," *Slavic Review* 39 (June 1979):377-402.

In the meantime, Bolshevik industrial managers had to run Soviet industry—a task that was becoming increasingly frustrating as political matters intruded ever more into economic concerns and as not only the specialists came under attack, but also their Communist bosses, who were seen as either incompetent or as overly protective of their "politically unreliable" staffs. Talented Bolshevik industrial managers—and indeed there were some—often found themselves at war with the Party Secretariat. Regardless of their political positions, Bolshevik leaders at the top of the industrial pyramid from Aleksei Rykov and Feliks Dzerzhinskii to Valentin Kuibyshev and Sergo Ordzhonikidze found themselves attempting to protect their talent while paying lip service to the drive to oust the non-Party specialists. Each in his own way tried to stand against the pressure of the Party apparatus, usually by quoting Lenin on the value of the specialists and on the nature of the NEP, which lent an air of authority to their continuing utilization of specialists. Each in his own way raised the issue of a legitimate separation between the demands of politics and economics, but they were drowned out in the noise of the new campaign.

Lenin had declared on a number of occasions that the NEP was a serious and long-term policy, but the NEP was running its course. The NEP had been successful in its principal purpose, of restoring the economy to its prewar levels, but in effect this had simply been a delaying device affording the hard-pressed Bolsheviks breathing space to develop their political base while the devastated economy proceeded along the familiar paths of prerevolutionary patterns. Now that the prewar levels were being reached, conscious decisions about the future had to be made.

The industrialization debates had established that the Bolsheviks were sharply divided on how to proceed along this largely uncharted course. Political struggles after Lenin's death were being resolved largely in Stalin's favor and the developing intricate alliances were determining the economic stands for each side. Fortuitously, the economic positions of the "right opposition" were closely linked to the views expressed by a large segment of the non-Bolshevik economic cadres who still predominated in the economic sphere—specialists for whom Stalin had long felt contempt. Though racked by internal debate, the Party also understood its failure to gain the genuine support of the masses even ten years after the Revolution, and sought ways to stamp the new regime with a distinctive Bolshevik flavor and ensure loyalty within the state apparatus. An obvious solution was at hand with the elevation of a younger generation of Party loyalists, who as soldiers or children of the Revolution had seen their paths for upward mobility blocked by a near monopoly on professional positions held by the prerevolutionary intelligentsia. The situation that prevailed in the economic sphere was little different from that in other professions or within the Party apparatus itself. Therefore, the General Secretary was able to take advantage of this desire for the just rewards of the Revolution claimed by this new generation and to use their support to stamp legitimacy on his own policies.

The purges of the late twenties are seen by most observers as important because they represent a dress rehearsal for the Great Purges of the thirties. In a larger sense, however, they have an intrinsic importance because they represent one further fundamental shift away from the society fashioned by Lenin toward a return to the insularity of Muscovy. In more general terms, it may be argued that these shifts ended the revolutionary era, which saw the rise of the professional intelligentsia beginning in the 1840s and 1850s. Those tainted with "freethinking" had to be removed and to be replaced with those loyal to the "cause" for whom interest ended at the border and who would deify the man and consecrate the policies responsible for providing their upward mobility.

To paraphrase both Lenin and Abram Tertz, Stalin's Russia took two steps back to the ideas and forms of the grandfathers, rejecting the still-born aspirations of the fathers, in order to take one step forward toward the ill-defined goal of creating the new Soviet society. In so doing, however, a fundamental problem of economic organization and the relationship of economics to politics, which had finally been raised in the prewar period, was summarily dismissed and declared resolved. The Red-expert debate was simply an extension of the debate that erupted in the prewar period between the state and the emerging entrepreneurial class. The major focus of the debate was the growing awareness that economic and political actors had fundamentally different roles to play, and that no matter how much of an overlap existed in interests and responsibilities, tension was bound to develop between the two groups. Perhaps the issue was already being resolved in the dying days of the old regime with the inevitable ultimate rejection of a Western entrepreneurial model. Nonetheless, Stalin's Russia firmly ended the debate fusing the two functions by eliminating the old specialists, replacing them with Red-experts, and decreeing the problem solved and thus not open to debate. The important point here is that the issue was resolved on political grounds. The new experts had won out, not by proving their experience or ideas superior, but simply by proving they were more loyal. Part of the battle involved charges that the disloyalty of the specialists led them to produce economic plans which were damaging to Soviet Russia's growth—thus the ideas of the specialists had to be rejected not because they proved unworkable but because they came from a disloyal source. To paraphrase Moshe Lewin's remarks on the Kulaks, the specialists were not removed because they were counterrevolutionaries, but were labeled as such so that they could be removed. The new Red-experts could not affirm the policies articulated by the specialists even though they may have been rational, and therefore they found that from the start their decision-making role was largely circumscribed by political considerations.

In reality, Stalin's decision only postponed the debate and, in a classic Russian pattern, forced it into convoluted forms in the coming decades. The problem has nonetheless remained, and Soviet leaders have had to deal with it. Even current Soviet leaders have on occasion recognized the fundamentally different roles that economic and political actors play, and although these roles may overlap and intertwine, tension between the demands of the varying functions actually exist. Moreover, they have recognized that these tensions do not simply arise from the disloyalty of one of the groups involved. Function then does have an important role to play in defining the nature of concerns and interest of individual actors. But, by definition these tensions should not and could not exist in the new society. Soviet economists were left to face a problem that many other groups in Soviet society have faced, namely, how to discuss and deal with fundamental problems that the leadership has already declared to be nonproblems and thus not legitimate subjects for discussion.

The Prerevolutionary Legacy

Private entrepreneurship had been the dream of very few Russians during the nineteenth century, although a number of isolated and eloquent voices were raised in support of the principle of moving economic decision making outside the confines of the state apparatus. Most, however, eventually succumbed to the realities of the Russian economic scene.[2] The state was not only the major investor in but also the major consumer of the products of industrial enterprises. Capital in sufficient quantities for major industrial undertakings was largely unavailable outside the state or, as in the case of foreign investment, without the active participation and support of the state. Russian economic thinkers, whatever their inclinations, had become conditioned to view the state as the focal point for economic activity, and the developments of the late imperial period, although offering opportunities for a new vision of economic activity, were not sufficient to change this viewpoint.

Not until the very end of the century, under the programs of Sergei

[2] See Guroff, "The State and Industrialization in Russian Economic Thought, 1909-1914" (Ph.D. dissertation, Princeton University, 1970). Also Joad F. Normano, *The Spirit of Russian Economics* (New York, 1945), and N. K. Karataev, "Dvorianski-liberalnaia ekonomicheskaia mysl' . . . ," *Istoriia russkoi ekonomicheskoi mysli* (herafter cited as *IREM*) (Moscow, 1959), 2, part 1.

Witte, did a self-supporting private sector begin to emerge. Witte himself shared few of the sympathies for private enterprise of his more liberal colleagues outside the government, but ironically it was his policy of rapid economic growth that made possible the emergence of an autonomous private sector.[3] Witte was first and foremost interested in the development of a strong industrial base to support Russia's great power aspirations. Slowly he came to realize that the political structure itself was a major obstacle to industrialization, and even more slowly did he understand that his goals and aspirations were often congruent with those of the emerging industrial class. But the fragility of the Russian industrial economy was exposed with a devastating downturn at the turn of the century, thereby undermining Witte's position and policies. Russia's depression was prolonged and deepened by foreign affairs debacles and the increasing domestic turmoil. While the rest of Europe began to recover from financial crisis, Russia became more mired in economic stagnation.

In the wake of the events of 1905, the Witte system appeared to be swept away and adjudged an interesting failure. Not until 1909 did Russia show signs of renewed industrial growth. In fact, the Witte system had partially succeeded in laying the foundation for this new industrial spurt, but one that differed greatly from the kind of development Witte had envisaged. As Alexander Gerschenkron has noted, after 1909 Russia began to approach the precedent pattern of economic growth of Western Europe for the first time.[4] However, the state was not in a position to contribute much to this new advance, for it was deeply concerned with questions of political order and stability and had precious little energy to devote to the economy. The Russian economy was slowly beginning to generate its own capital to finance expansion, absorbing some of the foreign debt, and making the most spectacular advances in industries that were not primarily dependent on government orders for their survival.[5]

During the relatively brief economic advance, cut short by the war, Russian industrialists were able to raise but not resolve questions about the fundamental relationship of economic activity to the state apparatus. Owners, managers, economic and technical cadres of industry, all shared to some extent the organizing zeal that had accompanied the upheavals

[3] S. Iu. Witte, *Konspekt lektsii o narodnom khoziastve* (St. Petersburg, 1912), esp. pp. 415-568; and Theodore von Laue, *Serge Witte and the Industrialization of Russia* (New York, 1963).

[4] Alexander Gerschenkron, "An Economic History of Russia," *Journal of Economic History*, 12, no. 2 (Spring 1952):157ff.

[5] Gerschenkron, "An Economic History"; Margaret Miller, *The Economic Development of Russia, 1905-1914* (London, 1926); and Richard Lorenz, *Anfänge der bolschwistischen Industriepolitik* (Cologne, 1965).

of 1905. They appeared to raise more self-confident voices about their ability to deal with the problems of Russia's industrial development.[6] This self-confidence of the industrial leadership was reenforced by the appearance of new cadres of managers, technicians, and economists, who made it less necessary to turn to the state apparatus for expertise. This flow of newly and better-trained economic cadres was partly a response to the increasing opportunities available in the private sector and partly a consequence of a shift in training made available after the turn of the century, which produced graduates interested in and capable of exercising independent economic judgments.[7]

Yet, Russian industrialists were quite conscious of the extreme fragility and volatility of the Russian economy. They were confronted with the choice of trying to act on their own in the face of economic uncertainties or trying to secure government cooperation in dealing with the vicissitudes of Russian economic life. Like many of their Western colleagues, but perhaps with a greater sense of urgency, they sought to reach an accommodation with the state in the hope that such an accord would guarantee a regularity to economic activity and a reasonable rate of return on their investments rather than the chaos they saw arising from the unfettered marketplace. At the same time, they found themselves confronted by a state apparatus that appeared dominated by agrarian interests and hostile to the needs of industry, in part because many of the industrial leaders did not come from the Russian Orthodox community. Nonetheless, the industrial community persevered unwilling, or perhaps unable, to acknowledge the fundamental nature of their conflict with the tsarist system.

Although several major issues animated state-industrialist relations in the prewar years, a few will give a flavor of the growing confrontation.

Industrialists recognized that the state itself was the single most important source of investment and sales of industrial goods. Thus industrial organizations urged the government repeatedly to try to introduce coherence and planning into future expenditures so that the industrialists could rationally plan their production and introduce a reasonable level of coherence into their own ventures. The state responded with only mild interest in these ideas, partially out of a desire to maintain control of the budget, and partially out of more venal instincts to use the state budget to reward friends and punish enemies. With Witte's departure in 1903,

[6] For a detailed discussion, see Ruth AmEnde Roosa, "The Association of Industry and Trade, 1906-1914: An Examination of the Economic Views of Organized Industrialists in the Pre-Revolutionary Russia" (Ph.D. dissertation, Columbia University, 1967), as well as her chapter in this collection.

[7] See Guroff, "The Legacy of Russian Economic Education: The Saint Petersburg Polytech," *The Russian Review*, 31 (July 1972):272-81.

no major governmental figure emerged who placed a high premium on rapid industrial development.

Secondly, industrialists interpreted the quite unequal trade treaty that Russia had been forced to sign with Germany in 1905 as a major indication of the state's unwillingness to support Russian industry in its battle with what was often perceived as German colonial dominance. Arguments used by the state that were based on the need to preserve a political balance in Europe and not alienate the Kaiser's empire were of little avail. For a number of years industrial groups sought to get the government to renegotiate or cancel the trade treaty with little apparent success.[8]

Finally, Russian legislation on industrial organizations was perhaps the most backward in Europe. Industrialists sought to achieve legal recognition of corporate and syndicate organizations. A state commission studied the problem for nearly five years with no resolution of problems until early July 1914. The legal changes that were achieved did not address any of the problems raised by the industrialists. Rather, the new regulations focused on limiting the amount of land industrial corporations could hold and on restricting the amount of "Jewish" capital that could be invested in any one venture.[9]

On the eve of war with Germany the Russian industrial community, backed by its technical cadres, found itself frustrated by the actions of what was perceived to be an agrarian government. The industrial community was as close as it had ever been to openly acknowledging its fundamental differences with the tsarist government. The government was forced to rescind its new regulations but the mutual hostility continued. When war came it served to dampen temporarily some of the more overt differences. Germany was the enemy of the industrial classes. Perhaps they, more than any other group, saw clear benefits that could arise from Germany's defeat. The industrialists publicly stood foursquare behind the war effort, convinced, as were most others, that the war would be short and ultimately won, because Germany could be starved into submission. They openly looked forward to the end of the war, which would bring the end of German industrial domination of Russia.[10]

[8] See Guroff, "State and Industrialization," esp. pp. 120ff. Also, A. Manuilov, "Industrializm i Russko-Germanskii torgovlyi dogovor," *Russkie vedomosti*, no. 52 (March 3, 1912):2.

[9] P. V. Kamenskii, *Znachenie torgovo-promyshlennikh trestov na zapade i u nas.* (Moscow, 1909), esp. pp. 1-10, 77ff.; N. S. Zhukov, "Burzhuaznye teorii imperializma," *IREM*, 3, part 1, pp. 332ff.; V. V. Oreshkin, "Voprosy imperializma i sotsializma," *IREM*, 3, part 1, pp. 122ff.; Roosa, "Association," pp. 280-83; and G. Tsyperovich, *Sindikaty i tresty v Rossii* (Moscow, 1919).

[10] See for example: P. P. Migulin, "Voina i nashe ekonomicheskoe polozhenie," *Novyi ekonomist*, no. 30 (July 26, 1914):2-6; I. Kh. Ozerov, *Na novyi put': K ekonomicheskomu*

Yet, within the first year of the war, the industrial community realized that the war would be longer than expected and the government was not capable of organizing the war effort. The subsequent creation of the War Industries Committees represents one of the most intriguing spontaneous organizational efforts in Russian history. Brought into being ostensibly to work hand in hand with the government, in coordinating the distribution of war materials, the Committees were greeted with considerable suspicion and hostility by the state. The War Industries Committees provided a crucible of common experience for managers, owners, and specialists alike. For many it was the first opportunity to discuss the national needs of particular economic sectors. The understanding of the problems faced and the hostility of the state apparatus led simply to greater alienation from the tsarist regime. At the same time that much of the industrial leadership was becoming convinced that the tsarist regime had to be abandoned, few thought of fundamental changes in state-enterprise relations. Recognizing their own weakness, they still perceived a society in which the state was the primary economic actor, although the new society would be dominated by industrial interests rather than by agrarian ones.[11]

When the tsarist regime collapsed in February 1917 and the Provisional Government took over, it was not surprising that many of those who had carried industry's battle and who had initiated the activities of the War Industries Committees—Guchkov, Konovalov, Riabushinskii and others—found themselves in positions of considerable influence and power. While this is not the appropriate place to analyze the failure of the Provisional Government, it is worth pointing out in this context that the industrialists' commitment to the war effort and an ultimate victory, coupled with their inability to find short-term solutions to the economic and social dislocations in part occasioned by the war provided little positive contribution to the prospects of the new government. Although within the confines of the War Industries Committees (WIC) many plans and policies had been discussed, there was little hope of realizing any new direction while the war raged on. The WIC had even attempted to initiate a dialogue, and cooperate with the workers, but these efforts were largely stillborn—opposed by the government and received ambivalently within the WIC.

---

osvobozhdeniiu Rossii (Moscow, 1915), pp. 320ff.; S. Zagorskii, "Voina i zadachi torgovoi politiki," *Izvestiia imperatorskago volnago ekonomicheskago obshchestva*, nos. 9-10 (November 16, 1914):1-4; and S. Dmitrievskii, "Na puty K emantsipatsii," *Izvestiia tsentral'nago voenno-promyshlennago komiteta*, no. 102 (May 31, 1916):1-2.

[11] Roosa, "Association," pp. 285ff.

The Bolsheviks and the Problem of Economic Organization

The October Revolution fundamentally altered the rules by which the game would be played, but this was only dimly perceived at first. For many in the industrial community it was hard to take the ragtag band of Bolsheviks seriously. There was even a tendency to view them as a temporary plague that would soon abate. Many proceeded to act as if the Bolsheviks would go away, carrying on business as usual and trying to reach temporary compromises with the Bolsheviks when necessary. As the Civil War reached a crescendo and it became clear that the Bolsheviks intended to hold on, gradually the industrial owners and elite began to disappear from the scene. Left in place, especially in the central industrial regions, were the organizations created by the WIC. Staffed by economists, technicians, managers, and scientists, they provided the framework for continuing discussion of Russia's economic problems. Confirmed Marxists of Bolshevik and Menshevik persuasion worked quite amiably with moderate and even right-wing professionals, concerned most often with professional dialogue and not politics. It is in this context that Leonid Krasin, the Bolshevik electrical engineer, first became acquainted with the economic views of Professor Grinevetskii, a man whose political views were to be characterized by Lenin as among the most reactionary he had ever encountered. Nonetheless, the professional dialogue continued, and Krasin was later to be responsible for bringing Grinevetskii's work to the attention of Lenin and others in the Bolshevik leadership.[12]

Within days after the surprising ease of the coup in Petrograd, the Bolsheviks had to begin wrestling with the problem of the role of non-Party specialists in the new Soviet structure. Bereft of the necessary economic cadres within his own party, Lenin moved quickly to try to attract these specialists into the new state apparatus of the Bolsheviks. He carefully employed the contacts of two leading Bolshevik engineers who had been active in the WIC, Krasin and Krzhizhanovskii.

From the outset Lenin cajoled and sometimes drove the Party to use all available talent and he sought to protect conscientious specialists from the wrath and jealousy of the Party apparatus. Battles erupted over the use of specialists in the Red Army (e.g., the Stalin-Trotsky standoff at Tsaritsyn), in the management of factories (e.g., the debate over workers' control), and in the economic organizations of state, but at each point

---

[12] Nikolai Valentinov (Volskii), *Novaia ekonomicheskaia politika i krizis partii posle smerti Lenina* (hereafter *NEP*) (Hoover Institution, 1971), pp. 176ff.; and V. Sarabianov, "Predislovie," to V. I. Grinevetskii, *Poslevoennye perspektivy russkoi promyshlennosti*, 2nd ed. (Moscow, 1922).

Lenin had his way and the role of specialists was temporarily assured. Yet, within the Party apparatus, suspicion and even envy of the specialists continued to smolder. Ideological considerations aside, it is clear that Lenin as well as Trotsky and other prominent leaders of the Party did not feel that the appearance of specialists in the Soviet structure was a threat to their personal positions. But members of the middle and lower levels of the Party, who had fought and won the Revolution, found that as Bolshevik power was being established, they often remained in positions subordinate to former enemies. Quickly, some members of the Party leadership identified themselves with the antispecialist position, most prominently, Joseph Stalin. The process of attracting specialists to the state apparatus was well under way even during the Civil War, but the end of the war and the announcement of the NEP in 1921 removed the last obstacles and opened the gates for the economic specialists to join the new regime in its efforts to construct a new society.[13]

After the initial disasters of workers' control, the role of non-Party specialists in the economic organizations of the country grew steadily. The number of specialists working in the Supreme Economic Council (Vesenkha) expanded along with its activities during the Civil War. The first major new economic venture, GOELRO, became the virtual domain of non-Party specialists. Lenin recognized this when he praised the GOELRO report and observed that "more than 200 specialists—almost all, without exception, opponents of Soviet power—worked with interest on GOELRO, although they are not Communists."[14] In fact, it can be argued that not only the work but the idea itself was suggested to Lenin by non-Party specialists.[15] The bulk of the specialists, recruited largely by Krasin and Krzhizhanovskii, the two electrical engineers in the party, had worked together in the WIC. But GOELRO was not an exception; when Gosplan was established in 1921, a staff of thirty-four included only seven Bolsheviks, only two of whom held professional positions. As late as 1924 when the Gosplan staff had expanded to nearly five hundred, there were still only forty-eight Party members and again most of the Party members held nonprofessional positions.[16]

[13] Lenin, "Ocherednye zadachi Sovetskoi vlasti," *Polnoe sobranie sochinenii* (hereafter *PSS*), 5th ed., 36:165-208. Also see Z. K. Zvezdin, "Iz istorii deiatel'nosti Gosplana v 1921-1924 gg.," *Voprosy istorii KPSS* (hereafter *ViKPSS*), 3 (1967):45-46; and Valentinov, *NEP*.

[14] Lenin, *PSS*, 44:51.

[15] The credit is often given to the work of V. I. Grinevetskii, *Poslevoennye perspektivy russkoi promyshlennosti*, 1st ed. (Kharkov, 1919). Valentinov, *NEP*, makes this argument at length. Also see Leon Smolinski, "Grinevetskii and Soviet Industrialization," *Survey*, no. 67 (April 1968):100-15, and Guroff, "Lenin and Russian Economic Thought," in Bernard Eisenstadt, ed., *Lenin and Leninism* (Boston, 1972), pp. 200-205.

[16] Zvezdin, "Iz istorii deiatel'nosti Gosplana," pp. 45-56.

The number of non-Party specialists who sought and found work in the economic organizations of the Soviet state increased rapidly with the announcement of the NEP in 1921. For many specialists who had remained on the sidelines during the Civil War and the period of War Communism, the NEP represented to them the abandonment by the Bolsheviks of their more extreme policies and a return to rational economic decision making. Nikolai Valentinov-Volskii, for one, argues that this perception was widely shared in non-Party circles and was the cause for the appearance in substantial numbers of technical cadres in Soviet agencies.[17] The Bolsheviks did little to dissuade the technical specialists from this point of view. While most agencies had a large number of non-Party specialists, it is hard to pin down the backgrounds of all of them. For the most part, the specialists represented left or socialist political positions, with many former Mensheviks among their number. Few had been professional revolutionaries, and the great majority had professional careers in the government, business, or academies before the war, and most had had extensive contact with the WIC during the war. In fact, the electrotechnical section of the WIC was the fertile recruiting ground for Krasin, its former chairman, for the GOELRO project.

Lenin's death in January 1924 deprived the non-Party specialists of their chief supporter and protector within the Party. The goals of the NEP had dovetailed well with the views of the bulk of the non-Party specialists. Lenin did not hide the fact that the NEP meant the consolidation of Bolshevik political control and that political opposition would not be tolerated. But for the specialists the Lenin of the NEP was a much less fearsome figure than the Lenin of War Communism, and the political control could be accepted as the price to be paid for economic progress. Lenin had first described the NEP as a political expedient, but the more it succeeded in restoring the devastated economy, the more Lenin appeared to support its continuation. Especially in his last year he ceased to speak of the NEP as a temporary policy, and the more he enjoined the Party to think of it as a long-term and serious policy, the success of which depended on maintaining of the good will of the hard-working and honest specialists. He also realized that economic progress was intertwined with the regime's ability to create a framework that would encourage and reward economic innovation and higher productivity.[18]

[17] See Valentinov, *NEP*.

[18] For Lenin's views see *PSS*, 45:343-451, esp. pp. 369-77 and 389-406. For an interesting and extended Soviet scholarly discussion of Lenin's attitude toward *NEP* see E. B. Genkina, "K voprosu o leninskom obosnovanii novoi ekonomicheskoi politiki," *ViKPSS*, no. 1 (1967):58-70; V. I. Kuzmin, "Novaia ekonomicheskaia politika smychka sotsialisticheskoi promyshlennosti s melkokrestianskim khoziastvom," *ViKPSS*, no. 2 (1967):46-47; A. A. Matiugin, "O khronologicheskikh ramkakh perekhoda ot 'voennogo kommunizma' k novoi

Lenin himself was fascinated by the possibilities of technological innovation, particularly given the state's lack of investment capital and consequent need to find rapid and inexpensive ways to break out of the traditional circle of low productivity in spite of a limited pool of skilled workers and technicians. Lenin had been an avid supporter not only of GOELRO but also of possible experiments, as he confided to Krzhizhanovskii, with X-rays and perpetual-motion machines.[19]

To what extent Lenin's thinking was influenced by the ideas of the non-Party economic and scientific cadres whom he supported and protected is debatable. I have argued elsewhere that Lenin's views were developed largely out of the Russian context and owe much more to this tradition than to either Marxism or foreign models.[20] He was thus quite susceptible to the influences of a group of professionals who represented a tradition with which he was familiar and with which he sympathized. It is likely that his fascination with electricity as a possible salvation came in part from his close friend Krasin and from the work on the quiet but devoutly counterrevolutionary Professor Grinevetskii from the Moscow Higher Technical School.[21] Be that as it may, the point is that as the NEP progressed and Lenin was increasingly pleased with the results—he had been able to consolidate political power without serious opposition and the economy was showing signs of recovering from the devastation of war, revolution, and civil war—he became firmer in his conviction that the correct path had been chosen. For Lenin the NEP was indeed a serious and long-term policy. Perhaps he would have wished otherwise, that War Communism could have been continued or that socialist forms had quickly come to predominate, but it is difficult to deduce this position from his later works. He saw on the horizon a socialist society, but this was a matter of faith and not of immediate policy.

It is clear that among the likely successors to Lenin, the non-Party specialists would find neither the clear-cut support for the NEP nor the individual protection that the founder of Bolshevism had provided. Trotsky had not been afraid to use specialists in either the government or the

---

ekonomicheskoi politike," *ViKPSS*, no. 3 (1967):66-72; R. N. Savitskaia, V. I. Lenin i izpol'zovanie gosudarstvennogo kapitalizma v period mirnoi peredishki 1918 g.," *ViKPSS*, no. 3 (1967):57-66; and E. I. Beliantsev, "Nekotorye zamechanii k obsuzhdeniiu problem novoi ekonomicheskoi politiki," *ViKPSS*, no. 5 (1967):51-52.

[19] G. Krzhizhanovskii, *Sobranie sochinenii* (Moscow, 1936), 3:87ff.

[20] Guroff, "Lenin and Russian Economic Thought"; also see Alexander Gerschenkron as quoted in *Industrialization in Two Systems: Essays in Honor of Alexander Gerschenkron by a Group of His Students*, Henry Rosovsky, ed. (New York, 1966), p. 155.

[21] See note 15 above; also *Bol'shaia sovetskaia entsiklopediia*, 1st ed., 19:391-93; Mikh. Vindelbot, "Pamiati prof. V. I. Grinevetskogo," *Ekonomicheskaia zhizn'*, no. 99 (May 10, 1919):1; and Lubov Krassin, *Leonid Krassin: His Life and Work* (London, n.d.), pp. 41-45.

army, but his economic policy positions were anathema to the majority of specialists. Stalin was feared and in some quarters hated not because of his policy positions but because of his well-known contempt for the non-Party specialists. Among the others, only Rykov, head of the Supreme Economic Council, had developed a relationship of mutual respect with the non-Party economic cadres. Ironically Lenin's mantle as staunch supporter of the NEP and protector of non-Party specialists fell to an extremely unlikely candidate, the "Red executioner," Feliks Dzerzhinskii, who was named to head the Supreme Economic Council. The career of Dzerzhinskii as an economic manager is an extremely interesting case study of the interaction between the political leadership and the economic cadres. Unlike Lenin, Dzerzhinskii, despite his short tenure as Narkom of Transportation, came to his new post as head of the Supreme Economic Council with little apparent interest in and no coherent views on economic policy matters. His views evolved through his interaction with the specialists of Vesenkha. The way in which Dzerzhinskii entered the economic debates is worth our attention.

No organization was more affected by the influx of specialists than the Supreme Economic Council, which more than any other agency dealt with the day-to-day coordination of the Soviet economy. The problem of how to control the increasing influence of non-Party specialists was widely debated in the Party. The problem in Vesenkha was more acute, for the Party had not provided effective leadership in the organization. Vesenkha had had three chairmen in its early years. Two of them, Osinskii (1917-18) and P. A. Bogdanov (1921-23), had been relatively ineffectual. Rykov, head of Vesenkha from 1918 to 1921 and then again from 1923 to 1924, had excellent relations with the staff, but his other Party duties, especially after Lenin's illness, left him little time to cope with the increasing bureaucratic tangles in the economy. Within the Party apparatus, criticism of the NEP was increasingly coupled with attacks on the non-Soviet character of the economic organizations and the lack of effective Party control.

In February 1924 during the administrative reshuffling that followed Lenin's death, the Party apparatus decided to move in a direction designed to curb the independence of the economic cadres. Rykov, who now became head of Sovnarkom, could no longer even nominally serve as Vesenkha chairman. The decision was made to bring in a real "boss" whose strength and loyalty were beyond question. Apparently, a wide search was conducted, and a number of prospective candidates such as Piatakov, Rudzutak, and Sokolnikov were dismissed. Piatakov was perhaps the most serious candidate, but his economic views and his abrasive personality probably disqualified him. Rykov said of Piatakov, "You have to watch him constantly or he'll break all the dishes." In the meantime specialists in Vesenkha made a demonstration of their respect for Rykov and particularly for his ability to treat the staff well. But as the specialists shuddered, the announcement was made that the new chairman of Vesenkha would be Feliks Dzerzhinskii and, to add emphasis, it was announced that he would also continue as chief of the secret police (Cheka).

It appeared that the Party had found its tough boss and that specialists in Vesenkha had considerable reason to shudder. Dzerzhinskii's loyalty to the regime was unquestioned and he had demonstrated his willingness to use brutal force against opponents of the Party. Lenin had chosen him as first head of the Cheka for precisely these reasons. The methods of the Cheka had also been used liberally when he served as Narkom of Transportation and attempted to put the devastated transportation system back together. His Party connections, in addition to the loyalty shown him by the Cheka, made him a powerful figure, for not only was he a longstanding member of the Central Committee, he was now a candidate member of the Politburo. Yet, he had on occasion declared his independence from the majority political position of the Party. He had maintained his opposition to the treaty of Brest-Litovsk and had often criticized the growing bureaucratism infecting the Party itself.

Until his appointment as Narkom of Transportation, he had evinced little interest in economic policy questions. All of his prerevolutionary and most of his postrevolutionary writings and speeches are concerned almost exclusively with the political struggle. His approach as Narkom of Transportation was extremely pragmatic, although his experience with the reorganization of the railroads led him to begin to articulate broader concerns with the restoration of the economy. By mid-1923 he had begun to take positions on economic policy, but beyond support for greater attention to the development of a metallurgical industry, little was known of his economic views.[22] In addition, Dzerzhinskii had been involved in the Georgian Affair, which brought only terror to the non-Party cadres. Now with Lenin gone and Dzerzhinskii appointed, the specialists waited.

The wait was not long. Although he brought with him some of his assistants from the Cheka, Dzerzhinskii indicated quite early and quite clearly that he was primarily interested in economic policy and conscientious work, and that he would not tolerate interference from Party cadres in the technical work of the Council. He echoed Lenin's earlier attacks on *komchvanstvo* (Communist self-conceit) and indicated his full support for specialists who worked honestly and conscientiously. He was contemptuous of Party members who felt that they ought to have more

---

[22] F. E. Dzerzhinskii, *Izbrannye Proizvedeniya* (hereafter *IP*) (Moscow, 1967), 1:397-413.

authority simply because of their Party cards. Dzerzhinskii quickly began to earn the respect and even the affection of the specialists in Vesenkha.[23]

Although he acquired considerable experience dealing with economic problems both as head of Vesenkha and as Narkom of Transportation, he rarely delved into economic theory and often yielded on technical questions to the staff or in Party meetings to his deputy Piatakov. Yet, he developed an approach to economic problems that was to stand him in sharp contrast to Piatakov and the emerging left opposition. He stated quite clearly that he believed in Lenin's position that the NEP was a long-term venture, and he attempted to follow its logic as much as possible. This position placed him closer to the majority of non-Party specialists and it seems quite likely that they had considerable influence in bringing him to this position.

His economic policy, then, emerges more from an analysis of the particular economic actions he took than from a coherent position that he articulated. He initiated a number of "economic" campaigns as head of Vesenkha, and when the elements common to each are extracted, a policy emerges which is quite compatible with what later emerged as the right opposition. He was clearly concerned with the development of the metallurgical industries and spoke passionately for their expansion, but his position differed sharply with the positions of Piatakov and the other leftists. He felt that the first priority for the metals industry was the provision of goods to the mass market—lamps, roofing material, nails, horseshoes, and so on.[24]

Dzerzhinskii's concern for developing a mass market and for the improvement of the standard of living, particularly in the villages, motivated two other "campaigns." The first was a campaign to lower wholesale and thus retail prices of finished goods.[25] He and his staff encountered enormous difficulties in this campaign, for despite massive efforts to control prices, there appeared to be little reflection in lower prices for consumers. Dzerzhinskii began to strike out at what he considered the insufferable bureaucracy that the Party had created. His criticism of bureaucratism went so far that even Trotsky, with tongue in cheek, suggested at a meeting that Dzerzhinskii ought to be careful for he might be classed with the opposition. The frustration with this effort led Dzerzhinskii to begin a campaign called the "regime of economy"[26] in which the same aim of lowering prices would be accomplished by attacking the

[23] On Dzerzhinskii's role in Vesenkha and his relationship with the specialists, see among others, Valentinov, *NEP*, and A. F. Khatskevich, *Soldat velikikh boev* (Minsk, 1970), pp. 385ff.

[24] Dzerzhinskii, *IP*, 2:26-30, 96-139.

[25] Ibid., pp. 42-48.

[26] Ibid., pp. 294-95, 314-22.

enormous waste and inefficiency of the administration of industry. He devoted much of the last months of his life to this venture and came into continual conflict with the Party apparatus. His concern for the expansion of trade and consumer goods led him to a final position that simply confirmed the distrust the left felt for him. He too was concerned with the accumulation of capital for the expansion of industry, but his emphasis on consumer goods led him to seek a source of capital accumulation that was rejected by the left. Rather than squeeze the peasantry, Dzerzhinskii proposed that the only feasible way to accumulate capital was to raise the productivity of labor, a campaign of labor intensification.[27] He argued that Soviet workers were overpaid and underemployed. Again, this campaign found him lashing out at the Party "businessmen," who served as heads of factories but whom Dzerzhinskii accused of doing little more than sloganeering. He charged that when experts were sent in to increase productivity, the Party members gave them no support and allowed the workers to rough them up. If the Party was going to move the country forward, then the Party bosses in industry would have to give support to and learn from the experts.

In general, Dzerzhinskii favored balanced growth with heavy emphasis on improving the lot of the common people and in particular the peasantry. He adhered to Lenin's dictum that if socialism were to succeed it would have to do so by proving that it was more efficient and productive, not by forcing out private ventures through administrative edicts. When Dzerzhinskii's views are analyzed he appears to stand even to the right of the leaders of the emerging right opposition, Bukharin and Rykov.

Dzerzhinskii found himself on occasion in open battle with members of the Party apparatus who felt he went too far in defending specialists or that his views on bureaucratism came too close to opposition. He had a few encounters even with Stalin, but he did not back away from the fray. Dzerzhinskii suggested that although he signed the directives of Vesenkha, he was usually not the author, and that he ought to share the limelight with the specialists who were in fact responsible for various documents. Here, he was attacked on the grounds that such an act would undermine the authority of the Party, but Dzerzhinskii responded directly by asserting that quite the contrary, such an act would convey the willingness of the Party to work with conscientious specialists and thus give greater confidence to the regime.

The paradox of Dzerzhinskii the Red Executioner, the scourge of the bourgeoisie, as friend and patron of the specialists was not lost on some astute members of the Party. In fact, in 1925-26 rumors abounded in Moscow that Dzerzhinskii was being considered as a potential successor

---

[27] Ibid., pp. 42-48, 185-88.

to Stalin as general secretary of the Party. There is no evidence that Dzerzhinskii participated in any of these discussions. Quite the contrary— he appeared to lack any aspiration to advance up the Party bureaucracy and seemed to feel that he had all the power and influence necessary. As chairman of Vesenkha he rarely invoked his second function to gain attention, but when he reminded people that he was also head of GPU, they knew that it was a matter of utmost seriousness to Dzerzhinskii. Perhaps he did not invoke his second title, for as his longtime friend Mantsev observed, "Feliks Edmundovich has changed drastically since he began working in Vesenkha. Before he wanted to be feared, even hated out of fear. This did not disturb him. As head of the Cheka he considered such fright was useful within the Cheka as well as outside of it. . . . But now it is unpleasant for him to hear that he calls forth terror from those under him or from those who work with him."[28] At the same time, while he refused to join factions within the Party, he maintained his independence and spoke out against abuses in and outside the Party as he saw them. Because the main thrust of this attack was against the left opposition, he was not under great pressure from the Stalinist apparatus. But his criticism was felt by the apparat.

In July 1926 he delivered an emotion-laden speech to a combined meeting of the Central Committee and the Control Commission,[29] in which he attacked both the left for its economic positions and the apparatus for its colossal inefficiency and corruption. But he was a sick man, and the emotional outburst took its toll, for his speech became halting and he obviously struggled to complete his oration. He finished his speech and had to be helped from the hall. Three hours later he was dead. The Party mourned its fallen comrade, but the truly spontaneous outpouring came from precisely those specialists who had two years earlier feared his appointment.

Dzerzhinskii's death once again created a situation of unease among specialists in Vesenkha. The appointment of Kuibyshev sealed their fate. Under Dzerzhinskii, many prominent specialists had easy access to the chairman, but now the situation deteriorated. Kuibyshev was viewed by many as Stalin's "creature" and Stalin's hatred for the specialists was well known.

While Dzerzhinskii's loss was to be felt by the specialists, perhaps more significant was his loss during the forthcoming Party struggles. He had fought to maintain his own independence throughout the last years of his life. He had opposed both the policy positions of the left opposition and the bureaucratism of the apparatus. While he had lost some battles,

[28] Valentinov, *NEP.*
[29] Dzerzhinskii, *IP,* 2:381-82.

he was not afraid to fight them. His sympathies lay with the emerging right opposition with which he had maintained cordial relations. In addition, he had the apparent loyalty and respect of the secret police. He was the only member of the right who had an independent source of power. Perhaps even with the alliance of Dzerzhinskii the right could not have succeeded, but it is interesting to ponder.

The Denouement

The great industrialization debates of the mid-twenties which preceded the adoption of the first Five-Year Plan by the Fifteenth Party Congress were the last gasp of the experimentation and relative intellectual freedom in the economic sphere provided by the NEP. These debates took place against the background of intense political infighting within the leadership of the Party after the death of Lenin and could not be divorced from the increasing factionalism at the top. The right opposition was often accused of attempting to introduce capitalism into Russia, but despite the hyperbole and epithets directed to all parties, the debates took place within the context of general agreement on certain principles.

Private enterprise, except in very limited and controlled circumstances, was not an issue in the debates. All of the participants—Party members and non-Party specialists alike—had come to accept the desirability, or at least the necessity, of a state-controlled, centrally directed economy. This proposition had been accepted by most of the specialists involved even before the Revolution. Within this framework, however, there was wide disagreement on specific policy issues: balanced growth (basically a continuation of the NEP versus heavy industrialization), the necessary sources for capital investment funds, and the role of material and moral incentives.

The right opposition rejected the arguments of the proponents of rapid industrialization and emphasized the need for a system of rewards and material incentives to encourage productivity and innovation. Their positions received the sympathy of the majority of the non-Party specialists, and for that matter the support of the bulk of the Party and non-Party economic cadres.

The plan ultimately adopted by the Fifteenth Party Congress represented a compromise, which, if anything, leaned toward more rapid industrialization than that proposed by Gosplan and Vesenkha. But, as adopted, the plan provided only a starting point for a program which was enacted administratively from the center during the gap between the Fifteenth and Sixteenth Congresses and which launched the drive to industrialize rapidly at the expense of the agricultural and the consumer sectors, although the proponents of rapid industrialization within the Party leadership had already been exiled or deprived of their positions.

In this context, the death of Dzerzhinskii had both real and symbolic significance. The specialists lost a protector and the right opposition lost a potential ally. During the ensuing struggles, the leadership of Vesenkha could not be counted on to provide a voice of moderation. Dzerzhinskii had maintained an independent status with a real, if limited, base of support. His replacement, Kuibyshev, was but one of a coterie of Stalin's lieutenants who had no status beyond his place in the camp of followers. But Vesenkha was not alone; throughout the professional community of the Soviet Union those with real or imagined independence were being set aside and replaced by "loyalists," not on the basis of talent or achievement, but on the basis of loyalty. The Party itself was being cleansed (particularly the sources of support of the Old Bolsheviks) through a process that would be completed by the purge of the right opposition in 1930. At the same time, a new Party was being created by a flood of new members; the so-called Lenin levy alone brought in 200,000 new members. This process further weakened the old Bolshevik nucleus, with its tradition of intellectual independence and sophistication. Between January 1924 and January 1928 membership grew from 472,000 to 1,304,400.[30] "To most of those who entered after 1924, Stalin was the leader and Lenin's successor; his rivals, for all their somewhat distant services during the Revolution, were people tainted with factionalism and intrigue. It is thus easy to understand how the purge or exile of such legendary figures of prerevolutionary or Civil War times as Trotsky, Zinoviev and Kamenev could be met if not with approval, then at least indifference, by the mass of members."[31] In particular, Trotsky's criticism of Socialism in One Country would fall on the deaf ears of those who were interested in their own careers; in the rebuilding of their own society, the international revolution was only a distant image for most of the members.

This process was not limited to the Party but proceeded everywhere in the professional world. New managers, technicians, and economists began to appear in great numbers in the economic sector. Private publishing was severely restricted and then ended in 1929. In all fields ranging from literature and publishing to architecture, from the universities to the state bureaucracy, new cadres were assuming control, cadres who owed their positions to the benevolence of the General Secretary. If there is a common denominator in these changes it is that those suspected of having independent positions were replaced by those whose ultimate

[30] Leonard Schapiro, *Communist Party of the Soviet Union* (New York, 1959), p. 309.
[31] Adam Ulam, *A History of Soviet Russia* (New York, 1976), pp. 78-79.

loyalty was unquestioned, those who would not be expected to take exception to any policy directive from the center.

Many of the specialists in the economic cadres had accepted the Leninist compromise of the NEP not out of loyalty but out of conviction. This policy and its formulator had gone far in the direction that many of the specialists had advocated or adopted even prior to the Revolution. To many, Lenin's articulation of the NEP was a sign that he had given up the radical ideas of the revolutionary period and moved into the mainstream of Russian economic thinking. The policy itself was perceived of as one that promoted industrialization within the framework of balanced growth, provided direction from the center with an appropriate amount of incentive and reward to encourage productivity and innovation. While the non-Party specialists lacked any real power base to oppose the new policies emanating from the center, they could not be counted on to support each turn in policy enthusiastically or to raise no questions. Even during the industrialization debates a number of specialists, Groman and Bazarov in particular, had been willing to raise their voices publicly against the proponents of rapid, coercive industrialization. They had not made a political alliance with the right opposition, but it was a possibility. To this extent, from the point of view of the Stalinist leadership, their removal was rational in terms of both the political and economic goals Stalin was intent on achieving.

The axe began to fall soon after Kuibyshev's appointment. First, the specialists had little access to the new leader, and soon their positions came under attack. Rather than simply dismissing them, the regime decided to make an example of them. Freethinking was not only to be treated as dysfunctional, but it was also to be equated with treason. A series of trials was arranged, which involved not only economic cadres, but also engineers, academics, and theoreticians.

New members of the Party were recruited to replace the old intelligentsia. They faced perplexing problems. Although they were trained, they had been chosen, not because they were better economists or engineers, but because they were more loyal. The policies, practices, estimates, and procedures that the specialists had produced during the twenties had been rejected as part of a concerted wrecking plot that the old specialists had undertaken. The new cadres were brought in, not to make policy, not to advise the leadership, but rather to implement policy unfailingly as it was passed down. The independent discussion and exchange that had within limitations existed during the twenties now disappeared. The new cadres were to define their goals as identical with those of leadership. It is small wonder that the economic bureaucracy ceased to have any major function in the early thirties, and that even Soviet economists have been forced to reconstruct almost every index for this period in order to gain an understanding of what was really happening.

Lenin had been willing to accept that economic failure could arise from inefficiency, poor organization, even from natural causes—Stalin acted as if all economic failure was the result of treason and sabotage.

For the interim, Stalin had solved a number of problems. He had achieved consolidated political power within the Party, he had responded to the desires for advancement on the part of an engorged Party apparatus, and he had effectively eliminated most voices that might object to his actions on the grounds of principle.

The failures of the economy were laid to the disloyalty of those who had run the economic organizations; now the situation was resolved by replacing those specialists with loyal Red-experts. But the precedent was established and most understood that economic failure would result in charges of sabotage; the price of failure was extremely high, and since few dared to fail, they reported success at all cost. To some extent, these new managers and technicians would suffer the same fate as their predecessors, but to a lesser extent than their colleagues in other sections of the Party. Stalin could still trot out the Old Bolsheviks and lay at their feet the blame for the economic dislocations of the early thirties.

The principles had been established and the debates ended. The functional distinctions between economic and political actors had been resolved by the fusion of their functions with the coming of the Red-Experts. Open debate was unnecessary, even treasonous, for the whole apparatus by definition now shared the same goals. Nonetheless, the problems of the economy would not dissipate and were not simply the function of shortages of resources; they involved fundamental organizational and structural issues. But generations of Soviet economists have found themselves frustrated because, while they could not ignore the issues, neither could they discuss them directly and openly.

XII

DAVID GRANICK

Institutional Innovation and Economic Management: The Soviet Incentive System, 1921 to the Present

This chapter concentrates upon one particular sphere of innovation: innovation in the structure of incentives given to the managers of individual Soviet enterprises by the large "firm" of USSR Incorporated, which can be considered as binding together in an administrative unity the various hierarchical levels of nonagricultural, and especially industrial, activity. Clearly, all innovation in this domain is the responsibility of hierarchical levels above the enterprise level; thus it is only at these levels that we find "entrepreneurial" activity as I define it by my focus of interest. Such entrepreneurial activity may be carried out by individuals whose posts range from those in the trusts and *glavki* to membership in the Politburo; my concern is not with the question of who in fact (if anyone) were the innovators or entrepreneurs, but rather with the nature and degree of the entrepreneurship exercised in the field of incentives.

While entrepreneurship can occur without any prior or expected change in the environment (including available information), it normally occurs as a reaction to such environmental change. It is in this latter fashion that I shall consider it. The issue addressed in this chapter is the following: Have alterations in the incentive system affecting enterprise managers, to the degree that such changes have been under the control of hierarchical levels above the enterprise level, represented appropriate adjustments to a changing environment and to a changing welfare function of central leaders? Have these alterations been such as to improve, or at a minimum

* This chapter was written with the aid of the Kennan Institute for Advanced Russian Studies of the Woodrow Wilson Center and of the Graduate School of the University of Wisconsin–Madison. I am indebted to Earl Brubaker, Michael Carter, and Jeffrey Williamson for their comments on an earlier draft.

maintain, the appropriateness of decisions made by enterprise managers to maximization of the welfare function of central industrial administrators, given constraints imposed by an environment that is outside the control of these administrators? In short, if one considers the incentive system as a set of positive and negative prices paid to enterprise management for particular types of enterprise behavior, has this set of prices changed over time in a fashion appropriate to the changing environment and changing central objectives? Optimum entrepreneurship is *defined* as the finding, and maintenance at each moment of time, of the optimum and changing set of incentive prices, where such an optimum set at any given moment is a function of the existing environment and existing central objectives.[1] Thus optimum entrepreneurship is defined as the solution of a dynamic programming problem and the successful implementation of this solution.

The above definition of entrepreneurship with regard to managerial incentives is quite consistent with Joseph Schumpeter's definition of entrepreneurship. Schumpeter defined entrepreneurship as the carrying out of new combinations.[2] Clearly, the implementation of a changing set of incentive prices is the carrying out of new combinations. Schumpeter's entrepreneurs need not be permanently connected with an individual firm; "financiers" and "promoters" may qualify.[3] My location of potential entrepreneurs as restricted to a set of individuals holding posts hierarchically superior to the individual Soviet enterprise is thus consistent with Schumpeter's treatment.

The decisions of enterprise managers that are here considered to be affected by the incentive system under which these managers operate are of two types; these decisions affect both the level of managers' own inputs into the production process (involving a trade-off between effort and leisure) and the combination of inputs and outputs of the enterprise as a whole. A third and important class of decisions by enterprise managers is excluded from treatment in this chapter: such decisions relate to the generation of information as such (rather than as unavoidable byproducts of their enterprise's physical inputs and outputs) to higher hierarchical levels.

In a centrally planned economy of the Soviet type, there is some arbitrariness in setting the boundaries for what should be treated as environment cum central objectives as contrasted with the incentive system.

[1] If one realistically imposes restrictions on the feasible rate of change of the set of incentive prices, then an optimum set at a given moment will be a function not only of the existing environment and central objectives, but also of central expectations as to the future environment and central objectives.
[2] Joseph Schumpeter, *The Theory of Economic Development* (New York, 1961), p. 75.
[3] Ibid.

The distinction to be used is that the former set includes all central decisions that are only negligibly influenced by considerations of efficiency at the enterprise level. This set includes not only such welfare decisions as those affecting the relative expansion of consumer versus producer goods, and such institutional decisions as central planning, materials allocation, and the setting of most prices through administrative rather than market mechanisms, but also the existence of the purges of the 1930s, and the absence of major purges thereafter in industry. All of these will be considered as exogenous to the incentive system, although they have clearly impacted on the reaction of enterprise managers to the various "prices" established by the incentive system itself.

This chapter's thesis is that, to a significant degree, the failure in recent decades of the Soviet central-planning model to meet political leaders' economic growth objectives results from the absence of successful entrepreneurial activity in changing the structure of incentives provided to enterprise managers. This is not to deny that features inherent in the Soviet central-planning model may be major contributors to these failures; this chapter does not attempt to estimate the quantitative role of entrepreneurial failure in accounting for performance failures. Its import is that the current Western tendency to regard observed Soviet performance failures as necessarily due to the Soviet central-planning model is exaggerated. Traditional analysis, by neglecting the issue of Schumpeterian entrepreneurship in the major field of managerial incentives, is incomplete in an important respect.

Section I presents the analytic framework of the chapter and the model employed. The experience of readers of an earlier draft strongly suggests that this section, leading to the results embodied in equations (8) and (9), is essential to the reader as a guide to the empirical sections II and III. Nevertheless, sections II and III are self-contained in the sense that they are informed by, but do not explicitly use, the model of section I.

Section II provides a periodization of Soviet industrial history with regard to managerial incentives, describing both the governing environment cum central objectives and the incentive system in force within each of the four periods. Section III analyzes the response of the incentive system to changes in environment cum central objectives as between the periods.

I

The model presented below is assumed to apply to the entire Soviet period since the 1920s; subsections (1) and (2) hold for the 1920s as well. The model per se has no periodization.

Periodization enters only in subsection (6) in the form of a change in an exogenous parameter after the war. The resulting equations employ the model to show the effect of this change on enterprise behavior.

In sections II and III I shall also introduce periodization with regard to the structure of the incentive system as designed explicitly for enterprise managers. But such periodization is at a level of generalization below that needed to find reflection in my model. Thus such changes are irrelevant to the present section.

(1) The model used in the chapter is that of agent-principal. The "principal" consists of all administrators situated at hierarchical levels above the enterprise; the principal's task is to choose enterprise managers, promote and demote them, and reward them in such a fashion as to attempt to motivate these managers to behave as the principal desires. (Clearly, the administrators who collectively constitute the "principal" also perform other actions: e.g., they allocate resources to the enterprises. But such direct activities carried out above the enterprise level fall outside our area of interest in this chapter.)

Such administrators are called the "principal" because they are viewed as representing the central leadership of the Soviet Union, whose welfare function is to be maximized.

The "agent" consists of the managers of a given enterprise. The agent is conceived as determining its own behavior, within constraints, and as acting in response to the reward system provided by the principal. The agent attempts to maximize its own utility.

The agent-principal problem is conceived as the problem of the principal alone; for the agent acts in a utility-maximizing fashion, given the procedures set down by the principal, rather than attempting to influence these procedures.[4] The problem of the principal is to devise and implement procedures that will lead to maximization of the net product produced by the agent, given the predicted reaction of the agent to these procedures. (Net product is defined as net of the payments given to the agent which reduce the total product available to the rest of the economy.)

This definition of the "principal" implies that this chapter is unconcerned with relationships among administrators above the enterprise level. I do not ask how ministries motivate their *glavki* to perform as desired. This singling out of the single level of the enterprise, within the complex hierarchical structure of the Soviet economy, for special attention as "agent" is justified partly by the fact that it follows traditional Soviet terminology in creating two subsets of organizations (business accounting or *khozraschet* and non-*khozraschet*) at different hierarchical levels, but mainly by the fact that nonbusiness-accounting Soviet administrative

---

[4] This follows from the existence of a large (*n*) of agents, with the resultant impracticality of collusion among them.

units have usually not been evaluated by means of the types of success indicators used for enterprises, nor have their administrators been rewarded through a similar type of bonus scheme.

All managers (defined as executives above foreman level) within a given enterprise are treated as sharing in some fixed fashion in the total income provided to the enterprise managers by the incentive system in force. It is assumed that all such managers within a given enterprise have the same behavioral reaction to a given incentive system. Thus the composite of management within a given enterprise can be treated as a single agent.

It is clear that this treatment of the managers of a given enterprise as all having the same reward function is empirically incorrect. But without such simplification I would be forced to analyze the reward structure within the enterprise, and the conflicting motivations of different managers inside the same enterprise. This would take the inquiry far afield. Moreover, the usual (although not invariant) similar treatment in the Soviet literature of the problem of rewarding enterprise managers suggests that my simplification of the "agent" reward problem is close enough to reality to be useful.

(2) As is customary in the agent-principal model, I assume that the agent's utility function is strictly economic. Specifically, I assume that it consists of a function of the discounted lifetime monetary earnings of the enterprise managers who collectively constitute the "agent."[5] I shall not use any assumption as to risk aversion by the agent; that is, the second derivative of the agent's utility with respect to discounted lifetime monetary earnings is allowed to take any sign.

The usefulness of this economic utility function lies precisely in its narrowness. Use of this function amounts to positing that the managers are uninfluenced by patriotism, Party spirit, or symbolic rewards such as medals. These strong and unrealistic assumptions allow me to proceed with a fairly well defined utility function, and to concentrate upon differences between periods that are much easier to treat than would be distinctions emanating from such amorphous concepts as Party spirit. Periodization, and the contrast of managerial activities between periods during the entire sixty years of the Soviet Union's existence, can be made dependent exclusively on changes in the factors affecting discounted managerial lifetime earnings and on changes in the constraints under which the managers have functioned. If this sparse and limited form of a man-

---

[5] One might more appropriately assume that it consists of a function both of the discounted lifetime earnings and (negatively) of the discounted lifetime level of effort of the agent. This more accurate function is collapsed to that of the text on the basis that the level of effort is implicitly assumed to be constant in all of the equations that follow. Equations (8) and (9), which embody the chapter's thesis, would be unaffected by use of the fuller function.

agerial utility function enables us to generate interesting results concerning historical change, it can be justified on the basis of Occam's Razor.

A critical underpinning of this function is the treatment of risk in my model (see below in this section): that risk avoidance by managers has no predictable effect on the aspects of their behavior that are of interest to us. Otherwise we would be hard put to ignore the fact that managerial failure of the late 1930s could be punished with the death penalty, while in the postwar era the highest usual penalty has been demotion. Clearly this should have made the managers of the 1930s more prone to adopt safety-first principles of behavior; but the point here is that pursuit of the "safety first" goals either provided no guide to managers in their decision making with regard to the variables of concern to us, or simply reinforced the direction of temporal change in the choices they would otherwise have made in maximizing a function of discounted lifetime earnings. Since this chapter is concerned with the direction of change over time, the question of risk can be ignored.

(3) Enterprise managers (the agent) attempt to maximize a function (U) of the following function:

$$Y_t = \sum_{t=1}^{n} f(B_t, C_t)/(1 + r)^t \tag{1}$$

where Y_t = discounted lifetime earnings earned in period (t)
   B_t = bonuses received in period (t)
   C_t = career level attained as of period (t)
   r = the rate of time preference of the agent
   n = average number of periods before retirement of the enterprise managers.

B_t and C_t are each functions both of the behavior of the enterprise managers and of choice variables determined by the principal, while r is a choice variable of the agent. (U) is an arbitrary constant if the enterprise managers are risk neutral.

B_t is included as an argument of the objective function because of the large contribution of bonuses to total managerial earnings throughout most of the years studied. C_t is a proxy for salary and fringe benefits in period (t); one might note that it would also serve as a proxy for hierarchical power if I had chosen to include this latter variable in the definition of the manager's utility function.

Maximization by the agent of $U(Y_t)$ leads to:

$$A_t = \gamma(Y_t) \text{ subject to constraints} \tag{2}$$

where A_t = enterprise behavior in period (t)

(4) Throughout the entire range of years following the 1920s, the principal is depicted as having maintained the following functional forms of B_t and C_t for the agent:

$$C_t = \sum_{i=0}^{m} g(Dm_{t-i}/Pm_{t-i}, Du_{t-i}/E(Du_{t-i})) \tag{3}$$

$$B_t = h(Dm_t/Pm_t) \tag{4}$$

where Dm_{t-i} = aspects of enterprise performance in periods $(t-m, t-m+1, \ldots, t)$ which are measurable in period $(t-i)$

Pm_{t-i} = the plan (generally annual) for period $(t-i)$ of those aspects of enterprise performance in periods $(t-m, t-m/1, \ldots, t)$ which are measurable in period $(t-i)$

Du_{t-i} = aspects of enterprise performance in period $(t-i)$ which are unmeasurable in period $(t-i)$

E = the principal's subjective concept of a "normal" value of the variable, given the principal's estimation of the agent's objective potential

(4a) With regard to career choices by the principal, the hypothesis asserted in this chapter (but, unfortunately, impervious to testing with the data available) is that the principal has failed to employ C_t as an instrument variable intended to influence A_t through the incentive path of equations (1) and (2). Rather, it is hypothesized that he has concentrated on making appointments and dismissals solely according to the criterion of placing the most effective manager in each post.[6]

Equation (2) is a formulation of the arguments of A_t which applies only from the agent's standpoint—that is, given the principal's prior decision as to which individuals should constitute the agent in period (t). But the principal's problem includes that of choosing those individuals who are to act as managers. Thus the appropriate formulation from the principal's standpoint, once we grant that managerial candidates are not all homogeneous, is

$$A_t = \gamma'(Y_t, \sum_{i=0}^{m} C_{t-i}) \tag{2'}$$

Faced with a trade-off between influencing A_t and future A_{t+i} in equation (2') directly through C_t, or indirectly through Y_t by means of the incentive

---

[6] This is in no sense to argue that political criteria, nepotism, backscratching, etc. do not affect career movements in the Soviet Union. The word "solely" refers to the absence of incentive criteria in career decisions by the principal.

route of equation (1), the principal has opted lexicographically for the first choice rather than the second or a mixed strategy.

Given this strategic decision of the principal, I posit that his choices as to career movements of managers are made as some function both of the manager's past performance and of his perception of the manager's potential for future performance. Having no way to model the evaluation of potential within the framework of this model, I take equation (3) as a description of the principal's criteria for determining career movements of managers. This means that he employs some combination of degree of plan fulfillment during the current and past years (as an objective measure) together with a subjective measure of performance along dimensions not measured in the plan.

(4b) In view of the hypothesis concerning the principal's strategy of career movements that was asserted in (4a), the principal is left with B_t as the only instrument variable available to him for influencing Y_t. The principal's concept of appropriate incentive strategy is perforce concentrated on the functional form which he gives to B_t.

Soviet bonus policy during the entire period since the end of the 1920s appears to have been dominated by the following four principles:[7]

A. The most important aspect of managerial behavior toward which a proper managerial-incentive system should be directed is managerial effort. It is such effort that should be maximized, subject to the constraints given by the manager's utility function and the objective of having a net payoff to the economy from increased effort after making the salary and/or bonus payments necessary to elicit it.

Another way of formulating this principle is that a proper incentive system should be directed to moving outward the production frontier of the enterprise (given all inputs except the level of effort) rather than assuring that actual output is on the appropriate ray-vector of output as measured in n-dimensions.[8] Clearly the second is also a desirable objective when it does not conflict with the first, but there exists a lexicographic ordering of these two objectives.

B. Enterprise managers operate in a stochastic world and are risk averse. This implies that the enterprise performance $(D) = \eta\,(e, \theta)$ where e is the managers' effort and θ is a random variable, and that for managers

[7] These principles are enunciated on the basis that they are all beliefs which could be held by reasonable men (whether or not they are correct as hypotheses concerning the real world of the Soviet economy), and that together they lead to the bonus policies that can be observed. It is not asserted that Soviet administrators have consciously held these principles in the forms to be outlined, but only that they have acted as though they did.

[8] A variant of this principle has entered the literature as the assertion of the primacy of X-efficiency over allocative efficiency. See Harvey Leibenstein, "Allocative Efficiency versus 'X' Efficiency," *American Economic Review*, 56 (June 1966):392-415 for an assertion of this viewpoint.

∂ utility$^2/\partial^2 D_t < 0$. Given these two conditions, an appropriate form of bonus (or progressive piece rate) will yield a higher net payoff to the principal than could be attained through the use of any straight salary paid to the manager.[9]

C. An effective bonus system should minimize the negative effect on the managers' effort of the fact that managers are both risk averse and have a positive rate of time preference. The first consideration dictates that bonus should be a function of enterprise performance (D) where the function is known beforehand by the enterprise managers. But if the function (h) of equation (4) is to be known beforehand by the managers, then the argument of the function must be restricted to the quantifiable aspects of D, that is, to Dm. The second consideration dictates both that the measurable performance of period (t) should be rewarded fully in period (t), and that period (t) should be as short as feasible. Thus, in equation (4),

$$B_t = \mathrm{h}'(Dm_t) \quad \text{rather than} \quad \mathrm{h}''\left(\sum_{i=0}^{m} Dm_{t-i}\right)$$

D. Bonus payments should be paid in some relationship to actual performance compared to standard performance. Interpreting the period's Plan as the proxy for standard performance, this implies that $B_t = \mathrm{h}'''(Dm_t, Pm_t)$, which constitutes an alternative form of equation (4).

Given the above four Soviet principles of bonus formation, the principal's room for maneuver in determining the appropriate structure of the agent's incentive is very restricted. The principal has only two decisions to make:

a. The decision of defining Dm. He must determine which aspects of measurable performance to reward and what relative weights are to be given to each aspect. The more appropriate the principal's decision in this regard, the greater the incentive to the agent (through B_t) to pursue the goals of micro-allocative efficiency. A subdivision of this problem is that of attempting to provide quantitative measurements in period (t) for aspects of performance which are important to the principal but which have in the past gone unmeasured and so have been subsumed as part of Du.

b. The joint determination of the functional form (h) and of Pm_t in equation (4). This composite decision has the goal of applying the first principle of Soviet bonus policy as it was described above.

[9] Tracy R. Lewis, "Bonuses and penalties in incentive contracting," *The Bell Journal of Economics*, 11 (Spring 1980):292-301. Lewis's result would apply to a wider class of bonuses than the one he discusses.

(5) The four principles of Soviet bonus policy, reasonable as they may appear, leave the Soviet incentive system with the profound problem that unmeasured performance (Du_t) is totally unrewarded by managerial bonus—despite the fact that bonus is the only instrument variable at the disposal of the principal for inciting managers to perform in the fashion desired by the principal. Du_t may be thought of as comprising two subvariables, each of which is of considerable significance to the principal.

The first subvariable constitutes a class of outputs in period (t) which remain unmeasured both in period (t) and in all future periods ($t + i$). One member (Du_1) of this class is the degree to which the enterprise produces the precise product mix that best meets the desires of customers. Since the Soviet economy is generally characterized by a sellers' market, the sales of the enterprise are not constrained by the need to reach more than a minimum value of D on this particular dimension of performance (that is, a constraint on maximization of Dm_t is that $Du_1 t \geq a$). Subject to this constraint, Dm_t is maximized by the agent when he sets $(\partial x_{j,t}/\partial I_j, t)/ (\partial x_{k,t}/\partial I_{k,t}) = y_{k,t}/y_{j,t}$ with $x_{j,t}$ = quantity of output (j) in period (t), $I_{j,t}$ = quantity of inputs going into the production of output (j) in period (t), and $y_{j,t}$ and $y_{k,t}$ are the prices set for outputs (j) and (k) in period (t). Since Soviet prices are set centrally, administrative considerations prevent authorities from changing the vector (y_j, y_k) except at infrequent intervals; yet in the interim, the production functions of (j) and (k) will vary dissimilarly. Thus, in the interim between price changes, authorities are unable to act on $Du_{1,t}$ through the incentive effect of change in ($y_{j,t}$, $y_{k,t}$). Unless the principal can transform $Du_{1,t}$ into a measured-performance indicator $Dm_{1,t}$ ($x_{j,t}$, $x_{k,t}$), the principal has no means of inciting the agent through equation (4) to set $Du_{1,t} > a$, no matter how desirable this may appear to the principal. However, given the large mix of products produced by each enterprise, it is administratively impossible for the principal to create measured-performance indicator $Dm_{1,t}$.

The second subvariable constitutes a class of outputs in period (t) that are unmeasured in period (t) but yield a measured result in period ($t + i$). One member (Du_2) of this class is the development by the agent of a new product x_r, accompanied by the necessary reorganization of total production so as to include x_r in the enterprise's product mix. Here, costs are incurred by the agent in period (t), but the increase of the enterprise's profits and output (which will occur if y_r is set appropriately) will occur only in future periods ($t + i$).

The problem for the principal in inciting the agent to develop product x_r lies in the definition of Pm_t, which is an argument in equation (4). Since the plan for period ($t + i$) is intended to be a proxy for standard performance in period ($t + i$), it must incorporate the principal's anticipation of the effect of $Du_{2,t}$ on $Dm_{t + i}$. However, since $B_{t + i} = $ h $(Dm_{t + i}/Pm_{t + i})$ in equation (4), the agent is indifferent in period (t)

to the expected value of $\partial Dm_{t+i}/\partial Du_{2,t}$ unless he believes that the principal's expected value of the partial derivative will turn out to be less than the true value. Without such a belief on the part of the agent—and there seems little reason for it—whatever the expected value of $\partial Dm_{t+i}/\partial Du_{2,t}$ the agent's expected value of

$$\partial\left(\sum_{C=0}^{n-1} B_{t+i}\right)\bigg/\partial Du_{2,t} < 0.$$

One might expect the principal to react to this problem by lengthening the period (t) sufficiently so that $\partial Dm_t/\partial Du_{2,t} > 0$. However, so long as the principal is extremely concerned with minimizing the effect of A_t in equation (2') that stems from the agent's positive rate of time preference, the principal is excluded from such lengthening of (t) by the third principle of bonus policy.

(6) All of the above model and its implications are assumed to hold throughout the period after the 1920s, while (1) and (2) hold for the period of the 1920s as well. Only one thing changes between the periods: the pace of managerial career movement both upward and downward. This pace is markedly slower in the postwar than in the prewar era. Such change of pace is the result of change in the Soviet environment and in the welfare function of the central leadership, but not in any of the aspects of agent or principal behavior that I have modeled.

Employing equation (3), we can express this change of career pace by a description of the total derivative $d(C_t)$. (Note that the agent maximizes $U(Y_t)$ by setting $d(Y_t)$, rather than $d(C_t)$, equal to zero.)

$$d(C_t), \quad \text{given} \quad d\left(\sum_{i=0}^{m} [Dm_{t-i}/Pm_{t-i}]\right) \quad \text{and}$$

$$d\left(\sum_{i=0}^{m} [Du_{t-i}/\mathrm{E}(Du_{t-i})]\right) \quad (5)$$

has a lower value in the postwar than in the prewar.

This reduction in the value of $d(C_t)$, given the value of its arguments, affects the agent's objective function through equation (1) and thus his optimal A_t through equation (2).

If we interpret equation (5) as constituting a postwar reduction in the value of (g) of equation (3), but no change in the form of the function (g), then equation (5) can be written in the form of the following two equations:

$$\left[\partial C_t\bigg/\partial \sum_{i=0}^{m} Dm_{t-i}/Pm_{t-i}\right]_{\text{Postwar}} < \left[\partial C_t\bigg/\partial \sum_{i=0}^{m} Dm_{t-i}/Pm_{t-i}\right]_{\text{Prewar}} \quad (6)$$

$$\left[\partial C_t\bigg/\partial \sum_{i=0}^{m} Du_{t-i}/\mathrm{E}(Du_{t-i})\right]_{\text{Postwar}} < \left[\partial C_t\bigg/\partial \sum_{i=0}^{m} Du_{t-i}/\mathrm{E}(Du_{t-i})\right]_{\text{Prewar}} \quad (7)$$

It is true that it is only either equation (6) or (7), but not both, which necessarily follows from equation (5). However, since I have assumed that the principal has throughout determined the movements without regard to their incentive effect, there is no reason why the relative weights of Dm_{t-i}/Pm_{t-i} and $Du_{t-i}/E(Du_{t-i})$ in equation (3) should have changed over time. Indeed, there is no empirical evidence available to suggest such a change. Thus we assume that equation (7) holds.

(7) We now turn back to equation (2) showing the result of the agent maximizing his utility $U(Y_t)$. Since $Y_t = F(B,C)$ from equation (1), while $C_t = G(Dm,Du)$ and $B_t = H(Dm)$ from equations (3) and (4), use of equation (7) provides us with the critical result of the model:

$$\partial A_t / \partial Dm_{t\text{Postwar}} > \partial A_t / \partial Dm_{t\text{Prewar}} \tag{8}$$

$$\partial A_t / \partial Du_{t\text{Postwar}} < \partial A_t / \partial Du_{t\text{Prewar}} \tag{9}$$

In short, the maximization of utility by the agent leads him to a reduction between the prewar and postwar periods in the relative attention given to unmeasured aspects of enterprise performance.

(8) My results are unaffected by considerations of risk on the part of the agent. If we take account of the nonmonetary risks involved in failure on the part of the agent, these should strengthen the relative importance of career compared to bonus considerations in equation (1). But these nonmonetary risks were much higher throughout the prewar period than in the postwar. Thus nonmonetary-risk considerations only strengthen my results as expressed in equations (8) and (9). Other aspects of risk avoidance on the part of the agent are irrelevant to the results.

II

The 1920s

The 1920s, and particularly the first half of this decade, appears from secondary sources to be a period in which State enterprises as well as private ones were profit maximizers. This was a period during which there was very little planning or centralized control of the economy, and in which the prime integrating forces at a microlevel were those of the marketplace.

Profit orientation is shown in the Decree of April 1923, which defined the legal status of industrial trusts, and which gave them independence in their operation with the objective of deriving profit.[10] More signifi-

---

[10] This was the first decree defining the status of the trusts, and it was not amended until 1927. (Alexander Baykov, *The Development of the Soviet Economic System* [Cambridge, Eng., 1947], pp. 110-11.)

cantly, it is revealed in the Scissors Crisis of 1923 and in the renewed price increases that began in the middle of 1925.

During the Scissors Crisis, the industrial trusts and syndicates acted as profit-maximizing monopolists operating without cash-flow constraints. The prices of industrial goods sold to the countryside were pushed up sharply, even though this policy required the reduction of the physical flow of industrial goods and the accumulation of finished-goods inventories by the trusts and syndicates. This policy of the trusts and syndicates was made feasible by current Soviet banking practice, which permitted them to borrow freely against their accumulated inventories. What is most revealing is that government instructions, moral suasion, and even directives to the trusts as to pricing policy were to no avail. The crisis was resolved only when the government adopted market mechanisms to force down industrial prices: primarily the restriction of bank credit to industrial and trading organs, thus placing them in a cash bind, but also— in special cases—even the importation of industrial goods so as to undercut the syndicate prices.[11] It is difficult to interpret this crisis, and particularly the nature of the tools used by the government to deal with it, without hypothesizing that profits constituted management's objective function.

Curiously, it is this first period (after the transition stage of War Communism) in Soviet economic history that is most difficult to interpret in terms of our model in which managers maximize a function of their private discounted lifetime earnings.[12] I suspect that this difficulty arises more from lack of research into the relevant aspects of the period than from the nature of the period itself. But alternative explanations suggest themselves.

During the period of 1923 and thereafter, managerial power in enterprises, trusts, and syndicates was shared by Communist party members (largely Red Directors without much formal education or business training) and prerevolutionary engineers, managers, and businessmen. In 1924, fifty-six of a total of sixty-four heads of industrial trusts were Party members; half of all these heads were Old Bolsheviks. Half of all factory directors were Party members. Yet if one adds enterprise directors together with the members of the administrative boards of the enterprises, three-quarters were non-Party experts.[13] Thus we are forced to explain

[11] Maurice Dobb, *Russian Economic Development Since the Revolution* (London, 1928), pp. 235-71.

[12] Earl Brubaker has suggested that it would have been surprising to see a fully coordinated economic policy in the confusion of the first half of the 1920s. Thus there may be nothing here requiring explanation.

[13] Jeremy R. Azrael, *Managerial Power and Soviet Politics* (Cambridge, Mass., 1966), pp. 45, 67, and 216.

the decisions of such disparate groups as educated Old Bolsheviks, un-
educated Red Directors, and non-Party experts.

Non-Party experts may well have believed that their earnings would
be higher in very profitable units than in those which were only marginally
profitable or were suffering losses, and that their positions would also
be more secure to the degree that they demonstrated business acumen
(their stock in trade) by achieving the profit goal set forth in the decree
defining the trusts' legal status. Thus it is not difficult to explain why
profits should have served as the maximand for these experts.

But why should this maximand have been equally accepted by the
Party members once the government had shown itself hostile to high
industrial prices? Subject as they were throughout the 1920s to the "Party
maximum" of monetary earnings, their current incomes could scarcely
have been increased by monopolistic behavior. One would have thought
that their security in past and future careers (and therefore their lifetime
earnings) would have been better advanced by obedience to national
Party and government policy than by following the legislation that was
intended formally to guide their trusts' activities. However, the period
has been studied too little to be sure of one's ground here.

Two other explanations of the behavior of Party directors during this
period, both alternatives to maximization of discounted lifetime earnings,
suggest themselves. The first is that the Party directors regarded themselves in economic matters as simple apprentices to the non-Party experts
and thus that they blindly accepted, as appropriate to NEP, the traditional
enterprise goals stemming from the prerevolutionary capitalist period.
After all, they could find support for such a policy in the April 1923
statute of the trusts. The second complementary explanation is that they
were influenced more by the Party opposition's policy toward industrial
prices[14]—an espousal of a form of primitive accumulation at the expense
of the peasantry—than by the official line. Both of these explanations,
of course, fall outside the domain of the analytic framework I have
suggested in section I.

The 1930s

The beginning of the 1930s is the period of the sharpest break in Soviet
managerial history that has yet occurred. This was connected primarily
with the creation of a system of annual obligatory national plans for
production operations, together with a system of materials allocations,
all brought down to the enterprise level. A secondary element was the
achievement of a virtual monopoly over managerial posts at the executive

[14] Dobb, *Russian Development*, pp. 254-55.

(as opposed to narrowly technical) level, at least in larger enterprises, by Party members who had either considerable managerial experience or the equivalent of a university-level education in engineering. At this period, Party membership still represented a considerable degree of political commitment by the member as well as of political trust by higher authorities; successful managers did not automatically join the Party. Thus the 1930s were characterized by the fact that the authorities typically reposed some measure of confidence in both the political and technical reliability of one and the same manager.

It is these features that fundamentally distinguish the 1930s from the NEP period. But what distinguishes them from later years? In my view, it is the fact that the 1930s constituted a period of enormous potential for career movement, up or down, for all those involved in industrial management. During this decade, future career development must have been the major factor determining the expected discounted lifetime monetary earnings of even those managers who had already reached middle-management levels in large enterprises. This seems not to have been the case during any later period, when bonus variation was more important.[15]

During the decade of the 1930s, as in the following two periods, the expected discounted lifetime earnings of managers can be taken as an indirect function of the first of the following variables, and a direct function of the other two.[16]

[L] The quality of the resources at the disposal of the manager's production unit, particularly when such quality is difficult to measure and is unlikely to have a significant effect on the level of the plans set for the unit.

---

[15] In the language of the model of section I, using B_t and C_t but not L_t as arguments of Y_t, and using (e) = managerial effort, the above sentences are a verbal expression of
$$[(\partial U[Y_t]/\partial C_t) \cdot (\partial C_t/\partial e_t)]/[(\partial U[Y_t]/\partial B_t) \cdot (\partial B_t/\partial e_t)] > 1$$
in the 1930s and < 1 in the postwar era.

[16] Discounted lifetime earnings of managers are a direct function of [B] and [C] below, but only an indirect function of [L]:

$$\text{Discounted lifetime earnings} = f_1(B,C) \quad (a)$$
$$B = f_2(L,X_1) \quad (b)$$
$$C = f_3(L,X_2) \quad (c)$$

where X_1, X_2 = matrices of independent variables

In equation (a), the independent variables appear by definition as arguments. In contrast, equations (b) and (c) are causal equations. Most of the discussion throughout this paper of variables [B] and [C] should more precisely be described as a discussion of, respectively:

∂ discounted lifetime earnings/∂X_1
∂ discounted lifetime earnings/∂X_2

A fourth very minor variable also affected discounted managerial lifetime earnings during the pre-1965 period, especially after 1936: this consists of profits earned by the enterprise, which served to provision the director's fund. The quantitative unimportance of this pre-1965 variable is such that it is ignored in this paper.

Among such resources, the critical one most under the control of the manager is the quality of the labor force attracted and retained by the enterprise. Given the fact that most labor was recruited at the factory gate, was free to move between industrial enterprises until 1938-40, and that there was very high labor turnover, the relative level of compensation provided to the labor force must have had a major influence on its quality.

[B] Bonuses earned by managers.

[C] Prospects for career movement of managers.

With regard to variable [L], earnings of manual workers were primarily a function of piece-rate earnings and of counterpart bonuses for hourly paid workers. These, in turn, were functions of the annual plan for the enterprise as to the wage fund per employee, and of the actual plan fulfillment of gross output (*valovaia produktsiia*) per employee as measured in constant prices or physical units. This last feature made gross output per employee an important intermediate objective of managers, as affecting the realized wage fund per employee—since the latter was a function not only of planned wage fund per employee but also of the ratio of actual to planned labor productivity. This objective must have been partly modified in the direction of total gross output, since in order to attract the relatively plentiful unskilled laborers it was not necessary to offer them the same proportion of earnings above their standard wage that was required for skilled labor, which was in much shorter supply.

Thus we have here an independent source of incentive to managers for laying emphasis on the goal of gross output. This incentive has continued to the present. But it must have been much less important as an incentive during the 1930s than in the two later periods for two reasons:

First, State Bank control was less effective in preventing overexpenditure of the enterprise wage fund during the 1930s than was the case afterwards.[17] Thus managers in the 1930s had more room for raising manual workers' nominal earnings without proportionately increasing measured output.

Second, the expected period in-post of a given manager was shorter during the 1930s than it became later.[18] Therefore, since higher or lower relative earnings of their enterprises' labor force would affect the quality of this labor force only with a time lag, managers were in a better position during the 1930s than afterwards to ignore this lagged quality effect on the ground that they themselves were likely to be elsewhere when the lagged variation in labor force quality in turn exerted its influence on the enterprises' performance.

[17] Franklyn D. Holzman, "Soviet Inflationary Pressures, 1928-1957: Causes and Cures," *Quarterly Journal of Economics*, 74 (May 1960), sections 3 and 5.

[18] David Granick, *Managerial Comparisons of Four Developed Countries: France, Britain, United States and Russia* (Cambridge, Mass., 1972), pp. 235-40.

With regard to variable [B], managerial bonuses were in theory linked to total enterprise performance relative to the annual Plan without any explicit weighting of the various indicators of such plan fulfillment. In practice, it seems clear that gross output was the indicator given overwhelmingly dominant weight.[19]

It would be incorrect, however, to exaggerate the importance of managerial bonuses during the period of the 1930s. The best indicator we possess is the ratio of bonuses to total monetary earnings of all managerial and professional employees (ITR) in industry. During the fall of 1934 in all industry for the single month for which we have data, this proportion was only 3.6 percent. (13.4 percent of all managerial and professional employees received some bonus in this month. Thus, for those receiving any bonus at all, the average bonus was 27 percent of the month's total earnings.)[20] We have no further data until 1940, by which time the ratio to total earnings in all industry had risen from 4 to 11 percent. It was only during the war and immediately afterward that the proportion rose to two and three times the 1940 level, even exceeding the ratios of the first half of the 1970s.[21] These figures suggest that almost certainly in the early and middle 1930s, and perhaps even until the end of the decade, managerial bonuses were relatively insignificant.

This comparative insignificance suggests that the weight of variable [B]—with its stress on the plan indicator of gross ouput—was relatively minor in the utility function of Soviet managers during the decade under consideration.

Thus one should turn to variable [C], career movement, in searching for the predominant factor in managers' objective function throughout the 1930s. During 1934 and 1936 in various branches of heavy industry, some 25 to 34 percent of all enterprise directors had held their post for

---

[19] This is much clearer in postwar Soviet writing about the 1930s than it is in the contemporary Soviet literature. (See David Granick, *Management of the Industrial Firm in the USSR* [New York, 1954], chapters 9 and 10, which draws exclusively upon contemporary sources and is a good deal less positive than the above statement.) It is possible that the postwar Soviet writing represents an exaggeration, particularly for the first half of the 1930s, and that in fact managerial bonuses were then less firmly attached exclusively to measured aspects of enterprise performance than was the case later. This possibility should be treated as a caveat to the statement in the text; but the critical point to recognize is that it is either irrelevant to (if all plan indicators were of the *Dm* type) or would only strengthen the basic argument of this chapter as embodied in equations (8) and (9) of section I.

[20] TsUNKhU Gosplana SSSR, *Zarabotnaia plata inzhenerno-tekhnicheskikh rabotnikov i sluzhashchikh v sentiabre-oktiabre 1934 g.* [Earnings of Managerial and Professional and other White Collar Personnel in September-October 1934] (Moscow, 1936), pp. 6-49. The total sample size was 125,000 managerial and professional employees, distributed among twenty-six branches of industry.

[21] Granick, *Managerial Comparisons*, pp. 277-79.

less than one year, and an additional 40 to 56 percent for between one and three years. Moreover, even during the pre-Purge period of January 1934 to March 1937, some 39 percent of those directors in heavy industry who changed their post and whose next position could be traced suffered a demotion.[22] Throughout the decade—although for very different reasons before and during the purges—managerial career mobility upward, downward, and laterally stood on a peak ridge as measured both by Soviet and by international standards.

But what determined the shape of individual careers? Clearly it can have been only one thing: the judgment by hierarchical superiors (as well as by Party and secret police organs) of the *overall* success of the managers in their previous and current positions as well as evaluations of "potential" (both managerial and political). The predominant influence of plan fulfillment as measured by gross output in the shaping of careers was possible only to the degree that superiors were willing to give it pride of place in their subjective evaluations.

To sum up, the 1930s seem to have been a period in which enterprise managers could best maximize their discounted lifetime monetary earnings through attempting to carry out their "Plans" by emphasizing those aspects of plan fulfillment that they expected would carry the greatest subjective weight with their superiors at ministry and its branch subdivision (*glavk*) levels and in the Party hierarchy when these superiors reviewed their accomplishments at a later date. In this respect, as will be seen below, the 1930s differed sharply from the postwar period. There were in the 1930s other aspects of the managers' reward structure and environment (incorporated in variables [L] and [B]) which bound them to give special attention to the criterion of gross output—but such aspects had relatively slight importance during this decade. To the degree that managers did emphasize gross output, and there can be little doubt that this degree was considerable, it was because of its importance in determining their career progress.

The import for technological innovation within Soviet industry of such subjective evaluation by superiors in the utility function of managers was that, in my opinion, the 1930s constituted a decade of extraordinary innovative accomplishments compared to the bleak record ever since. Designs and equipment radically different from those used earlier in the USSR were imported from abroad and put into reasonably effective operation: this represented a major process of successful implementation of innovations, a process that proved difficult to continue in future years when the designs and equipment were Soviet developed and thus should have been easier, *ceteris paribus*, to employ successfully. Foreign designs

[22] Granick, *Management of Firm*, pp. 290-96.

and equipment were quickly copied, with highly successful modification, for the building of "duplicate" plants.[23] It proved feasible for Soviet ministries and their subdivisions to alter radically and quickly the product mix of operating enterprises, a feat that later defeated their best efforts. The machine-tool industry, for example, was fairly quickly converted in the middle 1930s from a sector following a policy of large-scale production of a very narrow range of products to one in which expansion of range was given high and successful priority.

Most impressive of all, in view of the later Soviet record, was the fashion in which the mix of Soviet imports changed continuously and dramatically during the course of the decade. Major imports of a given year would fade into insignificance within a very few years as these products were mastered by domestic industry (see footnote 38). The growth in domestic output of these same products showed that such import reductions were not due to a change in the priority of these products in Soviet usage, but rather were a consequence of import substitution.

Thus Soviet enterprises in the 1930s were remarkably successful in carrying out the innovations required in order to copy foreign-developed technology and to modify it to domestic conditions. The speed of development of import-substituting production of specific capital goods and intermediate manufactures—as reflected in the declining share of such individual imports of high-priority products in the total Soviet import bill, especially notable since the total import bill was declining after the beginning of the 1930s—is a conservative indicator of such success, as it is either uninfluenced or influenced negatively by the size of the technological gap existing between Soviet industry and that of world leaders.

I believe that the chief reason for this success was managerial. To the degree that managers were rewarded in terms of their discounted lifetime monetary earnings for stressing those aspects of their work most important to their superiors, there was no reason that implementation of technical innovation could not be incited just as effectively as could emphasis upon gross output. It became a matter of what ministerial and *glavk* authorities wanted; never again has the Soviet managerial reward system been structured so as to give authorities above the enterprise level so much freedom to exercise choice of this type.

---

[23] See the construction of the Kharkov Tractor Plant on the model of the Stalingrad Tractor Plant. The Kharkov plant, using a much higher proportion of Soviet-constructed equipment, had a superior performance record as measured by a series of relevant performance criteria. (D. Granick, *Soviet Metal Fabricating and Economic Development* [Madison, Wisc., 1968], pp. 117-19.)

1940 to 1965

It is this third period in Soviet managerial history which the Western models of the Soviet enterprise seem to describe best. These are the years of the complete predominance of the criterion of gross output and of the neglect of other performance criteria.

In formal terms, nothing of significance altered between the second and third period. The objective function of managers in the third period can be analyzed in terms of the same three variables used for the second period. It is the relative significance of these three variables that changed dramatically.

The most important change was in variable [C], career development. The rapidity of expansion in the number of industrial enterprises to be managed ended with the major structural change of the economy that occurred during the second period. The political purges of the second half of the 1930s brought into office a generation of young executives who were to grow old in their posts, thoroughly clogging the lines of promotion during the entire third period.[24] These two developments could only be taken as "givens" by those Soviet authorities in the third period who shaped policy as to managerial careers. But there was also a third development over which such authorities did have control; the previous practice of widespread and rapid demotion for failure was abandoned, and managers were provided with a degree of security in their current job never granted in large American companies.[25] The managerial insecurity of the 1930s was replaced not only by relative political security but also by career security. Insofar as industrial managers were concerned, the Soviet system had stabilized into comparative ossification. Both the carrot and the stick, implicit in career development, almost disappeared; from having constituted the prime variable affecting the managers' objective function during the years of the 1930s, variable [C] exercised only a minor influence throughout the third period.

Variable [L], the quality of the labor force as a lagged function of worker earnings, must have become considerably more significant to managers in the third period than earlier. This is partly because managers now had a far higher probability of remaining in their posts long enough to gain or suffer from the lagged effects of these worker earnings. For this reason alone, the importance to managers of gross output per worker was bound to rise.

[24] Granick, *Managerial Comparison*, pp. 235-40, and Azrael, *Managerial Power*, pp. 230-31. The last source indicates that in 1962 an absolute majority of the directors of the leading enterprises of Leningrad had apparently held their posts for more than fifteen years.

[25] For some limited evidence, compare pp. 235-40 for Soviet managers and industry ministers with pp. 214-16 for executives in a postwar sample of large American corporations (Granick, *Managerial Comparisons*).

Probably even more significant was the fact that the Soviet economic control system had matured sufficiently by the late 1940s to prevent the huge overexpenditure of nominal wage funds that had characterized the 1930s. The royal route to increasing manual worker earnings as a proportion of base pay now took the form of expanding gross output per worker. The enterprise director of this latter period who slighted this indicator of plan fulfillment to the benefit of other criteria was creating major difficulties for himself with regard to his manual labor force.

Variable [B] (bonuses for managerial and professional employees) continued, as in the 1930s, to be linked primarily to plan fulfillment of gross output. But, in contrast to the earlier years, such bonuses had a major effect on managerial earnings through 1959; even during the 1960-64 period, when they were at a postwar low, their proportion of earnings was 230 percent of the 1934 level.[26]

To sum up, the 1940-65 period was one in which variable [L] became more strongly attached to the criterion of plan fulfillment of gross output than had been the case earlier, and in which variable [B]—always strongly linked to this indicator—increased enormously in relative importance. At the same time, variable [C], the only one that could be made relatively independent of gross output, lost its significance. The result was that, during this quarter of a century, expected discounted lifetime earnings of managers virtually became a function solely of the indicator of plan fulfillment of gross output.[27]

Less certain, but nevertheless probable, is that the "ratchet effect"[28] came to exercise an important influence on enterprise behavior during these years. This effect expresses the notion that annual plans for enterprises in year $(t + 1)$ are set as a function of their actual production in

[26] Ibid., p. 278.

[27] Earl Brubaker has pointed out to me that a high proportion of Soviet managerial earnings is made up of fringe benefits of an in-kind nature. The principles of distribution of such benefits are unknown, but may modify the argument of the text. To the extent that such fringe benefits are linked to the post held by the manager, the text's argument is modified only in the quantitative sense that bonus earnings—and thus plan fulfillment of gross output—are somewhat less important than has been suggested by the data as to the composition of managerial monetary earnings. To the extent that such fringe benefits are linked to the same measured success indicators to which monetary bonus is linked, then the text's argument remains intact.

It is only to the degree that such fringe benefits may be awarded differentially to managers at a given level, but according to total measured and unmeasured performance as judged *ex post* by superiors rather than according to a measurable indicator, that the postwar period may fail to depart from the 1930s in the importance given to measured-performance variables such as gross output. This could be the case if these fringe benefits have become more important in the postwar period than they were earlier.

[28] See Holland Hunter, "Optimum Tautness in Developmental Planning," *Economic Development and Cultural Change* (July 1961), part 1, pp. 561-72.

year (t), and thus that managers are motivated to restrain their degree of above-plan output—when such output is feasible—because of the likely effect of such excess on the standard against which they will be judged in the following year. However, the ratchet effect operated only to the degree that annual plans for enterprises were stable and not subject to revision during the course of the planning year as a function of enterprise output. The same is true with regard to the notion that managerial bonuses encouraged concentration on gross output since, to the degee that output plans were changed during the year, such changes may have been a function of enterprise performance along other dimensions than that of gross output.[29]

It is in these years that Soviet economic literature began seriously to reflect the working of the ratchet effect, although this effect does not find statistical expression in data at the ministry level.[30] (No statistical data are available at the enterprise level, which is precisely the level at which Soviet complaints have centered.) Of course, this effect was unlikely to be serious for enterprises faced with tight plans in year (t), but there must have been many for which the plans were loose.

There are two reasons why the ratchet effect on plan formation might be assumed to have had increased influence on managerial behavior after the 1930s. First, one would expect it to take some time before enterprise managers became aware of how their enterprises' plans were actually shaped, given the influence on such plans of a host of random factors that would tend to hide the effect of plan fulfillment in the previous year. Second, during the 1930s the enterprise manager in year (t) had reason to believe that he might well have been moved elsewhere by year ($t +$ 1), and thus would not personally suffer from the use of a higher standard of performance for the enterprise in that later year.

The greater influence during 1940-65 of the ratchet effect on managerial behavior had, in its turn, two effects. By far the greater must have been to relax the efforts put forth by enterprise managers once the achievement of their gross output plans were secured. But a second effect must have been to divert their efforts at this stage to other goals than that of gross output. This second effect—relevant only for those enterprises already assured of as much overfulfillment of the gross output plan

---

[29] For a limited discussion of the instability of annual enterprise plans, see David Granick, "The Ministry as the Maximizing Unit in Soviet Industry," *Journal of Comparative Economics*, 4 (September 1980):259-60.

[30] For six years of the first half of the 1950s, the percentage of plan fulfillment of gross output by the industrial ministry in year ($t + 1$) can be regressed against the same percentage achieved in year (t). The ratchet effect, if existing in a major form at the ministerial level, would make the sign of the coefficient negative. In fact, even when dummy variables are introduced for individual years, regression analysis shows that the coefficient was insignificant or significantly positive (ibid).

as their managers felt to be safe—reduced the net tendency caused by the development of variables [L], [B], and [C] described earlier. But such reduction appears to have been weak, applying as it did only to the most patriotic or ambitious managers.[31]

Post-1965

The fourth and current period of Soviet managerial history has seen a major effort to overcome the problems emanating respectively from the first, third, and fourth principles of Soviet bonus policy. Three principal goals have been pursued by central authorities: (1) the reduction of the relative importance of the gross output success criterion in managers' utility functions to the benefit of other quantitatively measured objectives; (2) the reorientation of managerial efforts toward the implementation of product and process innovations; (3) a significant reduction in the debilitating effects of the ratchet system of plan formation. The first of these goals represented an objective that was new (in the sense of being taken seriously) in Soviet history since planning to the enterprise level began around 1930. In contrast, the second and third goals should be interpreted—if I am correct in my understanding of the 1930s—as an attempt to reinstitute under a new guise the favorable features of the second period of Soviet managerial history.

To return to the three variables affecting managers' lifetime earnings, the one concerning which there is much uncertainty is variable [C] (career development). On the one hand, there is nothing of which I am aware in Soviet writing to indicate that the situation changed in this regard from that which existed during the 1940-65 period; certainly the same negative attitude toward managerial demotions seems to have prevailed.[32]

[31] It is probable that the change in another factor operated in the opposite direction, but with similar weakness, to increase the net tendency caused by the development of variables [L], [B], and [C] described above. This factor is the degree to which annual enterprise plans remained unchanged throughout the year for which they were intended to be current.

Although no data exist concerning this question, it seems reasonable to suppose that the greater experience with planning in the postwar period, combined with the greater ease of determining materials allocations that were balanced for the economy as a whole—due to the lessened variance in growth rates both within and between different sectors—should have led to a reduction in the number and extent of plan changes throughout the year. If this hypothesis is correct, such a development would have led enterprise managers to attach greater importance to fulfilling and overfulfilling their current plans; this is because the likelihood had grown that [L] and [B] would in fact be based on these plans rather than on revisions of them.

[32] See V. Iakushev and V. Iakhantov in *Literaturnaia gazeta*, September 2, 1970. During the three years of 1970-72, data for all of the industrial and construction enterprises of the city of Volgograd showed that the total annual turnover rate of directors of large (undefined) enterprises was 7.4 percent, of medium-size enterprises was also 7.4 percent,

On the other hand, there is the demographic evidence that the bottlenecks to managerial career advancement must have begun to break up as the generation which came to power at the end of the 1930s disappeared from the active scene; men who assumed positions of authority at the end of the 1930s must have been retiring by the middle 1960s. One would expect that such retirements would create a long series of career openings that would reinstate variable [C] as a major factor in managers' utility functions. Unfortunately, for lack of information, I shall have to abandon consideration of variable [C] in this fourth period with these cursory comments. It is a subject well worthy of research.

Variable [L] (the attachment of manual worker earnings to gross output through the mechanism of the wage fund) has continued unaltered as it had been during 1940-65.[33] The policy of change has been concentrated entirely upon variable [B] (bonuses) and upon the ratchet mechanism in plan formation.

After a five-year period of low bonuses for industrial managerial and professional personnel during 1960-64, there followed a sharp and steady rise at least until 1973 (no later data are available to me). Bonuses as a percentage of total earnings for this group rose from 8.9 percent in 1964 to about 27.5 percent in 1973—a figure at the level of 1944 and 1947 and far higher than that of any other recorded year. In 1973, one-third of the upper managers of all enterprises supervised by the Russian Republic office of the State Bank had total earnings that were at least double the base salary set for their post.[34] Whatever may have been happening nationally to the potential for career advancement of managers, Soviet administrators at the highest industrial levels have clearly desired to attach enterprise managers' utility functions closely to the success indicators reflected in the bonus schemes.

Bonus schemes since 1965 have been constructed on a basis that is fundamentally new in Soviet history. For the first time, a number of different success indicators have been used for determining the bonuses to be distributed within any given enterprise—with the weights of these

---

and of small enterprises was 18.5 percent. The annual turnover rate for reasons other than promotion was only 2.8, 5.2, and 5.9 percent, respectively. (G. K. Ivanov in *Nauchnoe upravlenie obshchestvom* (1973), no. 7, pp. 235-40, as referred to in Vladimir Andrle, *Managerial Power in the Soviet Union*, [Westmead, Eng., 1976], pp. 109-11.)

[33] In 1970, manual workers of industry received some 85 percent of their income from the wage fund, of which perhaps only 5 percent was paid dependent upon enterprise performance other than that measured by gross output. (See E. K. Vasil'ev and L. M. Chistiakova, *Effektivnost' oplaty upravlencheskogo truda y promyshlennosti* [Effectiveness of the Payment of Managerial Labor in Industry] [Moscow, 1972], p. 87.)

[34] Vasil'ev and Chistiakova, *Effektivnost'*, p. 87. Granick, *Managerial Comparisons*, p. 278; Iu. Artemov in *Voprosy ekonomiki* (August 1975), no. 8, pp. 40-42; V. Minaev, N. Ksenofontev and V. Iudin in *Ekonomicheskaia gazeta* (1975), no. 43 (November):10.

different indicators being set in advance at least for the current planning year. Although the relevant indicators have changed significantly during the post-1965 period itself, the basic principle of *ex ante* weighting seems to have remained unchanged.[35] While a close proxy for gross output has remained one of these indicators, others were also included which measured the inputs used and the quality of the products produced.

This new bonus principle in Soviet industry can be interpreted as a system of shadow-pricing—an awkward system, it is true, but the first such utilized since the beginning of planning in the early 1930s. To the degree that the managerial maximand can be taken as consisting of bonuses, a "shadow-price," measured in bonus, is set for each enterprise for actual performance divided by planned performance according to each individual indicator. Enterprise managers can use these shadow-prices to interpret the appropriate trade-offs among these indicators; superior administrative organs are in a position to guide change in such trade-offs by altering the weights given to each indicator in the bonus scheme of a given enterprise.

It is by this means that central Soviet authorities have attempted to use the managerial bonus scheme to guide enterprise managers to a "desirable" trade-off among centrally desired and quantitatively measured objectives. Here is a fundamentally new development in the current period of managerial history.

On the other hand, central pursuit of implementation at the enterprise level of product and process innovations has shown much less novelty. The difficulty here has been that such implementation, despite various efforts, could not be successfully incorporated into quantitative indicators to be integrated into the bonus scheme. The best that has been accomplished is to reduce the costs (measured in bonus) of such implementation of innovation.[36] But this is far from a positive incentive.

One means of testing the degree of implementation of product innovations is by analyzing the composition of Soviet imports from hard currency countries. During the 1930s, as was pointed out earlier, Soviet imports of means of production changed radically from year to year as Soviet industry mastered the output of one product after another. Given the strong desire of the Soviet regime in recent years to import new

---

[35] See David Granick, "Soviet Research and Development Implementation in Products: A Comparison with the G.D.R." in F. Levcik, ed., *International Economics—Comparisons and Interdependencies* (Vienna-New York, 1978), pp. 40-43, and U. S. Central Intelligence Agency, "Organization and Management in the Soviet Economy: The Ceaseless Search for Panaceas," *ER* 77-10769 (December 1977).

[36] Joseph S. Berliner, *The Innovation Decision in Soviet Industry* (Cambridge, Mass., and London, 1976), esp. chapters 6, 8, 9, 15, and 16; Granick, "Soviet Research," pp. 43-49.

technology from the West, and the fact that by the 1960s such imports seem to have been constrained primarily by the perennial Soviet shortage of foreign exchange, one might have expected a similar variation during the postwar years in the composition of imports of means of production from the West.

Individual important homogeneous products as a proportion of total such imports should have declined quickly after a few years, to be replaced by new or improved foreign products whose output had not yet been mastered in domestic industry. In terms of trade statistics, such new products might have been grouped into homogeneous categories that had been relatively unimportant earlier or, more likely, into heterogeneous categories that now rose sharply in importance. Indeed, such declines in the percentages of major homogeneous products should have been much easier to achieve by import substitution during the postwar years than in the 1930s, since total imports of means of production were increasing rapidly rather than declining.

One can test the degree to which such change has occurred during the postwar years by considering the imports of two relatively homogeneous groups of items (chemical equipment and pipe) as a proportion of all machinery, equipment, and pipe imported from the West (Finland excluded).[37] Together these categories constituted one-third of such imports throughout the twelve-year period 1965-76; their proportion had increased from 15 percent during 1955-59, to 40 percent in 1960-64, and thereafter held stable at 32 percent. This is a remarkable degree of stability compared to the record of the first half of the 1930s.

Results are shown in Table 1, where each of the two categories is treated individually, and where I employ unweighted annual averages expressed in current prices for *homogeneous periods*. The changes in the proportion of pipe imports are clearly not responsive to the main factor at work during the 1930s (the mastery of new products), but rather reflect nonsecular variations in total Soviet demand for oil and gas pipe. Move-

[37] Imports from Finland are excluded because of the special trade relations existing between Finland and the USSR (neither of the two selected categories has been imported from Finland). Data are taken from Ministerstvo vneshnei torgovli SSSR, *Vneshniaia torgovlia SSSR* [Foreign Trade of the USSR], Annual Handbooks.

Two additional important and relatively homogeneous product categories might have been added into the proportion examined (ships and ship equipment and equipment for the lumber and paper industries). However, they have been excluded because of the important role of Finland as an exporter of these products to the USSR. If one were to take unweighted five-year averages of the sum of all four product categories as a proportion of all machinery, equipment and pipe imported from the West (excluding Finland), one obtains: 1955-59, 50.5 percent; 1960-64, 65.3 percent; 1965-69, 52.0 percent; and 1972-76, 40.3 percent. The last nine years (1968-76) show no trend in this proportion, and the sole period of decline which represented other than annual fluctuations was 1967-68.

TABLE 1

Imports of Pipe and Chemical Equipment

(as a percentage of all machinery, equipment, and pipe imports from the West)

Homogeneous Periods	Pipe	Chemical Equipment
1955-58	1.4	4.8
1959-62	22.6	
1963-69	7.9	
1959-68		25.1
1969-76		13.1
1970-76	19.3	

ment in the proportion of chemical equipment imports over the last eighteen years is indeed in the direction expected from the extrapolation of the 1930s phenomenon, but the absence of trend over the last eight years is striking.[38]

How can one explain the continued heavy concentration in these two categories? Technical advance in the West in these products has been evolutionary rather than revolutionary; chemical equipment, in particular, has been primarily subject to a scaling-up effect on plant size. Furthermore, neither of the two import categories can be considered particularly heterogeneous. Unless one rejects the assumption that the Soviet government has given considerable weight to the desirability of

[38] A comparable analysis of different major components of total Soviet imports of all machinery, equipment, rolled steel, and pipe during the 1929-40 period points up the contrast between the periods. (Rolled steel is included in this earlier period because of its major significance then compared with the 1955-76 period.) It should be noted that this earlier period is one in which total post-1933 annual imports of the subtotal analyzed (expressed in current dollars) never exceeded 19 percent of the 1931 peak. Thus a component that represented a declining percentage of the subtotal during these years required a much larger domestic adjusting compensation in this product group than was the case during the postwar era.

Eight product groupings represented over 5 percent each of the subtotal in 1929; together they constituted 68 percent of the subtotal. Six of these eight (totaling 53 percent of the subtotal in 1929) showed very sharp declines in their percentages over the twelve years, totaling an unweighted annual average of only 20 percent of the subtotal during 1938-40 despite very large increases in Soviet consumption of these product groups during the period. A seventh (equipment for the food industry and light industry) is irrelevant to my argument, since its sharp percentage decline reflected the low priority of usage of these products. Only metalworking equipment (a mere 8 percent of the subtotal in 1929) rose throughout the period to peak in 1938-39; it is striking that this component is by far the most heterogeneous of all the product groupings analyzed, and in this respect the least appropriate to consider as a single product grouping viewed technologically. Ministerstvo vneshnei torgovli SSSR, glavnoe tamozhenoe upravlenie, *Vneshniaia torgovlia SSSR za 1918-1940 gg.* [Foreign Trade of the USSR during 1918-1940] (Moscow, 1960).

importing new Western technology,—a rejection that would seem particularly difficult to justify for the 1970s under tight balance-of-payments constraints—the explanation for the continued predominance of these categories among total Soviet imports of means of production would seem to lie in the incapacity of the Soviet economy—and of the Soviet Union's CMEA allies—to achieve the degree of new-product mastery that was accomplished during the 1930s.

The third goal of the current period—a reform of the ratchet system of plan formation—has been pursued by attempting to develop Five-Year Plans that incorporate annual objectives for each of the relevant years. The concept is to leave the standard of evaluation stable throughout the Five-Year-Plan period, thus permitting the ratchet effect on plan formation to be applied only once every five years instead of annually. It is hoped that this will cause managers to behave, at least during the early years of each Five-Year Plan, as though the ratchet system of plan formation did not exist.

While there are claims that such Five-Year Plans have been developed at the level of the individual enterprise, no serious supporting evidence exists. Greater success has been achieved at the ministerial level.[39]

To summarize, the current period of Soviet managerial history has been characterized by the pursuit of three goals. The two that consisted of restoring the virtues of the 1930s period, although by a new means, should be judged as constituting failures. The one goal which was indeed achieved was that of fashioning a managerial bonus scheme which could guide enterprise managers to a centrally desired trade-off among quantitatively measured objectives linked together in a system of shadow-prices measured in terms of bonus.

III

Having completed the periodization of the Soviet industrial system with regard to managerial incentives and the environments within which they have functioned, I now return to the original question as to the success of adaptations of the incentive system to changes in the environment cum central welfare function. Here I focus on the difference between periods.

From the 1920s to the 1930s

The major alteration—from an unplanned, market economy to an economy planned primarily in physical terms—is, of course, a change in the

---

[39] David Granick, "Industrial Growth: Hindrances to Labor Productivity and Management Problems," in NATO-Directorate of Economic Affairs, *The USSR in the 1980s* (Brussels, 1978), pp. 76-77.

external environment cum welfare function of the central leaders as I have defined the term above. The decision that requires analysis is the linkage of both bonuses and the wage fund to the criterion of gross output.

For me, the explanation of the decision has become clearer since I have recently had the opportunity of observing at close range two of the highest priority sectors of Algerian industry, sectors growing very rapidly both in capital resources and manpower in the same fashion as did much of Soviet industry during the first half of the 1930s. Based on my Algerian experience, I think that any Russian ministry which during the first half of the 1930s was able to maintain data at central level and with a time lag of no more than one or two months as to the total tonnage of production and the total number of employees within each of its major enterprises, had an internal information system worthy of some respect. If it went further, and was capable of assuring the receipt of production information by product groups, and then of processing this information through multiplying the production components by fixed prices and thus obtaining a weighted total of gross output, it was doing as fine a job as one might reasonably think possible. Tolerably accurate and prompt information as to materials usage and direct costs, let alone as to profits or capital value, must have been well beyond the realm of the feasible.

Thus it would seem to me that if managerial and white-collar earnings were to be linked to any success indicator, and if manual worker piece-rate earnings were to be subject to any limitation whatsoever imposed by levels above that of the enterprise, gross output was the only feasible choice.[40] The true alternative was between having no incentive system in industry (in the sense of *glavki* and ministries possessing no instrument variable which they both could and were willing to use as a direct influence on the discounted lifetime earnings of managers) and the linking of incentives to an indicator that was likely to distort decision making. After observing in Algeria the results stemming from having selected the alternative to the choice made by the Soviet leadership, I am impressed with the wisdom of the Soviet decision to introduce a workable incentive system regardless of its nefarious byproducts.

A second, somewhat more theoretic approach might be taken to the reliance on the gross output indicator during the 1930s. This approach abstracts from the problems associated with the lateness, scarcity, and poor quality of information, from the problem of determining the product mix of the individual enterprise, as well as from the trade-offs between

---

[40] The difficulty of getting reliable data as to even this primitive indicator may help explain why managerial bonuses were kept so restrained as a proportion of total managerial earnings in 1934, and why great reluctance was shown in giving the State Bank operational control over the size of wage payments to be made by the enterprise from the wage fund.

those enterprise outputs which are measurable currently and all other outputs.

Given the decision to set product prices administratively, and the absence of sufficient central administrative staff to revise relative product prices with any frequency, it was inevitable that the pricing system would be a bad reflection of relative scarcities. This was the case, not only because of the constant development of new bottlenecks, but also because of major changes in the technology, in the scale of output, and in the quality of the labor force involved in the production of different products. Thus monetary costs, ruble profits, or rates of profitability would all have been very poor guides to managerial decisions.[41]

In principle, the quantity of all inputs was planned (and thus fixed) for each enterprise over the course of a year. Taking all enterprise inputs as fixed, the correct statement of the economic problem of the enterprise was to maximize its value of gross output subject to these constraints. Thus, if we ignore the issue of product-mix choices by a single enterprise, and pretend that each enterprise produced for sale only a single and homogeneous product, the maximization of gross output by each enterprise was the appropriate enterprise objective according to the standard of efficient operation of the economy as a whole.

Aside from the force of random factors (including the personal influence and connections of the managers of different enterprises), there were two major reasons why input availability at the enterprise level was not proportional as among enterprises to the annually planned quantities. The first reason was that the quantity of labor force was not in fact allocated, but was rather determined primarily by the level of quits and of hirings at the factory gate. Enterprises could and did build the size of their staffs well above the planned level. Thus the size of the labor force must be taken as a variable rather than as a fixed factor.

While this variability of labor inputs at the enterprise level tended to make gross output an inefficient success indicator from the national economic standpoint, the national importance of this phenomenon was relatively minor during the 1930s. In terms of the welfare standard of Soviet leaders, there was a great excess of unskilled labor in the countryside;[42] additional labor could be brought into existing urban centers without

---

[41] Very poor guides, that is, against the standard of a pricing system either established on the marketplace or set administratively during more stable times.

[42] The later successful labor-intensive crop production on private plots raises the question of whether agricultural labor was really "surplus" in the 1930s. An answer to this query is that Soviet leaders were primarily interested in grain and cotton, as opposed to vegetable and fruit, production within crop agriculture; for these crops, particularly grain, it would appear indisputable that the marginal product of unskilled agricultural labor must have been extremely low throughout the 1930s.

any significant capital investment in overhead facilities (including housing); therefore, the shadow-price of unskilled labor was very low.[43]

The second and more significant reason for the variability of inputs at the enterprise level was that the rationed material inputs used for current production (as opposed to capital expansion) depended not only upon planned allocations but also upon the degree of informal priority given to the products of the enterprise. For the very highest priority enterprises, managers might virtually expect that the only major constraint to the expansion of production was their existing capital stock; for this group, maximization of gross output implied utilization of material inputs as though they were free goods. Thereafter, as one moves down the priority listing of products, the enterprises producing such products were increasingly constrained by the quantity of materials that they could expect to receive rather than by their fixed-capital capacities—and their current adjustments of technology were presumably determined accordingly.

It is true that this priority system, under conditions where individual enterprises attempted to maximize gross output, made for inefficient development of the composition of national industrial capital resources. But this was a problem of investment allocation, a decision concentrated above the enterprise level. Moreover, at least on a year-by-year basis, this combination of a priority system and of the gross-output enterprise objective made for a national production mix—and a use of intermediate material resources—which was reasonably well guided by central decision makers' views, changing during the course of the planning year, as to the relative importance of marginal amounts of different products.

The important and adaptive feature of the managerial incentive system of the 1930s was that current activity was measured by the simplest possible type of success indicator for whose calculation the Soviet information system proved capable of generating the necessary data with reasonable promptness. The waste of manpower inputs resulting from the use of this success indicator was of much less significance than it was to prove later in a changed environment. Moreover, both for environmental reasons and because of the incentive system, which set a low scale of managerial bonuses, the potential harm that could be caused by reliance on the gross output indicator was minimized. Most important, however, was the fact that managerial careers were allowed to advance or recoil rapidly; thus managers were very much concerned with their superiors' *ex post* evaluation of them. In the light of future Soviet ex-

---

[43] A significant caveat here concerns skilled labor. The size of the skilled labor force should also be taken as a variable factor. Yet, during the 1930s, the shadow-price of skilled labor must have been very high. Indeed, it seems likely that the ratio (shadow-price of skilled labor)/(shadow-price of capital) was even higher in the 1930s than in the postwar periods. I am indebted to my colleague Earl Brubaker for pointing this out.

perience, we can say that this last element was particularly vital in promoting rapid implementation of technological innovations.

From the 1930s to 1940-65

For the reasons indicated in section II, the environment cum welfare function of the central leaders changed between the 1930s and 1940-65 in such a fashion as to expand greatly the relative importance of the gross output indicator in enterprise managers' utility functions. The disadvantages inherent in reliance on this indicator—particularly the disadvantages related to choice of product mix by the individual enterprise and to implementation of product and process innovations—accordingly increased in importance.

Moreover, three additional factors of the environment were operating to worsen further the fit of the existing incentive system to the needs of the economy. The first of these factors was that unskilled-semiskilled labor was becoming increasingly scarce during the 1950s,[44] and thus the waste of labor implicit in the gross output incentives grew increasingly deleterious. The second was that the priority system of materials allocation began to break down after Stalin's death, at the time that it became increasingly important to the supreme Soviet leaders to achieve the planned goals for output of agricultural products and of manufactured consumer goods—even their political survival hanging in the balance. As the priority principle gradually lost its predominance as the mechanism for reconciling the actual deliveries of intermediate materials with the planned allocations, only random forces, exchange of favors among enterprises, and simple corruption[45] were available as replacements. The third factor was that the international pace of product and process innovation had speeded up considerably above that of the interwar level, and thus the demands for ever-renewed implementation of innovation within a given enterprise became increasingly severe. This was aggravated by the fact that within each administrative grouping and enterprise there were now many more minor products, requiring continuous modification of product and process, than had existed in the 1930s.

[44] See Murray L. Weitzman, "Soviet Postwar Economic Growth and Capital-Labor Substitution," *American Economic Review*, 60 (September 1970), and the discussion of his data in Granick, "The Internalizing of Externalities in Socialist Enterprises and in Subunits of Large American Firms" in W. G. Shepherd, ed., *Public Enterprise: Economic Analysis of Theory and Practice* (Lexington, Mass., 1976), p. 80.

[45] Assuming that Gregory Grossman is correct in his belief that a great expansion in the extent of the black market has occurred in the Soviet Union since the death of Stalin (Grossman, "The 'Second Economy' of the USSR," *Problems of Communism*, 26 [September-October 1977]:36), the demise of the priority principle may be a partial explanation of the timing.

The shift in the postwar years away from the administrative readiness of the 1930s to make frequent use of managerial demotion for nonpolitical reasons presumably had two causes. The first was the fact that by the postwar period the most ineffective managers had already been weeded out. The second was the central leaders' desire for achieving greater stability throughout Soviet society after the shakeups due to the purges of the middle and late 1930s. This second factor would seem to have had considerably greater force for the post-Stalin half of the period than for the first half. In any case, what matters is that the sharp reduction in the use of managerial demotion must be interpreted as a change in environment cum welfare function of the central leaders, rather than as a change in the incentive system employed by Soviet administrators above the enterprise level.

The positive response of industrial administrators to the changing environment was negligible. Their first principal action was an attempt during 1959-65 (apparently, from later Soviet accounts, not very successful) to shift bonus attachment partly to a cost-reduction indicator, thus placing some emphasis on the reduction of inputs by enterprise managers. The second action was the sharp reduction during 1960-64 in bonuses of managerial and other white-collar personnel as a proportion of their total earnings. This latter move implied some shift from gross output (to which these bonuses were attached) to gross output per member of the labor force (to which the wage fund was attached) in the utility function of enterprise managers, thus encouraging them to economize on the increasingly scarce factor of labor. Probably more important, by reducing the strength of managerial incentives in general, it may have been hoped that the degree of pressure upon enterprise managers to make bad decisions would be reduced.[46]

Other actions were to have significance for the incentive system in the post-1965 period, but probably not until then. The first of these was the normal improvement one might have expected over time in the information system within industry—extending both to the physical use of inputs and to financial summary data. The second was ideological: the increased acceptance, both in decision making and in the evaluation of enterprises' financial performance, of one or another form of capital charge and of rent.

Overall, the weakness of administrative response to a changing envi-

[46] It has been suggested that this action may be better perceived as part of Khrushchev's income-equalization policy rather than as an adjustment to a changing environment for managers. I think this argument may possibly be applied to managerial and professional bonuses, but not to those of the remaining white-collar personnel who did not have high earnings compared with those of manual workers. Both, however, seem to have been affected by the 1960-64 development.

ronment (i.e., the absence of entrepreneurship in the face of new conditions) was striking. In essence, Soviet administrators attempted to live with some consciously designed incentive system—reinforced indeed until 1960 through the larger share of managerial bonuses—which had functioned with reasonable effectiveness during the 1930s. Small wonder that the first half of the 1960s constituted a low point in Soviet industrial success.

From 1940-65 to Post-1965

After a quarter century of stagnation in the design of managerial incentive systems, the most recent period has seen considerable innovation. Much of this has been unsuccessful to date, but genuine change has occurred both in linking managerial (and, indeed, all white collar) bonuses to a broader set of criteria than that of gross output, and in strengthening the relative importance within managers' utility functions of this new type of bonus compared with the gross output per employee criterion to which manual workers' earnings remain tied.

But even abstracting from potential institutional changes that lie outside of the considerations going into the agent-principal model of section I, reformation of the incentive system has proceeded within narrow bounds. There has been no serious change in the approach of linking monetary payments to manual workers to short-run group output achievements, and there has indeed been reinforcement of the binding of managerial and other white-collar monetary payments to enterprise achievements as measured by one or another indicator of measured short-run success. Soviet administrators have continued to reject the East German approach of providing administrators with considerable discretion in defining enterprise success not *ex ante* but *ex post* (thus including unmeasurable dimensions of performance in the definition), and of linking managerial bonus awards to this *ex post* definition.[47] Thus the potential "arbitrariness" of administrators has been restricted, and Soviet enterprise managers have continued to be given objectives that are reasonably well defined in a quantitative fashion *ex ante*. In my view, one price of having maintained these bounds on the incentive system is that little could be achieved in better promoting enterprise implementation of technical innovations.

Conclusion

Western literature on the Soviet economy is filled with comments to the effect that the Soviet central-planning model was well designed to meet

[47] David Granick, *Enterprise Guidance in Eastern Europe* (Princeton, 1976), chapters 6 and 7.

the economic growth objectives of the political leadership of the 1930s, under the economic conditions of the time, but that it has become increasingly inappropriate as the Soviet Union has developed. Some doubt is cast on this view of central physical planning, as being peculiarly poorly adapted to the conditions of developed economies, by the experience of the German Democratic Republic; for that country has had a very respectable economic record by the standards of the other CMEA nations and of the German Federal Republic[48] during the last twenty years.

This chapter has focused on the changing congruence between economic development and an extremely secondary aspect of the Soviet system, rather than upon the congruence of development and the main Soviet model. One would think that the basic Soviet central-planning model could be combined with very variegated managerial incentive systems without doing violence to this model. Thus adaptation of the incentive system to changing conditions seems to be a customary problem of organizational adaptation, quite comparable to the historical adaptation problem within individual large American companies that has been the concern of Alfred Chandler[49]—rather than constituting a broad socioeconomic-political issue.

I have suggested that the first years of the operation of the Soviet central-physical-planning model were precisely those in which the fit of the incentive system and the environment cum welfare function of central leaders was the best. Thereafter, despite the environment changing rapidly, there was virtually no positive adaptation (i.e., entrepreneurship) during a quarter of a century and only weak positive change since. This failure of Soviet industry to meet the organizational-adaptation entrepreneurial standard suggested by Chandler as characterizing American big business helps—to an unexplored degree—to explain the increasing difficulties of Soviet industry.

[48] Paul Gregory and Gert Leptin, "Similar Societies under Differing Economic Systems: The Case of the Two Germanys," *Soviet Studies*, 29 (October 1977):519-42.

[49] Alfred D. Chandler, *Strategy and Structure: Chapters in the History of the Industrial Enterprise* (Cambridge, Mass., 1962).

XIII

ROY D. AND
BETTY A. LAIRD

The Soviet Farm Manager as an Entrepreneur

[Lenin] . . . taught how to combine "the democracy of the toiling masses with iron discipline during working time and unconditional obedience to the will of a single individual, the Soviet leader, during time of work."[1]

In this study we will attempt to examine the farm manager[2] in his entrepreneurial capacity and determine the degree to which he functions as an organizer and manager, and to which he assumes risk.

Soviet Farms, Then and Now

Although space limitations do not allow more than a cursory look at the essential elements of a Soviet farm, a brief discussion of some of the basics is required in order to put entrepreneurship in the countryside in perspective.

There is a great historical paradox about rural Russia (and much of the rest of the USSR). Imposition of the socialist sovkhozy and kolkhozy on the villages in the 1930s brought about a profound transmutation of the private agricultural activity that flourished in the "golden era"[3] of the New Economic Policy (NEP). Yet, we suspect that if a collectivized peasant of the 1980s could return to a farm predating the emancipation

---

* The authors wish to thank the Hesston Foundation and the University of Kansas, whose assistance helped to make this study possible.

[1] A. Klimov and N. Chernykh, "The Leader and the Collective," *Kommunist*, no. 12 (August 1972):37.

[2] We use the term *farm manager* to denote both the kolkhoz (collective farm) chairman and the sovkhoz (state farm) director, since much of the time we will be considering them jointly.

[3] A term used by Fedor Belov in his *The History of a Collective Farm* (New York, 1955).

in 1861, he would be astounded by the similarities between agriculture under the socialist system and that under the tsarist landlords. True, the implements would be more primitive and horses instead of tractors would provide the draft power, but the organizational and social structure would seem quite familiar, for the old village commune was in some ways a primitive kolkhoz. Then the peasants received their guidelines from the mir through meetings of the village elders. Today, the same function is carried out by general meetings of the able-bodied members of the collective or of their representatives. Then the landlord's manager was all powerful. Today, as we shall document, the kolkhoz chairman (or the sovkhoz director) is the all-powerful resident manager, under a new landlord, the state.

Whereas in the beginning there were very few sovkhozy, and the average kolkhoz, created on the basis of the old villages, probably encompassed a score or two of households, by 1940 both types of farms had grown significantly larger, their numbers including 235,500 kolkhozy (excluding fishing collectives) and 4,200 sovkhozy. Starting in the 1950s, under Khrushchev's leadership, the amalgamation drive resulted in a dual transformation of the countryside. As summarized in Table 1, the kolkhozy were greatly reduced in number (with a more than fivefold increase in size) and with the simultaneous transformation of many of the "weaker" kolkhozy into sovkhozy (plus the opening up of the "virgin lands" to gigantic grain-growing state farms), the sovkhozy grew up in both size and number. Thus, whereas by 1976 the sovkhozy numbered 19,617, there were then only 27,300 kolkhozy.

Theoretically, the kolkhozy are collectives. All land in the USSR is state-owned, but the land in the kolkhoz is said to be in the charge of the farm members in perpetuity—that is, unless a decision is taken to transform a collective into a sovkhoz. The organizational form is dictated by the so-called Model Charter, first issued in 1930, slightly changed in 1935, and updated in 1969. Although euphemistically named, that document is the basic law for all kolkhozy. A major provision in that document is that all important on-farm decisions, including the "election" of a chairman, are to be taken by vote in periodic general meetings of the membership. In fact, however, published accounts of proceedings make abundantly clear that (with the rarest of exceptions) the general meetings are not decision-making bodies. They are educating, indoctrinating, legitimizing institutions where the farm members learn of plans and decisions already set in cement. Votes are taken, but as in Soviet elections, virtually all the results are a foregone conclusion.

New kolkhoz chairmen are voted on, but with the exception of a time of relaxed outside controls during World War II, rarely has the nominee come from inside the farm. Indeed, the record indicates that the vast

TABLE 1
Some Kolkhozy and Sovkhozy Averages

	1940	1960	1976
Kolkhozy			
Total number	235,500	44,900	27,300
Per Farm			
Workers	110	445	542
Specialists	—	4.9	20
Sown Area (hectares)	500	2,746	3,597
Head of livestock (cattle, hogs, sheep, and goats)	297	3,031	4,509
Tractors	4.4	14.4	39
Value of production (Million rubles/yr.)	—	—	1.7
Sovkhozy			
Total number	4,200	7,400	19,617
Per Farm			
Workers	381	783	559
Specialists	—	22	33.6
Sown area	2,750	9,081	5,680
Head of livestock	3,033	10,279	6,171
Tractors	20	54	57
Value of production	—	1.6	2.0

SOURCES: *Narodnoe khoziaistvo SSSR v 1961, Narodnoe khoziaistvo SSSR za 60 let*, 1977, *Sel'skoe khoziaistvo*, 1960 and 1971.

majority of such candidates are total strangers to the farm membership. Although raion party officials may engineer the elections, they select farm chairmen from the oblast party unit's *nomenklatura* (appointment list).

Not only does the chairman have the final word in all on-farm decisions not predetermined by outside controls—e.g., state delivery requirements will determine the minimum number of hectares to be planted to a particular kind of grain, but the chairman dictates which land will be sown to which crop, and he determines who among the membership will cultivate it—but he controls the lives of the farm members as thoroughly and completely as the commander determines the affairs of those who live on a military post.

As shown in Table 1, the average farm has more than a score of specialists, plus others such as brigade leaders who comprise the managerial and technical staff. A select number of such individuals will comprise the management board. In addition to the chairman, most such boards include a vice-chairman, a chief accountant, a head agronomist, head zootechnician, and the inevitable Party secretary. All serve at the chairman's pleasure, with the possible exception of the Party secretary who, as in all Soviet enterprises and institutions, usually is the second most powerful person on the farm and may, on occasion, force the chairman to temper his decisions so as not to incur Party displeasure. However, since virtually all chairmen and directors are now Party members, the evidence suggests that on most farms the Party secretaries work closely with the managers, subjecting their actions to his direction. Prior to the amalgamation of the smaller farms into today's huge enterprises, which occurred in the 1950s, most of the kolkhozy did not have a Party-member chairman or Party units. This, along with the universal adoption of a guaranteed minimum wage for the kolkhozniki, inaugurated in the 1960s, served to remove most of the important differences between the kolkhozy and sovkhozy. As low-level state bureaucrats, the sovkhoz directors had always been under the tight discipline of Moscow. As state employees, sovkhoz workers have almost always received their wages, regardless of the success or failure of a crop. Today, although different methods may be employed (e.g., kolkhozy contribute to a crop insurance scheme, which helps assure that the kolkhozniki will receive their guaranteed wage), for all practical purposes the kolkhozy are as tightly held by outside controls as are the sovkhozy, and today's kolkhoznik is nearly as much a hired hand as is his sovkhoz counterpart, even though the average sovkhoz worker's annual income remains higher than that earned by the worker on the kolkhoz fields. In the formative years and during the relaxed controls of World War II, many chairmen acted in a spirit of considerable independence. Some, but far from all, performed in ways that they felt would best serve the farm members. Today most of that independence has gone by the wayside, as administrative boards demand an accounting and threaten the manager with dismissal if standards are not met.

Outside Chairmen

As documented in Table 1, until recently, the kolkhozy dominated the rural scene. In the beginning, farms were created on the base of the former villages. Most chairmen were selected from among the membership, even though they lacked the talent to survive under the demands of the time. Almost from the beginning the central authorities' insatiable quest for maximum controls, rooted in political, ideological, and economic contributions, led to an increasing practice of imposing outside chairmen on the farms. Moreover, a major cost of forced collectivization made the practice imperative in most cases. *Raskulachivanie* (destruction of the kulak class) had removed the best of the nation's farmers from the land.

Whether the sons of better-off farmers inherit superior intelligence, receive better training, or are given economic advantages (surely a combination of all three is at work in most instances), as can be seen the world over, the best farmers tend to be sons of men who, in their day, were the best farmers in a region. Stalin's decision to eliminate the kulaks worked so successfully that even today some of the shortcomings of Soviet agriculture may be linked to the human tragedy of the early 1930s. In this judgment, we go even beyond the time limit suggested by Lazar Volin, who observed: "One . . . point cannot be stated too often: with the large number of the best farmers driven off the land or exterminated, the result of dekulakization, the qualitative depletion of human resources was bound to impair the productive capacity of Russian agriculture, at least temporarily. . . . [Thus] the Kremlin had to rely on nonfarmers, . . . or on mediocre farmers for leadership in the kolkhozes."[4]

In L. E. Hubbard's accounting: "Probably not less than five million peasants including families, were deported to Siberia and the Far North, and of these it is estimated that 25 percent perished."[5] Elimination of the kulaks involved a deliberate removal from the land of those most capable of entrepreneurial activity. Nor did the drive end there. The new farm managers were desperate for help, at least someone who could read, write, and do simple accounting. Many, perhaps most, of the talent the managers recruited were "former kulaks and children of kulaks, merchants, and priests" who came to be major targets of the "mounting purge hysteria," regardless of how sorely needed their skills were.[6]

Imposition of outside chairmen became an imperative of the regime. More often than not they were urban agricultural illiterates. The practice continues to the present, although nearly all of the chairmen of the 1980s do have some training in agricultural pursuits. The record implies that in most years hundreds of urban leaders (predominantly Party members) have been sent to take over the farms.

In 1929 25,000 city workers were sent to act as chairmen and rural functionaries.[7]

In 1933 18,000 city workers were sent to the MTS politdely and sovkhozy.[8]

In the early 1950s a total of 32,078 outsiders were sent to be farm chairmen.[9]

---

[4] Lazar Volin, *A Century of Russian Agriculture: From Alexander II to Khrushchev* (Cambridge, Mass., 1970), p. 237.

[5] Leonard E. Hubbard, *Economics of Soviet Agriculture* (London, 1939), p. 117.

[6] Merle Fainsod, *Smolensk Under Soviet Rule*, (Cambridge, Mass., 1958), pp. 303-5.

[7] Naum Jasny, *The Socialized Agriculture of the U.S.S.R.* (Stanford, Calif., 1949), p. 335.

[8] Volin (supra, n. 4), p. 240.

[9] Jerry F. Hough, "The Changing Nature of the Kolkhoz Chairman," in James R. Millar, ed., *The Soviet Rural Community* (Urbana, Ill., 1971), p. 111.

If more than one in ten U.S. farms were to experience a change in management every year, rural America would be seen as in a state of chaos. Yet, as of the early 1970s, more than that number of kolkhoz chairmen were in their jobs for less than a year. Fortunately, the recent rate of turnover is much lower than it was in earlier decades. (See Table 2.)

The Powerful Rural Bureaucrat

AS AN ORGANIZER

Not since the collectivization drive of the 1930s has any Soviet rural leader had the opportunity to organize a farm in the sense of building a new enterprise according to his vision. All soviet farms exist at the behest of the Party-state leadership.

As noted earlier, the Model Charter is the basic law for all kolkhozy; however, it is supplemented by a continuing flood of Moscow-initiated laws and administrative orders. According to the Charter, the farm chairman is elected to a three-year term (with the right of recall) by a general meeting of collective farmers. His function is spelled out in one sentence: "The chairman of the collective farm exercises day-to-day direction over the collective farm's activity, ensures the fulfillment of the decisions of the general meeting and the board, and represents the collective farm in its relations with state agencies and other institutions and organiza-

TABLE 2
Tenure of Kolkhoz Chairmen
(percent)

	Less than 1 Year	1-3 Years	3 Years and More
1934	30	—	—
1938	54	—	—
1939	48	—	—
1946	41	—	—
1953	23.8	35.6	40.6
1956	29.7	33.9	36.4
1959	4.6	38.9	56.5
1965	14	28	58
1971	13	21	66

SOURCES: Jerry F. Hough, "The Changing Nature of the Kolkhoz Chairman," in James R. Millar, ed., *The Soviet Rural Community*, Champaign, 1971, pp. 103-20; Naum Jasny, *The Socialized Agriculture of the USSR* (Stanford, 1949), p. 334; and *Sel'skoe khoziaistvo*, 1960 and 1971.

tions."[10] In practice, of course, the name of each prospective farm chairman is presented to the general meeting for their approval which, except in the most extraordinary cases, is dutifully given.

Such pretense to the democratic process is not necessary in the sovkhoz, where the director is appointed (and dismissed) by the trust, association, or combine to which the state farm is subordinated.[11] His assignment is virtually the same as that of the kolkhoz chairman. "[He] organizes all the work of the state farm, represents it in all institutions and organizations, handles, in accordance with the law, the property and resources of the enterprise, concludes contracts, issues powers of attorney, opens accounts in the bank and, within the bounds of his competence, issues orders, hires and dismisses personnel, rewards and reprimands the workers."[12]

Thus the farm manager is not in an enviable position as an organizer. Having had no control whatsoever over the initial organization of his farm, he is then assigned full responsibility for organizing the work within an already prescribed production labor plan and structure from which he may not deviate without special permission from above.

Since the early 1970s, however, a peripheral organizational opportunity seems to have become available to some farm managers; this is in the development of subsidiary enterprises within the public sector. Frequent articles in the Soviet press have pointed to this method of increasing farm income and improving labor and raw-material utilization. Taking advantage of newly available bank loans for the purpose, farm managers, on their own initiative, through the encouragement of their staffs, and with pressure from above, have organized thousands of these subsidiary enterprises, including canneries, flour mills, wineries, creameries, folk-art shops, carpentry and woodworking shops, sawmills, brick, tile, concrete and asphalt plants, quarries, and slaughterhouses.[13] Needless to say, the manager must have the approval of his superiors to attempt such an undertaking, and the project must fit within the guidelines established.

AS A MANAGER

Both the kolkhozy and the sovkhozy are operated on the basis of one-man control, but presumably on democratic principles. The kolkhoz chairman, for example, functions as chairman of the kolkhoz board,

[10] "Text of the Model Collective Farm Charter as Adopted," *The Current Digest of the Soviet Press*, 21 (1969) no. 50, 14.

[11] G. M. Loza, "State Farms—Socialist State Agricultural Enterprises," in L. Kolesnikov, ed., *Agriculture of the Soviet Union* (Moscow, 1970), p. 42.

[12] Ibid., p. 52.

[13] K. Khavronin, "Subsidiary Enterprises and Works," *Sovetskaia Moldaviia*, July 16, 1972, p. 2.

theoretically making joint decisions on the basis of orders from the general meeting of the kolkhoz membership. In practice, however, most of the kolkhoz chairmen, under the eye of the Party secretary, exercise virtually dictatorial powers, overruling board members and presenting decisions already made to the general meeting of the membership for rubber stamping. Since general meetings need not be called more than four times a year, they do not present much of a problem for a determined chairman. Furthermore, if the farm membership is so large as to preclude the gathering of all members in a single room at one time (and it usually is), the general meeting may be constituted of elected representatives, offering another opportunity for the chairman to stack the deck in his favor. A description and schematic diagram (see Figure 1) of the kolkhoz management structure—first established in the 1930s to 1940s—are provided us by Candidate of Economic Sciences M. Darii.

> The production structure of kolkhoz management and the organizational structure conformable to it led to the predominance of the linear-staff type of management based on a combination of linear management on the part of the line supervisors (chairmen and brigade leaders) and functional management on the part of the agricultural specialists (agronomists, zootechnicians, etc.). This basically insured adherence to the principle of one-man control, unity of supervision, and subordination of all the workers (through a linear management apparatus) directly to one person—the kolkhoz chairman in conjunction with a collective leadership—in making decisions at board sessions and general meetings of the kolkhoz farmers. This was accompanied by the exercise of simultaneous functional management on the part of the various agricultural specialists.[14]

Darii suggests that the old form of management is outmoded and generally should be replaced by a model that would reduce considerably the number of persons directly subordinate to the kolkhoz chairman. His argument is that under the present system the chairman is compelled to resolve a myriad of temporary, minor production problems that could as well be solved by subordinates, thus relieving him of an excessive workload which distracts his attention from major, long-range problems, the solutions of which affect the entire farm. Darii's concern reflects the fact that most chairmen apparently are reluctant to release control of any facet of the kolkhoz down to the most minute detail. Clearly, there are some kolkhozy operating under a more democratic system, depending partly on the personality and philosophy of the chairman involved, but

[14] M. Darii, "Improving Kolkhoz Production Management," *Kommunist Moldavii*, no. 4 (April 1973):57.

FIGURE 1
Schematic Diagram of Kolkhoz Management

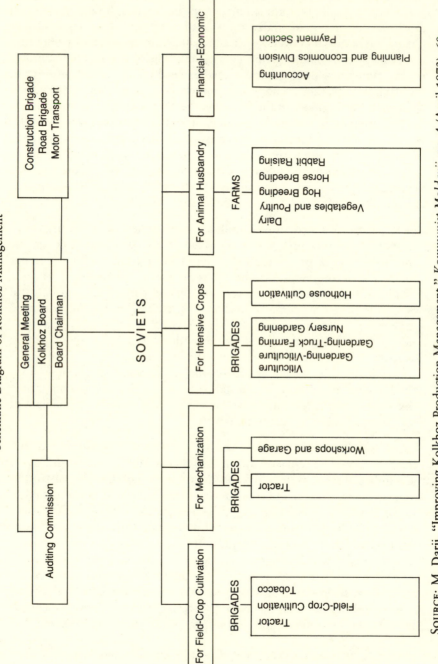

SOURCE: M. Darii, "Improving Kolkhoz Production Management," *Kommunist Moldavii*, no. 4 (April 1973), 60.

in general, the kolkhoz chairmen remain enormously powerful bureaucrats, administrators who are, from the average peasant worker's point of view, virtually as powerful as the tsarist landlords. Manipulating the rubber stamp of the general meeting so as to legitimize his actions, a chairman can even move to have a kolkhoznik expelled from the farm. Indeed, according to former chairman Fedor Belov, at least as late as 1948, such expulsion could include banishment to Siberia for several years.

Whatever the kolkhozniki may think of their bosses in private, publicly they treat the managers with awe, often literally approaching them with hat in hand. Other observers of the Soviet rural scene have made similar points. According to Jan and Arthur Adams: "Like the *pomeshchiki* (landowners) of old the collective farm chairmen and state farm directors are in almost total social and organizational control over their farms and the people in them."[15]

Certainly the sovkhoz director is no more democratic than the kolkhoz chairman, if that much. Indeed, the director does not even have a sovkhoz board with which to consult. Theoretically, he makes a collective agreement with the local trade-union committee as representative of the workers, which establishes rules, bonuses, incentive funds, and awards, and distributes living space. Meetings of workers' representatives and trade-union meetings are supposed to promote discussion and generate input, but, again, their major function is to approve the director's recommendations. The sovkhoz director also keeps in his hands the strings to every operation of the farm. One director we visited during a trip to the USSR in 1970 was especially delighted with the farm's new telephone communications network, enabling him to know at all times how every sector was functioning. Finally, although the director does not hire and fire the main specialists on his sovkhoz, the superior agency that does usually acts on the director's recommendations. Like his counterpart on the kolkhoz, the sovkhoz director generally guards his powers jealously, and from our limited observations, revels in his Little-Caesar role. "Spying the director, the old muzhik halted abruptly, jerked off his hat and held it to his chest, bowing with the short repeated jerks of a humble peasant of imperial times. The director *was* the farm."[16]

AS THE ONE WHO ASSUMES RISK

As documented below, at least in the past, being a farm manager was to place oneself in an extremely high-risk position. Indeed, the evidence is that for many years the average tenure in office of farm managers was

---

[15] Arthur E. Adams and Jan Steckelberg Adams, *Agriculture in the USSR, Poland, and Czechoslovakia: Men Versus Systems* (New York, 1977), p. 31.

[16] Ibid., pp. 55 and 63.

only some two years. From the 1930s to the present the first remedy for a farm with serious problems has been to replace the manager in command. True, not all were destined to sink into oblivion, since over the years numerous complaints have been made in the press concerning managers who were fired as the head of one farm turning up later as managers of another farm in trouble, or in some other responsible position. For example, Kolkhoz Chairman Juozas Minkauskas was fined by the People's Court in 1974 for embezzlement of kolkhoz funds, and although he was not reelected as chairman, two years later he was head bookkeeper of the same kolkhoz.[17]

Obviously, however, the risks of the profession are high in terms of career security for the individuals involved. Moreover, as Professor Hough has suggested, what is known of biographies of kolkhoz chairmen leads to a conclusion that such jobs hardly are stepping stones to higher office for an ambitious Soviet citizen.[18]

On the other hand, with the exception of land lost to urban and industrial expansion, no matter how poor the performance, Soviet farms never die—although many have been absorbed into larger units. Unlike earlier times when many, perhaps in some years most, kolkhozy paid no money income to the workers—a key price of Stalin's use of the countryside to subsidize industrial growth—today's farms are heavily subsidized. According to the official in charge of setting all the prices in the USSR, the subsidy rate reached a staggering 22 billion rubles annually in 1978.[19] At the worst, an ailing kolkhoz is tranformed into a sovkhoz. No Soviet authority has ever repudiated the oft-repeated claim that the sovkhoz is the ultimate, highest agricultural form. For such reasons there is no more risk involved in the survival of a farm than there is to the continued existence of a key munitions plant. Indeed, there is less, since technology can eliminate some kinds of manufacturing, whereas the need for food will remain as long as there are people to eat it.

Innovation, Reward, and Punishment

Beyond money income, some three times that of the average kolkhoz workers, the perquisites and windfalls of Soviet farm managers must mean their standard of living is relatively high. The nature of the job demands that cars, trucks, and drivers be constantly at their call. Cer-

---

[17] J. Meskauskas, "The Readers Suggested the Subject of the Moral: He Considered Himself Infallible," *Tiesa*, September 1, 1977, p. 4.

[18] Hough (supra, n. 9), pp. 103-20.

[19] David K. Willis, "The Man Who Sets 10 Million Prices," *The Christian Science Monitor*, June 21, 1978, p. 3. This is an interview with Nikolai Timofeevich Glushkov, chairman of the State Prices Commission of the USSR.

tainly, samples of the best of all the food grown on the farm find their way into the boss's kitchen. For at least those fortunate enough to manage successful farms that attract visiting delegations, such chairmen must have no bill for spirits. The state repays the farms for playing host and, as we have observed on several occasions, in spite of gargantuan efforts on the part of the hosts and guests, vodka and wine are left over after such confrontations. Managers in similar situations the world over live high off the hog. Moreover, managers in such positions of power as Soviet farm managers are confronted constantly with the temptation to take even more.

Thus we read of a kolkhoz chairman who requisitioned for his own use some 11,000 rubles out of 32,000 reserved for prize money for his kolkhozniki. He lessened the chances of being caught by directing some of those funds into the pockets of his specialists.[20] Or a recent example of a manager whose farm operated at a 300,000-ruble loss, in spite of which he assigned himself a 900-ruble bonus.[21] An even more energetic sovkhoz manager in Azerbaidzhan, with the assistance of several employees, embezzled 169,771 rubles by falsifying accounts.[22]

Most cases that we read about of cheating by the farm managers, however, seem to be for the general welfare of the farm rather than to increase the personal wealth of the leader, although the two are tied inextricably together. Indeed, there may be nowhere else in the world where farm managers in general face as great a need to break the rules just to avoid failure as in the Soviet Union. As in Soviet industry, Soviet farm managers who may avoid cheating for personal gain are forced to employ *tolkach* (an expediter) and *blat* (the practice of manipulation) in order to keep an enterprise going. For example, with the chronic shortage of fertilizer, if a farm manager can arrange for a shipment of fertilizer destined for another farm to be diverted to his own, he may be able to increase his yield enough to meet the plan.[23] Or if he can negotiate on the side with a construction brigade to acquire their off-schedule services for constructing a sorely needed storage bin, he may save a large portion of the farm's grain from rotting on the ground.[24] Or if he supplies speculators with fruit or vegetables from an overabundance that is spoiling

[20] I. Lukin, "In Accordance with the Rules," *Pravda*, November 16, 1973, p. 2.

[21] A. Platoshkin and V. Posokhovi, "In a Thorough and Businesslike Manner," *Pravda*, April 24, 1978, p. 2.

[22] "With a Stroke of the Pen," *Bakinskii rabochii*, March 26, 1978, p. 4.

[23] A. Mukhamedov, "Guarding the Interests of the Kolkhozes and Sovkhozes," *Turkmenskaia iskra*, August 12, 1975, p. 2.

[24] N. Brizhan, "Supervision of Observing Laws on Kolkhoz Property Maintenance," *Sotsialisticheskaia zakonnost'*, no. 11 (1973):31.

for lack of transportation to the city, he can increase the farm's income and transfer the badly needed produce to the consumer as well.[25]

Making a profit is important. Guaranteed minimum wages exist. However, for the kolkhozniki, and especially the managers, receipt of bonuses can mean the difference between just getting by, and having a life with some comforts. Bonuses are dependent primarily upon fulfilling and overfulfilling the plan. The plan is the most important of all economic indicators. Other infractions of the rules can be overlooked, or result in minor reprimand or punishment, but repeated failure to meet the plan without the best of excuses will result in the sacking of a manager. Surely, there is a strong correlation (at least in recent years) between the rate of turnover of farm managers and the number of farms that fail to meet the plan.

Without a marketplace from which to purchase crucial equipment and supplies (each year the papers are full of complaints about shortages of spare parts to keep the machines going), most managers would be faced with some kind of annual input catastrophe if they did not engage in extralegal maneuvers to avoid disaster. Every successful manager must have an uninventoried horde of chains, tractor generators, spark plugs, wheel bearings, and other items in anticipation of breakdowns at such times as the harvest, when normal supply channels are even less reliable than usual.

This is hardly a new concept. For centuries the peasant, who knew that wagon wheels and axles wear out faster than the wagon box, prepared himself for winter by laying in a supply of axles. One kolkhoz chairman who found himself in a difficult situation with a shortage of tractor parts during harvest was advised by an old mechanic to search the lofts of houses formerly belonging to tractor drivers who had left the farm. There, sure enough, the chairman found the needed parts.[26] During calving, if a storm were to destroy livestock sheds, a barrel of nails to make instantly needed repairs could save the day. Managers who survive not only must have anticipated their needs, but in case they have failed to horde the right thing, or in the right quantity, they must have connections with neighboring farms and enterprises where a needed load of lumber can be obtained for a few hams or a quantity of leftover paint.

Such outside-of-plan activity is illegal in the USSR, but since most

---

[25] George Malarchuk, "What to Do with the Surplus?" *Literaturnaia gazeta*, June 25, 1975, p. 10.

[26] D. Kuzovlev, "The Concerns of a Villager," *Novyi mir* (October 1973):206. How these extra parts are acquired by the peasants is another story. Some are purchased legitimately, but many come from pilferage of unattended machines. The story is told that once an entire tractor was dismantled and carried away, bit by bit, over a period of several weeks by workers who thought the parts might come in handy.

officials realize that without the lubrication that makes the system work (*tolkach* and *blat*), production would grind to a halt, they look the other way, at least until the sweetener in such transactions grows to a point that individuals become rich as a result. Serious violations of the economic rules can result in serious consequences for those involved. Nevertheless, the impression is that major infraction of the law is frequent. For example, in recent years more than one report has told of one means used by managers to assure meeting state purchase plans. Livestock produce is deliberately sold below cost in state stores. Thus, if a manager knows he will not be able to deliver his farm's butter quota, he can arrange to have enough butter purchased from state stores to add to the farm's output to the point that the plan is fulfilled. There are, of course, many ways to skin a cat. As noted in *Pravda*, April 24, 1978, in an article dealing with problems on the collective and state farms in Tula Oblast, "there are still plenty of people who are fond of claiming nonexistant achievements and padding when it comes to writing reports."

There are, fortunately, a number of entirely legal directions that innovative management can take. A manager may wish to set up a machine-repair shop on the farm rather than rely on the raion repair shop or a neighbor for major alterations.[27] Again, however, many of the parts necessary for the shop likely will come from illegal sources. Some managers encourage their workers to invent and construct labor- or time-saving devices that can enhance production. (Examples include loading and unloading equipment, potato bins for temporary storage and loading, and hay-scalding apparatus.)

One kolkhoz chairman, A. Buznitskii from Kievskaia Oblast, believes that innovative farm management not only is possible, but is no less important than capital investment to the success of the farm. He proved his point by noting that on his farm, spreading chemical fertilizer by airplane, the "modern method," resulted in uneven spreading, with heavy coverage in some areas and nothing at all in others. Retaining his sense of humor in spite of adversity, he explained:

> The wind rises, covering with fertilizer a cow barn or a settlement, which does not benefit either the cows or the people. The wind may also take the fertilizer into your neighbors' field. Yet, it is not your neighbor who paid for the airplane . . . or worse a higher wind will take the fertilizer to the upper atmospheric strata, on the edge of outer space. We believe it premature to apply fertilizer to outer space.[28]

[27] V. Gafiatulin, "Kazakhstan: The Grain Won't Wait," *Trud*, September 1972, p. 1.
[28] A. Buznitskii, "How the 'Golden Calf' Is Born," *Literaturnaia gazeta*, October 17, 1973, p. 11.

Buznitskii and his staff reequipped a planter and began applying their fertilizer directly to the roots of their crops, thereby increasing their yield as much as ten quintals. His innovation, in 1973, was regarded with considerable suspicion by his superiors and by agricultural scientists who maintained it was untested. Only with repeated successes and frequent pleading of his case did he gain acceptance of his "doubtful" improvement, and then mostly by other farm managers who could arrange to have fertilizing machines constructed by their mechanics.[29] By spring of 1977, apparently Buznitskii's idea had made some impact, for by then fertilizing machines were being tested, although they were not yet available from the factories.

Unfortunately, farm managers are frustrated at every turn by pressures and restrictions from above. In spite of an attempt in 1965 to grant the individual farm greater autonomy, what the right hand giveth the left hand taketh away. Viktor Perevedentsev, the well-known Soviet sociologist who writes on farm problems, reported a chairman's complaint, common among farm managers. "I do not see any special distinction between the present and the former systems. . . . Formerly the number of hectares to be planted to wheat was planned for us, while now we are told how much wheat we are to deliver. It is six of one and half a dozen of the other."[30] As late as 1976 an agronomist reported, "We don't enter any figures into the industrial-financial plan on our own, we go to the administration office and there we are told what crops to grow and how much should be sown."[31]

In his farm's particular case, this meant that in spite of urgent need for careful clean-fallow practices, the farm was forced to grow crops on virtually every hectare, resulting in a steady and accelerating annual decrease in yields. Waving her hands in despair, another agronomist complained of other bad cropping practices forced on her farm by the administrative office, resulting in no rest time for the soil between summer harvest and fall planting.[32]

Chairman Buznitskii protested such interference in his article:

It is known in the Ukraine that by the end of August the telephones begin to ring from the top to the bottom: "Undertake the harvesting of sugar beets. Undertake . . . Undertake . . ." Yet, undertaking the harvest at that time is impossible. Beets are harvested precisely when they have reached their full weight and sugar content: this is the "peak."

---

[29] I. Lakhno and I. Totskii, "On the Field's Orders," *Pravda*, April 15, 1977, p. 2.

[30] Viktor Perevedentsev, "For All and For Each—Notes of a Sociologist," *Nash sovremennik*, no. 1 (January 1974):144.

[31] Leonid Ivanov, "Harvest Affairs," *Nash sovremennik*, no. 4 (April 1976):154.

[32] Ibid., p. 157.

Give beets another 20 days to "fatten up," and the country would receive additionally thousands of tons of sugar and the kolkhozes would earn additionally thousands of rubles. Yet, the telephones keep ringing: "Undertake . . ."[33]

Directors of sovkhozy are even more hamstrung than kolkhoz chairmen, for as economist Iu. I. Krasnopoyas pointed out in a December 1978 article, while the kolkhoz is given "full independence in resolving all routine production issues," the sovkhozy are subject to daily intervention "in the operational administration of production" by "the raion Party, soviet, and agricultural organs."[34]

Such strict supervision from above and frequent interference with farm activities greatly restricts the manager's ability to function in a managerial capacity and must exert considerable negative influence on any innovative potential. Some managers, like Buznitskii, simply ignore minor instructions, preferring to risk the consequences of insubordination, but a manager bold enough to ignore the plan and major directives will not be a manager for long.

Unfortunately, legal innovation is often difficult to initiate, not only because of reluctant superiors, but because of the dearth of equipment and parts that may be needed to put the new concept into effect. This, however, is only the beginning of the story. Farm machinery of all kinds is in short supply. Further, since parts that are available frequently have been stolen from machinery in transit, new trucks, tractors, combines, and so on often arrive unable to operate or, indeed, unable even to be driven to the farm from the railroad station. Much of the equipment is outdated or faulty to begin with. Grain combines, for example, are famous for their leaks, through which many centners of small grain are lost back into the field as is virtually all the chaff, which could otherwise be used in feed mixes.[35] A conscientious farm manager will order his machinists to plug the leaks as well as they can to save the grain, but the chaff is probably a total loss.

Add to the manager's headaches the appalling road and transportation problem and a score of other obstacles set in the path of production, and one wonders what kind of person would undertake such an impossible managerial position.

[33] A. Buznitskii, "An Embarrassment of Riches," *Literaturnaia gazeta*, October 31, 1973, p. 10.
[34] Iu. I. Krasnopoyas, "Intersector and Sector Problems of Administering Agricultural Production," *Vestnik Moskovskogo universiteta*, December 22, 1978, p. 60.
[35] A. Buznitskii, "Reckoning with the Designer," *Literaturnaia gazeta*, October 24, 1973, p. 10.

Who Are the Farm Managers?

One Soviet writer suggests:

> The management of modern agriculture is complicated. Solid prepa-
> ration is required on the part of the kolkhoz chairman or sovkhoz
> director: He must know the fundamentals of agriculture and cattle-
> breeding, he must be well versed in economics, construction and en-
> gineering, he must have a knowledge of jurisprudence and law, and
> finally, he must be a fairly good sociologist. And what is most impor-
> tant, he must have a keen sense for that which is new.[36]

A later source tells us that the farm manager must be more than this,
that,

> as a trainer and organizer he must unite the collective and bring about
> a striving on the part of each worker to labor in a selfless and creative
> manner. He must skillfully utilize incentive measures and punishment
> measures and he must create a circumstance of mutual trust and a
> general striving to achieve the established goal.[37]

One author, a Ukrainian Party official, believes that a good manager
should instill "Party style" into this managing.[38] Although he does not
explain how this is to be done, we suspect that he would agree with a
Kazakh Party secretary who writes,

> Some managers, for example, do not go deeply into questions of party
> theory and policy and certain comrades have only a superficial knowl-
> edge of the most important CPSU documents.

Fortunately, to his way of thinking,

> Daily political and educational work has become an integral part of
> the activity of many of our managers . . . [who] are also propagandists
> who regularly give lectures and reports to workers.[39]

Several authors point out that a good manager should be able to accept
criticism from the workers, but apparently not all managers meet that
criterion.

> Criticism? From above, as much as one likes. He may even appeal for
> the development of criticism and for the sharp formulation of problems.

[36] Kuzovlev (supra, n. 26), p. 210.

[37] A. I. Timush, Report on conference, "Social Development of the Countryside During
the Building of Communism," *Nauchnyi kommunizm*, no. 2 (1976):142.

[38] A. F. Vatchenko, "Party Style for All Units of Administration," *Kommunist Ukrainy*,
no. 8 (August 1974):13.

[39] Ye. Auel'bekov, "Maturity Tested with Deeds," *Pravda*, April 28, 1973, p. 2.

Yet, should anyone try to criticize him, he may frequently regret it. It is in such circumstances that the initiative of the people gradually dampens. They lose interest in the bold objectives of the collective which becomes corroded by relations marked by alienation and mistrust, and intrigues, alien to socialist collectivism.[40]

And thus, for want of *kritika i samokritika* (criticism and self-criticism), the kingdom is lost. The same authors suggest that training in sociopsychological aspects of management might be helpful, and judging from some of the disputes that seem to develop among subordinates and between the manager and his superiors, we are inclined to agree. Finally, a skillful public-relations man could do wonders to inspire "socialist competition" among the workers and thereby increase yields.

In general, our observations and reading lead to the same conclusion as that offered by Alec Nove in 1967. Farm managers are a mixed bag.[41] Some few undoubtedly are outright scoundrels, such as the Azerbaidzhan embezzler. Some, perhaps even a majority, genuinely try to further the interests of the farm membership. Yet, as underscored above, none can forget for one moment that his tenure in office is at the sufferance of higher Party officialdom, and not ballots cast in a general meeting. True, Fedor Belov in his *History of a Soviet Collective Farm*, does relate one instance in the late 1940s when a farm membership was able to rid itself of a particularly unsavory chairman, but such successes must be rare.[42]

Although a majority of the workers are women, very few ever become chairmen or directors. The typical chairman of the 1930s, according to Fainsod's analysis of the material in the Smolensk archives, "was hard driving, hard drinking, blustering, and threatening, frequently abusive and foul of mouth." These traits, with some important additions, probably still apply generally today. Now that telephones allow constant contact with raion headquarters, managers must learn to be responsive and polite to their superiors, but for those under them on the farm they surely are "too powerful."[43] Even though most may try to improve the conditions of the membership, they probably tend to share the outside officials' view that the peasants are "tricky and untrustworthy,"[44] and that many of their immediate assistants on the board of management are "fools."[45]

Admittedly, Western visitors see only the better farms directed by the

[40] Klimov and Chernykh (supra, n. 1), p. 32.

[41] Alec Nove, "Peasants and Officials," in Jerzy Karcz, ed., *Soviet and East European Agriculture* (Berkeley, 1967), pp. 57-62.

[42] Fedor Belov, *The History of a Soviet Collective Farm* (New York, 1955), p. 111.

[43] Adams and Adams (supra, n. 15), p. 31.

[44] Nove (supra, n. 41).

[45] Adams and Adams (supra, n. 15), p. 55.

most effective leaders. Of the several farms we visited on trips to the rural USSR in 1960, 1970, and 1977, the average tenure in office of the managers was well over five years. Within that sample, however, all proved to be powerful personalities, proud of their farms and their accomplishments. None exhibited "a feeling for the new, personal modesty" recently advocated by the first secretary of the Pskovskii Obkom.[46] All proved to be highly intelligent leaders, the type of men found in charge whatever the setting. Unlike the earlier managers, however, all (or virtually all) are now Party members, and the great majority have had at least some specialized education for the task. Indeed, as of 1977, 93.5 percent of the kolkhoz chairmen, and 98.3 percent of the sovkhoz directors had secondary or higher specialized training.[47]

Like his American counterpart, the truly successful Soviet farm manager in the 1980s must possess a wide range of specialized knowledge, not only about plants and animals, but also about machinery and chemicals. However, there are important differences between the two types of managers. Change has put business acumen at the top of the list for American farmers. Today, success is determined by one's ability to know what to buy and when, what to sell and when; in every sense of the word they are entrepreneurs who organize, manage, and assume the risk of a business enterprise. In contrast, although the Soviet manager risks his career as a boss, any risk of the enterprise is taken by the state, and the major talent required of the manager is the skill of an administrator who makes sure that those under him perform in ways that satisfy Moscow's orders.

Peasant Private Enterprise

Although our major purpose has been to examine the farm manager as an entrepreneur, we cannot ignore the individual peasant, who exercises a considerable degree of entrepreneurship in a sea of socialism by clinging tenaciously to his tiny vestige of private enterprise, the household plot. Indeed, the importance of the private plot and the level of entrepreneurship practiced by the peasants suggests a wholly separate study, which has been undertaken in part by these and other authors in earlier works. (See, especially, Karl-Eugen Wadekin, *The Private Sector in Soviet Agriculture.*)

However small, averaging some 0.3 hectares and occupying only some 3 percent of the total sown area in the USSR, the plots are enormously important to both the Soviet economy and the livelihood of the vast

[46] A. Rybakov, "Who Will Head the Collective Party Life at the Front Line?" *Pravda*, May 16, 1978, p. 2.

[47] *Narodnoe Khoziaistvo SSSR za 60 let* (Moscow, 1977), p. 378 and 379.

majority of the nation's rural inhabitants, as well as many urban inhabitants who have acquired the use of similar plots.

Private peasant enterprise is the major outpost of agricultural entrepreneurship in the fullest sense of the word. When there is little or no meat in the state stores, the consumer can go to the kolkhoz market and usually find what is wanted—that is, if he is willing to pay the price. In the spring, when vegetables and fruits in the north are still weeks from ripening, we have ridden in airplanes filled with peasants carrying baskets bulging with produce headed for the kolkhoz markets of Moscow, Leningrad, and other northern cities. Given the relatively inexpensive air fare and the demand for fresh produce, a peasant can pay for his or her ticket and other travel costs, go to a city, sell the produce, and still return home with several rubles in profit.

On some farms, the individual peasant is forbidden to sell his produce privately until the farm's plan in those particular fruits or vegetables has been met. Rather than sell to the farm for low prices, many peasants box their produce, hide it along the road to town, and contract with a passing truck driver to haul the vegetables, melons, or whatever to a city market. Initial contact with potential truckers is made by sitting beside the road and displaying a sample of the crop tied to a stick. Sometimes truck drivers may be persuaded to abandon a less valuable load on the roadside in order to make room for the more profitable produce.[48]

Sometimes enterprising individuals can turn a considerable (though illegal) profit in the market. In an article about such activities in Alma Alta, for example, F. Zevriev tells us:

some market workers confirm, as do police, that a significant portion of marketplaces are occupied by the same people day after day. Moreover, they sell the most varied articles, which it is impossible to cultivate on one's private plot.

The following facts speak of who these individuals are. A certain Z. Rogovenko systematically bought up cleaned chickens from city stores and sold them in the market for 3 rubles per kilogram, or for double the original price. She was arrested 23 times by the police for speculation with products, and only recently has a criminal case been brought against her.

A. Fomina bought 13 cases of tomatoes, a total of 568 kilograms, from kolkhoz workers and began to sell them with a 50-kopek increase.

[48] Anatoliy Ivashchenko, "His Garden Plot and the Field Behind Him" (2nd part), *Chelovek I Zakon*, March 14, 1978, p. 44.

T. Kakharov acquired two sheep from a nearby village for a good price, but at the market he sold 1 kilogram of lamb for 6 rubles.[49]

Such black-marketeering appears to be extensive. In one Moldavian village, for example, we are told that "dozens of the village's residents do not work anywhere for years on end. They are exclusively engaged in black-market activities."[50] Several elderly peasants near Kiev were called to task for making wine from their own grapes and selling it locally. The quality of the vintage produced by V. M. Konovalov was questionable, but it had the desired effect for several pupils from the higher grades who had been frequenting his cottage. The chairman of the executive committee of the village soviet tells us what was done about the infraction:

> We invited Konovalov to a meeting of the executive committee and scolded him severely. One would think the very walls would blush with shame, but the guilty party was calm. He knew how everything would end. We would send the case to the administrative commission, and there he would be fined 10 rubles. And in the protocol it would be necessary to note "alcoholic beverages." That was because if you wrote "wine" the decision might be overturned. Then he would bring me a receipt for the fine, and would blubber that this was the last time. And I could see in his eyes that he was lying. It would be necessary to haul him into court again. And again the whole thing would end with a 10-ruble fine.[51]

Although Khrushchev tried to restrict the private plots, Brezhnev, in his resolve to improve diets, has presided over a move to encourage the increase of such production. No wonder, as of 1978 the private farming activity furnished over 25 percent of all agricultural products,[52] and in 1976, 34 percent of all livestock products and 10 percent of all crops.[53] In Belorussia in 1976, permanent kolkhoz and sovkhoz workers (thus excluding others with private plots) held 23 percent of all cattle, grew 50 percent of all vegetables and potatoes, produced one-third of the milk and meat and 50 percent of the eggs. From this activity, they derived 40 percent of their personal income. Not surprisingly, the official estimate

---

[49] F. Zevriev, "Where There Is No Agreement," *Kazakhstanskaia pravda*, July 31, 1977, p. 2.

[50] Ivashchenko (supra, n. 48) (1st part), *Chelovek i zakon*, February 10, 1978, p. 88.

[51] A. Sakva, "Aunt Khristia's 'Limanskoe,'" *Pravda Ukrainy*, January 10, 1978, p. 4.

[52] Krasnopoyas (supra, n. 34), p. 78.

[53] A. M. Yemel'ianov, "Means and Mechanism for Implementing the Party's Economic Strategy in Agriculture," *Vestnik moskovskogo universiteta*, no. 4 (July-August 1976):3-16.

is that rural workers devote some one-third of their working time to their private enterprise.[54]

True, a significant portion of the fodder for the private livestock comes to the peasant by way of payment in kind for her or his work on the collective, plus an additional untold amount by way of midnight requisitioning. As Karl-Eugen Wadekin observed in his monumental study, how else, except by theft, can one explain the size of the private livestock holdings?[55] Author N. Boroznova in a *Sel'skaia Zhizn'* article points out:

> The minutes of the comradely court provide precise figures. Of the ten sessions held in six months, six were devoted to thefts of concentrated feed from the farms. It is typical that virtually every comradely court session winds up with the administration's recommendation to write off concentrated feed for personally owned livestock.[56]

Another article in *Sel'skaia Zhizn'* relates:

> During the harvest it is nothing for a tractor or truck driver to stick a sack of grain under his seat and later cart it off home. Grain disappears from the threshing floor. And when the potatoes are lifted, it's impossible to count how many buckets, bags and nets filled with potatoes disappear from the fields.[57]

In his foreword to Wadekin's book, Gregory Grossman summed up much of what needs to be said:

> The private sector is of course an anomaly in the socialized, centralized, planned economy of the USSR. Economically it is backward, ideologically it is alien, politically it is suspect, and morally it stands in the way of the creation of the new socialist and communist man. But it utilizes labor, land, energies, and drives that would otherwise be largely lost; it produces an important part of the food supply; and it provides income where the socialist economy fails to do so.[58]

In recent years, however, numerous articles in the Soviet press strain to justify the existence of and, indeed, to encourage these private activities. "Thus the private subsidiary farm is the sphere not only of private, but also of public interest. Here the public and private interests intertwine,

[54] V. Tarasevich and V. Leshkevich, "Importance of Private Subsidiary Farming," *Ekonomika sel'skogo khoziaistva*, no. 2 (February 1978):77-85.

[55] Karl-Eugen Wadekin, *The Private Sector in Soviet Agriculture* (Berkeley, 1973), p. 229.

[56] N. Boroznova, "Livestock Fed Bread in Kaluzhskaya Oblast," *Sel'skaia zhizn'*, July 27, 1972, p. 4.

[57] Quoted from *Sel'skaia zhizn'* in Allan Kroncher, "Just One Sovkhoz . . . ," Radio Liberty Research Bulletin no. 307-75, July 25, 1975.

[58] Wadekin (supra, n. 55), p. xv.

interpenetrate and supplement one another." Or again, "Since the producer working at a private subsidiary farm is simultaneously a worker at a kolkhoz or sovkhoz, the private subsidiary farm participates in the reproduction of manpower for socialist agriculture, in the creation of a necessary product."[59]

In an interview, the Latvian minister of agriculture stressed the traditional aspect of the private plot: "We need to take into account the force of the traditions of those who have lived in the countryside for generations. Children take their first steps on the road of life in the household plot, learning there a love of labor and a caring, thrifty attitude toward the land and nature, grasping there the ABC's of agronomic science."[60]

Various kinds of assistance beyond the fodder are now provided at least on some farms. One kolkhoz chairman arranges for the sale of mineral fertilizer and insecticides to peasants, and has helped to install small irrigation systems to half of the plots on his farm. The common incubators provide hatchlings (we assume for a fee) for the peasants to raise at home. Beekeeping and rabbit raising are encouraged. Frequently, peasant field plots are cultivated by farm tractors, usually for a fee, but not always at the desired time. The peasant has learned that a gift to the tractor driver in the form of an extra 3 rubles or a half liter of vodka will usually expedite the plowing, unless, of course, the driver consumes the latter while working, which is not unheard of.[61] Unfortunately, the farm machinery is designed for work on huge fields and is not always satisfactory for small plots. Sometimes it wreaks havoc, tearing up the roots of nearby fruit trees and grapevines. Much of the work still must be done by hand. Here, however, the peasant usually has free rein to make his own decisions, an opportunity completely lacking in the public sector. We use the word *usually* because recently there have been several articles stressing the fact that since the private plot is really public land, the farm has a responsibility to see to it that the plot is properly cared for and made adequately productive, which suggests interference in the peasant's private domain.

Of even greater significance, although more subtle, may be the efforts of the consumer cooperatives, in response to L. I. Brezhnev's appeal at the Sixteenth Congress of USSR Trade Unions, to influence production on the private plots by contracting with individual peasants for their

[59] G. I. Schmelev, "The Private Subsidiary Farm as a Sphere of Public Interest Under Socialism," *Izvestiia akademii nauk SSSR; Seriia ekonomickeskaia*, no. 6 (November-December 1975):86-87.

[60] Interview with Kazimir Semenovich Anspok (Latvian SSSR minister of agriculture) by Ye. Kiriliuk, *Kommunist Sovetskoi Latvii*, February 21, 1978, p. 74.

[61] V. Golubev, "The Private Plot," *Sovetskaia Latviia*, April 1, 1978, p. 2.

produce as far ahead as two years. Higher purchase prices are being offered, though certainly not as high as those that the goods would command at the peasant's market, and the offer is being sweetened by cash advances upon the signing of the contract. Some consumer cooperatives (in Moldavia, for example) go so far as to promise to make scarce industrial goods and construction materials available for purchase by the peasant upon fulfillment of his contract. Whether or not the consumer cooperatives will be able to keep their end of the bargain remains to be seen.[62]

Theoretically, cooperatives' employees are "obligated . . . to recommend the variety of crops, to offer assistance in the purchase of seed of vegetables of the best strains, orchard and garden tools, fertilizer, toxic chemicals, as well as young livestock and fowl, to see to it that the private farms receive the amount of fodders and forage, which is stipulated by the contracts."[63]

In spite of all these inducements, however, apparently the peasants are not flocking to sign the contracts, for we read that only where consumer-cooperatives personnel "show the proper initiative" in pursuing such agreements are they in fact being made. Perhaps, as with previous attempts, these latest maneuvers to invade the peasant's bastion of individualism will fail.

Certainly, there have been no recent attempts to reduce the amount of land or livestock managed by the peasant. Quite to the contrary, we read articles deploring the reduction of private livestock holdings. Poultry, pigs, rabbits, and sheep seem still to be abundant, but fewer and fewer families are keeping a cow and a calf.[64] Part of the reason seems to be the scarcity of feed, fodder, and pasturage. Enterprising peasants, however, learned some time ago that if they could not steal adequate feed they could purchase bread at the state store for relatively little and use it as feed, although there was a general outcry against such a practice.[65]

More recently, peasants have been buying fine-ground cereals by the sackful or truckload as they are hauled from the mill to the store. The trucker pockets 3 or 4 rubles per sack on the transaction, the peasant has feed for his livestock, and the Soviet consumer complains about a shortage of cereals in the stores.[66]

The major complaint one reads today against the private plot is not that it is needed to supplement the supply of food produced in the socialist

[62] I. Bodur, "An Important Source," *Sovetskaia Moldaviia*, August 3, 1978, p. 3.
[63] Ibid.
[64] V. Grebeniuk, "A Cow on a Personal Plot," *Leninskoe znamia*, April 21, 1977, p. 2.
[65] Boroznova (supra, n. 56).
[66] Ivashchenko (supra, n. 48) (2nd part), p. 47.

sector, but rather that it is sometimes the means for private speculation. In a hard-hitting article written in 1977, A. Sharovskaia quotes from a letter:

> "As a rule, the prospering garden owners are those who are in no hurry to help out on the kolkhoz field. Their own plots are in exemplary condition, though. Everything they raise is of the highest grade and— for the market. They fatten their pigs until they are a sight to behold. Also to sell."

Then she goes on to say:

> Of course we cannot place all of the personal plotholders on the same level. It would be a grave error to consider on the same level those who conscientiously work for the good of society and care for their personal plots at the same time, selling the surpluses, and the open money grubbers who have turned state land into a source of unabashed profit making. In our nation the land is of course state property, belonging to all the people. To turn it into a source of profit is to grossly flout public interests, to think only of one's own benefit that is, to go counter to the moral principles of our life, the laws of socialist communal living.[67]

Thus the battle over the private plot goes on while the peasant steadfastly maintains his foothold as an entrepreneur in Soviet society.

The Schizophrenia of the Soviet Rural Dialectic

Limited as they are in their entrepreneurial activities, we conclude that Soviet farm managers are, at most, quasi-entrepreneurs.

Even more, they are a new breed of rural bureaucratic administrators, caught in the schizophrenia of the Soviet rural dialectic. From a Marxian point of view, the private plots are remnants of the old thesis, eventually to be transformed by the antithetical forces of the kolkhozy and sovkhozy. Yet the modern private peasant enterprise is hardly that which existed in rural Russia under the old regime. Considering the number of articles appearing in the last few years condemning actions to block expanded private enterprise, and those advocating positive changes in their favor, we wonder whether economic reality in the form of an increasingly pressing need for more food has not thrown a new antithetical wrench into the machinery of Soviet history. The schizophrenia is that the countryside is ruled by farm managers tightly restricted from above, but insulated

[67] A. Sharovskaia, "A Vegetable Garden or a Latifundium?" *Sovetskaia kirgiziia*, July 15, 1977, p. 4.

from any risk of the business enterprise, who are dependent for the success of the collective enterprise upon a bastion of millions of small entrepreneurs who would rather maximize their time and efforts on hoeing their own rows, because that is the part of their lives over which they have control. In any event, unless Brezhnev or some future successor should effect a reversal of recent policy, the tiny family enterprises seem to have a brighter future than has been their past.

XIV

GREGORY GROSSMAN   *The Party as Manager and Entrepreneur*

> The Party has always regarded and continues to regard accomplishments in economic development as the main payoff of the organizational and political work of all its bodies and organizations.[1]

Jerry Hough's masterful study of the "Soviet prefects"[2] drove home to sovietologists the realization that the Soviet economy—the vaunted principle of *edinonachalie* notwithstanding—is in fact managed simultaneously by two parallel hierarchies, the economic-administrative hierarcy and that of the Party. In common with other political scientists, he naturally tends to look at the problem of Party-management relations from the standpoint of the Party's role in society and of the historical evolution of that role.[3] In his analysis, Hough draws on the prior work of certain economists, particularly the classic studies

* The author gratefully acknowledges the beneficial effects of conversations on this and related topics with George Breslauer, Aron Katsenelinboigen, and Alexander Yanov. He profited from the ventilation of some of the ideas in this paper at the colloquium on "Party and Society in East Europe" in the summer of 1973 at Berkeley, and takes this opportunity to thank the cochairmen of the colloquium, Andrew C. Janos and Kenneth Jowitt. He is grateful to Pauline Andrews and Alexander Bennett for able research assistance, and to the Center for Slavic and East European Studies of the University of California, Berkeley, for the financial support.

[1] M. Voropaev, first secretary of the Cheliabinsk oblast committee of the CPSU, in *Kommunist*, no. 11 (1974):64. My translation.

[2] Jerry F. Hough, *The Soviet Prefects* (Cambridge, Mass., 1969).

[3] In addition to Hough's study, the monographs by Enno Barker (*Die Rolle der Parteiorgane in der sowjetischen Wirtschaftslenkung 1957-1965* [Wiesbaden, 1973]), and William J. Conyngham (*Industrial Management in the Soviet Union: Role of the CPSU in Industrial Decision-Making, 1917-1970* [Stanford, 1973]), are devoted to the Party-management relationship. Philip D. Stewart (*Political Power in the Soviet Union: A Study of Decision-Making in Stalingrad* [Indianapolis, 1968]) also in large measure addresses himself to this issue with specific reference to the Stalingrad *obkom*.

by Granick[4] and Berliner.[5] On their part, these and other economists who have addressed themselves to problems of Soviet management (management in the usual sense of the word, which will be the one employed hereinafter) have been primarily concerned with the way the Party affects managerial behavior and success.

The present exercise, therefore, requires an excuse for its existence as well as a specification of its limited scope. Our approach is not primarily historical; rather, it focuses on the post-*sovnarkhoz* (i.e., post-Khrushchev) period, though some of our evidence necessarily comes from before 1965. For the sake of convenience and in deference to venerable precedent, when we refer to economic activity we shall think primarily of the *industrial* firm (or association) and its superordinate planning and administrative entities up to the industrial ministry and the high-level planning commission. Last and perhaps not least, we attempt to invoke certain concepts that have lately enjoyed increased currency in economic analysis, such as "externality" and "social responsibility of business," in order to understand better the role of the Party as manager and entrepreneur.

For the present purpose we ought not define the "Party" too broadly. We certainly do not mean the totality of sixteen million members of the Communist party of the Soviet Union (CPSU), a category so broad as to be largely meaningless, if only because it encompasses nearly all the managerial personnel with which the "Party" has to deal. What is the significance of mere membership in the "vanguard of the proletariat" if, according to Hough's calculation, at least 50 percent of all males with completed higher education can claim it?[6] Rather, for us the relevant category is that of the *professional Party functionaries*—the first secretaries, other secretaries, their full-time lieutenants, and other responsible officials of the Party organizations. Taken together, the Party organizations form a clear hierarchy or pyramid that embraces the whole society. Except at the very top and the very bottom, the pyramid is territorially structured. Lowest-level Party organizations have at least one professional functionary; the more important ones have many more.

However, what we have in mind is not the whole pyramid of Party organizations. We discard the Party leaders and functionaries above the

[4] David Granick, *Management of the Industrial Firm in the USSR* (New York, 1954).

[5] Joseph S. Berliner, *Factory and Manager in the USSR* (Cambridge, Mass., 1957). Mention should be made of the pioneering work on Soviet management by Gregory Bienstock, S. M. Schwarz, and A. Yugow, *Management in Russian Industry and Agriculture* (Ithaca, N.Y., 1948; originally published in 1944), which devoted a chapter to "Industrial Management and the Communist Party."

[6] Jerry F. Hough, "Party 'Saturation' in the Soviet Union," in Paul Cocks, Robert V. Daniels, and Nancy Whittier Heer, eds., *The Dynamics of Soviet Politics* (Cambridge, Mass., 1976), Table 7.5, p. 125.

republic level, not because they are unimportant but because they are too important. At this high level—which means primarily the Politburo, the other secretaries of the CPSU, and the apparat of the Central Committee—the crucial entrepreneurial and managerial decisions are continually made for what Alfred G. Meyer has called USSR, Inc. The consequences of these decisions are for us to see. But we know too little of the process by which they are reached and of the relations between the top of the Party and the top of the governmental planning and administrative hierarchy (insofar as the two are not fused, as they often are at the very peak) to bring this level into our analysis.

The bottom tier of the Party pyramid, which includes the "primary Party organizations" at the level of the firm, is also of limited interest for our purpose. Its members are employees and workers of the firm, almost always including the director himself and other top management. While the relationship between the firm's Party secretary and the director is ill-defined and complex, as well as a matter of the interaction of two personalities, there is, as a rule, sufficient coincidence of the interests and points of view of the two to consider the Party secretary as virtually part of the firm's management.[7] To be sure, in part, this coincidence is a consequence of the preselection of managerial personnel by the Party thanks to the Party's control (exercised at suprafirm levels) of managerial appointments and promotions in the first place. As a *Pravda* correspondent put it in describing a specific instance of secretary-director conflict (by quoting approvingly from a letter to the editor): "It is odd that the secretary of a (primary) Party organization could not arrive at a harmonious working relationship [*ne mog srabotat'sia*] with an experienced and knowledgeable director of an enterprise."[8] The "harmonious relationship" may, however, also take legally questionable turns, such as a secretary's connivance with—if not outright involvement in—a director's illicit machinations, whether for the good of the enterprise as such (and indirectly for the benefit of the director's and secretary's careers) or for sheer personal peculation.[9]

Therefore, in what follows we focus on suprafirm levels, i.e., on the

[7] For the relationships between the director and the firm's Party secretary see especially Jerry Hough, *Soviet Prefects*, pp. 86-97. At the heart of this relationship is the "right to control" (*pravo kontrolia*) over management enjoyed by the primary Party organization. Hough devotes much attention to this "right" and its implications for *edinonachalie*; see also Conyngham (supra, n. 3), passim.

[8] N. Borzenkov, "Sekretar' i direktor," *Pravda*, November 29, 1976, p. 2. In Hough's view, "the more serious danger has been that of domination by the director over the Party secretary than that of the secretary over the director." ("Party 'Saturation' in the Soviet Union," p. 96.)

[9] By way of random example, see a long account of such goings on in N. Mironov, "Vyvodov ne posledovalo," *Pravda*, March 6, 1975, p. 2. Cf. Conyngham (supra, n. 3), pp. 243-44.

so-called local (*mestnye*) Party committees: the district committee (*raikom*), both rural and urban; the city committee (*gorkom*); the provincial and territorial committees (*obkom, kraikom*) and those of the autonomous republics, there being little difference between the three for our purpose; and the republican committees in the case of the smaller union republics. For an extensive account of the structure of the local Party organs the reader is referred to chapter 2 in Hough, *The Soviet Prefects*.

Lastly, we are not here concerned with the place of managers in Soviet society, except incidentally in a few respects, or with their past, present, or potential political roles in the system.[10]

The Soviet firm has many bosses in addition to its direct hierarchical superiors. Innumerable planning bureaus can wreak havoc with its production program and its supply flows. The State Price Board can make or break its profits and therefore the source of bonuses and premiums for managerial and other personnel. Financial organs have their own power over the firm. (Nor are such bureaucratic bene- and malefactors unknown to the Western enterprise.) And then there is the Party. As a rule, none of these authorities bears any legal or factual responsibility for the damage it may inflict, by dint of its "planning acts," on the enterprise as such, on its management, its other workers and employees, and on various third parties. Bureaucratic conscience apart, there are only two kinds of constraints on the arbitrary actions of the many administrative, planning, and Party authorities: their self-interest, which may protect the firm when their own success indicators overlap with the firm's, and, secondly, yet higher authority to which the damaged party (with a small *p*) may appeal.

Why, then, single out the Party for our exercise? (1) The Party is, after all, prior to and above all other entities in the Soviet system as the seat of power, authority, and policy making. Taken as a whole, it is the last—and frequently the first—instance of appeal. Of the Party as such, it can be truly said "Roma locuta est, causa finita est" (though the CPSU is no more than Rome a political monolith or an unfailing master of its own will in society). This alone places the Party in a class by itself among the firm's bosses. (2) Formally, the Party's power and authority extend into

---

[10] Regarding managers as a professional and interest group, see John P. Hardt and Theodore Frankel, "The Industrial Managers," in H. Gordon Skilling and Franklyn Griffiths, eds., *Interest Groups in Soviet Politics* (Princeton, 1970). As for managers being collectively a significant force for political change, a forceful negative answer is provided by Jeremy Azrael's well-known monograph, *Managerial Power and Soviet Politics* (Cambridge, Mass., 1966); while Alexander Yanov's analysis (*Detente After Brezhnev* [University of California, Berkeley: Institute of International Studies, Policy Paper No. 2, 1977]) contains a close observer's view of the possible potential role of management in the Soviet polity.

every fold and seam of the social fabric. Thus, ideally, it looms before
the firm and the firm's management as the enforcer and guardian of all
of organized society's values and priorities, extraeconomic as well as
economic. It is the monitor and enforcer of the firm's social responsibility
in the broadest sense. No other element of the Soviet power structure
(except possibly the secret police) has so broad a concern backed up with
legitimate authority and means of enforcement. (3) Because of its territorial organizational structure, the Party performs the important function
of intraregional coordination of economic activity. To be sure, the local
government (the *ispolkom*) and local planning bureaus, the local *sovnarkhoz* in its day, and other regional bodies may and do play the same
role. Yet the fact is that the other bodies do not begin to compare with
the local Party committee—and particularly the heads of these bodies
with the Party committee's first secretary—in power and authority, and
in the respect and fear that they command. Indeed, nowhere is the first
secretary's power as many-sided (to use a favorite Soviet term) as vis-à-
vis the other organs of local political administration, such as the *ispolkom*
and firms subordinated to it. Not unexpectedly, both Taubman and Stewart found this to be the case in their studies of Soviet local government.[11]
The Soviet press is replete with confirming information. So is Soviet
fiction: For example, Denisov, Kochetov's positive hero of an *obkom*
first secretary, says with transparent false modesty (somewhat reminiscent
of Khrushchev in his public appearances) that he is quite sure that the
city soviet will respond favorably to a suggestion from him.[12]

In regard to firms subordinated not to local government but to their
respective administrative pyramids, whose apexes are often in Moscow,
the local Party committee's and the local Party secretary's authority and
power are still great but cannot be exercised on quite so broad a front
as in the case of local government bodies and their production enterprises.
And yet, because the first secretary holds in his hands enough cards to
be of crucial importance even for a large, high-priority enterprise on his
territory, his position as the true boss of the given region or district is
not in doubt even in the eyes of big business.[13] Power begets, attracts,
and perpetuates power, and the first secretary remains the local boss so
long as he stays in the good graces of his superiors.

The power of the local Party committee derives in the first instance
from the national monopoly of political power of the Party as a whole.
But more concretely, it derives from the *nomenklatura* system that places

[11] Stewart (supra, n. 3), and William Taubman, *Governing Soviet Cities: Bureaucratic
Politics and Urban Development in the USSR* (New York, 1973).

[12] Vsevolod Kochetov, *Sekretar' obkoma*, in *Sobranie sochinenii*, vol. 4 (Moscow, 1975;
originally published in 1961).

[13] Yanov (supra, n. 10), pp. 22ff.

the local Party in such a strong position, and which in turn, in the aggregate, helps guarantee the national political monopoly of the CPSU. The *nomenklatura* is of course the roster of local positions for which the consent of a given local Party committee is required for appointment, promotion, demotion, or dismissal. Nearly all managerial positions of significance are within the *nomenklatura* of *some* level in the Party hierarchy. In addition, nearly all managerial positions of importance are held by Party members, a result that is itself the product of the *nomenklatura* system, placing the incumbents in these positions, as individuals, under Party discipline. The extreme form of intra-Party disciplinary sanction is expulsion from the Party, which is usually tantamount to the termination of one's managerial career. Less extreme forms, e.g., reprimands (especially when repeated), can also be very harmful to the manager's future. Consequently, almost everyone of any importance in management knows that his tenure in office, his future promotions, and his whole career are at the mercy of the Party's professional *apparat*. Hence, the Party's power in the economy on the local level.[14]

To be sure, this power can be abused. It can be abused by the moral corruption that the very existence of power may engender, or by the individual's tendencies for self-protection (as in the questionable acquisition of scientific degrees by apparatchiki) and for self-enrichment (abetted by the corrupting advances of local clients).[15] The abuses may, up to a point, be protected and encouraged by the indifference of the higher leaders so long as the Party official "delivers the goods," or even invited

[14] At one point Kochetov's Denisov acts as though any directorial vacancy in the oblast is his to fill, even if for reasons of "human compassion" for a particular person; Kochetov (supra, n. 12), p. 353.

[15] In addition to many important privileges and perquisites received in common with the rest of the Soviet elite (cf. Mervyn Matthews, *Privilege in the Soviet Union* [London, 1978], passim), local Party leaders and functionaries receive a steady and rich flow of gifts and "tribute" (*pobory*), not to say bribes, from their de facto subordinates, as is amply attested by the accounts of recent émigrés. Nor are they always above extortion; cf. the following instance vividly described in an article by a prosecutor's investigator (*sledovatel'*), since immigrated to the United States, who stumbled on the matter while examining another case. In 1960, in a rural district of Moscow oblast on the outskirts of the capital itself, he discovered that the woman director of a vegetable warehouse had been forced, on pain of dismissal from her position, to pay regular graft to several of the Party and government chiefs of the given district. One figure mentioned in the article is 15,000 rubles (pre-1961, presumably, equal to 1,500 "new" rubles) per season. Those with smaller establishments were said to be paying 5,000-10,000 rubles per season to the same individuals. (F. Neznanskii, "Gusev protiv Sakharova," *Novoe Russkoe Slovo*, New York, June 4, 1978.)

Local Party leaders and officials, especially but not exclusively those in the Asian republics, figure prominently in Simis's striking eyewitness account of corruption in the USSR (Konstantin Simis, "The Machinery of Corruption in the Soviet Union," *Survey*, 23, no. 4 [Autumn 1977-78]:pp. 33-55). He speaks specifically of extortion from a Moscow food shop (p. 37).

by the leaders' own example. But, abuse or no, the mere fact of power
in the hands of the local Party secretaries and other functionaries can
hardly be denied.

With all this power, what functions do the local Party authorities
exercise in the economy?[16] First, they are a partial substitute for the
missing market mechanism. In this respect the Party is not alone; the
whole elaborate structure of Soviet planning and economic-administrative bodies is a substitute for the market mechanism in bringing about,
what perforce must happen, the allocation of the economy's scarce resources and a certain distribution of income and wealth. But the Party
does more than that in the economy. Among other things, it undertakes
certain functions that the market mechanism frequently fails to perform
in a market economy; in other words, in the Soviet economy the Party
also in effect corrects for what in a different context would most likely
be "market failures." Even more often it undertakes functions which the
market mechanism performs tolerably well, but which in the Soviet nonmarket economy tend to suffer conspicuously. We might call them "nonmarket failures."[17] And, at least at first glance, the Party does all this as
a "generalist," as the chief guardian of the official set of values and
preferences.

The economist's concept of "externalities" is germane to the issue. One
kind of externality—an external economy—is something of social value
that *does not pay doing* by a given decision unit, such as a firm. For
example, in a market economy it frequently does not pay to employ and
train unskilled youths because at first their low productivity does not
compensate for their wages, and because, once trained, they need not
remain in the same firm's employ (worse still, transfer to the firm's competitor). Another kind of externality—an external diseconomy—is something of social harm that *does not pay not doing* by a given decision
unit. In this case the examples are even more familiar: polluting the
environment, congesting traffic, and the like. The economist says that in
the first case the decision unit, for some reason, cannot "internalize" the
benefits that may redound to the community or society at large, and
therefore, if rational, the unit will not incur the expense to bring the
benefits about. In the second case the decision unit does not internalize

[16] Again, the reader is referred to Hough, *Soviet Prefects*, Conyngham (supra, n. 3), and
Barker (supra, n. 3), for extensive discussion of these functions.

[17] Since completing the final version of this essay, we came across a penetrating article
by Charles Wolf, Jr., which uses the identical term in very much the same sense, though
without direct reference to the Soviet or any Soviet-type economy: "A Theory of Nonmarket
Failure: Framework for Implementation Analysis," *Journal of Law and Economics*, 22
(April 1979):107-39.

the costs of what society would prefer it to do, such as abate pollution when the discharge of pollutants into the environment is costless or nearly costless to the unit; hence, it will not, if rational, incur the expense to avoid inflicting the social harm. To repeat, these are the kinds of externalities that are familiar to us in our own market-economy setting, where supply and demand are assumed to be roughly in equilibrium at the actual prices. Let us designate such externalities with the symbol "Ex1." As we know, Ex1 exist in the Soviet Union (and other Soviet-type economies), too, as both external diseconomies committed and external economies forgone. We now know of the widespread presence of environmental disruption in the USSR, despite both state ownership and planning (despite earlier Soviet disclaimers). Furthermore, we also know, for example, that if left to their preferences many Soviet firms are reluctant to hire unskilled youths even in the face of a general labor shortage.

But the Soviet economy is not a market economy. The controlled prices, both retail and wholesale, are often too low, in the sense that demand at these prices exceeds supply. A repressed inflation prevails. Magnified by clumsy planning and administration, the well-known (and not uniquely Soviet) consequences of repressed inflation are shortages, formal and informal rationing, the seller's market, and various concomitant negative phenomena, such as reduced variety (actually, a kind of shortage), impaired quality, and considerable expense of procuring and adapting goods from the buyer's standpoint, and—not the least—sluggish innovation. These nonmarket failures impose significant costs on society, costs that would, or at least might, be avoided in the absence of microdisequilibrium and its necessary concomitant, command planning. These are externalities that generally do not appear in a market economy; let us designate them "Ex2."[18]

The *amount* of damage inflicted upon society by Ex1 and Ex2 depends on one's appreciation of the damage, i.e., on one's set of ultimate values and the corresponding set of preferences, or, in the economist's jargon, on the particular social welfare function (SWF). There are very many distinct sets of preferences held by members of any society at any one time; moreover, each member's set of preferences can change over time. But there is one set of preferences which is of more than ordinary importance in an authoritarian society, namely, that set which is held at a given time by the dictatorial leader, if there is one, or in some sense collectively by the ruling leadership group.

However, one ought to distinguish between the leaders' "effective" preferences, those that are actually being pursued at the given time, from

---

[18] The symmetry-seeking reader may wish to add Ex3 for the situation that is the mirror image of the usual Soviet one: namely, a state of sluggish aggregate demand, buyer's market, and the associated unemployment of resources and costs of selling.

their "ideal" preferences, which the leaders may hold in the abstract or which they may wish the world to believe they hold.[19] Effective preferences reveal themselves in deeds and are subject to all the difficulties of policy making and policy enforcement in the real world; ideal preferences are spelled out in May Day slogans and speeches on Red Square. Our concern here is with effective preferences, for it is these that the Party at all its levels presumably safeguards and enforces.

In the normal course of their daily activity, Soviet enterprises and industries generate both Ex1 and Ex2. Some of the externalities may be of little import from the standpoint of the official SWF, even if they occasion inconvenience and displeasure on the part of the ordinary consumer, worker, and citizen. Other externalities tend to weigh more heavily with the official set of preferences, and traditionally in the USSR they have tended to be more of the Ex2 than the Ex1 kind. Examples are interruptions in the flow of producer goods, "unplanned" bottlenecks, lower-than-planned quality of materials and equipment, deviations from the planned assortment of producer goods, delays in innovation, and similar dysfunctional effects of the conscious decisions of enterprises and industries. (Surely, the plans can be "bad" to begin with, but we abstract from this cause at the moment.) The conscious decisions in question are presumably suboptimizing decisions by enterprises with reference to their own "success indicators" and weighted by the positive and negative incentives aimed at the decision makers. Consequently, the decision makers—say, managers—are continuously exhorted and enjoined to keep the social good (i.e., the official SWF) in mind and to forestall the dysfunctional effects of their actions on the rest of the economy. There would seem to be little chance that given a regime of repressed inflation in both the household sector and the state (production) sector, and given large managerial bonuses, externalities of the Ex2 as well as the Ex1 kind can be substantially avoided.

In sum, the Soviet firm needs a considerable measure of what has come in the United States to be known as "social responsibility of business." A great deal has been written on and around this topic in connection with the American economy, especially in the sixties and in the first half of the seventies[20] (less so since then as this country's macroeconomic problems have tended to push other concerns more into the back-

[19] For a discussion of "effective" vs. "ideal" preferences in the Soviet setting, see Lenore Shever Taga, "Externalities in a Command Economy," in Fred Singleton, ed., *Environmental Misuse in the Soviet Union* (New York, 1976), pp. 75-100.

[20] See, for instance, the various contributions to James W. McKie, ed., *Social Responsibility and the Business Predicament* (Washington, D.C., 1974); a good, brief treatment relating social responsibility to economic efficiency is Kenneth J. Arrow, "Social Responsibility and Economic Efficiency," *Public Policy*, 21 (Summer 1973):303-17.

ground).[21] The concept, vague in both content and scope, has been often understood to encompass not only business responsibility for the externalities (Ex1) caused by its productive activity, but also for the welfare of society in a more general sense. This broader understanding of social responsibility would not be out of order in the Soviet setting, where in theory everyone is responsible for everyone else and for everything.

Generally speaking, business—whether capitalist or socialist—can be tamed for a broader social benefit in a variety of ways:[22]

1. It can be *regulated*, i.e., coerced by governmental authority to desist from certain acts and to undertake others when such action (or inaction) is contrary to the firm's perceived self-interest. In the USSR, there is some regulation of this sort by planning and administrative entities—we leave the Party aside for the moment—in regard to Ex1, though with mixed results (as elsewhere in the world). There is much more regulation in regard to Ex2—central allocation of materials and equipment, legal specifications in regard to quality, "plans for new technology," etc.—and, as we know, also with mixed results.

2. Public authority can artificially make environmental disruption (and other external diseconomies of the Ex1 kind) *costly to the offender* by imposing effluent charges, taxes, and so forth, thereby causing the external diseconomy to be "internalized" by the firm. Similarly, fines can be levied on the firm that does not deliver on time, or in the wrong assortment, or otherwise sins with regard to Ex2. In the USSR, laws and regulations often provide for payment of fines, but they seem to do little good, primarily for the reason that with state ownership and in a climate of planners' tension and repressed inflation, enterprises as such and their managers are insufficiently sensitive to monetary sanctions.

3. The commission of external diseconomies of the Ex2 kind can be contained by the offender's *liability* to injured parties under civil law, and in a market economy is indeed typically so handled. In the Soviet economy, too, it is quite common for injured firms to file complaints under the system of State Arbitration against offending firms, even to the point of excessive litigiousness. But the behavior of producers and sellers does not seem to be much affected thereby. Owing to the seller's market, the buyer frequently prefers to accept the damages of Ex2 rather than offend the seller; and monetary penalties decreed by State Arbitration have little effect on the losing side for the reasons just mentioned.

4. Then there is the possibility of social responsibility of the decision maker thanks to a conscious commitment to an *ethical code*. In our instance we must distinguish between two kinds of ethical code. There

---

[21] Cf. "A Social Lapse," editorial in *The Wall Street Journal*, January 17, 1975, p. 8.
[22] Cf. Arrow (supra, n. 20), 310ff.

is, first, the generalized code, "the moral code of the Communist," which supposedly separates right from wrong at any point in time. Since nearly all decision makers of some importance are members of the Party, this would seem to do the trick. Of course, it does not, if only because mere membership in the Party falls far short of guaranteeing full adherence to the "moral code of a Communist." The other kind of ethical code, the particularistic one of a given profession—and management might be regarded as a profession for this purpose—could possibly protect outsiders from abuse of a profession's special powers. Thus, a professional code can be socially beneficial in regard to both Ex1 and Ex2, up to a point; it cannot, however, guarantee the safeguarding of general social values and priorities. And neither code can effectively respond to frequent and swift changes in priorities.

We are, therefore, left with institutional solutions that rely on administrative or political internalization of the externalities.

5. *Administrative* internalization requires at once (a) vertical integration of enterprises (in a sellers' market, usually "backward" integration); and (b) centralization of functions in the supra-enterprise hierarchy. The former is largely the rationale of the campaign to form "associations" (*obedineniia*) that has been in progress since 1973. On the other hand, (b) helps explain the persistent phenomenon of "creeping recentralization," the slow but steady recentralization of functions in administrative and planning organs following any one-time decentralizing reform. Neither vertical integration of enterprises nor the centralization of functions in the hierarchy can by itself fully take care of Ex1 and Ex2. They only shift suboptimization to higher levels of the administrative hierarchy, those of the association or of a branch of the economy (*otrasl'*); they do not by themselves ensure the proper safeguarding and enforcement of the values and priorities of the top leadership. Moreover, administrative internalization of externalities engenders its own costs and rigidities, and, hence, sooner or later leads to calls for new reform.[23]

6. We are left with the political solution for the internalization of externalities in the economy, or, more generally, for the safeguarding and enforcement of the top leaders' values and priorities. This political solution is, of course, the use of the Party and especially the use of its local apparat,[24] as a kind of comanager of the economy, in order to

---

[23] Cf. the interesting conclusions by Granick regarding the general inefficacy of handling externalities by the Soviet administrative hierarchy (David Granick, "The Internalizing of Externalities in Socialist Enterprises and in Subunits of Large American Firms," in William G. Shepherd, *Public Enterprise: Economic Analysis of Theory and Practice* [Lexington, Mass., 1976], pp. 79ff.). While he has in mind both Ex1 and Ex2, he does not class them separately.

[24] We do not exclude here the Party's various helpers, such as the Komsomol, the organs

ensure that business management behaves in what would be seen as a socially responsible manner by the country's top leaders at the given time.

The Party parallels and penetrates all economic sectors, organizations, and firms. It is, as much as anything, a monitoring hierarchy.[25] Its carefully selected local leaders and functionaries presumably fully subscribe to and hold the official values and priorities. It has, supposedly, full power to enforce the proper kind of social responsibility on business managers, and therefore to thwart the managers' tendency to focus solely on their own success indicators at the price of the broader social welfare (again, as officially understood).

And indeed, the economic functions of the local Party committees very largely focus on externalities, and especially on those of the Ex2 variety. One need only run one's eye over the captions of articles on Party work in *Kommunist* and its republican counterparts, *Partiinaia Zhizn'*, *Pravda* and other Party organs, and the titles of chapters in the innumerable analogous books to establish that a very large proportion of them are concerned with such topics as quality of output, "rhythmic" flow of supply, breaking of bottlenecks, honoring of contracts, intraregional coordination of economic activity, innovation, and other aspects of Ex2.

The official line is that the local Party organs must, first and foremost, reject narrow departmental or local interests in favor of the overall aims of the Party and the state. They must emphasize management's social responsibility. To quote from an editorial in *Kommunist*, one of many such pronouncements:

> A Party-like [*partiinoe*] attitude toward the leadership [*rukovodstvo*] of the economy is a political activity that is inconsistent with a narrowly economic, let alone technocratic, approach to management. The development of the economy must be seen as more than just a process of accretion of quantities of production and consumption, structural changes brought about by new scientific and technological possibilities, etc. . . . It must not be forgotten that while automated systems (of data processing) do facilitate the preparation, computation, analysis, and taking of decisions in regard to economic projects, naturally, they cannot perform the basic function of a business leader, the informed making of decisions on the *political plane*, that is to say, with reference to the overall objectives of the state and to Party directives in the economic realm. . . .

Soviet businessmen [*khoziaistvenniki*] are not just highly competent

---

of People's Control (prior to December 1965, Party-State Control; prior to November 1962, State Control; etc.), the trade unions, and certain professional and mass organizations.

[25] On the theory of separate monitoring hierarchies in hierarchically structured organizations see Anthony Downs, *Inside Bureaucracy* (Boston, 1966), pp. 148ff.

specialists, but are first and foremost the trusted agents of the Party and the state.[26]

Or, for a more recent statement on social responsibility one may quote from a public address by I. V. Kapitonov, a secretary of the CC CPSU, who, citing General Secretary Brezhnev as his authority, calls for "a fundamental reorientation of the thinking of (Party and other) officials, a new approach to the evaluation of the results of business activity. It is no secret that we still frequently judge the performance of enterprises basically in terms of sold output, overlooking indicators of labor productivity, production cost, quality of output, and the adoption of new technology. It is clear that such an approach is now obsolete and is at odds with the Party's policy regarding the enhancement of production efficiency."[27]

Nothing said so far, however, is meant to suggest that local party committees and their responsible functionaries are always effective in bringing about the social responsibility of Soviet business. To try to answer this question we must, first, take a closer look at what the local committee and its secretaries and other officials do. We have already taken note of one of their most important tasks, *nomenklatura* work, the selection and confirmation of leading personnel in the economy and all other spheres of society. Much of it apparently takes place relatively high up in Party hierarchy, which may be an indication of the doubts at the top as to the degree of *partiinost* that lower officials will exercise in personnel matters. Another important activity is "mobilizing the population," which can be translated to mean making large numbers of people do what they do not want to do. Specifically, in the economic sphere this means organizing socialist competitions (which often are more show than substance), mounting various campaigns, such as collecting scrap and economizing energy, and organizing *subbotniki*. Finally, there is the traditional "mobilizing" of the peasants at crucial times to do what they are expected to do in socialist agriculture, but for which they have limited incentive and enthusiasm, and the annual dispatching of millions of city people and a great deal of equipment to help bring in the harvest.

The mobilizing is supposedly done by educational and indoctrinational

---

[26] *Kommunist*, 1975:12, p. 14; our translation and emphasis. The editorial goes on to condemn, among other things, bureaucratism, departmentalism, and localism. Experienced readers of Party prose will recognize that the indicative mood is a thinly veiled imperative mood, and that the injunction to businessmen is also a directive to the Party authorities who supervise them.

[27] *Sotsialisticheskaia industriia*, October 18, 1978, p. 1. Kapitonov goes on to mention other indicators, such as adherence to contracts, as hitherto having been incorrectly neglected by Party and other officials.

means, and while these may indeed be of some importance, say among the young, any acquaintance with Soviet reality quickly convinces the observer that, in the large, mobilization is achieved primarily by dint of pressure on the individual at places of work, study, and residence. There also seems to be little doubt that the productivity of labor mobilized under pressure is not remarkably high for want of both adequate motivation and proper organization, while the economic (opportunity) costs to the country are substantial, to say nothing of damage to public morale. Why then are things still being done in this way? Because in the near term there *are* no alternatives, and no one cares much for the long term? Because of inertia and lack of social imagination? Because, so to say, the medium is the message—revolutionary values are kept (supposedly) alive, while many people in and around the Party can still flex their social muscle? If so, this may be yet another obstacle in the way of the rationalization of the economy by turning more functions over to managerial decision on the basis of meaningful parametric information. In the meantime, the mobilizational work is one of the ways in which the Party substitutes for the market mechanism, and in the process justifies its existence in the eyes of top leadership.

All authorities agree that a very considerable part of the local Party committees' job is assisting in the procurement of material supplies from outside the given region or district,[28] and the redirection of materials, labor, and equipment within the given area.[29] Much of this work is thrust upon the local Party organs, simply because no one of all those close enough to production has the Party's clout to deal with the wretched supply problem. Especially important is its role in the many emergencies.[30] Here, again, the Party substitutes for the market mechanism, guided by the officials' perception of national priorities yet doubtless mixed with parochial zeal and local political considerations. In doing so, however, the first secretaries may well deal in a kind of politicoeconomic market,

[28] Berliner (*Factory and Manager*), Hough (*Soviet Prefects*), Conyngham (supra, n. 3), and Barker (supra, n. 3) all heavily stress this role of the local Party authorities. Conyngham goes so far as to characterize the local Party organization as a *tolkach* (pusher). On the other hand, in his important article on Soviet plan execution in the face of shortages, Raymond P. Powell ("Plan Execution and the Workability of Soviet Planning," *Journal of Comparative Economics*, 1 [March 1977]:51-76) barely mentions the Party (p. 57n) as an important actor in the process.

[29] Cf. Yanov's vivid eyewitness account of both the humiliation of the director of a high-priority enterprise in seeking local Party intervention in a sudden supply shortage, and the eventual "theft" of the needed materials from a lower-priority industry in the area (supra n. 10).

[30] As a random example in the Soviet press, cf. the account of emergency shunting of skilled labor and transport from other enterprises to a favored enterprise by *gorkom* in E. Leont'eva, "Vcherashnie prichiny," *Pravda*, March 31, 1978, p. 2.

the market for the exchange of mutual favors *among themselves*.[31] This is perhaps yet another Soviet economy, in addition to the "first" (command) and "second" (private and/or illegal) economies, that might some day attract the researcher's attention.

Closely related is the local Party's function of intraregional coordination,[32] whose importance arises from the conjuncture of two characteristic aspects of Soviet reality. (1) Soviet planning is notably weak in bringing about intraregional coordination and balance. It can barely achieve its primary objective of coordination among industries; to do so additionally region by region in an effective manner has so far proved to be beyond the system's capacity. (2) Thus, if any authority on the local level is to redress even partially the intraregional balance on its own, it must have sufficient force both at the national center and within the region to go against the grain of Soviet product-line planning. Only the local Party qualifies.

Its work in this regard is twofold. First, it lobbies for the allocation of additional resources to the region, preferably while the plan (medium- or short-term) is still under preparation. We know little about such lobbying, except that the speeches of the assorted first secretaries at Party Congresses and on other reported occasions are generally replete with pleas for additional resources to their districts to meet very specific needs. We do not know how much effect the pleas produce, let alone the mechanism of "log rolling" or whatever brings results. Secondly, local Party authorities can and apparently do reallocate resources and require specific production for local needs in the course of plan execution, in order to achieve a better intraregional balance (as they understand it, at least). As Hough correctly stresses, this frequently carries the Party beyond the limits of the law. Thus, the text of a recent joint decree by the Central

[31] Cf. Hough, *Soviet Prefects*, p. 230. Compare the following by the first secretary of the Bashkir *obkom* (Z. Nuriev, "Rukovidit' ekonomikoi, ne podmeniia khoziaistyennye organy," *Kommunist*, 1965: 16, p. 65): "When plan fulfillment is at stake, Party committees take upon themselves the solution of business problems, dispatch pushers, and send out numerous letters and telegrams pleading to hasten the delivery of certain equipment or materials. Thus, just in the course of the first nine months of this year we received from *Party* organs of other oblasti and republics 813 telegrams dealing predominantly with supply matters. On our part, we dispatch similar letters and telegrams to other Party committees." (Our translation and emphasis.) Note that the *sovnarkhozy* were still in effect during those nine months, which may have enhanced the role of Party committees.

[32] Cf. Hough, *Soviet Prefects*, chap. 11. See also Granick, *Management of the Industrial Firm*, chap. 12; Aron Katsenelinboigen, "Some Regional Problems in the USSR," August 1978 (unpublished paper), pp. 16ff.; and N. N. Smeliakov, *S chego nachinaetsia rodina* (Moscow, 1975), pp. 146ff. N. N. Smeliakov's is an interesting instance of the same person having been enterprise director, *gorkom* first secretary, *obkom* first secretary, and *sovnarkhoz* chairman, all in Gorki, and high foreign trade official (still active). These are his memoirs.

Committee, CPSU, and the Council of Ministers, USSR (8 August 1978), complains of the large-scale illegal diversion of investment funds and transfer of physical capital from agriculture to other branches of the economy, with local Party organs expressly accused of having taken part in the reallocations.[33]

One of the more significant effects of the Party's active role in the local economy is the enhancement of the tendency toward local self-sufficiency (*mestnichestvo*, "localism"). Under conditions of widespread and persistent shortages, no prudent boss of a region or district would act otherwise—unless, of course, his Party conscience would never allow him to compromise the higher interests of the country and its leadership. The latter does not seem to be the case in the event, and local Party organs have been subjected to a steady barrage of lectures and warnings against local bias over the years. Numerous anecdotal accounts in the press attest to the involvement of Party authorities in conspicuous cases of *mestnichestvo*.[34]

Whatever it may do to legality, the criss-cross structure—the Party territorial and the state hierarchy primarily by "branch"—does make a good deal of sense under Soviet conditions in balancing the one organizational bias against the other. Khrushchev's *sovnarkhoz* solution may have been politically astute in that it strengthened the "prefects" on whom Khrushchev's power at the time rested[35] (though they did not save him in the end), but economically it made less sense in biasing the organizational structure too much on the territorial side.

Lastly, in spurring technical progress and innovation, the local Party organs perform a function that rates very high on the central authorities' scale of values. Yet in fact, the Party's importance in promoting and accelerating technical progress and innovation is not very clear. To be sure, the countless books and articles about "Party work" devote considerable attention to this function, and, naturally, find reasons to pat the Party on its collective back. Indeed, in a study of certain cases of diffusion of managerial innovations, Robert Campbell finds that the important "Saratov system of defectless work" in industry owed its diffusion, first within the oblast and then in the whole country, to the crucial

[33] *Sobranie postanovlenii Pravitel'stva SSSR*, 1978: 19, pp. 379-80, here cited from C. Duevel, "Joint Decree Reveals Large-Scale Diversion of Agricultural Resources," *Radio Liberty Research*, RL 214/78, October 2, 1978 (mimeographed).

[34] As an example, see the vivid account in Iu. Makhrin, "Svoe i 'chuzhoe'," *Sotsialisticheskaia industriia*, June 11, 1978, p. 2.

[35] Cf. Alec Nove, *Was Stalin Really Necessary?* (London, 1964), pp. 99ff. However, there is reason to believe that the *sovnarkhozy* quickly lost power and industry was in effect largely run from Moscow on the branch principle; see Andris Trapans, "A Study of Soviet Industrial Administration: The Sovnarkhoz Experiment, 1957-1965," unpublished doctoral dissertation, University of California, Berkeley, 1978.

role of the Party at the oblast and (later) higher levels. He surmises that only the Party could have crossed the barrier between secret and nonsecret work to effect the initial transfer of the technique, and to have bypassed the administrative hierarchy and gained access directly to the enterprise. Nevertheless, "on balance we should probably conclude that the Russians have not succeeded in getting this innovation diffused. These transfers by official campaigns are likely to be only superficially effective. . . . If the potential adopters of the innovation do not have an inherent interest in it . . ."[36] Something of this sort may have also happened in the case of the much publicized Shchekino system of raising labor productivity (a kind of Soviet Scanlon Plan).[37] And in his comprehensive study of innovation in Soviet industry, Berliner concludes flatly that Party activity is not "central" to the problem, and that the subject "may be studied independently of the Party's role."[38]

In truth, we seem not to know very much yet about the role of the local Party organs in promoting both technical and managerial innovations within existing enterprises. But what we do know does not suggest that it is always successful in overcoming strong inherent resistance to innovations where it exists.

The Party—its local leaders and functionaries—plays a number of important roles in the economic life of the district or region in its charge. Its power to play these roles is great, in some respects virtually unlimited. How it uses this power in the performance of its economic functions and in what directions it makes its weight felt depends surely on the values of the national Communist leadership of the given time, and especially on the particular configuration of the official values that the given *local* Party leadership holds at the moment. Yet the Party is also a hierarchy, a territorially structured bureaucracy that shares not only a set of values and a strong instinct for corporate self-preservation but also, as with all hierarchies, dependence of the subordinate on the superior for evaluation, reward, sanction, and punishment. Taken together, a Central Committee consisting largely of regional first secretaries can overthrow a Khrushchev

[36] Robert W. Campbell, "Management Spillovers from Soviet Space and Military Programmes," *Soviet Studies*, 23 (April 1972):593. Hough (*Soviet Prefects*, pp. 119-20) and Barker (supra, n. 3, pp. 107-12) do seem to assign some efficacy to Party intervention in innovation, though they apparently ran into difficulty assessing its significance. Conyngham (supra, n. 3, pp. 116, 237, 277) takes a more negative view of the matter. On the variety of instruments employed in promoting innovation in Soviet industry the reader is referred to Gregory Grossman, "Innovation and Information in the Soviet Economy," *American Economic Review*, 41 (May 1966):118-30.

[37] Cf. Jeanne Delamotte, *Shchekino, enterprise soviétique pilote* (Paris, 1973). The role of the Party is briefly stated on pp. 119 and 146.

[38] Joseph S. Berliner, *The Innovation Decision in Soviet Industry* (Cambridge, Mass., 1976), p. 41.

and install a Brezhnev at the apex of its own hierarchy, but at any time the individual first secretary is more or less at the mercy of his superiors, just as his junior secretaries and his professional staff are pretty much at his mercy. The first secretary, just like his subordinates, has to "deliver"; he has to meet certain expectations of his performance higher up. He is responsible for his region or district, or some functional aspect of the territorial unit. He is judged by a set of success indicators. What are they?

By the nature of the case, answers to this question can be only tentative with the information at hand. Nonetheless, the weight of informed opinion leans heavily toward identifying the local first secretary's economic "success indicators" with the main plan-fulfillment indicators of the given district or region, or those of the leading industries or firms therein. Such were, by and large, Berliner's findings from his interviews with former Soviet citizens based on their prewar experience (supra, n. 5, pp. 268ff.). Writing about the early thirties, Conyngham states: "To fulfill the Plan was the local Party organs' central task from the beginning of the Five-Year Plan" (supra, n. 3, p. 40). With respect to a more recent period, Hough concludes: "Yet the [local] Party officials can never forget that they themselves are judged on the basis of plan fulfillment, particularly plan fulfillment in such an important area as industry",[39] and further clarifies that it is the fortunes of the *leading* industries and enterprises in the oblast or district or city that are particularly relevant to the Party secretary's own success and career.[40]

Here is Brezhnev himself, in 1968: "work done by Party organizations . . . must be judged first and foremost by how production assignments are fulfilled, by how labor productivity is increasing, by the state of labor discipline."[41] The order in which the three criteria are listed by Brezhnev is presumably not random. At the time, following the reform of 1965, labor productivity as such was temporarily not a formal success indicator for the firm (management), though soon to be reinstated in this capacity. And we may note that labor discipline, always a problem in the Soviet Union, and presumably always of concern to management, is also, of course, invariably of concern to the local Party as well.

So far it would seem that the motives of the local Party in the economic sphere coincide quite closely with those of management and the latter's administrative superiors, and that, with the important exception to be

[39] Hough, *Soviet Prefects*, p. 177.

[40] Ibid., pp. 146, 201, 256ff. Hough cites the evidence from Smolensk Party archives (Merle Fainsod, *Smolensk Under Soviet Rule* [New York, 1958], p. 76), dating back to the early thirties, that the first secretary of that agricultural oblast with heavy specialization in flax growing considered his success indicator to be the size of the flax harvest.

[41] *Pravda*, March 30, 1968, pp. 1-2. Here quoted from Conyngham (supra, n. 3), p. 348, n. 148.

presently noted, the Party only reenforces the strengths and weaknesses, and the biases toward externalities, of management itself. Accordingly, one would not expect strong pressure on the firm's management from the side of the Party in the direction of social responsibility of socialist business.

Furthermore, as seen by some close observers of the Party's personnel, there has been notable growth of technical competence and experience on the part of the local Party's leadership, including the cooptation to such positions of outstanding technical specialists from industry, agriculture, and other branches of the economy.[42] To this we might add two other important developments under Brezhnev: lengthening job tenure on the part of *obkom* first secretaries (and those on lower levels as well?) and a greater tendency for them to be recruited locally (the latter an openly proclaimed policy).[43]

The exception is that the Party is concerned not with just one firm or one branch of the economy, but with many firms and at least several branches within its territory. In directing its attentions and efforts, in prodding and mobilizing, in shunting supplies and adjudicating conflicts, it must choose between favorites and the rest. As already noted, it does so presumably with reference to what its superiors regard to be the "leading" industries and lines of production in the given region or district, where the national priorities fall at the moment, and what happens to be the current object of a "campaign." This is how the Party functionary's and the Party secretary's (and, especially, the "first's") reputation is presumably built up. If so, the effect of the Party's comanagement of the economy may be not only to uphold the leader's priorities but to intensify them. Just as DDT becomes concentrated as it passes through the food chain, so priorities may well become progressively concentrated and intensified as they pass down the Party's command chain. The effect on the economy need not be always salutary, even from the standpoint of the national leaders' objectives and values.

The Party's role in the local economy may, however, be felt in directions other than those that enjoy high priority at superior levels. Thus, we have already noted the likely contribution of the Party to the ever-present tendency toward local autarky, often in clear contravention of policy at higher levels. Nor would one be surprised if the local Party also looked favorably on those industries in the given region that produce valuable trading chips for the Party's own interregional market (supra)—which, incidentally, like any free trade, may be beneficial to the national econ-

---

[42] Cf. T. H. Rigby, "The Soviet Regional Leadership: The Brezhnev Generation," *Slavic Review*, 37 (March 1978):1-24. For the changing trend in the recruitment of *gorkom* secretaries see Hough, *Soviet Prefects*, pp. 66-67, 74.

[43] Rigby (supra, n. 42), pp. 12-13; Hough, *Soviet Prefects*, p. 70.

omy, partially compensating for the failures of formal planning and administration.

Perhaps of greater significance is the fact that the local Party authorities are responsible not only for production successes but also for public order, morale, and labor discipline in their respective territories. Consequently, one might expect them to intervene not only in favor of the high priority industries and lines of production, but in some measure also at the other end of the spectrum, i.e., on behalf of branches and industries producing goods and services that raise order, morale, and discipline. Such intervention in favor of (shall we say) consumer welfare in the given region may take place primarily in the form of lobbying at the top— whence most of the welfare flows—with results that are hard to know for the outsider (but may be in some measure mutually cancelling among regions, as already noted). Yet to some extent there may be also Party-directed reallocation of the region's own resources in favor of uses with (nationally) relatively low priority but of importance for upholding the morale of the local population. In the latter respect the Party may perform a role not unlike that of the ubiquitous underground (or, at least, informal) economy, by diverting resources to meet preferences and values that diverge from the officially approved ones. It might be added that the Party is far from innocent of involvement with informal and underground activities, despite their illegal nature. Not only does the Party as such tolerate many of these activities, but particular Party officials frequently protect, and sometimes promote and encourage them, not without considerable material benefit to themselves. This sort of corruption is quite widespread, judging by hints in the official press as well as by explicit émigré accounts.

So far so good, but what of the Party's "generalist" function as the guardian of the full range of official values and priorities and as the watchdog over management in the name of social responsibility in a broad sense. What motivates the Party in these roles? Some might say that it is the local Party officials' and functionaries' unquestioning adherence to the official ideology of the CPSU and in each individual's moral code of a Communist. Others, in refutation, might minimize any generalist function, pointing to sheer careerism, technocratic or even professional standards (as distinct from the official ideology), bureaucratic attitudes (in the colloquial sense), and even ordinary self-serving tendencies to the point of graft and corruption, that seem to have encroached upon the Party's consciousness in the course of time. To some degree, perhaps, the answer lies in the direction of Granick's pioneering work on comparative management (management in the narrower sense, not including the Party). In attempting to explain the differences between managerial behavior in several countries, both East and West, in regard to adherence to the broader values and objectives of the larger entity, such as a corporation or the whole Soviet economy, as against suboptimization to the benefit of a single subdivision thereof, Granick finds a strong explanatory factor in managerial career patterns. Where the career patterns are such that management's fortunes are closely tied to a given part of the larger entity, suboptimization seems to be pronounced, with inevitable negative externality effects on the larger entity. Where, on the contrary, there is no such identification, but the individual manager's career is closely bound with the top leadership and the larger entity, the tendency to suboptimize at the lower levels seems to be weaker.[44]

Much has been written by sovietologists on the careers of intermediate-level, as well as top, leaders of the CPSU. Notably, the first secretaryship of an oblast or union republic is a standard stepping stone to membership not only in the Central Committee but also to the highest positions within the CPSU, including the Politburo and even the general secretaryship. This much seems to be well established.[45] But what kind of behavior earns for the first secretary of a republic or an oblast the coveted promotion to the Kremlin? The literature is more ambiguous on this question. Is it an outstanding record of meeting the requisite success indicators, in the sense discussed above? If so, the career pattern would not seem to induce the first secretary (and, a fortiori, the subordinates in his own apparat) to be much of generalist in upholding the broader official values and priorities. Or is the key to the "first's" promotion to the Kremlin unstinting personal loyalty to whomever does the promoting at the moment? In this case the broader official values and priorities may also not be entirely relevant.

To conclude: Soviet firms are guilty of serious faults of both omission and commission from the standpoint of official values (as well as common sense), as they follow the behavioral rules mandated from above and as they adapt to the prevailing environment of widespread shortages and the seller's market. Some of the faults are similar to the undesirable effects on society that occur in market economies (externalities Ex1), others (Ex2), on the whole probably the more serious, are typical of nonmarket systems, and might therefore be called "nonmarket failures." The system's directors do attempt corrective measures along a number of dimensions, though short of a radical systemic reform so far. Among such dimensions is the (local, regional) Party, which, with its authority and

---

[44] See David Granick, *Management Comparisons of Four Developed Countries: France, Britain, United States, and Russia* (Cambridge, Mass., 1972), and "Managerial Incentives in the USSR and in Western Firms," *Journal of Comparative Administration*, 5 (August 1973):169-99.

[45] The reader is referred, inter alia, to the works by Hough, *Soviet Prefects*, Rigby (supra, n. 42), and Stewart (supra, n. 3).

power and its supposed commitment to official values and priorities, plays an important role as a kind of parallel managerial hierarchy, which at once intervenes in essentially managerial decisions and monitors the commitment of management proper to a sense of social responsibility. (Responsibility is, of course, to official values and priorities.) Its most basic function, which invests it with great power, is control over all important personnel appointments in the business sector, and in many cases also the possibility of removal of such personnel. It intervenes directly in the mobilization and redistribution of local resources, and to some extent even in direct production decisions. It adjudicates disputes on the local level.

The just-listed functions are essentially managerial rather than entrepreneurial, although some risk taking, an entrepreneurial trait, necessarily attaches to such decisions taken by individual Party leaders and functionaries. Evidently, the Party is not a perfect automaton in the hands of the top leadership; the consequences of its comanagement need not always effectively advance the top leadership's desires, nor stop short of excesses in that direction. Local Party authorities have their own axes to grind, rows to hoe, and pockets to line, and, as we have seen, they grind, hoe, and line them. As Conyngham stresses, the Party, like any political entity with economic functions, faces the dilemma of efficiency versus power, and it resolves the dilemma not necessarily to the advantage of efficiency and innovation.[46] Valid as the observation may be, it should not distract us from appreciating that in the Soviet-type system, which lacks both an autonomous market mechanism and an efficient bureaucratic command structure to manage the economy, the Party does, withal, have a constructive though probably limited function as comanager, adjudicator, and watchdog of social responsibility.

Whether the Party (on intermediate levels) can be said to play a real entrepreneurial role is somewhat problematical. Perhaps it comes closest to this when it acts, as it often does, in the role of advocate of its own region or district before superior authorities, and especially as it attempts to redress some intraregional imbalances engendered by Soviet-type product-line-oriented planning.[47]

[46] Conyngham (supra, n. 3), pp. 286-87.

[47] Finally, it should be noted that we have not taken a historical view of the Party's role in the economy, rather focusing on a brief, recent period. This role has not, needless to say, remained invariant thanks to important socioeconomic changes over the decades as well as the evolution of the technological parameters of production. For historical perspective of the Party's relationship to the economy the reader is referred to the able and insightful treatments by Paul Cocks ("The Rationalization of Party Control," in Chalmers A. Johnson, ed., *Change in Communist Systems* [Stanford, 1970], pp. 153-90; and "Administrative Behavior, Political Change, and the Role of the Party," in Karl W. Ryavec, ed., *Soviet Society and the Communist Party* [Amherst, Mass., 1978], pp. 41-59); Hough (*Soviet Prefects*, chap. 13); and Conyngham (supra, n. 3), among others.

XV

PAUL COCKS

Organizing for
Technological Innovation
in the 1980s

Technological innovation has become a dominant issue on the Kremlin's political agenda in the 1980s. Early in the last decade Brezhnev singled out the application of R & D results as the most important but also the most deficient aspect of Soviet science and technology policy. "If we examine all the links of the intricate chain that binds science to production, we shall easily see that the weakest links are those relating to the practical realization of scientific achievements, to their adoption in mass production." It was necessary, the general secretary stressed, "to create conditions compelling enterprises to manufacture the latest types of products, literally to chase after scientific and technical novelties and not to shy away from them, figuratively speaking, as the devil shies away from holy water."[1] Similarly, five years later he told the Twenty-fifth Party Congress, "Today the practical application of new scientific ideas is no less important a task than their development."[2] Again at the 1981 congress, Brezhnev called the promotion of scientific discoveries and inventions "the decisive, most critical sector" in economic policy. The removal of all obstacles to the introduction of new technology, he warned, was "absolutely necessary for the country, for the people, and for our future."[3] The main brake on Russia's technical progress is seen to be not the absence of scientific achievements—much less an inability to produce excellent science—but poor organization and management of technological application. Indeed, a major challenge of the day consists in formulating a science policy and appropriate institutional structures to promote the innovation process.

To be sure, the need to accelerate technological development and de-

---

[1] *XXIV sezd KPSS: Stenograficheskii otchet* (Moscow, 1971), 1:80-81.
[2] *XXV sezd KPSS: Stenograficheskii otchet* (Moscow, 1976), 1:72.
[3] *XXVI sezd KPSS: Stenograficheskii otchet* (Moscow, 1981), 1:61.

livery is not a new theme in Soviet politics. The process of translating scientific ideas into new products and processes has long been a veritable obstacle course plagued by endless delays and difficulties. Khrushchev complained almost as much as his successors about the "divorce of science from production" and the need for better coupling. Nor have the problems surrounding innovation, for the most part, changed fundamentally in the last two decades. What has changed and broadened are Soviet perceptions of these problems and of the innovation process itself along with official motivation to use science and technology as an instrument of policy and tool of economic progress.

Wrestling with the obstacles to innovation, Kremlin authorities have devoted particular attention to organizational problems and approaches. Admittedly, organizational structure is not the whole cause of the innovation problem. Nonstructural factors, such as prices, decision rules, and incentives, play an important role in poor Soviet performance. "But part of the explanation," Berliner writes, "is due to strictly organizational matters—primarily the separation of R & D establishments from the enterprises that ultimately introduce the innovations."[4] Significantly, Soviet science-policy analysts and administrators have become increasingly aware of the importance of linkage in moving ideas from the lab into use and of the need to structure more explicitly and effectively the vital interfaces in the transfer process. This chapter deals with some of the underlying assumptions and practical forms of the new architecture for integrating research and production that evolved in the 1970s and provides the structural underpinnings for technological advance in the 1980s.

Technological Imperatives in A Revolutionary Age

The keen, almost consuming interest in accelerating innovation and change reflects the extent to which a perceived "technological imperative" has come to dominate and divide the Kremlin leadership in recent years. Two important discoveries have prompted this official concern. First is the rather belated awakening of the ruling elite to the full significance of the development and role of science and technology in the world, roughly since mid-century. These changes have been dubbed the "contemporary scientific and technical revolution" (STR), largely a euphemism for the computer age. The changing conditions and new demands associated with this new stage of industrial revolution are seen as placing unprecedented importance on scientific and technical progress. Such progress becomes not only the key force driving modern society forward but also

---

[4] Joseph Berliner, *The Innovation Decision in Soviet Industry* (Cambridge, Mass., 1976), p. 102.

a major arena of competition between the world's two opposing social systems. Underlying the notion of the STR is also implicit—and sometimes explicit—recognition of Russia's relative backwardness and growing technology gap with the West, especially the United States. As a letter of appeal from dissident but concerned Soviet scientists to Party and government leaders in March 1970 noted frankly with respect to the computer age: "We are simply living in a different era. The second industrial revolution came along and now, at the onset of the seventies, we see that far from having overtaken America, we are dropping further and further behind."[5] Thus, a "historic" task facing the USSR today, as defined by General Secretary Brezhnev at the 1971 Party congress and reaffirmed by the 1976 and 1981 congresses, is "to combine organically the achievements of the STR with the advantages of the socialist economic system, to unfold more broadly our own, intrinsically socialist forms of fusing science with production."[6]

Second, there has also been growing realization that the Soviet economy is approaching the limits of "extensive" growth and entering a new era that calls for more "intensive" methods of development. Declining supplies of manpower and material resources require a basic shift in development strategy and greater emphasis on qualitative improvements rather than quantitative increases of inputs as the main source of future growth. Already at the end of the 1960s, Brezhnev declared firmly that intensification "becomes not only the main way but the *only* way of developing our economy." Moreover, in this approach he told the 1971 Party congress, "the acceleration of scientific and technical progress forges into first place both from the point of view of current tasks and of the long-term future." A decade later against the backdrop of a continuing slowdown of the economy and growing squeeze on resources, Brezhnev emphasized to the Twenty-sixth Party Congress, "The circumstances in which the national economy is to develop in the eighties make the acceleration of scientific and technical progress even more pressing. No one needs convincing of the great significance of science. The Communist party proceeds from the premise that the construction of a new society is simply unthinkable without science."[7]

International and domestic pressures have combined, therefore, to make

---

[5] Andrei Sakharov, Roy Medvedev, and V. F. Turchin, "Letter of Appeal of Soviet Scientists to Party and Government Leaders of the USSR," March 19, 1970, reprinted in *Survey*, no. 76 (Summer 1970):161-70.

[6] *XXIV sezd KPSS*, 1:82, and *XXV sezd KPSS*, 2:237; *XXVI sezd KPSS*, 2:160.

[7] L. I. Brezhnev, *Ob osnovnykh voprosakh ekonomicheskoi politiki KPSS na sovremennom etape: Rechi i doklady* (Moscow, 1975), 1:418; *XXIV sezd KPSS*, 1:80; *XXVI sezd KPSS*, 1:60.

the acceleration of scientific progress a major issue of the 1970s and 1980s. Just as he had defined this to be the "key task" of economic policy in 1971, Brezhnev also listed it first among the "key problems" of the period of the Tenth Five-Year Plan (1976-80). Indeed, he affirmed, "In our entire economic development perhaps no tasks are more urgent and more important." Looking at the current decade, he reminded the 1981 Party Congress, "We cannot forget that it is precisely during these years that the foundations will be laid for the national economic structure with which the country will embark upon the twenty-first century."[8]

Two key factors of intensification, two main levers for speeding economic development, have been singled out and stressed by Brezhnev: modern technology and modern management. Already at the turn of the last decade he observed, "The solution to many of our economic problems should now be sought at the junctures between progress in science and technology and progress in management."[9] Throughout the seventies the general secretary continued to emphasize not only their importance but also the impossibility of having one without the other.

Underlying these ideas is enhanced awareness of a direct correlation between technology and structure. Technical progress and organizational development are seen increasingly as being interrelated and interdependent. N. S. Kalita and G. I. Mantsurov, for example, note, "The level of organization and management of production to a significant—if not decisive—degree now predetermines the rates of scientific and technical progress." They acknowledge "a direct dependence between organizational and technical factors of production, between the nature of its structure and the rates of technical advance." Boris Milner, a top authority on industrial design, also observes that qualitative changes in organization and management "are becoming a premise and a result of progress in science and technology."[10]

Accordingly, the adoption of a new strategy for technological innovation is seen by some to require organizational and administrative adaptation as well. As Brezhnev noted in 1971, the new demands on organization and management "do not allow us to be satisfied with existing forms and methods, even where they have served us well in the past." P. M. Masherov, then a candidate member of the Politburo, told the Party congress in 1971, "Still not all of our executives fully understand that it is impossible to 'squeeze' the revolution in science and technology

---

[8] *XXV sezd KPSS*, 1:73; *XXVI sezd KPSS*, 1:62.

[9] *Pravda*, June 13, 1970.

[10] N. S. Kalita and G. I. Mantsurov, *Sotsialisticheskie proizvodstvennye obedineniia* (Moscow, 1972), pp. 3-4; Boris Milner, "Organization of the Management of Production," *Social Sciences* (Moscow), 7, no. 3 (1976):48.

into the framework of old methods and organizational forms of work."
Two specialists on innovation, P. Danilovtsev and Iu. Kanygin, similarly
insist, "To attempt to put the research-production cycle into traditional
forms of organization and management is like trying to use a steam boiler
to harness thermonuclear energy."[11] Experience has also demonstrated
the difficulties of applying new techniques of planning and management,
including computerized information and control systems, within established structures. More and more, then, there is movement toward the
view, advanced by numerous Western writers on innovation, that "structure follows strategy," that organizational forms, to be effective and
sound, must adapt to changes in technology strategy.

To phrase the issue somewhat differently, there is growing recognition
in the USSR that the phenomenon designated the STR is not only a
scientific and industrial revolution but a managerial revolution as well.
The task of the times is to develop not just modern technological hardware but also a distinctive managerial software appropriate to Russia's
conditions. Indeed, this is the essence of Brezhnev's call for combining
the achievements of the revolution in science and technology with the
advantages of the socialist economic system, for building and managing
an effective innovation process in an intrinsically Soviet way. At issue,
then, are really two broad categories of innovation—technological and
administrative. The latter deals with changes in the methods of running
business operations that make more effective use of resources. These may
include changes in organizational structure, policies, and procedures.
Administrative innovations are increasingly seen as necessary to supplement technological innovations.

What has been most notable about the contemporary scientific revolution, and probably what characterizes it as a revolution, has been the
increasing speed with which theoretical discovery has found its way into
practical application. Meanwhile, the slow and ineffective passage of
ideas into practice remains the principal deficiency of Soviet science and
technology organization. Not more than 30 to 50 percent of completed
R & D finds its way into production. The remainder is either not utilized
at all or assimilated so slowly that it is already obsolete by the time of
its introduction.[12] Enhanced interest in accelerating the development and

[11] *XXIV sezd KPSS*, 1:90, 179-80; P. Danilovtsev and Iu. Kanygin, *Ot laboratorii do
zavoda* (Novosibirsk, 1971), p. 40.

[12] See Louvan E. Nolting, *Sources of Financing the Stages of the Research, Development,
and Innovation Cycle in the USSR* (Washington, D.C., 1973), p. 3; V. N. Arkhangelskii,
Organizatsionno-ekonomicheskie problemy upravleniia nauchnymi issledovaniiami (Moscow, 1977), p. 33; V. I. Kushlin, *Uskorenie vnedreniia nauchnykh dostizhenii v proizvodstvo* (Moscow, 1976), p. 3.

transfer of technology throughout the economy has led to important reconceptualization of the innovation-diffusion process itself.

Changing Perceptions of Innovation

At the outset it should be mentioned that such notions as "innovation process," "technology transfer," and "realization cycle," which figure prominently in Western writings, are relatively unknown in the USSR. Soviet analysts, on the contrary, tend to use terms like "research-production cycle," "scientific and technological complex of work," and "complex of preproduction work" to describe the sequencing, organization, and stimulation of scientific research and development. For the most part, their concepts have revolved around phase-dominant models of innovation with emphasis on separate functions and individual work efforts performed in isolation from one another and cut off from the application of results into production. Only recently have they begun to adopt a more *process* view of innovation with the focus on final results and overall integration.[13]

Also only recently has a predominantly linear-causal view of innovation been called into question. This model emphasizes a relatively simple and orderly forward flow of work from theoretical conception to practical use. The notion that innovation involves a complex and helixlike stream of events and stages with significant feedback coupling is not commonly held. Accordingly, various stages of work are planned predominantly in sequence rather than simultaneously and in parallel. The result is significant losses of time between phases and a lengthening of the process as a whole.[14]

Generally speaking, the Soviet approach to structuring the innovation cycle is premised on the image of technology transfer that prevailed largely in the West until the early 1960s. According to this view, the transfer process is envisaged as "the passage of disembodied 'ideas and methods,' endowed with some quasi-independence in the manner of genes, from one state of existence or milieu to another." The underlying assumption is that technology is primarily "an assemblage of pieces of information which can be extracted or expelled from one sector of organized creativity and transposed to another to produce different out-

---

[13] See Iu. M. Kanygin, *Nauchno-tekhnicheskii potentsial (Problemy nakupleniia i ispolzovaniia)* (Novosibirsk, 1974), pp. 157-59, 179-80.

[14] E. I. Gavrilov, *Ekonomika i effektivnost' nauchno-tekhnicheskogo progressa* (Minsk, 1975), pp. 283-84; Iu. Kanygin, *Nauchno-proizvodstvennyi tsikl: Voprosy teorii i organizatsii* (Novosibirsk, 1971), and *Nauchno-tekhnicheskii potentsial*, pp. 179-82.

puts."[15] The whole process is reduced to clerical reporting, to a kind of mechanical transmission of documents and routing of information through formal communication systems.[16]

Basically, the Soviet research-to-production process has been broken up in time, task, and territory. Planning and financing are carried out primarily on an *institutional* basis by functional type of performer rather than by stages of the research-development-innovation cycle, much less by the cycle as a whole. Thus science and technology tend to be built around organizations instead of around programs and projects. Not only is the process structurally fragmented and shapeless; it also lacks basically a unifying goals framework. Coupling is loose and disjointed, and sometimes it is next to impossible to unravel the chain of events. Individual and institutional participants are not fully aware that they are involved in a connected process. Indeed, they tend to take a very narrow view of their roles, responsibilities, and interests. As Berliner explains, their concern with the end result of work is a concern that ends with their stage of it.[17] The whole activity chain moves through different links without the integrating force of common purpose and sense of teamwork.

Technological innovation in the Soviet Union is distinguished, above all, by its inherently bureaucratic nature. The whole process takes place primarily through bureaucratic interactions between functional performers and higher ministerial authorities who serve as administrative "gatekeepers" at the critical transfer points. There is little direct interplay and collaboration among actual individual and institutional performers. External transactions between organizations are handled and mediated, for the most part, by various ministerial offices and departmental channels. Upon completion of its assigned work a research institute or design bureau, for instance, will report its results to one of the technical administrations, branch *glavki*, or industrial associations to which it is subordinate. The latter, in turn, decides what should be the next phase of work, by whom, and where. The whole system operates by hierarchical referral and bureaucratic relay—situations are referred upward in the hierarchy for resolution. Communications and work must go up and down long organizational lines to get across the various functional interfaces in the cycle.

This bureaucratic structure and procedure affect the decision process

[15] Tom Burns, "Models, Images, and Myths," in William H. Gruber and Donald G. Margues, eds., *Factors in the Transfer of Technology* (Cambridge, Mass., 1969), pp. 11-23.

[16] One of the best discussions of Soviet views of innovation is by Kanygin. See his *Nauchno-tekhnicheskii potentsial*, pp. 151-213, and *Nauchno-proizvodstvennyi tsikl: Voprosy teorii i organizatsii.*

[17] Berliner, *The Innovation Decision*, p. 107.

in at least two important respects. First, the need to get endless approvals and agreements at various stages produces decision delays and prolongs the research-production cycle. The creation of a new machine, for example, requires typically twenty-five approvals at different levels. To build a new technological system of ten to fifteen machines may require as many as four hundred to five hundred favorable clearances.[18] In general, these agreements are obtained sequentially and not in parallel.[19] Forward movement is constantly interrupted and stalled by numerous rounds of negotiation, by waiting for approval of reports by departmental and interdepartmental expert commissions, for the return of tests on prototypes, by the absence of supplies and financing, and so forth. Considerable time is spent on correspondence and on trips to ministries in pursuit of support for innovation. The path from conception to commercialization can be especially long and precarious if the technology entails new processes or products unrelated to established interests and activities or involves much interministerial negotiation.

According to studies by the State Committee for Science and Technology, it frequently takes as much time to secure agreements and to transfer documents from one organization to another as it does to conduct the necessary scientific development.[20] That is, the bureaucratic process of moving research results consumes as much time as the research and development process itself. Even excellent ideas must "stand in line" to be included in the work plan of the organization designated to conduct the next phase of the process. They, too, sometimes fail to pass the approval stage. Among the nearly seven hundred completed R & D projects that were proposed by the Siberian Division of the USSR Academy of Sciences for practical use between 1960 and 1970 but were not introduced, about 40 percent had become obsolete while waiting for higher approval.[21]

Secondly, the quality of decision making is reduced, because structure forces decisions to the highest levels away from the information and knowledge that are most relevant to deal with them. Each additional level distorts objectives and misdirects attention. The vision of individuals and managerial units is directed toward separate efforts rather than on the overall enterprise, results, and performance. Every link in the ad-

---

[18] Kanygin, *Nauchno-tekhnicheskii potentsial*, p. 225.

[19] L. S. Bliakhman, "Nauka kak otrasl' proizvodstvennoi deiatelnosti," in L. S. Bliakhman, ed., *Voprosy ekonomiki i planirovaniia nauchnykh issledovanii* (Leningrad, 1968), p. 15.

[20] K. I. Taksir, *Integratsiia nauki i proizvodstva pri sotsializme* (Moscow, 1975), p. 14 and Kushlin, *Uskorenie vnedreniia nauchnykh dostizhenii v proizvodstvo*, p. 122.

[21] V. I. Shteingauz, *Ekonomicheskie problemy realizatsii nauchno-tekhnicheskikh razrabotok* (Moscow, 1976), p. 118.

ministrative chain creates one more source of inertia, friction, and slack. All along the line there is constant danger a project will lose momentum and fall into incompetent or unsympathetic hands. Months of lost motion and dissipation of effort are frequently the result.

These factors assume special importance in the branch ministries, where the quality of managerial personnel is appreciably lower than in the academy system. The management of academic science is exercised by scientists themselves, and it is not nearly as fragmented and hampered by departmental limitations as so-called branch or ministerial science. Research and development work in the ministries, on the contrary, is directed by people who are not scientists. "They themselves do not perform scientific research, and many of them have only a vague notion of how it is conducted."[22] To be sure, scientific and managerial competence varies across ministerial lines. Nonetheless, the traditional "production bias" of the branch ministries that discriminates against new technology and the relative lack of highly qualified personnel oriented to R & D issues and interests have not contributed to the cause of innovation.

Significantly, some of the traditional perceptions and assumptions regarding scientific and technological development that underlie the structural organization of, and bureaucratic barriers to, innovation are being increasingly questioned and replaced by a more dynamic and systems view. Established structural arrangements, in turn, are giving way to new organizational approaches and institutional frameworks. One of the major Soviet discoveries about innovation in the 1970s, in fact, was the importance of the "management connection." The very phrase "research-production" cycle is said to be somewhat of a misnomer, because action throughout must be negotiated and mediated. It is better to speak in terms of a system of "research-management-production," to use the words of some Soviet analysts. Such terminology, they note, conveys a more adequate image of this complex process. It also explicitly identifies and emphasizes the management function and linkage.[23]

Finally, it is important to mention the growing recognition in the Soviet Union of the need to make the management of R & D a distinct and separate form of managerial action and specialization. In the past, innovation was not made a managerial responsibility. Both the researcher and manager have been characterized by noninnovative role definitions. The introduction of new technology fell entirely outside the normal duties of enterprise executives and workers. No explicit or uniform rules existed

[22] A. Zalkind, "An Academy for the 'Nonacademic' Sciences," *Literaturnaia gazeta*, no. 12 (March 24, 1976), p. 11.

[23] See V. I. Berlozertsev, "Soedinenie nauchno-tekhnicheskoi revoliutsii s preimushchestvami sotsializma," in *Problemy soedineniia dostizhenii nauchno-tekhnicheskoi revoliutsii s preimushchestvami sotsializma* (Voronezh, 1974), pp. 11-12.

to regulate technological change. Each new product or process was introduced largely in its own way. Nor is this surprising, since the introduction of new technology was an extraordinary event. Management was geared to repetitive and unchanging production operations. Increasingly today, however, technological change, at least in certain sectors, is becoming a normal and continuous situation. To accommodate a more rapid rate of technological growth, some Soviet experts argue that a new kind of management is needed which is oriented to innovation. The management of R & D must be developed and included as an integral part of the system of managing the enterprise, the branch, and the economy as a whole. In addition, this new managerial function must be put on a par with the management of production, of finances, and of supply.[24] More and more, then, Soviet specialists appear to be coming around to the view shared by numerous American writers that innovation cannot be a subordinate and part-time task. The problems and obstacles are too obstinate to yield to only occasional attention and halfhearted action.

Structuring and Managing the Research-to-Production Cycle: A Systems Approach

With gradual movement away from a strictly phase-dominant to a more process view of innovation, the need for a systems model of organization and management has become more and more apparent. The traditional approach to innovation, based upon extreme functional specialization by institutional performer, has left the process structurally fragmented. Structural barriers have been created all along the innovation chain. In essence, the research-production cycle has been unorganized and unmanaged.

To overcome the fragmentation of this cycle, special emphasis is now being put on the integrative aspects of management. The significance of integration has also risen with growing realization that innovation is increasingly a social and complex process. Expressing this view, E. Kosov asserts, "Scientific activity is not simply an act of creativity but a complex system of coordinating the activity of separate scientific organizations."[25] Iu. Kanygin also stresses the idea that innovation involves a series of several interdependent steps that must be successfully joined and coor-

---

[24] See G. Kh. Popov, *Effektivnoe upravlenie (perspektivy razvitiia)* (Moscow, 1976), pp. 12-13; G. A. Dzhavadov, V. N. Varvarov, and A. V. Sobrovin, "Organizatsiia ratsional-izatsii upravleniia nauchno-tekhnicheskim progressom v otrasli," in G. Kh. Popov, ed., *Problemy organizatsii sovershenstvovaniia upravleniia sotsialisticheskim proizvodstvom (Seminar g. Kalinin 1-10 fevralia 1974g)* (Moscow, 1975), p. 253.

[25] E. Kosov, "Ekonomicheskie problemy upravleniia nauchno-tekhnicheskim progressom," *Ekonomicheskie nauki*, 7 (1971):52.

dinated.[26] This is the task of management. Its role in integrating people and processes so they can perform as a unified whole becomes not only more important but also more difficult. Gvishiani emphasizes, "The problem of ensuring *continuity* of the process at every stage of research and development work, including the introduction of results into mass production, is now being brought to the fore as the most complex organizational task. It is quite obvious that this process requires integrated management."[27]

Because it focuses attention on interrelationships, interdependencies, and integration, the systems approach is regarded by many to be a more viable conceptual framework for analyzing and solving structural design problems. Writing about the particular attraction of this approach, Gvishiani notes, "What interests us is its basic conclusion as to the need for a complex, all-around approach to management, and the disclosure of its integrative function."[28] Its emphasis on study of organization of the research-production cycle as a total system is new and underscores the emerging broader view of organizational structure as a means of facilitating decision making, motivation, and control. The application of a systems model transforms the innovation process allegedly into "a unified and self-regulating dynamic system." The research cycle becomes "a continuous and goal-directed process."[29] Iu. Mikhnevich speaks, in fact, of the "structuralization" of the research-to-production process that underlines recent organizational reforms. Kanygin also observes, "This is a process whose effective management requires a definite structure; that is, a definite composition of elements and means of fusing them."[30] In effect, a systems approach to structuring organizations and guiding organizational processes toward innovation objectives is seen as the new cure for overcoming Russia's perennial linkage problems.

In line with this approach, a variety of new structural configurations have sprung up since the late 1960s to promote technological innovation. While they assume generally the shape of large-scale research and pro-

[26] Kanygin, *Nauchno-tekhnicheskii potentsial*, p. 183.

[27] D. M. Gvishiani, "The Scientific and Technological Revolution and Scientific Problems," *Social Sciences*, 1, no. 7 (1972):52. Emphasis added.

[28] D. Gvishiani, *Organization and Management: A Sociological Analysis of Western Theories* (Moscow, 1972), p. 146. He adds, "This approach makes it possible to see the whole managed system as a complete set of interrelated elements, united by a common aim, to reveal the integral properties of the system, its internal and external links" (p. 142).

[29] L. S. Bliakhman and A. F. Ivanov, "Nauchno-proizvodstvennoe obedinenie kak forma sistemnoi organizatsii tsikla 'issledovanie-proizvodstvo'," *Izvestiia Akademii nauk SSSR, seriia ekonomicheskaia*, 6 (1971):39; K. I. Taksir, *Nauchno-proizvodstvennye obedineniia* (Moscow, 1977), p. 16 (hereafter cited as *NPO*).

[30] Iu. Mikhnevich, *Ekonomicheskie problemy upravleniia nauchno-tekhnicheskim progressom* (Leningrad, 1974), p. 5; Kanygin, *Nauchno-tekhnicheskii potentsial*, p. 183.

duction complexes, these new associational forms contain different combinations of scientific and engineering talents. The distinct kind of clustering of research activities and manufacturing operations depends largely upon the extent of involvement of the complex in the innovation process. This factor also determines which unit—research institute, design bureau, experimental plant, or production enterprise—will be the main link that bears the "structural load" of the final edifice. Each complex represents an attempt to build a unified organizational system rather than an unrelated or disjointed array of tasks, functions, and individual efforts. Basically, the new integrated and integrating structures are designed to give institutional expression and coherence to the innovation process. Some science-policy experts in Moscow argue, in fact, that only through such research and production complexes can the "research-*to*-production" cycle be effectively carried on from beginning to end.[31]

A major aim of these institutional reforms is to make the innovation process more managed and manageable. Stated somewhat differently, it is to create a managerial cycle whereby the development and application of new technology is more effectively controlled. Organizational separation and administrative fragmentation have resulted in both divided responsibility and diluted authority. The new complexes seek to concentrate managerial responsibility and authority for the R & D process as a whole, to centralize decision making in order to achieve greater unity and order, and to minimize the probability of conflict and delay. In short, the new arrangements seek to build a managerial structure that spans and links the various subsystems of the organization, a decision center that can act as a common superior and coordinating body for the complex as a whole. With the formation of such complexes, all the organizational preconditions are supposedly laid for comprehensive systems planning and management of scientific and technical progress.[32] Much like Western organizations responding to new environmental uncertainties and complexities, then, Kremlin authorities are expanding organizational boundaries and bringing within internal control those forces creating complexity and anxiety. As Berliner notes, the new corporate form of Soviet innovation amounts essentially to an "internalization of what were formerly external transactions. It transfers certain flows of goods and services out of the domain of central planning into that of internal enterprise administration."[33]

A second and no less important objective of the new complexes is to establish a more effective framework for cooperation and interorganizational actions through the creation of a unifying goals structure. The

[31] L. Bliakhman, "Associations Link Science and Industry," *Pravda*, December 1, 1971.
[32] Mikhnevich, *Ekonomicheskie problemy*, p. 148.
[33] Berliner, *The Innovation Decision*, p. 526.

accent on objectives and end results in programmed-goals planning and systems-management approaches currently in vogue is designed to help build commitment and a sense of common purpose that can fuse structure and people in cooperative joint efforts. Through the new complexes and associational forms, the authorities hope to reshape the attitudes of R & D personnel and to create a coincidence of interest among all participants in the smooth and rapid transfer of technology. Instead of being guided by its own special interests and parochial perspectives, each unit is to be motivated by common objectives, by "only one concept: ours." The new complexes are seen as means by which to transform "awkward external cooperation into harmonious intrafirm cooperation."[34] Such integrating structures are expected to build a more favorable climate for innovation and to help foster needed team play. Indeed, the Russian term most frequently used to describe these complexes—*obedinenie*—comes from the verb "to unite" or "to join." It captures the explicit design emphasis on integration and teamwork.

A discussion of the array of new partnership arrangements and structural designs coupling science with industry is beyond the scope of this chapter. One piece of the emerging Soviet architecture of linkage does warrant detailed analysis, however. This is the so-called "science-production association," *nauchno-proizvodstvennoe obedinenie* (NPO). According to one of the most informed American specialists on Soviet science policy, the creation of NPOs is "probably the most significant consequence" of recent Kremlin reforms from the perspective of the future organization of Soviet science.[35] Of all the new organizations, the NPO is singled out universally by Russian writers as not only the most comprehensive but also the most successful form of integrating and accelerating the research-to-production process. To what extent are these claims justified? Are the NPOs, in fact, effective models of systems organization, planning, and management? Do they really represent "the innovative organization"? What are their advantages and their deficiencies? What obstacles impede their performance and institutional development? Are NPOs the answer to Russia's innovation problems? These are questions to which we now turn.

Organizing for Innovation: The Science-Production Associations

Science-production associations first appeared as a "qualitatively new form" of organization and management in the late 1960s. Special impetus

[34] A. Bachurin, "The Industrial Association and Technical Progress," *Ekonomicheskaia gazeta*, no. 43 (1970):5-6.

[35] Louvan E. Nolting, *The Financing of Research, Development, and Innovation in the USSR, by Type of Performer* (Washington, D.C., 1976), p. 10.

to their creation was provided by the Party and government decree of September 24, 1968, which set in motion a major overhaul of Soviet R & D practices and structures.[36] By January 1, 1972, there were 63 NPOs. Five years later they numbered 128 and by 1980, nearly 250.[37] Though they exist in nearly all branches of industry, NPOs are concentrated mainly in machine building, especially the electrical engineering, electronics, instrument manufacture, and aviation sectors, as well as in the chemical and petrochemical industries. Associations have also been organized in agriculture, construction, transport, communications, geology, and other nonindustrial branches. Though they are now found in several cities of the USSR, NPOs continue to be located predominantly in Moscow and Leningrad.

Set up explicitly to organize innovation as a distinct and major task, the associations function as special nurseries for the creation and application of fundamentally new technology of the highest quality and in the shortest time possible. They give ideas "a ticket to life." At present, it is possible to differentiate within industry three basic types of NPO according to their final product: (1) those that specialize in developing primarily new products and technological equipment for their manufacture; (2) those that concentrate on creating new means of mechanization and automation of production, including management information systems; and (3) those that engage in the development of new materials and technological processes. The third type is less prevalent than the other two. A few NPOs, like Mikrobioprom (microbiological industry), Soiuznauchplitprom (wood processing), and Plastpolimer (chemical industry), engage simultaneously in developing new products, new processes, and new kinds of equipment and automated devices.[38]

NPOs also differ in terms of the scope of their specialization and product use. The majority are of branch importance. However, some NPOs like Plastpolimer are primarily subbranch in focus, and still others are essentially interbranch in nature. The latter include Soiuznauchplitprom and Soiuzsteklomash (glass machine building), which develop articles used in construction, electronics, and defense as well as in the automobile, electrical engineering, instrument manufacture, light, food, chemical, and medical industries. Similarly, the All-Union NPO Soiuz-

---

[36] See Nolting, *The 1968 Reform of Scientific Research, Development and Innovation in the USSR* (Washington, D.C., 1976).

[37] V. Sominskii and L. Bliakhman, eds., *Ekonomicheskie problemy povysheniia effektivnosti nauchnykh razrabotok* (Leningrad, 1972), p. 178; *Pravda*, March 14, 1977; F. M. Rusinov, V. A. Pokrovskii, et al., *NPO: Formirovanie, razvitie, effektivnost'* (Moscow, 1981), p. 3.

[38] Taksir, *NPO*, pp. 42-53, 57-58; Iu. Subotskii, *Novyi etap razvitiia obedinenii v promyshlennosti* (Moscow, 1973), p. 26; L. N. Andrukhovich, *Upravlenie kachestvom* (Novoe v zhizni, nauke, tekhnike—seriia nauka upravleniia), 10 (1976):47.

transprogress was formed in 1974 to design, develop, and install transport container systems throughout the country.[39]

In general, numerous benefits are ascribed to these new integrated structures. The process of creating and applying new technology has been reduced in some NPOs by two and even three times.[40] The quality of research, development, and innovation is also higher. In electrical engineering the share of output stamped with the seal of highest quality is 1.5 to 2.5 times greater in NPOs than in the branch as a whole.[41] In the associations from 40 to 50 percent (and climbing to 80 to 90 percent) of the completed R & D is actually implemented while in autonomous scientific and technological organizations only 15 percent is successfully utilized. Labor and material costs are reduced because of less duplication, greater specialization, better organization of design work, fewer documentation errors, greater standardization of parts, and more extensive automation of work processes. In addition, NPOs are credited with harmonizing the actions, goals, and interests of different performers and with creating a favorable climate for innovation. They enjoy greater possibilities of applying network planning methods and computer techniques to the innovation cycle, of using matrix organization and project management concepts to improve the decision process and to build more dynamic and flexible innovative structures. Above all, they are said to generate favorable conditions for the conduct of uniform policies and integrated leadership throughout the associations.[42]

As Berliner notes, however, much of the evidence on NPOs deals with the performance of individual or groups of associations. Aggregate data in systematic form are still lacking.[43] It is hard to get a good "qualitative fix" on these organizations as a whole. Nonetheless, there is sufficient fragmentary information and critical analysis to suggest a much more mixed record of performance and diverse development. Not all associations have been resounding successes. Even those NPOs that have been

[39] Taksir, *NPO*, p. 57; G. A. Dzhavadov, *Upravlenie nauchno-tekhnicheskim progressom* (Moscow, 1976), p. 23.

[40] Taksir, *NPO*, p. 132; B. I. Tabachnikas, "Ot edinstva organizatsionnogo—k ekonomicheskomu," *EKO*, 8 (1979):20.

[41] Ibid., p. 145; V. Pokrovskii, "Perestraivaias' na marshe," *Sotsialisticheskaia industriia*, July 13, 1977, p. 2.

[42] Taksir, *NPO*, pp. 125-54; Subotskii, *Novyi etap razvitiia obedinenii*, p. 18; Shteingauz, *Ekonomicheskie problemy*, pp. 120-22 and her "Novye organizatsionnye formy sviazi nauki s proizvodstvom," *Ekonomika i organizatsiia promyshlennogo proizvodstva* (EKO), 3 (1973):46-47; G. A. Dzhavadov, "NPO—forma integratsii nauki, tekhniki, proizvodstva," *Sovetskoe gosudarstvo i pravo*, 1 (1975):37, 43-44; N. E. Drogichenskii, *Sovershenstvovanie mekhanizma khoziaistvovaniia v usloviiakh razvitogo sotsializma* (Moscow, 1975), pp. 168-71; and Andrukhovich, *Upravlenie kachestvom*, pp. 48-50.

[43] Berliner, *The Innovation Decision*, p. 135.

held up as stellar examples, like Pozitron and Plastpolimer, have important problem areas. Despite individual accomplishments and some remarkable gains, serious deficiencies and gaps persist in both the theory and practice of science-production associations. The ostensible advantages of these new complexes are not always or, to use the Soviet phraseology, not "automatically" realized.

One area of criticism and controversy concerns the optimal structure and composition of NPOs. Basically at issue here are conflicting views about the essential purpose and function of these associations. There is general consensus that in promoting the rapid creation and smooth transfer of technology the associations are to encompass the entire research-production cycle. Disagreement exists, however, over what should be the precise role and form of participation of the NPO in the initial and concluding phases of the cycle.

As regards the latter question, there are two main schools of thought. One holds that the task of the association should be limited essentially to the development and testing of prototypes. According to this view, which finds partial support in the official statute on the NPO, the business of series and mass production of new technology belongs not to the NPO but to the production associations and enterprises. If these two tasks are not delimited organizationally between science-production and production associations but are done within the NPO, then confusion and a distortion of functions takes place. The inclusion of enterprises engaged in series production leads to an expansion of manufacturing operations to the detriment of R & D activity. The main function of the NPO—prototype development—becomes subordinate to the task of fulfilling current production programs.

Indeed, the claims and fears of those adopting this view are confirmed by experience. In several NPOs the share of scientific research and experimental design work comprises only 5 to 15 percent of the volume of industrial production activity. Some NPOs, like Istochnik in Leningrad and Akkumuliator in Podolsk, both of which fall into this category, were renamed production associations in 1976. In Elektrokeramika the proportion of series production has risen to more than 90 percent of the total work plan of the association. Because of this, R & D results are accumulating and cannot find an outlet either at the association or at other enterprises of the branch. The share of new products originating in the NPO and assimilated into series production has also declined in recent years at Elektroapparat and Kondensator. More than half of the workload of series production facilities at some NPOs deals with assignments that have nothing to do with the activities of their own R & D units and sometimes even fall outside the specialized profiles of the associations. NPOs having major enterprises of series and mass production have shown a strong tendency to become interested mainly in improving production indicators and not in accelerating innovation. To weaken the desire to maintain production runs of the same items and to encourage greater product mix and renewal, a new rule has been introduced. If an NPO issues a particular product more than three years, deductions to its incentive funds are then reduced by 50 percent.[44]

On the other hand, many specialists insist equally strongly that series or batch production is an integral part of the NPO. The role of series production facilities is not to increase industrial output but to serve as an arena within which the NPO can test and perfect its innovations under actual production conditions. If NPOs lack series production capability, this forces them to transfer the assimilation of new products and processes to other organizations that prolongs the process and reduces the quality of innovation. A proponent of this view is Dr. Kim Isaevich Taksir of the Academy's Institute of Economics and one of the foremost authorities on NPOs. It is precisely the capacity to produce unique or small batches of new technological items, he claims, that distinguishes the NPO from a complex research institute.[45] V. I. Shteingauz and V. N. Arkhangelskii share a similar opinion. Without this function, the latter points out, the NPO is excluded from the most important stage connected with the implementation of R & D results and cannot perform its role of connecting link between science and industry. Other Soviet writers also maintain that when the NPO concentrates mainly on "preproduction" work, it cannot really qualify as a "science-production" association.[46]

Differences of view—though less sharply defined—also exist with respect to the place of the NPO at the research end of the innovation process. For that matter, there is no agreement in the Soviet Union about the place and role of basic research generally in the "research-production cycle."[47] Until recently, major NPOs like Pozitron themselves performed fundamental research at the level of nearly 10 percent of their total scientific research effort. It became necessary to abandon this practice by the mid-1970s, however. While a few NPOs still engage in some exploratory research, the majority rely upon institutes of the Academy to

[44] See Dzhavadov, "NPO—forma integratsii nauki, tekhniki, proizvodstva," p. 37; Yu. V. Subotskii, *Razvitie obedinenii v promyshlennosti: Voprosy teorii i metodologii* (Moscow, 1977), pp. 66-67; V. Kochikian and V. Kushlin, "Osnovy khoziaistvennogo rascheta v nauchno-proizvodstvennykh obedineniiakh," *Planovoe khoziaistvo,* 7 (1977):25-26; Taksir, *NPO,* p. 39; Pokrovskii, "Perestraivaias' na marshe," p. 2.

[45] Taksir, *NPO,* pp. 35, 39-40.

[46] Shteingauz, *Ekonomicheskie problemy,* p. 124; V. N. Arkhangelskii, *Planirovanie i finansirovanie nauchnykh issledovanii* (Moscow, 1976), pp. 158-60.

[47] Iu. Kanygin and S. Kostanian, "Nauchno-proizvodstvennyi tsikl," *Voprosy ekonomiki,* 12 (1976):61.

conduct fundamental research for them on the basis of contracts.[48] Befitting their role and development as "branch" institutions, NPOs focus predominantly on applied R & D.[49]

At the same time, the scope and volume of scientific research and development vary considerably among NPOs. In some associations the share of R & D may be less than 10 percent of the total cost of production activity while in others it may account for as much as 50 percent. Table 1 reveals this range of diversity for a few selected associations.[50] Some specialists believe that a fixed percentage should be established for the ratio of "science" to "production" activity as a mandatory condition for the functioning of NPOs. Though he disagrees with this view, Taksir notes that when a complex is headed by a small research institute which conducts an insignificant volume of R & D (less than 10-12 percent), then the NPO is generally unable to direct effectively the research-production cycle. Arkhangelskii also stresses that experience has shown that the capacity of the R & D center must be nearly 20 percent of the production capacity for an NPO to perform successfully its various functions.[51]

TABLE 1
The Share of R & D and of Industrial Production in NPOs
(expressed in terms of total cost)

NPO	R & D	Industrial Production
Plastpolimer	24.0	76.0
Pishchepromavtomatika	23.2	76.8
Elektroapparat	10.0	90.0
Elektrokeramika	6.0	94.0
Bummash	20.3	79.7
Pozitron	33.0	67.0

SOURCE: K. I. Taksir, *NPO*, p. 110.

[48] Mikhnevich, *Ekonomicheskie problemy upravleniia nauchno-tekhnicheskim progressom*, p. 57.

[49] B. E. Paton, president of the Ukrainian Academy of Sciences, has raised the idea of creating a new academy-based research complex called an academy scientific-technical association (*akademicheskoe nauchno-tekhnicheskoe obedinenie*), which could encompass the spectrum from fundamental research to the production of experimental prototypes. This proposal was supported at a meeting of the USSR Academy in late 1976 by A. P. Aleksandrov, president of the Academy. See *Vestnik Akademii nauk SSSR*, 2 (1977):51, 57.

[50] This information is cited by Taksir, *NPO*, published in 1977, but it may be substantially out of date. These same percentages were used by Bliakhman and Ivanov in their 1971 article, "Nauchno-proizvodstvennoe obedinenie kak forma sistemnoi organizatsii tsikla 'issledovanie-proizvodstvo'," p. 44.

[51] Taksir, *NPO*, p. 111 and Arkhangelskii, *Planirovanie i finansirovanie*, p. 162.

This aspect acquires special importance, because the NPO is intended to serve as the scientific-technical center for the branch or subbranch in the area of its specialization. In fact, this is seen as a distinguishing feature of the NPO that differentiates it from a production association and other research and production complexes that may also contain R & D subdivisions. In the NPO these units are expected to conduct general-purpose or branchwide R & D, developing innovation for the industrial branch as a whole. In production associations, however, scientific organizations are usually of local significance and confine their research-development-innovation work primarily to the production needs of the associations. The "head" organization is also different in these two kinds of structures. While this role belongs to an industrial enterprise in the production association, it is performed generally by a powerful research institute in the science-production association.

As branch Science and Technology (S & T) centers, NPOs are assigned several tasks. Their responsibilities include, for example, long-range planning of the main directions of research; developing forecasts and programs to solve the most important scientific and technical problems in the branch, especially those related to improving production efficiency and product quality; and making recommendations about the use of R & D results in both the branch and the economy as a whole. NPOs are expected to coordinate scientific research, experimental design, and engineering work done by other organizations and production associations in their spheres of specialization, regardless of the departmental affiliation of these units. In addition, they perform other branchwide services, such as supplying scientific and technical information, doing economic analysis and engineering feasibility studies, conducting work on patents and licensing, setting branchwide technical standards, forecasting the demand for new products and processes, and providing management training and advice on production organization with respect to new technology. The associations are also expected to develop and provide special services for introducing new technology, its assembly, start-up, and adjustment to other enterprises and organizations.[52] In exercising these functions, the NPO clearly assumes (or shares) certain of the responsibilities formerly held by the ministry technical administration and other staff units.

To be sure, several NPOs do perform these tasks and act as the principal organizers of technical progress in their branches. Soiuznauchplitprom,

---

[52] These tasks are listed in the statute on the NPO. See "Polozhenie o nauchno-proizvodstvennom obedinenii," *Sobranie postanovlenii pravitelstva SSSR*, 2 (1976):24-25. See also Subotskii, *Razvitie obedinenii*, p. 67 and Dzhavadov, "NPO—forma integratsii nauki, tekhniki, proizvodstva," pp. 38-39.

for example, plays this role in the wood-processing industry. One hundred and five enterprises of the USSR Ministry of Timber and Wood Processing Industry and 67 enterprises of other ministries produce items developed by the NPO. Mikrobioprom is the S & T headquarters for the micro-biological industry. More than 70 enterprises work on projects originating at the association. Plastpolimer is the leading center for plastics and has overall responsibility for high pressure polyethelenes, polystyrenes, fluoroplastics, and polyvinylacetates. Between 1969 and 1973 the NPO introduced 117 technological innovations into Soviet industry. More than 300 sugar plants in the USSR produce products that utilize developments of the NPO Sakhar. In the cryogenic engineering industry nearly 90 percent of all machinery and equipment produced is based on designs developed at the industry's NPO Kriogenmash. In radio electronics Pozitron is the S & T center. Ritm occupies this position in shipbuilding. During the Ninth Plan (1971-75) 40 percent of all improvements in labor productivity at shipbuilding enterprises were to be based upon the application of engineering ideas developed at the NPO.[53]

It is also clear that not all NPOs serve as the scientific and technical headquarters for their branches. Some associations serve only a few enterprises and contain very small R & D units. Others that do exercise branchwide functions do not provide all the special services mentioned above. Some NPOs are unable to perform broad S & T responsibilities, because they lack a research institute altogether or, if one is present, it is not the leading link in the association.[54]

These basic differences in perception and practice, moreover, find expression in the structure of science-production associations. Not surprisingly, a variety of institutional forms have evolved. While as many as six or seven separate kinds of NPOs are described by some specialists, they generally fall into three main types: (1) a technical or scientific-technical association, which engages in general prototype development and innovation; (2) a science-production association per se, which conducts R & D, prototyping, testing, first series production, and assimilation of new products and equipment; and (3) a production-technical association, which is occupied primarily with the assimilation, assembly, installation, and debugging of new processes and products.[55] As Taksir points out, however, what are called scientific-technical associations are essentially complex scientific research institutes, while production-technical associations are really specialized organizations for the introduction

[53] Taksir, *NPO*, pp. 43-79.

[54] Ibid., pp. 38-39, 74-79; Kushlin, *Uskorenie vnedreniia*, p. 111.

[55] For a description of the various kinds of NPOs, see Nolting, *The 1968 Reform*, p. 17, and Taksir, *NPO*, pp. 29-34.

of new technology. Neither type envelops the entire research-production cycle.[56]

Generally speaking, NPOs are mergers in various combinations of branch scientific research institutes, design bureaus, project-design and development engineering organizations, experimental plants, industrial enterprises for series production, assembly, start-up, and installation facilities, centers for management training, divisions for various scientific-technical services, and so on. It is not necessary for an NPO to contain *all* of these units, however. Table 2 gives information about the structural makeup of fifteen leading NPOs. All these associations include both a

TABLE 2

The Structural Composition of Selected Science-Production Associations

Name of the NPO	Subdivisions Included in the Association							
	Scientific Research Institute	Design Bureau	Design-Technological Bureau	Project Organization	Experimental Production Plant	Series Production Facility	Assembly, Startup and Installation Organization	A Training and Methods Center
Agropribor	+	−	+	+	+	+	−	−
Soiuznauchplitprom	+	−	+	+	+	+	+	−
Sakhar	+	+	−	−	+	+	−	−
Sistema	+	−	+	+	+	+	−	−
Istochnik	+	−	−	+	+	+	−	−
Mikrobioprom	+	−	−	+	+	+	−	−
Soiuzsteklomash	+	−	+	+	+	+	−	−
Znamia Truda*	−	+	−	−	+	+	−	−
Plastpolimer	+	+	−	+	+	+	−	−
Bummash	+	−	−	−	+	+	−	−
Pozitron	+	+	+	−	+	+	−	−
Pishchepromavtomatika	+	+	−	+	+	+	+	+
Ritm	+	−	−	−	−	+	−	−
Soiuzavtomatstrom	+	−	−	−	−	+	+	−
Turan	+	−	−	−	+	+	−	−

SOURCE: Taksir, *Nauchno-proizvodstvennye obedineniia*, p. 34.

* The head organization of the NPO is the Central Design Bureau for Construction Engineering, which is essentially a scientific research institute.

[56] Taksir, *NPO*, p. 32.

scientific research institute and a series production unit. Thirteen have an experimental production capability. Other evidence suggests, however, a less uniform picture for NPOs as a whole. In a study of forty NPOs, V. I. Kushlin notes that 10 percent had no series production unit, while 8 percent lacked a scientific research subdivision. Eighteen, or 45 percent, of the NPOs had no experimental production or testing facility.[57]

Particularly absent, it seems, are facilities such as start-up and adaptation organizations and training centers that can promote more rapidly and effectively the implementation of R & D results. A few NPOs, like Pishchepromavtomatika (food processing), Soiuznauchplitprom, and Impuls (minicomputers) have established special services that help introduce new products and processes directly at customer enterprises and train their personnel in the use and repair of technology. Other associations have created at series plants of their branches special departments (affiliate services of the NPO), which include design engineers and technologists who assist the plants in retooling and manufacturing new products.[58] In general, though, this set of important functions is not yet being performed by the majority of NPOs.

Underlying these issues of the optimal structure, composition, and functions of science-production associations is the problem of what in American business terminology is called product differentiation. Given the array of new structural designs and associational forms that have evolved since the late 1960s, the NPO has had difficulty in gaining and maintaining a distinct identity. Lacking a precise definition of the NPO, some ministries have been rather arbitrary in classifying and creating the new complexes. What are labeled NPOs are, in fact, production associations or complex scientific institutions. Some NPOs have experienced difficulty in preserving their fundamentally dual character. Overdevelopment of their scientific functions turns the NPO into a traditional research institute, only larger. Hypertrophy of production operations, on the other hand, transforms the complex into a production association. The problems of maintaining a "dialectical unity" of functions have led some experts to press for some kind of fixed ratio or at least minimum levels regulating these activities.[59]

The problem of product differentiation is made all the more difficult because in some instances it is practically impossible to distinguish between an NPO and a production association that contains its own large R & D complex. For example, the Uralmash Production Association includes a scientific research and engineering design institute of heavy

[57] Kushlin, *Uskorenie vnedreniia*, p. 111; Pokrovskii, "Perestraivaias' na marshe," p. 2.

[58] Taksir, *NPO*, pp. 48-49, 139-40.

[59] Ibid., pp. 32, 37, and *Problemy sovershenstvovaniia upravleniia sotsialisticheskoi ekonomikoi* (Moscow, 1976), pp. 135-36.

machine building, which has more than six thousand workers and does business by contract with more than sixty R & D establishments in the country. During the Ninth Plan the association developed more than one hundred prototypes of new machines and equipment. Other POs which conduct major scientific research and development include AvtoZIL, Svetlana, and Elektrosila. The distinction becomes especially fine when a production association creates new products in small series or single lots and is one of the major producers of this type of product, as in the case of Elektrosila.

On another level, the relations of science-production associations with higher ministerial authorities are not uniform and regularized. In some branches there is no permanent body to lead NPOs. Where such organs exist they sometimes fail to take into account the distinct features of individual associations and regard them as all alike. Some ministries and agencies approach NPOs as ordinary research institutes or industrial enterprises. The lines of subordination also vary. A few NPOs such as Soiuznauchplitprom and Mikrobioprom report directly to the ministry (frequently to a deputy minister). The majority, however, operate on a three-link system (NPO—*glavk*/industrial association—ministry). They report either to one of the *glavki* or main administrations in their respective ministry or to an all-union industrial association. Plastpolimer provides an example of the latter pattern, which will probably become more common as the ministries reorganize and the *glavki* are liquidated or transformed into industrial associations. The majority of NPOs function as the first link of management. Yet a number of them conduct from 30 to 100 percent of all R & D done in the branch. In addition some NPOs are essentially all-union associations. These differences are not reflected in their legal status, however. This causes some specialists to argue that certain NPOs should have additional powers and prerogatives in comparison with other NPOs.[60]

Internal organizational development has also been marked by problems and diversity. The key issue here has been the degree of legal authority to be exercised by the central management or head organization as against that retained by the constituent units. "The criteria for establishing a happy median between loose or formal merger and overcentralization of decision making are apparently difficult to arrive at," observes Louvan Nolting.[61] The aim of creating these new complexes, it will be recalled, is to break down structural barriers, to bring the multiple participants in innovation into close association and even under common administration.

[60] Taksir, *NPO*, pp. 36, 55-56, 78, 157-58; Shteingauz, *Ekonomicheskie problemy*, p. 124; Tabachnikas, "Ot edinstva," pp. 22-23.
[61] Nolting, *The 1968 Reform*, p. 16.

Meanwhile, two negative tendencies found expression in the institutional evolution of NPOs up to 1976. On the one hand, integration stopped far short of the model of a truly unified system. Amounting to little more than a mechanical conglomerate of autonomous units, the NPO was transformed into "an administrative superstructure, a superficial link on the path from the ministry and *glavk* to science and production."[62] Even among the earliest and most touted NPOs institutional consolidation was slow and incomplete. An investigation of nine major NPOs by the Institute of Economics in 1974 found that a council of directors had not yet been formed in three of the complexes. One still lacked a scientific-technical council for the association.[63]

On the other hand, centralization was sometimes carried to an extreme. Constituent units of an NPO were denied any autonomy, even in operational management and control. This situation proved especially debilitating when the association contained subdivisions that were highly diverse and geographically dispersed. As a result the NPO became unmanageable. The decision process became frozen as each unit was forced to go to the highest levels and much time was lost in getting agreements and approvals. In short, association members became caught in the familiar bureaucratic chain from which they were supposedly to be liberated.[64]

Of these two tendencies, the first was the most dominant. The retention of autonomy by component parts almost everywhere impeded, if not prevented, the development of an integrated planning and management structure for the association as a whole. Indeed, this was the conclusion that several NPOs, including Ritm and Pishchepromavtomatika, drew after two or three years of operation.[65] The pressure subsequently mounted on Moscow authorities to impose greater centralization. The official statute on the NPO, which was finally approved by the USSR Council of Ministers on December 30, 1975, stipulates that all units joining an NPO lose any legal autonomy. At the same time, the ministries and union republic officials have been given some discretion in applying this requirement, and they continue to make it the exception rather than the rule.[66] By 1981 most NPOs still do not control their member organizations and operate as constitute single units. Internal divisions within

---

[62] Sominskii and Bliakhman, *Ekonomicheskie problemy*, pp. 188-89, and Dzhavadov, "NPO—forma integratsii nauki, tekhniki, proizvodstva," p. 40.

[63] Taksir, *NPO*, pp. 54-55.

[64] Sominskii and Bliakhman, *Ekonomicheskie problemy*, p. 189, and Gavrilov, *Ekonomika i effektivnost' nauchno-tekhnicheskogo progressa*, p. 296.

[65] B. Tabachnikas and M. Skliar, "Khoziaistvennyi raschet nauchno-proizvodstvennykh obedinenii," *Voprosy ekonomiki*, 12 (1976):73, and Gavrilov, *Ekonomika i effektivnost' nauchno-tekhnicheskogo progressa*, pp. 295-96.

[66] "Polozhenie o NPO," p. 23.

NPOs are compounded by divisive forces bearing on each of the units from outside, imposed by higher authorities, usually separate ones, to which they continue to report.[67] Nor are NPOs recognized yet by the Central Statistical Administration as a distinct entity. All accounting continues to be done strictly according to individual structural subunits.[68]

On the whole, centralization of planning and management functions within science-production associations remains both uneven and incomplete. Professor Dzhavadov goes so far as to assert, "Practice shows that NPOs are created on the basis of existing research institutes, design bureaus, and enterprises without any radical changes in the structure of management."[69] A few associations like Plastpolimer have built new and separate management bodies to run the complex. However, the majority organize administration around the managerial staff of the head unit. As a rule, this structure is too small and inadequate for servicing the association. Additional personnel from other subdivisions of the NPO must be brought in to beef up existing departments or to form new administrative sections at the head organization. Since no unified staff list has been developed for the management of NPOs, each person is paid according to the salary scale and bonus system of his particular subdivision. Wages and incentive systems are not the same in research institutes and production units. As a result, association executives doing identical work are frequently paid in different ways, and they are motivated to fulfill different indicators and in varying degrees.[70] Not surprisingly, these factors have impeded the recruitment and development of a strong and competent management team for the NPOs. To help remedy the situation the official statute on science-production associations gives to the general director of an NPO greater powers to apply more flexible wage structures and to effect organizational change. The ministries have also been permitted to raise the salaries of managerial officials by 10 to 15 percent at the largest NPOs.[71]

[67] See the excellent discussion on NPOs by Thane Gustafson, *Selling the Russians the Rope? Soviet Technology Policy and U.S. Export Controls* (Santa Monica, 1981), pp. 42-50.

[68] Gustafson, *Selling the Russians the Rope*, p. 44, and Yurii P. Inin, "Rol' i otvetstvennost' NPO," *Ekonomicheskaia gazeta*, no. 31 (1981):7.

[69] Dzhavadov, "NPO—forma integratsii nauki, tekhniki, proizvodstva," p. 41.

[70] Arkhangelskii, *Planirovanie i finansirovanie*, pp. 168-69; Taksir, *NPO*, p. 56.

[71] "Polozhenie o NPO," pp. 53-55; "Postanovlenie Soveta Ministrov SSSR ob utverzhdenii Polozheniia o nauchno-proizvodstvennom obedinenii," *Sobranie postanovlenii pravitelstva SSSR*, 2 (1976):19-20; A. Vershinina, "Nauchno-proizvodstvennye obedineniia i stimulirovanie tekhnicheskogo progressa" *Sotsialisticheskii trud*, 7 (1976):32-36. For a discussion of how the NPOs Burevestnik (Leningrad) and Analitpribor (Tbilisi) have tried to cope with these problems, see the trip report prepared for the National Science Foundation by Morris Bornstein, et al., *The Planning and Management of Industrial Research and Development in the USSR* (Washington, D.C., 1980), pp. 1-7, 17-24.

Planning and financing are two areas in particular where NPOs have major problems. As regards the first, long-range planning is still undeveloped in the associations. Though a few like Plastpolimer have drawn up plans for five years and scientific forecasts for twenty-five to thirty years in areas of their specialization, they are clearly the exception. It is said to be possible now to have in the NPOs truly major projects extending over the long term rather than minor themes as prevailed in R & D units in the past. So far, however, medium-range planning has been minimal. During the Ninth Plan, in fact, NPOs received five-year plans only for production, not for R & D, which continued to be conducted mostly on an annual basis.[72] Nor have NPOs been successful in integrating research-development-innovation-production plans for the complexes as a whole. Ministries and higher planning bodies have persisted in issuing plans to separate NPO units rather than to the association leadership. Work plans are approved "in pieces," at different times and by different deputy ministers or administrative divisions in the branch, and they are brought to the association without being coordinated.[73] By the early 1980s science policy experts and NPO managers were still complaining that the associations lack a single and well-integrated plan.[74]

Divided authority and fragmented administration also prevail in financial matters. As a rule, NPOs have no centralized funds and reserves. Financing is done through multiple channels, and resources are allocated separately to each subdivision. Characteristic of Soviet budgeting generally, financing is oriented to maintaining institutions (research institutes, design bureaus, and enterprises) and not to supporting programs and projects. At least until recently the central management or head organization of NPOs lacked authority to redistribute assets, investments, and funds of the constituent units.[75] Development of a unified incentive structure has also been a special problem. Up to now each subdivision formed and spent its own fund for material incentives and the NPO did not have any right to these funds. As a result, top management could not utilize these resources or part of them as an economic instrument. Furthermore, the magnitude of bonus payments for developing new technology varies substantially among subdivisions, reflecting their different orientations and interests. The absence of unified funds and more uniform bonuses has prevented NPOs from using monetary incentives to get as-

[72] Tabachnikas and Skliar, "Koziastvennyi raschet NPO," p. 73.

[73] Taksir, *NPO*, p. 77; Nolting, *The 1968 Reform*, p. 16.

[74] Tabachnikas, "Ot edinstva," pp. 22-25, and Inin, "Rol'i otvetstvennost' NPO."

[75] K. I. Dubrovskii and Yu. Yu. Ekaterinoslavskii, *Upravlenie nauchno-tekhnicheskim razvitiem proizvodstvennykh obedinenii: Informatsionnyi aspekt* (Moscow, 1976), pp. 18-20; Dzhavadov, "NPO—forma integratsii nauki, tekhniki, proizvodstva," pp. 42-43; Nolting, *The 1968 Reform*, p. 16.

sociation members to pull in the same direction.[76] To enable the NPOs to overcome these problems and to apply economic stimulation as a means of promoting throughout the complexes planning and management by objectives, Kremlin authorities adopted new regulations in the fall of 1976. These decisions set down new guidelines for the formation and utilization of common bonus funds in NPOs.[77] Nonetheless, an editorial in *Pravda* on January 12, 1978, devoted to a ten-year assessment of this institution, observed, "There is [still] no precise financial and economic system that, taking into account the distinctive characteristics of the association, could provide a solid support for the organic merging of science and production, and promote the efficient development of new technology." Although a few NPOs have since made some progress in dealing with these matters, financial policy and management remains a critical problem area.

Underlying these problems of the continuing fragmentation of planning, finance, and management of the NPOs are serious methodological questions about how to evaluate these structural entities coupling science with production. Basically, new integrated performance criteria have not been devised. This explains partly, in fact, why ministries and higher planning and financial agencies persist in issuing plans and funds to separate NPO subdivisions. Many performance indicators still relate to the activities of R & D and production units in their previously independent status. Existing indicators do not differentiate between R & D subdivisions that belong to NPOs and those that do not. According to current methods of accounting and statistical reporting, it is not possible to aggregate the results of activity of organizations that relate to material production and to the world of nonproduction.[78]

To be sure, some efforts are being made in this direction. Some norms have been devised for determining the average length of the research-production cycle and are used in measuring performance of NPOs. According to Tabachnikas and Skliar, however, these norms are established rather arbitrarily, largely "by eye." No fixed and uniform methodology exists yet for this purpose. In other associations indicators are used to determine the degree to which the research-production process has been

[76] Arkhangelskii, *Planirovanie i finansirovanie*, p. 162; Taksir, *NPO*, pp. 111-13.

[77] For the text of the regulation, see "Polozhenie o poriadke obrazovaniia i ispolzovaniia fondov ekonomicheskogo stimulirovaniia nauchno-proizvodstvennykh obedinenii," *Ekonomicheskaia gazeta*, no. 36 (September 1976): 15-16. For the procedures for awarding bonuses, see ibid., nos. 48 (November 1976) and 49 (December 1976):1.

[78] See Tabachnikas, "Ot edinstva," pp. 25-27; Inin, "Rol'i otvetstvennost' NPO," and Nolting, *The 1968 Reform*, p. 16; Gavrilov, *Ekonomika i effektivnost'*, pp. 297-305; B. Tabachnikas and M. Skliar, "Otsenka raboty i printsipy obrazovaniia fonda material-nogo pooshchrenniia nauchno-proizvodstvennykh obedinenii," *Planovoe khoziaistvo*, 2 (1974):123-24.

reduced over time. Taksir points out, however, that this kind of norm is of dubious value because reduction of the innovation cycle obviously has a limit.[79] What methodological progress has been made in devising integrated evaluative indicators and norms for NPOs is still largely confined to experiments. Not everyone realizes yet that the NPO is not simply the sum of its parts but represents a qualitatively new type of organization.

Looking back on the first decade of its life, therefore, we can say that this new institutional form has still not found its proper face and place in the Soviet scheme of things. Very few NPOs have approached—much less accomplished—the goal of creating an organizationally, technologically, and economically integrated system for promoting innovation. They have not yet in general successfully closed the gap between science and industry through organizational design. In most, "science" and "production" continue to lead separate lives. The administrative and psychological barriers between them have not been effectively broken down. Organization building has been marked by much confusion and diversity, not to mention bureaucratic opposition and lethargy. In the absence of clear guidelines from the center, branch ministries created NPOs as they saw fit, often obliterating the boundaries between different kinds of research and production complexes. Sometimes NPOs were put together without any systematic research and analysis of design and development problems. Little consideration was given to their place in the context of future directions and needs of the branch as a whole.[80] Initially, the lack of a formal statute permitted needed room for flexibility and experimentation. It also reduced the danger of putting these new structures into an organizational straitjacket and monolithic mold. More and more, however, the absence of a document establishing the legal status of the NPO and defining its basic functions and principles of organization had prevented the solution of a number of complex problems. The associations were recognized as being frozen in their units, forms, and relations.

A new stage of development came in 1976. After confirmation of the NPO statute, Kremlin authorities stepped up efforts to impose greater clarity, order, and direction in the affairs of the associations. A drive was launched to make the Tenth Five-Year Plan a period of "development not only in the breadth but also in depth" for research and production complexes of all kinds, and not just NPOs. As regards the latter specifically, their number was to grow to between 200 and 250 by 1980.[81]

On the whole, however, implementation efforts have been slow and

---

[79] Tabachnikas and Skliar, "Khoziaistvennyi raschet NPO," p. 77, and Taksir, *NPO*, pp. 101-2.

[80] Gavrilov, *Ekonomika i effektivnost'*, pp. 294-95, and Mikhnevich, *Ekonomicheskie problemy*, pp. 71, 85.

[81] Subotskii, *Razvitie obedinenii v promyshlennosti*, p. 5, and Taksir, *NPO*, p. 158.

half-hearted. Little institutional or bureaucratic breakthroughs have been made. In this regard the situation at the NPO Sistema of the Ministry of Tractor and Farm Machinery, reported in *Pravda* in March 1978, is instructive. Despite the fact that the NPO was formed eight years before, its assistant general director admitted, "There are certain shortcomings and rough edges since Sistema is still trying to find itself." Indeed, to date the association, we are told, had produced almost no articles relating to automated control systems, the area of its alleged specialization. Detailing a "list of all kinds of foul-ups and absurdities" in the NPO's activity, the *Pravda* reporters attributed most of these problems to a pro forma approach taken when the association was created. "Ministry officials gave no thought to the necessary correspondence between the form and content of the new research and production association." The reporters added, "It was assumed that in time everything would work itself out and fall into place. But, as we see, this has not happened. Now, eight years later, no one in the ministry wants to admit the mistake, since such an admission would make it necessary to name the specific parties responsible for such an unsuccessful experiment. As a result, a search is underway for all sorts of half-measures to get the hastily formed association moving." In concluding their piece of investigative reporting, the authors noted that Sistema's unlucky story is by no means exceptional. "Nowadays calling a research institute merely an institute or a plant merely an enterprise seems clumsy, an admission of one's backwardness," they say.[82] In the era of the scientific and technical revolution, organizational nameplates must be changed to keep pace with the times.

At the same time, expectations for the NPOs seem to have cooled in recent years. Much of the initial optimism that surrounded them has dissipated. The accumulation of a variety of unresolved problems in the course of their development has diminished the institutional glow of the NPO as a possible panacea for the innovation problem. As one Soviet observer noted already in the summer of 1976, "One can hardly find now defenders for the view that every branch institute should be turned into an NPO. The opinion is growing slowly but steadily that the number of NPOs in industry cannot be big, perhaps three or four in one ministry." "And if this is so," he continued, "then it is necessary to recognize directly that the NPO is a partial solution to the problem of [strengthening] the ties between science and production."[83] V. I. Shteingauz also concludes, "The NPO must be regarded as a successful but far from the only form of integrating research with production."[84] The NPO is still expected to play an important, and even increasing, role in accelerating innovation

[82] G. Ivanov and G. Iakovlev, "Under a New Name-Plate," *Pravda*, March 26, 1978.

[83] R. M. Shteinbok, "Komu vnedriat novuiu tekhniku," *EKO*, 6 (1976):78-79.

[84] Shteingauz, *Ekonomicheskie problemy*, p. 125.

and technical progress, but there is growing realization that other kinds of integrating structures will have to be developed and that each can contribute to innovation in different ways.

Applying R & D Results: The Institutionalization of Entrepreneurship

Along this line, Soviet interest has mounted in recent years in establishing a network of specialized innovation organizations whose task is explicitly the implementation and spread of new technology and production techniques.[85] Since this function is not the main job of either scientific or production organizations, a new type of institution is needed for this purpose that is neither a research institute nor an industrial enterprise, some specialists argue. They see innovation—the exploitation and application of new ideas and designs—as a distinct activity that is fundamentally different from both research and production. Hence, they maintain that new technology transfer vehicles are required to perform vital but neglected innovation functions. Such specialized organizations are depicted as new connecting links between science and industry, which serve as important "middlemen" facilitating and mediating the research-to-production process.[86]

Attention to these new structural forms has grown, in part because the science-production associations have proven to be more successful at creating new technology than at applying it. Although a few NPOs conduct extensive innovation activities, they are clearly the exception rather than the rule. The majority of associations lack the services and staff needed to perform these functions on any meaningful scale. NPOs have other limitations as well that prevent them from acting as a significant force for the mass introduction and diffusion of R & D results. The creation of NPOs strengthens the production ties of only a few research institutes. It does nothing for other branch R & D units that do not belong to the NPOs. They remain as isolated and insulated as before. Moreover, even the most specialized enterprise cannot be satisfied with the services of only one scientific organization to solve all the problems of its technological development. Since NPOs generally produce new items at best in small lots of a hundred or so, their volume of output is

---

[85] Such organizations have been given a variety of names: "innovation" or "introducing" firms (*vnedrencheskie firmy*), specialized associations for the introduction of new technology (*spetsializirovannye obedineniia po vnedreniiu novoi tekhniki*), and associations for scientific-technical services (*obedineniia po nauchno-tekhnicheskomu obsluzhivaniiu*).

[86] See Taksir, *Sushchnost' i formy soedineniia nauki s proizvodstvom pri sotsializme* (Moscow, 1974), pp. 92-104; V. Pavliuchenko, "Ot stola konstruktura do zavodskogo konveiera," *Pravda*, June 13, 1971, and his *Ekonomicheskie problemy upravleniia nauchno-tekhnicheskim progressom* (Moscow, 1973), pp. 202-13; Shteinbok, "Komu vnedriat novuiu tekhniku," pp. 76-85.

clearly insufficient for the needs of the branch as a whole. In addition, the NPOs are obliged to implement their own R & D. Their experimental production capacity is usually too small to handle research and engineering results produced by outside organizations. In short, the NPOs are closed and relatively confined complexes, walled off from many R & D organizations and production establishments in their branches. What is needed are organizations specializing exclusively in translating R & D results into practical use. They must be distinguished by their universality and capability of introducing ideas generated by many sources; they must be places where any R & D unit or industrial plant can turn for assistance.[87]

Actually, the idea of innovation firms is not new. Taksir describes five kinds of organizations that have evolved since the late 1960s and are oriented specifically to the utilization of new technology.[88] One type includes institutions, like Energotekhprom within the USSR Ministry of Power and Electrification, that are fully geared to develop and transfer R & D results into application. Established in 1965, this experimental production and engineering facility provides a broad array of innovation services in the amount of more than 14 million rubles a year. Besides installing and debugging new products and processes, Energotekhprom trains personnel at client enterprises. The firm also helps research institutes formulate their work agendas to incorporate specific requests from industry.

A second type of adaptation organization is of a more mixed profile. Along with introducing new technology, it also engages in repair and construction work. Examples include several associations that have been set up by the USSR Ministry of Non-Ferrous Metallurgy. Enterprises in this branch are generally not able to conduct technological modernization and improvements on their own. Some of these innovation associations have a specific technical specialty; Uralenergotsvetmet, for example, installs evaporative cooling equipment in metallurgical plants, pneumatic transport systems for loose and pulverized materials, and special pneumatic dust-collecting devices. Economic savings from the innovations by this one association alone are estimated to have been about 30 million rubles for the period 1971 to 1975.

Soiuztekhosnastika represents the third variety of introduction organization. This association deals mainly in the installation of different interbranch engineering devices. One of its chief tasks is the creation and

[87] Shteinbok, "Komu vnedriat novuiu tekhniku," pp. 70-80, and L. Davydov and R. Shteinbok, "Formy organizatsii vnedreniia novoi tekhniki," *Voprosy ekonomiki*, 9 (1977):134.
[88] See Taksir, *NPO*, pp. 24-25.

broad dissemination of a uniform system of standardized multipurpose assembly and readjustable equipment.

A fourth group of innovation organizations is made up of the Centers for Scientific Organization of Labor at various research institutes. Conducting all their work through economic contracts, these centers resemble, to a certain extent, management consulting firms in the West. They serve essentially as organizational intermediaries between R & D establishments and the world of production. Their business involves not only the introduction and diffusion of new technology but also the propagation of knowledge and advanced production experience. The Center for Scientific Organization of Labor and Production Management under the All-Union Institute of Economics and Labor Organization in the oil and gas industry falls into this classification.

From a Western perspective, the fifth category of introduction organization identified by Taksir is perhaps the most interesting. This group is comprised of what can best be described as profit-maximizing engineering or management consultant firms. They are created and sustained through largely private initiative of technological entrepreneurs seeking to exploit scientific advances. Offering a broad profile of services, these organizations exist essentially outside the formal economic system and beyond official planning and control. Paradoxically, this is both their greatest strength and their greatest weakness. In accord with the initial decentralizing spirit of the 1965 economic reforms, more than a dozen of these new technical firms sprang up across the Soviet Union. They included, for example, Fakel (The Torch) in Novosibirsk, Novator (Innovator) and Khikmet (Wisdom) in Baku, Neva in Leningrad, Iskra (The Spark) in Tomsk, Poisk (Search) in Severodonetsk, and Temp (Tempo) in Moscow. By the early 1970s, however, most of them were forced to close their doors. Others continue to lead a semilegal life. In general, these structures have not been stable and surviving additions to the Soviet science and technology establishment. This is not because they have been inefficient but, on the contrary, because their success and viability have not been acceptable in ideological and political terms.

Indicative of the nature and fate of these entrepreneurial ventures is the "tale of the Torch."[89] Fakel was set up by a few young scientists-entrepreneurs in 1966. It had no budget, no material supplies, no paid staff, and no office space. After compiling a list of prospective consultants and their specialties, the founders simply set up headquarters in a dormitory of the University of Novosibirsk and began soliciting contracts. Consultants would be chosen to work on problems in their spare time.

[89] See the excellent article by John Lowenhardt, "The Tale of the Torch: Scientists-Entrepreneurs in the Soviet Union," *Survey*, 20, no. 4 (Autumn 1974):113-21.

Various organizations were paid for the use of their equipment and facilities during nonworking hours. The Torch received 3.5 million rubles from 263 contracts for the period up to June 1970. Allegedly, the innovations introduced by it resulted in a savings of 35 million rubles. These included the development of "an optimal plan for forest exploitation" in Novosibirsk Province, a system of computer analysis of seismic materials for a local geological expedition, and an experimental model of a Torch-built swamp vehicle for oil exploration in the western regions of Siberia. Other projects were in such diverse fields as gold extraction, the use of manure, development of coloring substances, and of control devices for the Novosibirsk Power Station. Despite support from the Presidium of the Siberian Division of the Academy of Sciences, not to mention the local Komsomol authorities under whose wing Fakel formally operated, however, this efficient but unconventional organization came under strong attack and eventually closed down in May 1971.[90]

One of the few firms of this kind to have survived—in modified form—is Novator. Formed in 1967, it was reorganized by the leaders of the Azerbaidzhan Republic in 1971 and placed under the jurisdiction of the republic Trade Union Council. It has since been put under dual subordination to the republic Ministry of Local Economy and the State Committee on Inventions and Discoveries. Basically, the firm seeks and screens relatively simple "orphaned inventions" from institutes throughout the USSR that cannot exploit them. By 1976 Novator was doing an annual business of over a million rubles. Since its creation the firm has developed and disseminated more than 120 innovations. Some of these have been awarded state medals, and others have been displayed at the Leipzig international trade fair.[91]

Scientists in particular attempt recurrently to revitalize and legitimize these entrepreneurial firms. Recently in the Academy's main economic journal Taksir and M. Krasnokutskii argued that these institutions were viable and desirable. They urged that these products of private initiative be turned into state organizations with a firm legal basis.[92] Their recommendation has yet to find strong endorsement from the political leadership, however, and so far little action has been taken along this path. The central issue is the institutionalization, if not bureaucratization, of entrepreneurship. The problem is how to preserve these innovating forms without destroying their spontaneity, independence, and élan vital—the very foundation of their success. Some Soviet specialists recognize that

[90] Ibid., pp. 117-18.

[91] K. Taksir and M. Krasnokutskii, "Formy organizatsii vnedreniia novoi tekhniki," *Voprosy ekonomiki*, 1 (1977):50; V. Pokrovskii, "Novaia tekhnika: Dorogi i porogi," *Ekonomicheskaia gazeta*, no. 10 (1976):10.

[92] Taksir and Krasnokutskii, "Formy organizatsii vnedreniia novoi tekhniki," p. 50.

entrepreneurship is frequently associated with specific and special personality traits. Like R. M. Shteinbok, they reason then, "If there are people, there can be organizations as well."[93] The fundamental and problematical elements involved in institutionalizing the innovative spirit are not fully appreciated or addressed.

In general, all five kinds of innovation organizations are severely limited in their capacity for introducing new technology. There are very few of them. Their legal status remains ill-defined. No formal statute establishes their goals and functions, rights and responsibilities, organizational and administrative relations. Their activity is not properly planned, monitored, or stimulated.[94]

Since the Twenty-fifth Party Congress there has been renewed interest in expanding and developing this net of specialized innovation associations. A national conference devoted to the problems of accelerating innovation in the economy, held in Voronezh in December 1976, endorsed the idea of creating special diffusion organizations. A proposal was made to establish under the State Committee for Science and Technology a national center that would be responsible for organizing the practical utilization of R & D results. Such a center should exercise methodological leadership over specialized diffusion agencies as well as oversee the innovation services at production and science-production associations. Such centers, it was pointed out, do exist in other socialist countries, notably Hungary and Poland.[95] Meanwhile, also under consideration is a proposal to establish under the USSR State Committee on Inventions and Discoveries and the All-Union Exhibition of Achievements of the National Economy an interbranch association in charge of developing, testing, and making the first application of important inventions.[96] In short, the debate about and search for new forms of speeding technological modernization continues.

Soviet opinion remains hotly divided, however. Some commentators feel that structures specializing exclusively in innovation have a "right to exist." Given the constraints on existing production and research units, many recognize that new instrumentalities can be useful. Others stress that innovation is the proper function of production units. What is needed is a more favorable climate for innovation at plants. Indeed, the formation of special introduction facilities carries the possible danger that they, like R & D units in the past and even still today, will become organizationally separate from the production sector. As a result, a set of superficial links

[93] Shteinbok, "Komu vnedriat novuiu tekhniku," p. 80.

[94] Taksir, *Integratsiia nauki i proizvodstva pri sotsializme*, pp. 47-48.

[95] See *Voprosy ekonomiki*, 2 (1977):151-53; *Ekonomicheskaia gazeta*, no. 52 (1976):14; Taksir and Krasnokutskii, "Formy organizatsii vnedreniia novoi tekhniki," pp. 52-53.

[96] Pokrovskii, "Novaia tekhnika," p. 10.

may be created. Innovation functions themselves may become distorted and exaggerated, and lead to the introduction of unprofitable and unnecessary technological change. The vital interface problems that plague the research-to-production process today would not only persist but be compounded by still another set of administrative barriers.

Special innovation firms, therefore, should also be seen to be only a partial solution to the problem of modernization. As one Soviet observer notes, "Until the economy itself begins to work fully for the introduction of new technology, no organizational structures by themselves will guarantee success."[97] While there is growing awareness that new approaches and perhaps even radical organizational changes are needed to provide the stimuli, the incentives, and the opportunities for innovation, there is still no clear consensus about the shape these solutions should take. Though the important role of individual entrepreneurs is glimpsed, the art of fostering technological entrepreneurship is not well understood or developed. The care, feeding, and coupling of such creative people have not received prominent attention or analysis.

Innovation and the New Architecture of Linkage:
Complexities and Constraints

In the beginning of this chapter, I noted that technological innovation has long been a problem area in Russia and the Soviet Union. Since at least the mid-1960s a variety of steps have been taken to speed up the rate and to spread the incidence of technology transfer into the economy. Despite these efforts and some gains, however, the barriers to innovation have persisted. In Siberia the gap has grown between the number of ideas proposed for application by the Siberian Division of the Academy and the number being introduced. In the early 1960s nearly 25 percent of finished R & D recommended by the Division did not find practical application, then a decade later this figure had climbed to 40 percent.[98] A similar situation has developed in the Ukraine as well. Though the lead time between the ending of R & D and its introduction decreased between 1970 and 1975 in the USSR ministries of heavy machine building and of the electrical-engineering industry, this gap actually increased for

[97] *EKO*, 5 (1977):160. These differences of view are expressed in the debate in this issue of *EKO* (pp. 143-46) under the subject, "Komu vnedriat novuiu tekhniku?" This was the same title that Shteinbok used in his article in *EKO* the year before. The discussion in the May 1977 issue contains reactions and reflections to Shteinbok's article and call for specialized innovation organizations. By 1981 the debate was still not resolved and little headway had been made to restructure and reorient successfully the economy to promote technological innovation.

[98] Kanygin, *Nauchno-tekhnicheskii potentsial*, p. 243.

other all-union and union-republic ministries in the Ukraine.[99] Advances in science and technology have outpaced the ability of industry and of institutions to deal with them.

These developments have caused Soviet policy experts to take a consuming interest in integrating research more effectively with production. In approaching these coupling problems, they have given considerable attention to structure, to improving the architecture of linkage. Through new institutional forms and structural arrangements it is hoped that organization can be made a force that fosters rather than impedes innovation. Given the heavy emphasis on organizational issues and approaches, the key to innovation seems, at times, to be simply "management by structure."

As regards prospects for improvement, however, there are important complexities and constraints at work in the system that necessarily limit the effectiveness of structural solutions. These can perhaps be grouped into three broad areas. First, restructuring itself is a formidable task. Established organizational structures and processes have an inexorable momentum of their own, a built-in continuity difficult to break. Gvishiani writes, in fact, that Soviet science has a surplus of stability and even of conservatism. At the same time, he admits, "It is extremely hard to recast the structure of a scientific establishment that has taken decades to shape."[100]

Second, structure is an ambiguous variable that is not easily disentangled from other elements with which it interacts. Modifications in organization are usually accompanied by improvements in planning, the use of new incentive systems, the application of computers, and changes in personnel also. It is difficult, if not impossible, to determine the consequences and benefits of structural change alone. This is particularly true at present because the Soviet architecture of linkage is in transition. It is still evolving. Old structures and links are clearly ineffective and cumbersome. At the same time, new institutional forms and relationships have not yet acquired what in American political science terminology is called "enabling effectiveness." They are still largely experimental structures, coexisting with the old. Until they gain status, borne of the experience of their adequacy, these structural designs will continue to inhibit as much as they enable innovative action.

Finally, one should stress the importance of nonorganizational factors and broader environmental features that affect structural developments. The problems underlying innovation in the USSR—and elsewhere—are fundamentally human problems. People and relationships, not structure,

---

[99] V. P. Aleksandrova, *Problemy planirovaniia i effektivnosti razvitiia nauki i tekhniki v Ukrainskii SSR* (Kiev, 1976), pp. 53-54.

[100] Gvishiani, "The Scientific and Technological Revolution and Scientific Problems," pp. 55-56.

are the key. Proper attitudinal changes must keep pace with structural reforms. The creation of large integrated research-and-production complexes requires a psychological remolding of collectives that are used to working in isolated groups. Structure is merely a means for accomplishing purposes and overcoming obstacles. Inspiration, will, and teamwork are the real motive forces that bring about innovation.

On balance, the new architecture of linkage appears to be more supportive of innovation than the old mechanisms of technology transfer. Many basic problems, nonetheless, remain unresolved and incapable of solution by structural means alone. Though the 1970s brought conceptual changes and greater awareness of the multiplicity of factors involved in moving ideas from the laboratory into use, Soviet understanding of the innovation process is still incomplete. Above all, practice continues to lag behind perception. The major challenge facing Soviet leaders in the 1980s is to carry out and build upon the policy and structural designs they began to fashion in the last decade but then failed fully to implement. Success will depend ultimately as much on their political commitment and ability to break the bureaucratic barriers of complexity and inertia as on their imagination and ingenuity to frame effective innovation policies.

The Scientific-Technological Revolution and the Burden of Russian History

Since the mid-1960s the phenomenon perceived in the USSR as the contemporary scientific-technological revolution (STR) has become a major frame of reference for both Soviet domestic and foreign policies.[101] Under the spell of the STR, Kremlin leaders have come increasingly to see science and technology as the main pacemakers of modern industrial progress and the key pillars upon which to build the future of Soviet society. As Brezhnev emphasized on the occasion of the 250th anniversary of the USSR Academy of Sciences and repeated at the 1981 Party congress, "Socialism and science are indivisible. Only by relying on the latest achievements of science and technology is it possible to build socialism and communism successfully."[102] In responding to the challenges posed by the STR, Soviet leaders have begun to shift to a new development strategy that gives greater place to technological innovation as a source of economic growth. They have also taken steps to modernize the or-

[101] See Erik P. Hoffmann, "Soviet Views of the 'Scientific-Technological Revolution,' " *World Politics*, 30 (July 1978), and Paul Cocks, "Rethinking the Organizational Weapon: The Soviet System in a Systems Age," Ibid., 32 (January 1980).

[102] *Pravda*, October 8, 1975 and February 23, 1981.

ganization and structure of the research-to-production process in order to accommodate—indeed to facilitate—technological change.

Significantly, however, there has been little effort to modify the innovative spirit or to alter the essentially bureaucratic environment in which innovation takes place. Kremlin authorities have not abandoned their basically centralized approach to science and technology policy, even in face of the growing size and complexity of their R & D enterprise. On the contrary, they have pressed all the more strongly in the 1970s and the 1980s for new techniques and structures oriented to systems planning and management. Their commitment to central planning remains firm. "The scale and complexity of these problems," writes Gvishiani, "are such that in present-day conditions they can be tackled only on the level of state policy." Indeed, the prevailing view emphasizes, "It is necessary to centralize the management of technical progress more than any other area of economic management."[103]

For all practical purposes, the dominant Soviet approach to technological innovation remains fundamentally management-centered rather than entrepreneur- or market-centered. Just as industrial advance is the product of state initiative and administration, the spur to innovation also comes from central political authorities. State ownership of R & D results and detailed plans permit considerable direct government involvement and intervention throughout the research-to-production cycle. New products and processes are deliberately planned and introduced by administrative bodies. If they are not explicitly provided for in "the plan," innovations have little prospect of garnering the requisite supplies and services and thus little chance of success. Since the mode of advance is predominantly "innovation by order" from the top down, heavy reliance is placed on administrative levers and bureaucratic instruments to drive the whole process. Indeed, this fundamental characteristic of the system explains, in large part, the almost excessive Soviet concern with organizational and procedural solutions to science and technology problems.

Similarly, the integration of research, development, and innovation is basically a bureaucratic function assigned to and assumed by a many-headed hierarchy of special agencies. Decisions regarding the movement of research results are left to an administrative process. There is little direct collaboration among R & D performers. Most external transactions are managed through superior ministerial offices and departmental channels. Interorganizational connections are essentially administrative

[103] See D. Gvishiani, "The Scientific and Technological Revolution and Scientific Problems," p. 42; G. Kh. Popov, *Effektivnoe upravlenie*, p. 136. For more general discussion of these themes, see Paul Cocks, *Science Policy in the Soviet Union* (Washington, D.C., 1980), and "Rethinking the Organizational Weapon: The Soviet System in a Systems Age," *World Politics*, 32 (January 1980):228-57.

in nature. Linkage takes place primarily through formal directives and approvals. The accent throughout is on hierarchical organization, extensive use of rules, and multiple clearances. Within such an environment there is little room for informal contacts and autonomous entrepreneurial activity directed at promoting innovation. The tasks of production, procurement, and distribution are handled bureaucratically in the Soviet setting and not through any market mechanisms operating under conditions of independent actors and competitive alternatives as is the case in a free-enterprise system. In effect, entrepreneurial functions are exercised by bureaucratic authorities who serve as administrative gatekeepers at critical transfer points in the translation of scientific ideas into new products and processes.

Indeed, the difficulties met in organizing for innovation in the 1980s reflect the deep-seated distrust of spontaneity and strong regime bias against autonomous innovative action. On the one hand, authorities recognize the need for greater organizational flexibility and more decentralized modes of operation. On the other hand, bureaucratic uneasiness over a variety of structural forms and diversity of operating practices among the science-production associations persists and underlies continuing efforts to impose uniform solutions and monolithic forms on these new complex organizations. Similar biases and fears were evident in the closing down in the early 1970s of special innovation firms like The Torch that arose a few years before largely on private initiative and operated much like profit-maximizing entrepreneurial firms in the West. Contending that they are both viable and desirable additions to the architectural landscape, some spokesmen continue to press for the restoration of these special innovation and diffusion organizations but in the form of regularized state institutions operating on a fully legal basis. In general, suspicion still runs deep of any innovation activity that falls basically outside the formal system of planning, finance, management, and control.

On a broader level, current innovation practices and recent responses to the STR reflect not only distinctive Soviet influences but also the continuing effects of inherited Russian scientific traditions and patterns. Brezhnev's emphasis on the indivisibility of socialism and science echoes the definition of communism as "Soviet power plus electrification," formulated by Lenin more than half a century ago. Similarly, the "historic task" of combining organically the achievements of the STR with the advantages of the Soviet system, laid down by the Brezhnev leadership in 1971, has a familiar ring. Early in the life of the regime, Lenin, too, insisted, "The Soviet Republic must at all costs adopt all that is valuable in the achievements of science and technology. The possibility of building Socialism will be determined precisely by our success in combining the

Soviet government and the Soviet organization of administration with the modern achievements of capitalism."[104] The Bolshevik leader, however, was following the path taken by Russian rulers, as far back as Peter the Great, who looked to science and technology as indispensable tools for overcoming Russia's backwardness. The practice of using the bureaucracy to foster development and change is also a well-established pattern in Russian history. Indeed, the problem facing Kremlin leaders in the 1980s is largely the same one that has bedeviled their predecessors for centuries: "how to run a country effectively with the sole aid of an outmoded autocratic system, and at the same time aspire to modernization."[105]

To phrase the issue somewhat differently, the real challenge of the STR consists in breaking the continuity of history and developing within the Soviet system a capacity for innovation and adaptation that has been fundamentally lacking in the past. It is true that the Soviet Union has demonstrated remarkable innovative behavior in military technology. But the military sphere operates under different rules, motivations, and institutional arrangements from the civilian economy. Outside the defense sectors the regime has never been very successful at innovation and technical progress, except in a few select areas. The absence of an internal dynamic and adaptive capacity has resulted in the general pattern throughout Russian history of change largely by "fits and starts." Intermittently, the state is forced to administer the shocks of adjustment in the form of modernizing "revolutions from above." Typically, change is accomplished by heavy doses of technological borrowing from abroad and administrative coercion from within.

The extent to which Brezhnev's successors are able to master the STR and to overcome Russia's technological backwardness while avoiding the traditional "terror and progress" syndrome depends, in large measure, on how successful they will be in achieving breakthroughs in what have always been intractable problem areas in the past. Indeed the "scientific and technological revolution" itself, according to one prominent Western observer, "is the Soviet hope for a *deus ex machina* solution to the USSR's problems."[106] At issue from the Soviet perspective is not the question of building an "innovative society" per se, since the participation of "so-

[104] Cited in Merle Fainsod, "Bureaucracy and Modernization: The Russian and Soviet Case," in Joseph LaPalombara, ed., *Bureaucracy and Political Development* (Princeton, 1963), p. 252.

[105] Leonard Schapiro, *Rationalism and Nationalism in Russian Nineteenth-Century Political Thought* (New Haven and London, 1967), 168.

[106] Observation by Murray Feshbach in John R. Thomas and Ursula M. Kruse-Vaucienne, eds., *Soviet Science and Technology: Domestic and Foreign Perspectives* (Washington, D.C., 1977), p. 247.

ciety" in the innovation process is still seen in rather limited and controlled terms. Rather, the real issue turns on how to prod, persuade, teach, and transform the ruling establishment into an "innovative bureaucracy." Consciously or unconsciously, willingly or unwillingly, contemporary Soviet leaders—like their predecessors—are finding themselves thrust into the role of a modernizing elite. How able they are to perform as a new industrializing elite will depend substantially on how well they respond to the changing conditions and new demands of the times.

Significantly, as the USSR moves into the 1980s, Party agencies themselves are assuming a more activist and interventionist role in promoting technological modernization. The deepening involvement of Party organs underscores the inability of the regime to manage and execute its new strategy for science, technology, and economic growth, its failure to reorient effectively its structures and processes toward technical progress. To put the issue somewhat differently, the expansion of Party involvement is prompted both by design and by default. It is prompted in part by a conscious desire by the Party leadership to maintain the leading role of the Party in society and to increase Party control over that sphere of action which is developing the fastest, is the most visible, in which the country's prestige is deeply engaged, and which has the largest potentiality for influencing the future development of the USSR and its place in the international order but which also has fallen largely outside the Party's control. At the same time, however, this growing intrusion of Party organs is prompted in part by default as well—by the failure of the Brezhnev regime to implement meaningful reforms to improve the system's performance and capacity in innovation. Expanding the use of the Party to perform linkage and integration functions reflects the failure to erect effective coupling and coordination mechanisms within the system to facilitate and speed the innovation process. Here the Party is not so much usurping a role as trying to fill a functional and institutional void that continues to persist. Similarly, the increasing resort to traditional mobilization techniques and political pressure tactics, such as socialist competition, in S & T programs reflects the failure to build an adequate incentive structure for innovation.[107]

[107] For a discussion of this issue and recent developments, see Paul Cocks, "The Role of the Party in Soviet Science and Technology Policy," a report prepared for the National Council for Soviet and East European Research (Washington, D.C., 1980).

XVI

FRED V. CARSTENSEN
AND GREGORY GUROFF

Economic Innovation in Imperial Russia and the Soviet Union: Observations

Every society must confront the problem of ordering the use of its human, natural, and technological resources to satisfy the material needs of its members. That ordering of productive activities can take many forms. A broad typology of economic systems can differentiate those forms according to the degree to which economic units have autonomy in determining the uses and disposal of the factors of production and output under their jurisdiction. Such units can be individuals, firms, productive associations, *sovkhozy* or other corporate and associational forms. In the West, that autonomy of action has been relatively large, and Western societies have been polycentric with a substantial separation between economic and political spheres of activity. Russia, in contrast, appears to have largely retained, even in periods of rapid industrial expansion, an autocratic or patrimonial system (single-centered), which has sharply limited autonomy of economic units in the use and disposal of resources, and which has preserved for those in political control the right, if only de jure, to determine the pace and pattern of economic development.

While it is fruitful to differentiate systems on this macroeconomic level, there is an increasing recognition that all systems share fundamental properties—prices, decision rules, incentives, and organizations—within which individual actors must operate. Joseph Berliner's recent work[1] on innovation is the most salient example of this approach. Development economists such as T. W. Schultz[2] have expanded our theoretical and

---

[1] Joseph Berliner, *The Innovation Decision in Soviet Industry* (Cambridge, Mass., 1976).

[2] Theodore W. Schultz, "The Value of the Ability to Deal with Disequilibria," *Journal of Economic Literature*, no. 1 (1975):827-46.

empirical understanding of the concept of entrepreneurship to embrace all economic actors seeking to reorder their use of resources to maximize their utility on the basis of their values and within given systematic constraints. Both the persistence of an autocratic environment in Russia and our increased understanding of the entrepreneurial function invited the broad consideration of continuities and discontinuities in entrepreneurial response from Imperial Russia to the contemporary Soviet Union.

The conference of which these essays are the product was conceived of as an investigation of how Russian/Soviet society has addressed these fundamental allocative and organization issues. As part of such an investigation, we wanted to identify those aspects of Soviet economic behavior, particularly responses to problems of organization and economic growth, that are functional results of Communist ideology and central planning per se, and those that grow out of traditional Russian patterns. Unfortunately, such identification is not entirely feasible because the choice is not strictly dichotomous, thus muddying the analytical waters. Moreover, in the process of carrying through the conference, the focus subtly broadened from one primarily on enterprise management and the identification of the entrepreneurial individuals or groups to an assessment of how Russian/Soviet society has accomplished the functions normally associated with entrepreneurs. Within this perspective, we have still tried to keep in mind the central question of what elements represent historical continuity and which, for the Soviet period, reflect functional exigencies. It would be nice if the answers that the various contributors offer could be as simple and direct as the question. But, as should be clear from the preceding essays, each author approaches a topic from an individual perspective and often speaks only inferentially to the underlying issues. Nonetheless, taken as a whole the essays provide significant insights into and suggest a number of observations about the patterns of Russian/Soviet economic development. Some of these conclusions also challenge Alexander Gerschenkron's widely influential interpretative paradigm for the late imperial period, which emphasizes the critical leading role of the state in promoting industrial development.

The essays by Samuel Baron and Paul Cocks, which bracket this collection, suggest broad parallels if not continuity between sixteenth/seventeenth-century Imperial Russia and late twentieth-century Soviet Russia. Baron reveals how the rational Western observer, schooled in Western concepts of property, contract, and due process, saw the potentialities for economic development that the vastness of Russian resources offered; Cocks suggests how the continuing Soviet struggle to devise a command structure as effective as Western corporate forms invites the hope that Soviet institutions can accommodate efficient management principles. Yet, as each author argues, neither the resources nor the institutional reforms lived up to their promise for bringing the Russia of either period optimal economic growth. The political institutions and ideology in both periods restrained economic forces and actors from realizing their potential. Thus bracketed, the remaining essays, implicitly if not explicitly, assess the evolving sources of and strictures on entrepreneurial response.

The perspective that emphasizes the degree to which Russian society can be interpreted in terms of the dominance of traditional, ideological, or other hierarchical or state-centered values and institutions is in fact common to many studies. For example, Richard Pipes has suggested the Weberian concept of a patrimonial society is especially relevant to understanding the structure and function of Imperial Russian society to at least the 1880s. Such a patronage structure ultimately reached the central source of legitimacy in the tsar.[3] Boris Anan'ich, in his contribution to this volume, suggests a possible continuation of this pattern as the state bureaucracy and the tsar in the period from the 1880s to 1914 proved unable to accommodate themselves to the logic of economic development and preferred instead to cling to the vestiges of dominance and patronage. Sir John Hicks has characterized Imperial Russia in a complementary way as a "revenue state." He argues that the exigencies of raising large quantities of revenue to support the tsar, the bureaucracy and military corps took precedence over other objectives, constantly thwarting development of a vital autonomous sector.[4] Arcadius Kahan, in his assessment of the Witte program, first suggested just such a scenario and simultaneously questioned the accuracy of the Gerschenkron/Von Laue positive assessment of that program.[5]

This perspective, which relies primarily on the paradigm of the patrimonial system with its emphasis on the distinctions between Russian/Soviet experience and Western experience, has been applied to other periods as well. Hedrick Smith, in his incisive analysis of the pace, pattern, and perception of Soviet life, suggests the cultural and ideological distance that separates Soviet Russia from the West.[6] Smith, without specifying what the roots of such differences might be, argues that in some idiosyncratic ways Russians are similar to Westerners, but, if we may simplify the argument, Russians are culturally and ideologically as inscrutable to most Westerners as are the proverbial Chinese. Writing primarily as a journalist/humanist, Smith does imply that Russians are so different not strictly because they live within a Soviet society that is just the recent

---

[3] Richard Pipes, *Russia Under the Old Regime* (New York, 1974).

[4] Sir John Hicks, *A Theory of Economic History* (New York, 1969).

[5] Arcadius Kahan, "Government Policies and the Industrialization of Russia," *Journal of Economic History*, 27 (1967):460-77.

[6] Hedrick Smith, *The Russians* (New York, 1974).

creation of the Bolshevik Revolution or Five-Year Plans. Those differences are, it seems, the results of something imbedded deeply within the collective, historical Russian legacy of ideology, institutions, and culture. This is to argue neither that Russia was not influenced in important ways by the West nor that in every way Soviet Russia is but the continuation of Imperial Russia. Neither position would be tenable. It is to suggest that in critical ways Russian society has remained essentially hierarchical or patrimonial even as the Soviet system has changed the location and focus of entrepreneurial function and economic decision making.

Harold Berman, in his seminal study of Soviet justice, supports Smith's view. Berman, in seeking the roots of Soviet conceptions of law, argues that Russia did not share in the fundamental revolution in legal doctrine and judicial ideology that the Renaissance brought to both civil- and common-law traditions of Western Europe and North America.[7] Though Russian and Soviet law share with the West that common legal ancestor of Roman law, Berman stresses that in the West concepts of equity, reasonableness, and growth transformed the Roman legacy. Thus, Russian law had only a veneer of Western attachment, a veneer strengthened by the legal reforms of the 1860s, which were largely without lasting impact on the society.[8] It is also tempting to see in the irrationality of the planning apparatus that Gregory Grossman describes a reflection of those rigid formulaic legal traditions.

Scholars working on the pre-imperial period have tended to take a similar perspective, putting the Russian experience as one outside the mainstream of Western development. George Fedotov provides a striking example of this approach in his work on early Russian Christianity. He reveals how, in Russia, Christianity lost its individualistic drive, which was, as Tocqueville noted, so critical a component of its influence on Western culture, becoming instead a collective ideology subservient to the needs of the state.[9]

Western scholars have long had a more ambivalent view of the pattern of development during the imperial period. While acknowledging the extraordinary gulf that the Petrine reform created between the service-gentry elites and the serfs, peasantry, and lower classes, Western scholars have also been fascinated and partly persuaded by Russia's self-conscious attempts to Westernize herself. Only rarely have Western scholars wrestled with the full implications of Kliuchevskii's comment that Peter wanted to make the gentry "at home with foreigners"—i.e., with West Euro-

---

[7] Harold Berman, *Justice in the USSR* (New York, 1963).

[8] Richard Wortman, *The Development of Russian Legal Consciousness* (Chicago, 1976).

[9] George Fedotov, *The Russian Religious Mind* (New York, 1960). For similar interpretations see also Nicholas Berdiaev, *The Russian Idea* (New York, 1948), and James Billington, *The Icon and the Axe* (New York, 1964).

peans—but only made them "foreigners at home." For Kliuchevskii, as for Smith and Berman, Russia may occasionally show a face seemingly familiar to the Westerner, but it is a superficial appearance.

For the late imperial period, the ambivalence is surely most pronounced, especially in economic history. In part, this reflects the very substantial material progress Russia did achieve after 1880 and its primary role within the European political system during the whole of the nineteenth century. Perhaps it also reflects a desire by Western scholars to see Russia in 1917 as being on the verge of becoming a great economic power under a system of constitutional monarchy or democracy, a development that only the Bolshevik Revolution prevented. Soviet scholars have had no reason to disagree with such a view; for them the Bolshevik Revolution represented the fulfillment of a historical process, a process essentially defined by Marx, Lenin, and Luxemburg on the basis of European experience. But, as Alec Nove has cogently observed, the hope for Russia's metamorphosis into a Western-style polity with sustained economic expansion seems unreasonably optimistic.[10] Both Anan'ich and Ruth Roosa, in their contributions to this volume, emphasize strongly the inability of the imperial government to accommodate such changes and its successful resistance to a full participation by those individuals and groups seeking strong developmental policies and institutional changes.

We can illuminate their analysis with another example. In the first decade of the twentieth century, the tsarist government, under pressure from the business community, created an imperial commission to revise Russia's archaic corporate laws. After years of effort, marked by both cooperation and conflict between Russia's business community and state bureaucrats, the Commission reported in the summer of 1914. In early July, the tsar issued not the hoped-for regulations modernizing Russia's corporate laws, but rather regulations that limited the amount of land corporations could own outside of their own factories and set quotas on the percentage of "Jewish" capital in various organizations. The fact that the tsar was forced to rescind these regulations shortly after the war began did little to alleviate the feeling among the business community that this was one more act which confirmed that the tsarist regime was determined to maintain traditional structures and values, regardless of the cost to enterprise. As Ruth Roosa points out, the war began and continued amidst deep suspicion between Russia's business community and the government, which was manifest in the constant infighting over the War Industries Committees and the diminishing support the industrialists were willing to give the imperial regime.

Denial of the strength of the forces pushing Russia into a more West-

[10] Alec Nove, *An Economic History of the USSR* (London, 1969), p. 28.

ernized form (limited monarchy or democracy joined to a relatively open market) does not thereby confirm the Soviet interpretation. The papers in this volume suggest to us that the history of Russian economic growth was not simply a variant on the West European pattern of economic development and modernization. However one might see the question of the inevitability of the Bolshevik Revolution, it should not be interpreted as the unavoidable fulfillment of Western capitalist development. More important, recognition of the peculiarities of the Russian historical economic experience should remind us that Gerschenkron's influential concept of relative historical backwardness is not a culturally or ideologically bound paradigm. It is a typology of the expected interaction or interdependence between the level of development a country has achieved, in absolute terms and, critically, relative to its competitors, and the range of policy options and institutional mechanisms available to a state to carry out a policy of accelerating economic development, of reducing the relative backwardness. Europe, therefore, should be seen no more clearly in the Russian mirror than in the Indian or Japanese mirror.[11]

Economic historians have recently given increased attention to the importance of the legal structures in the West. The discussion has focused on forms of property and legal guarantees of mechanisms (contracts, torts, and due process) used to carry out market transactions. This work has emphasized that it was in significant measure a congenial legal environment, especially in England and America, which explains the strength of Western economic development. Berman identified precisely this difference in legal traditions as one of the salient factors separating the Russian historical experience from the Western. Baron's essay here emphasizes exactly this institutional environment and its attendant uncertainty as a critical ingredient in understanding the effective strictures on Russian entrepreneurship in his period.

Thomas Owen's discussion of the differing patterns in the use of corporate forms in St. Petersburg and Moscow suggests to us an interpretation along the same lines. The St. Petersburg enterprises adopted a Western form devoid of much of its Western content, which was associated especially with releasing economic energies. The St. Petersburg firms were often subservient to political needs and objectives, and often were the vehicles for government bureaucrats. Witness also I. Kh. Ozerov's incisive criticism (quoted by Anan'ich) of the failure of the Russian government to modernize corporate law to make it an instrument of enterprise rather than state hegemony. Nonetheless, the traditional corporate forms favored by the Muscovite community reflected a significant market-oriented entrepreneurial vigor with a long-term horizon.

---

[11] Alexander Gerschenkron, *Europe in the Russian Mirror* (Cambridge, 1970).

Owen ironically recasts the problem as one between modern technology and the free market. But the materialist fixation on process technology—the techniques for the production of goods—is one common to Peter the Great, Witte (in his early years), Stalin, and Brezhnev (and one that Marxism shares). It is reflected to this day in the use of material balances and the lack of attention within the Soviet planning apparatus to marketing institutions, or more broadly the product technology by which products are distributed and sold. Typically, Russia looked to process technology to save itself from the consequences of its institutional arrangements. The traditional forms of Moscow, while possibly representing a slower adoption of the most advanced process technologies, may have represented a far stronger modernizing influence than the modern forms of St. Petersburg. This transformation of traditional forms' function can be an important process. The Rudolphs have argued for India that traditional forms often have the flexibility to subsume modern functions while preserving the legitimacy of tradition.[12] Japan is another example of a society that has successfully manipulated tradition to adapt selected Western concepts.[13] Japan surely, and India possibly, represent efforts more successful at modernization—as distinct from industrialization—than those in Russia.

The use of the terms *modernization* and *industrialization* requires some reflection. For these purposes industrialization is but one possible component of the broad process of modernization. It is useful to distinguish between the terms because the thrust of our argument is that Russia failed to modernize even though it industrialized. To put the matter in somewhat different form, Russia wanted, and to a significant degree acquired, the industrial brawn of the West, but not the "brain" of Western development, the complex matrix of institutional arrangements that created a polycentric society which tended to devalue tradition, to emphasize functional specialization, to separate spheres of activity, and to promote individualistic behavior. That is, to use Weber's schema, to create a legal/rational type of society. Modernization here refers to the processes that lead to such a legal/rational structure. Clearly, it is entirely possible to achieve a high level of industrial development without being modern in the specific sense to which we would confine that term, as it is equally possible for a society to be modern without being industrialized.

Turning back to the issues under discussion in this volume, it strikes us that three broad schools were contending with each other through the period under consideration. First, the traditionalists, like Plehve, sought to preserve as much of traditional, agrarian, autocratic Russia as possible.

---

[12] Lloyd I. and Suzanne H. Rudolph, *Modernity of Tradition: Political Development of India* (Chicago, 1967).

[13] Cyril E. Black et al., *The Modernization of Japan and Russia* (New York, 1975).

They were largely opposed both to industrialization and modernization, especially the rationalization of peasant agriculture and the creation of a fully articulated set of property rights, contract, and due process.

Second, there were the industrializers, like Peter the Great, Witte in his early years as minister of finance, and Stalin, who accepted the necessity of or believed directly in the importance of Russia's developing a powerful industrial base as an indispensable foundation for national power. But these industrializers were rarely willing to permit, let alone promote, significant institutional transformations, especially those that tended to diminish the power and legitimacy of the center. Nor was the tsarist government willing to provide the social overhead capital necessary to encourage broad-scale industrialization and modernization. Indeed, in the early part of the nineteenth century, Minister of Finance Egor Kankrin went so far as to oppose government support for railroads on the grounds that they would promote physical mobility of the population and thus had the potential of threatening the social underpinnings of the imperial system. Kankrin's position was like that of a great many government figures who were to continue to assume a direct conflict between the preservation of the tsarist order rooted in the agrarian system and any moves which would broaden the base of the industrial system beyond that needed for national security and defense—as well as the needs of the privileged elites.

Third, there were modernizers, the weakest group. Anan'ich suggests that Bunge had some real vision of transforming (modernizing) Russian institutions, but when Witte, under Bunge's influence, suggested such a course, he was forced from office. Bukharin and Lieberman might be added to the list of modernizers, whether conscious or not of the implications of their position. Stolypin may have been the most revolutionary of all, and deserved Lenin's howling condemnation, for he came closest to transforming the basis of Russian society. If Russia remains throughout a patrimonial or hierarchical society, the death of the imperial regime marks the end of the traditionalists in debates on economic policy; the Bolshevik regime clearly accepted and retains the primary objective of industrial development. In that sense, as Ruth Roosa describes, it co-opted some of those elements which argued for a more rational industrialization policy. But, as Guroff and Cocks show, the debate over modernization was rarely heard and has always been settled in favor of the industrializers.

The individual chapters divide almost evenly between two different perspectives on the relationship between the state and economic change. The works of Armstrong, Kahan, Owen, Carstensen, Laird, Grossman, and Granick detail how various groups within a society—Russian, Soviet, or other—respond to their milieu and simultaneously identify the sources of entrepreneurs. That milieu includes, as Armstrong suggests, differences in security, access to education, and the desire to secure such advances; Kahan then gives a deeper insight into these processes with his study of the Jews and their entrepreneurial struggle. Both papers simultaneously construct social-scientific behavioral explanations for the varying patterns of willingness to undertake economic risk and suggest cultural differences, especially for the Jews, for whom the high regard for education has necessarily (but perhaps unintentionally) had particularly strong economic effects.

Owen and Carstensen set forth how various groups within late Imperial Russian society were attempting to make the best of the opportunities that they had, much as Baron does for an earlier period. They both share a basic social-scientific presumption that, whether dealing with the behavior of English managerial and technical personnel working for Russian firms or Muscovite enterprise and Russian proprietors, all actors shared a common quality of trying to maximize benefits within the constraints they faced. The English differed in their participation in the Russian economy from other foreigners and from Russians apparently because of differential access to private capital, differences in training (human capital formation) and preexisting employment networks between British textile firms, machinery suppliers, and Russian enterprises—networks that stretched back into the early and mid-nineteenth century. Owen also suggests how for Russian entrepreneurs economic nationalism could be used to overcome cultural hostility to enterprising behavior among ethnic Russians.

Taken as a group, this set of essays on the imperial period also suggests strongly that there was a substantial supply of entrepreneurial energy from both within and without the empire. The obstacles to the full development of that energy seemed to lie not in some intrinsic weakness within the Russian market or in a peculiarly low level of commercial integrity that would frustrate coordinated efforts. Not even the venality of Russian officialdom looms very large among the barriers to entrepreneurial vigor. Rather, it appears that government fiscal policies, the absence of proper enabling legislation for capital-market intermediaries, and the paucity of social overhead investments created uncertainty of property rights and limited access to capital, markets, and skills. If this is the case, then, contrary to Gerschenkron, Russia was not so much demand-constrained and therefore in need of a substitute market as it was constrained by institutions and policies that restricted supplies of critical factors and created uncertainty. Policies that supported expansion of the autonomous sector might then have generated an even better record of growth than that which the Witte program achieved.

The Lairds, Gregory Grossman, and David Granick all suggest that in the Soviet period the same behaviorial characteristic is observed, namely, that any individual or group strives, within the constraints imposed upon them and given their particular endowments, to do the best they can. Therefore, we can approach Soviet behavior at the microlevel with reference to the universalistic criteria of the nature of the incentive structure, the price system, the decision rules, and the command system. This emphasizes again the vitality of entrepreneurial response even within the Soviet command economy and that such microbehavior is inherently rational in its response to factor costs, prices, and rewards. The distortions or barriers emerge, as Baron suggested for his period, from the nature of the institutional structure and policy objectives. There is even some grudging adaptation through co-opting peasant markets and expediters into the formal structure. What is perhaps most striking, however, is Granick's argument that the Soviet structure generated efficient behavior in the initial stages of the industrialization drive. This seems similar to the success of Peter the Great and Witte in achieving short-term objectives, and Granick also suggests a familiar evolution. The successful policies for one period fail to evolve in a manner that permits and supports further growth; the positive policies of one period become the barriers to expansion at later stages.

Recognizing the apparently recurrent pattern of institutional rigidity suggests another broad characterization of Russian historical development. The institutional patterns in Russia were largely the creations of particular dominant personalities, such as Peter the Great, Alexander II, Witte, and Stalin. The function of the institutions that these individuals created was to carry through the objectives of the particular leader. They were neither an organic result of the needs of society itself nor vehicles intended to permit public participation in policy debates. One example of this pattern was the peculiar Russian notion of local self-administration, which conferred on local officials only the right to carry through centrally set policies, not to participate in policy formulation or to develop independent local policies.

This conception of institutions contrasts sharply with the more varied purposes of Western, especially Anglo-American institutions, which served historically not only to administer activities but also to permit, even encourage, relatively wide participation in policy debates and often preserved the right to develop many local policies. Moreover, Anglo-American institutions, as William Blackstone lays out so brilliantly in his *Commentaries*, had overlapping and interdependent jurisdictions and authorities. Thus the legislative function came to be divided among three separate elements as the government itself was divided among the legislative, administrative, and judicial branches. Public policy therefore became the product of the interaction of these relatively independent institutions; Blackstone liked the Newtonian analogy of intersecting (vector) forces, none of which alone could determine the ultimate direction of the policy.

For Russia, lacking this institutional form and function, the bureaucratic and administrative agencies found their energy and rationale in the single personality that created them. They were thus specific, almost personal administrative hierarchies intended primarily to transmit orders downward. Once the creating and guiding hand was gone, there was no organic or societal procedure which permitted a continuing adjustment and evolution of these institutions and hierarchies. From this flowed the rigidity of institutions and the recurrent need for yet another dominant leader to recast them. The Lairds, Grossman, and Granick all identify this rigidity, but find that even within this inflexible formal structure, farm managers, enterprise directors, and middle-level Party functionaries all demonstrate significant entrepreneurial vigor. This important process is often ignored in the scholarly literature that favors the perhaps more exciting story of the entrepreneurship related to the extensive activities of the "second economy" in the Soviet Union.

The papers that describe the microeconomic decision-making process are interesting in and of themselves, but none take as their central concern the process of policy formation within the state or Party apparatus. It is that policy formulation which shapes the institutional environment surrounding and shaping economic life. Only when these papers are placed with the others that treat this problem does a balanced picture of the behavior of entrepreneurship in Russia and the nature of the evolution of the Russian context emerge. Baron, Anan'ich, Roosa, Guroff, and Cocks remind us of the continuing, persistent importance of the Russian state and its policies. Baron and Cocks provide, as noted above, strikingly parallel studies, suggesting how in some salient ways the command system and the incentive system of Russia have changed but little. In reviewing government policies and activity, Anan'ich reveals how inimical government remained to lines of autonomous development or what we would call modernization during the late imperial period. Roosa remarks how, even in the face of a devastating war, the bureaucratic elites would not cooperate with the industrial leaders whose enterprises formed the indispensable basis of any war effort. It is easy to understand the industrialists' growing disillusionment with and separation from the government, a process that Haimson has suggested was well advanced before the war began.[14] And Guroff shows the degree to which, even as the

---

[14] Leopold Haimson, "The Problem of Social Stability in Urban Russia, 1905-1917," *Slavic Review*: Part one, 23 (1964):619-42, and part two, 24 (1965):1-22.

state/Party apparatus accepted the primary goal of industrialization, it tolerated neither independent institutional arrangements nor a decentralization of economic power. The other side of this coin was the inability of groups such as Guroff describes—like Baron's merchants—to preserve their position. Thus all these papers indicate how the exigencies and ideology of state hegemony, tsarist or Communist, stifled autonomous initiative, diffusion of power and, ultimately, entrepreneurial response.

In categorizing the above chapters, we return to the basic questions with which this essay began. Fundamentally, these chapters challenge the periodization of Russian history that takes the Revolution of 1917 as the great watershed and point of discontinuity in Russian history. They force us both to recognize the long-term continuities in Russian history, continuities that join, in some fundamental ways, the Russia of Peter the Great with that of Brezhnev. But they also suggest that the period from the mid-nineteenth century to the early 1930s was one of enormous tension within Russian/Soviet society. The conflict was among three contending forces: those factions and interests trying to preserve a traditional, agrarian, tsar-oriented hierarchical society; groups and individuals trying to push industrialization to give Russia the basis to sustain its world political status; and persons trying to promote the emergence of a polycentric "Westernized" society. Perhaps Russian/Soviet history since 1700 should be divided into three segments that give special recognition to this period when the forces for modernization, however weak, played an identifiable and not inconsequential role.

There is another way of characterizing this period that helps to clarify the tensions. Individual discretion in the use and disposal of economic resources is both the product of the political-ideological system that identifies and defends such individual economic liberties and itself produces a measure of political power. Thus the range of individual discretion is inherently a function of the political culture and ideology that animates a particular society. In Russia, the state has never been able or willing to provide a framework within which such individual power was secure. Stolypin's reforms aimed at such a transformation but did not have time to mature. Nor did they have support among traditional bureaucratic elites who opposed such modernizing land policies. Indeed, these elites had been largely successful in undermining Stolypin's position with the tsar—and thus Stolypin's ability to carry through his reform— well before his assassination.

As a corollary of this observation, it is fair to say that Russia has never had, except for a brief time at the end of the imperial period, anything like a Western conception of individual property rights. The state had always viewed all alternative sources of power with suspicion; it never accepted the legitimacy of having a multipolar or polycentric society, a virtual corollary of property rights. Even in the late imperial period, as Anan'ich makes clear, in all its weakness, the regime would not give up the symbols of de jure power even if de facto power had long left it. But this ability to retain such symbols of authority and legitimacy is testimony to the inability of the middle classes of managerial, technical, and professional peoples to coalesce into a substantial political force that could impose changes on the regime. Part of the weakness of the middle classes was their vision of society, which for many did not embrace the conceptions central to the Weberian legal/rational or modern society described above.[15]

Stolypin's reforms held the same implications of diminished state power as did Bukharin's recommended economic program and Oskar Lange's vision of consumer sovereignty within the framework of central planning. The appeal of Preobrazhenskii's program, of Stalin's vision of "Socialism in one country," or of the power that the Five-Year Plans conferred on a state and Party to select and impose priorities in resource utilization ought to be understood, not simply as expedient solutions that satisfied state/Party psychology or ideology, but as consistent with traditional Russian views of the relationship between state power and individual discretion.

If the chapters here persuade us of the broad similarities of behavior over a long span of Russian history and of the continuing tension between the maintenance of state hegemony and the permitting or facilitating of economic change, there is still the question of understanding that persistence. Economists and political scientists might tend to argue that the persistence of circumstances sustains the behavior. Historians and other humanists might argue that the perceptions or ideology which collectively create the institutions of a society have largely persisted. Thus, to use a simplistic formula, Marxism added a proindustrial presumption to the dominant traditional Russian ideology based on a single-centered, hierarchical society in which legitimacy emanated only from the tsar or Party. The contrast in approaches may be in part a function of the social scientists' usual preference to deal with shorter periods of time where perceptions are presumed stable. We hope that this collection encourages scholars to see the insight and support they can draw from both approaches.

Beyond this restructuring of the temporal divisions of Russian/Soviet history and an invitation to reach across disciplines for new insights, these chapters suggest several areas for future research. Most obviously, we need to know much more about the range, nature, and vitality of

---

[15] One of the best discussions of the institutional transformation in the West that relies on the Weberian paradigm is David Little, *Religion, Order and Law* (New York, 1969).

entrepreneurship during the late imperial period. This includes expanding our studies of foreign firms and, especially, foreigners active in Russia. Even more important, because of its relative neglect, is the study of Russian enterprise and entrepreneurial groups, both in the traditional centers of St. Petersburg and Moscow and also in other centers like Kiev, Odessa, and Warsaw. The vitality in the agrarian sector where so much of the Russian population still worked in 1914 deserves equal attention. Such studies might lead to a thorough reevaluation of Gerschenkron's argument that Russia was largely constrained by the venality of officialdom, the low level of commercial honesty, and the paucity of demand in the domestic market. Such studies would also need to look more closely at the development of political ideology and policy formulation. We know the broad dimensions of this process, as Anan'ich ably points out, but we do not fully understand the maturity of the thought of people like Ozerov and the degree to which there was a school of Westernizers who really understood the full institutional and ideological consequences of that process.

For the Soviet period, this collection invites a closer look at the links between traditional conceptions of the polity and the existing structures as well as a deeper probing of the range of entrepreneurial vigor within the state/Party apparatus instead of the common concern with studying the pathology of the black market. On a comparative level, these chapters suggest that scholars may find useful insights in the historical approach for understanding the divergent patterns in and success with centrally planned command economies in Eastern Europe, the Soviet Union, China, and Cuba.

The Contributors

Boris V. Anan'ich is a member of the Academy of Sciences (USSR) Institute of History in Leningrad.

John A. Armstrong is Philippe de Commynes Professor of Political Science at the University of Wisconsin, Madison.

Samuel H. Baron is Alumni Distinguished Professor at the University of North Carolina, Chapel Hill.

Joseph S. Berliner is Professor of Economics at Brandeis University.

Cyril E. Black is Director of the Center for International Studies and Shelby Cullom Davis Professor of European History at Princeton University.

William L. Blackwell is Professor of History at New York University.

Fred V. Carstensen is Associate Professor of Economics at the University of Connecticut.

Paul Cocks is a Soviet affairs analyst with the Central Intelligence Agency.

David Granick is Professor of Economics at the University of Wisconsin, Madison.

Gregory Grossman is Professor of Economics at the University of California at Berkeley and past President of the American Association for the Advancement of Slavic Studies.

Gregory Guroff is Chief of Soviet and East European Research for the International Communication Agency. He is currently serving as Cultural Affairs Officer in the American Embassy in Moscow.

Arcadius Kahan was Professor of Economics and History at the University of Chicago.

Betty A. Laird is an independent research analyst in the fields of Soviet agriculture and Kansas history.

Roy D. Laird is Professor of Political Science and Soviet and East European Affairs at The University of Kansas, and founder (in 1962) of the International Conference on Soviet and East European Agricultural Affairs.

Thomas C. Owen is Assistant Professor of History at Louisiana State University.

Ruth AmEnde Roosa was adjunct Professor of History, Briarcliff College and Senior Fellow at the Russian Institute, Columbia University. She is currently Resident Fellow at the Russian Institute.

Index

A. M. Luther (Co.), 154
Academy of Science, 313, 322, 338, 340, 342
Adams, A. and J., 267
agent-principal model, 226-27, 256
agrarian policy/question, 131-35
agricultural-implement industry, 155-56
Aksakov, I. S., 79-80
Alexander II, 61, 69, 77-78, 83, 106, 126, 128, 136, 356
Alexander III, 9, 97, 126, 131-32, 136
All-Russian Industrial-Trade Conf., 135
All-Russian Union of Towns, 174, 176
All-Russian Union of Zemstvos, 174, 176
All-Union Exhibition of Achievements of the National Economy, 339
All-Union Institute of Economics and Labor Organization, 337
Altai, 137
Ambruger, E., 85
Amur River, 111, 117
Archangel, 35, 44, 55, 137
Archer, E. H., 154
Arkhangelskii, V. N., 322-23
Armenians, 9, 35, 62, 87, 93
arms industry, 152, 162, 177. *See also* war materiel
Asia Minor, 65
Association of Exchange, Trade and Agriculture, 177, 185
Association of Industry and Trade, 7, 160-86
Association of Southern Mine Owners, 166
Astrakhan, 34-35, 38, 40, 44-45, 47, 55, 117
automobile industry, 72
Avdakov, N. S., 160-61, 166-69, 171-73, 177-79, 181
Azerbaidzhan Republic, 338
Azov Sea, 117
Azov-Don Bank, 121

Babst, E. F., 81
backwardness, 3, 27, 34, 54, 75, 82, 183, 199, 308, 334, 345, 352; comparative, 192-93
Baku, 111, 160
balance of payments, 143, 145
balance of trade, 50
Baltic Germans, 19, 25, 87, 98, 99, 100-102. *See also* Germans
Baltic Sea, 31, 39, 120
bankers, 78, 109, 119, 127, 169
banking, 47, 55, 65-66, 71-72, 76-77, 94, 108-10, 121-22, 129, 146, 235
banks, commercial, 17, 109-10, 129, 142, 158; foreign, 118, 121
Baring Bros., 79
Bark, P. L., 138
Barone, E., 191, 196
barshchina, 65
Basel University, 161
Bazarov, 221
Beaulieu, A. L., 23
Belov, F., 267, 275
Benardski, D. E., 65
Bender-Galatz railroad, 118
Bennigsen, A., 93
Berdiansk, 156
Bergson family, 108n
Berlin (Germany), 19
Berliner, J. S., 300, 312, 317, 320
Berman, H., 350-52
Bezobrazov, A. M., 138
Bialystok, 109, 114
Bienstock, G., 284n
bill of exchange, 61
Billington, J. H., 201
black market, *see* second economy
Black Sea, 19, 31, 106
Blackstone, W., 356-57
Blackwell, W., 65, 69
blat, 269
Bloch, I., 20

(363)

Library of Congress Cataloging in Publication Data
Main entry under title:

Entrepreneurship in Imperial Russia and the Soviet Union.

Includes bibliographical references and index.
1. Industrial management—Soviet Union—History—
Addresses, essays, lectures.   2. Business enterprises—
Soviet Union—History—Addresses, essays, lectures.
3. Technological innovations—Soviet Union—History—
Addresses, essays, lectures.   4. Businessmen—Soviet
Union—History—Addresses, essays, lectures.
5. Entrepreneur—History—Addresses, essays, lectures.
I. Guroff, Gregory, 1941-   . II. Carstensen, Fred V., 1944-
HD70.S63E43   1983   338'.04'0947   82-15056
ISBN 0-691-05376-6
ISBN 0-691-10141-8 (lim. pbk. ed.)